STUDIES IN SOCIAL POLICY AND WELFARE XXI

RESPONSES TO POVERTY:
LESSONS FROM EUROPE

Studies in Social Policy and Welfare
Edited by R.A. Pinker

STUDIES IN SOCIAL POLICY AND WELFARE XXI

RESPONSES TO POVERTY: LESSONS FROM EUROPE

Edited by
Robert Walker
Roger Lawson
Peter Townsend

HEINEMANN EDUCATIONAL BOOKS · LONDON

Heinemann Educational Books Ltd
22 Bedford Square, London WC1B 3HH

LONDON EDINBURGH MELBOURNE AUCKLAND
HONG KING SINGAPORE KUALA LUMPUR NEW DELHI
IBADAN NAIROBI JOHANNESBURG
EXETER (NH) KINGSTON PORT OF SPAIN

© Robert Walker, Roger Lawson and Peter Townsend 1984
First published 1984

British Library Cataloguing in Publication Data

Responses to poverty. —(Studies in social
    policy and welfare).
    1. Poor—Europe—Political aspects
    I. Walker, Robert L.
    II. Lawson, Roger   III. Townsend, Peter, 1928—
    IV. Series
    305 5'69'094   HC240.P6

ISBN 0-435-82908-4

Typeset by The Castlefield Press of Northampton
in 10/12 Journal Roman, and printed in Great Britain
by Biddles Ltd, Guildford, Surrey.

Contents

The Contributors

Claude Ameline: employed by the Ministry of National Solidarity in Paris. He was formerly the Counsellor for Social Affairs at the French Embassy in London.

A. A. M. von Amelsvoort: Deputy Head of the Department responsible for employed persons' insurance at the Dutch Ministry of Social Affairs.

Dr Peter Coleman: Lecturer in the Department of Sociology and Social Administration and the Department of Geriatric Medicine at the University of Southampton.

Doreen Collins: Senior Lecturer in Social Administration at the University of Leeds.

Dr Karl Furmaniak: Director of the German research programme on job satisfaction and formerly headed the Planning Group of the Federal Ministry of Labour and Social Affairs in Bonn.

Helmut Hartmann: member of the Institute for Social Research and Economic Policy in Cologne.

Dr Wim Huizing: Director of the Policy Planning Unit for Social Security in the Ministry of Social Affairs, The Hague.

Roger Lawson: Senior Lecturer in Social Administration at the University of Southampton. He is joint editor (with Professor Vic George) of *Poverty and Inequality in Common Market Countries*.

Antoine Lion: Adviser for Research in the Department of Social Action at the French Ministry of National Solidarity. He led the team responsible for the French National Report on Poverty prepared for the European Commission.

Professor Peter Townsend: Professor of Social Policy at the University of Bristol and was formerly Professor of Sociology at the University of Essex. He is author of *Poverty in the United Kingdom*, *The Last Refuge*, *Sociology and Social Policy*, *The Social Minority*, *The Family Life of Old People*, *The Family and Later Life*, and other books.

Dr Robert Walker: Research Fellow, Personal Social Services Research Unit, University of Kent. He is joint editor (with Professor Cedric Sandford and Chris Pond) of *Taxation and Social Policy*.

Preface

Throughout much of the post-war era the countries of Western Europe have enjoyed unprecedentedly high rates of economic growth. During the same period governments have, without exception, directed an increasing proportion of the new-found wealth towards expenditure on social welfare and particularly on social security. However, certain countries have been markedly more successful than others in combating poverty: in providing adequate, and sometimes generous, benefits for the old, the sick and the unemployed; in giving special assistance to families; and limiting the numbers without entitlement to benefit or who fail to obtain benefits to which they are entitled. Moreover, significant differences in emphasis are beginning to emerge as governments respond to demographic changes and to the worsening economic climate which is placing increasing strain on established systems of social security.

In the light of these developments, the Civil Service College organised a seminar to review the measures to combat poverty adopted by other European countries with a view to providing a wider perspective on policies and policy options in the UK. It is this seminar, which was chaired by Professor Peter Townsend, then Professor of Sociology at the University of Essex, and bringing together civil servants and academics from the UK and the Continent which provided the initial stimulus for this book. However, while all the contributors attended the seminar, each contribution has been written since. In so doing we have sought a greater unity than would otherwise have been possible and wherever feasible descriptions and statistics have been standardised to July 1980. Detailed comparative sections and a concluding chapter drawing lessons for the UK have also been added. It must be stressed, though, that the opinions expressed remain those of the individual authors and do not necessarily reflect the views of other participants in the seminar, or the policy of any government, government department or other organisation with which they are associated.

The 'fight against poverty' has been an important stimulus to political action and to social reform in the UK, but different conceptions of poverty have held sway at different times, and have been held concurrently by different sections of the community. For example, Beveridge's welfare state was grounded on an absolute, subsistence-style concept of poverty (the 'giants' of 'want' and 'squalor'). The 1967 reform of national assistance was based more upon the relativist notions of poverty which were involved in the idea of a minimum income guarantee although benefit levels did not increase to the extent anticipated by its advocates. More recently, some, most notably Townsend,[1] have argued for a 'relative deprivation' concept of poverty. This would embrace all those people without sufficient resources to be able to participate fully in their own society and fulfil the social roles and obligations allotted to them. However, others certainly do not go as far and take a more limited approach to the meaning of the term, restricting it to signs of physical deprivation, for example, malnutrition.

Various conceptions of poverty are evident in Europe. Deference was paid to the notion of relative deprivation in some of the national reports prepared for the European Commission and the definition originally adopted by the Commission[2] does the same but, in general, different formulations have been used in domestic political debates in policy formulation. Indeed in many instances the substantive problem of poverty — as well as the problem of defining it — has effectively been ignored for the past 20 or 30 years. Questions of meaning and of theory have been dealt with implicitly in the development of generic social policy provisions. (France, Italy and Ireland may, like the UK, be exceptions to this last generalisation but in each case poverty is interpreted differently.)

All this makes the task of international comparison more difficult but no less important. Peter Townsend discusses problems of definition and measurement in Chapter 1 where he also looks towards a structural explanation of poverty bringing out the role of multinational conglomerations and international political associations as well as national factors. However, for much of the volume, necessity forces a more limited definition of relative income poverty to be employed and in Chapter 2 existing information on the nature and extent of this form of poverty in Europe is assembled and considered in relation to national resources and welfare expenditure. These two chapters, thereby, provide a context in which to view developments in individual countries.

However, meaningful international comparisons in social policy must be based on a detailed understanding of the politics, policies and institutions of the countries involved. It follows that the scope of any comparative analysis must be severely limited both in the policy areas and the

1 Townsend, P. 1979, *Poverty in the United Kingdom*, Harmondsworth, Penguin.
2 European Commission, 1981, Final Report from the Commission to the Council on the first programme of pilot schemes and studies to combat poverty, Brussels.

countries covered. In this volume three policy areas are examined — policies affecting unemployment and low pay, policies concerned with family poverty and policies to combat poverty in old age — in France, The Netherlands, West Germany and, in the case of low pay and unemployment, Denmark. In each case, the authors were encouraged to provide a brief history of relevant institutions, to describe the broad policy objectives and emphases within the policy mix, to consider the aims of the main policy programmes and to evaluate these programmes in relation to the stated objectives and their broader consequences. While these common guidelines were necessary to facilitate comparison, the authors freely interpret their material so as to convey the flavour of the national debates. Moreover, in meeting their briefs, the authors focus not so much on specific anti-poverty measures but on those social and economic policies which in some way influence the extent of poverty.

The resultant chapters (Chapters 3—12) are arranged thematically with the national studies being grouped in three policy sections. Each policy section is prefaced by an editorial overview which provides standardised comparative material for each country (and for the UK), and includes national information missing from individual chapters on account of the particular interpretation taken by the authors. The 'overviews' also seek to identify significant differences and common policy themes and contingencies which add to understanding of the development of social security in Europe. Finally, in Chapter 13, the UK provisions are reviewed in the light of European experience in order to illuminate the options for policy reform.

The structure of the book facilitates it being read in different ways according to the objectives of the reader:

(a) the reader seeking knowledge of a particular country will read the appropriate national chapters;

(b) the reader interested in trends and relative performances in a policy area will read the editorial review and sensibly qualify his interpretation by reference to the individual national chapters;

(c) the reader wanting to gain an overview of social policy development in Europe would do well to read the three individual overviews but should remain aware of the book's central focus on poverty;

(d) finally, the reader concerned with (or about) the future of social policy or poverty policies in the UK or merely interested in how the UK differs from or rates against European countries in terms of its provisions, could turn straight to Chapter 13. They might do even better, however, from reading other chapters so as to formulate their own opinion as to what the UK can learn from her European neighbours. Not least they should read Chapters 1 and 2 to remind themselves of the potential and limitations of the comparative method and to acquaint themselves with the qualifications that underlie this book.

Acknowledgement

The editors thank Marie Walsingham and Sheila Bishop who prepared the typescript and Pamela Park whose editorial support was invaluable.

Part I The Problem of Poverty

1 Understanding Poverty and Inequality in Europe
Peter Townsend

Poverty is increasingly acknowledged to be a significant phenomenon in the richer Western and Northern parts of the world and it is to the better understanding and explanation of this phenomenon in Europe that this book is addressed. We start from the belief that despite some obvious difficulties there is a great deal to be gained from studying poverty comparatively. National and parochial viewpoints can be put better into proportion. Techniques and observations developed elsewhere can begin to be applied to one's native country. And through an exchange of knowledge some of the puzzles about social conditions and structure can be ordered and explained, so that policies more sensitively related to human needs can be drawn up.

The Theoretical Challenge
Let me state the theoretical objective — to which, of course, this book can make only a small contribution. The world is made up of nation-states which vary astonishingly in their wealth and income. For example, the Federal Republic of Germany is the fifth richest country in the world, with $11 730 per head in 1981, compared with India, the 109th country, with only $190 per head. Within nation-states, including the richest as well as the poorest, wealth and income are also distributed highly unequally. Thus the richest 20 per cent in Germany have 46 per cent and in India 49 per cent of total household income, whereas the poorest 20 per cent have 6½ per cent and 7 per cent respectively (see World Bank 1981). As a consequence of this dual structure of inequality but also as a result of different styles of living and different job demands placed upon citizens, there is extensive, but very uneven, deprivation. Such deprivation takes many forms — ill-health or disability; risk of early death; poor physique; malnutrition; poor or overcrowded housing and lack of household facilities, such as heating and light; poor water supply, sanitation and washing facilities; poor conditions of work; lack of access to standard national services, amenities and environmental or community

facilities; poor education and lack of access to the media of communication; inability to fulfil social (e.g. parental) roles and participate in standard social customs. A European research group has been endeavouring to agree on such a list for standard investigation (ECSWTR 1979). These forms of deprivation are highly intercorrelated (Townsend 1979). They apply to individuals drawn from all sections of a population or to minorities, communities or the populations of local areas or regions within countries. They can be defined and measured only in relationship to standard reference points — to other members of the same societies, to national conditions and, in some instances where trading, military and political associations between states belittle national frontiers, to multinational situations, populations and spheres of influence.

This complex world pattern of resource distribution, privilege and deprivation is in constant flux. For example, the lifetime of any individual represents a tiny part of the history of human life on earth and yet in less than half the lifetime of older people alive in Europe today the relative prosperity of some nation-states has changed remarkably. By the criterion of income *per capita*, Japan has moved since 1957 from 46th to 3rd in rank order among nation-states, the USA from 2nd to 8th and Britain from 10th to 19th (Russett 1965; World Bank 1981). But it is not simply that for internal as well as external reasons the crude percentage of the world's resources commanded by any nation or group of nations is changing. Four other elements in the social equation will be changing too. These are:

(a) the distribution of resources internally;
(b) the spread of expectations (including job demands) placed on the citizens of each nation;
(c) the style of living of national populations and the institutional infrastructures underlying these styles;
(d) the relative balance of national and transnational economic, political and military associations.

Any responsible theory for the severity and prevalence of poverty must treat each of these elements at length.

This is a preliminary theoretical statement, which begs a number of questions and itself requires explanation. In this chapter attention will be given to four stages of analysis which have to be considered in turn before their indivisible inter-relationship can be fully understood. These are the conceptualisation, measurement, explanation and policy management of poverty. A brief introduction to the history and treatment of the concept will be given, followed by some account of its measurement in Europe — though illustrations in much greater detail will be found in later chapters. Next will be a section on the institutional or structural explanation of poverty in Europe, necessarily tentative but attempting to bring out the role of international political associations like the European Community (EC) and the Organisation for Economic Co-operation and Development (OECD), as well as multinational conglomerates, in controlling current trends. Finally, some of the implications of the analysis for policy will be briefly discussed.

The Conceptualisation of Poverty

There is more than one meaning of the term 'poverty'. Our task will be to explore the meanings that have been given to the term historically in order to develop a better understanding of how a systematic definition can be consistent across countries. In principle that consistency must extend beyond the scope of the member-countries of Europe and draw in the poorest countries of the world. Progress will only be possible in terms of an internationally comparable and scientific approach.

A hundred years ago the rich and the powerful dominated the interpretation of poverty as a condition of life that was regrettable but unavoidable. Poverty was felt to be a necessary element in society, since only by feeling the spur of want could the labouring poor be driven to work. The divisions between the classes were believed to be 'natural' and the conditions of the poor were felt by some to be biologically ordained. The old Poor Laws and, in later years, early schemes of public assistance attached punitive conditions for relief. Many of those in the colonising countries like Britain, France, The Netherlands and West Germany adopted fatalistic attitudes towards the destitution and wide experience of poverty in their own countries and also interpreted such phenomena in terms of individual weakness of character and lack of capacity (Rose 1972). Theories of poverty were primarily individualistic and were derived from *laissez-faire* economic theory. Since several of the European countries were also imperialist powers poverty in their midst was also excused and even maintained by predatory activity overseas.

Within a short span of years around the start of the twentieth century the first steps were taken to establish the Welfare State in several European countries. Among the forces which led to the emergence and adoption of its guiding principles — like the 'national minimum', the 'subsistence standard' and 'citizenship rights' — were the rise of Labour movements in different countries and the extension of the franchise, and a recognition of the need for mass armies of workers as well as soldiers in good health, together with a concern about the moral and material effects of poverty, inspired by religious movements and some of the newly educated middle classes. Industrialisation and the spread of new technologies contributed to a change in the climate of opinion but the political struggle in several countries contributed most to the promotion of 'minimum rights for the many' as one of the principles or conditions on which market capitalism would now have to be based. The ensuing struggle was over the interpretation of that principle in practice. In Bismarck's Germany social insurance benefits were introduced between 1883 and 1889. Several countries passed workmen's compensation schemes in the later 1890s. Denmark, Ireland, France and the UK were among countries enacting unemployment and health insurance measures during the first years of the twentieth century.   Although schemes developed in one country were readily taken up in another few national politicians called much attention to the borrowing which went on between countries.

The standards of benefit which evolved in the new national insurance schemes and schemes for public assistance tended to be drawn from the more generous precedents adopted under the former Poor Law legislation, particularly with reference to the standards of diet of Poor Law institutions. In Britain, the work of Charles Booth (published from 1889; Booth 1903) and especially of Seebohm Rowntree (1901) did much to assist the translation of the country to that of an embryonic welfare state. Rowntree defined families whose 'total earnings are insufficient to obtain the minimum necessaries for the maintenance of merely physical efficiency as being in primary poverty' (1901: 86). He made good use of studies by nutritionists who had established the levels of nutrients required by people of different ages. He translated these needs into quantities of different foods and then converted the result into the cheapest cost of buying those foods on the market. He also added minimum sums for clothing, fuel and household sundries according to size of family. The total cost represented his poverty standard. Rent was treated as an unavoidable addition to the total and was counted in full. A family was defined as being in poverty if its income minus rent fell short of the poverty standard.

This approach was eagerly taken up nationally and internationally. In Britain there was a stream of studies in the early decades of the twentieth century (see, for example, Bowley and Burnett-Hurst 1915). In 1941 Lord Beveridge explicitly adopted the Rowntree poverty standard as a basis for deciding the rates of benefit to be paid out under the new social security plan after the war. Both this definition of poverty and the measures adopted in policy were to be influential in former colonies like Canada, Australia (Henderson *et al.* 1970; Australia 1975; Halliday 1975; Henderson 1980; SWRC 1980) and South Africa (Maasdorp and Humphreys 1975). For example, there was a series of studies in South and Central Africa using the so-called 'poverty datum line', developed by Geoffrey Batson on the basis of Rowntree's work. The poverty datum line provided 'the barest minimum upon which subsistence and health can be theoretically achieved' (Batson 1941–4, 1945; Bettison 1960; Pillay 1973 and Maasdorp and Humphreys 1975). A number of governments still draw heavily upon the subsistence conceptualisation in framing the objectives of their development plans. For example, India defines a poverty line as the midpoint of the expenditure class in which calorific requirements are met (India 1978). A recent report from Malaysia provides another example (Malaysia 1976).

The subsistence concept lies at the heart of measures of poverty in the USA. The US government's 'poverty index' is based on estimates prepared by the Department of Agriculture of the costs of food needed by families of different composition. A minimum guide was worked out by the National Research Council, which conformed with the kind of diets actually followed by American families (as shown by food consumption surveys), and this is translated into a market cost. Non-food costs are estimated by taking food costs as a fixed percentage of the average budget. This procedure has been followed throughout the 1960s and 1970s (Orshansky 1969; USA 1976). The American methodology, which was developed in part to meet the political problems of the American 'war' on poverty in the 1960s, takes more account of budgetary behaviour than did Rowntree and Beveridge, but it maintains the emphasis on minimum dietary sufficiency and subsistence. One of the difficulties of this approach which puts it under strain intellectually is that food accounts for a declining share of the average American budget (as elsewhere) and those in charge of the procedures recognise that there are 'no accepted standards of need . . . for non-food items' (USA 1976: 74).

There are two other approaches to the concept of poverty which have been operationalised or partly operationalised. First there has been the development of a broader concept of 'basic needs', sponsored first of all by the International Labour Office (ILO) and then the World Bank, and also incorporated in the Brandt Report (Brandt 1980). This has a close affinity to the subsistence approach. Although the approach itself has a long history in international study and discussion it was adopted formally at the ILO's World Employment Conference, held in Geneva in 1976. Basic needs were stated to include two elements.

> First, they include certain minimum requirements of a family for private consumption — adequate food, shelter and clothing, as well as certain household furniture and equipment. Second, they include essential services provided by and for the community at large, such as safe drinking water, sanitation, public transport and health, educational and cultural facilities . . . it is important to

recognise that the concept of basic needs is a country-specific and dynamic concept. The concept of basic needs should be placed within a context of a nation's overall economic and social development. In no circumstances should it be taken to mean merely the minimum necessary for subsistence; it should be placed within a context of national independence, the dignity of individuals and peoples and their freedom to chart their destiny without hindrance. (ILO 1977).

The need to transform social structures, 'including an initial redistribution of assets, especially land', was accepted as being 'often' required (1977: 24—5). However, the claim that this goes beyond traditional formulations of subsistence or basic needs is rather doubtful (Townsend 1981). The ILO itself has admitted that 'it is both legitimate and prudent to concentrate first on meeting basic needs in the absolute sense' (ILO 1976: 33).

Despite the adoption of the basic needs concept in a variety of publications (see also ILO 1977; Ghai *et al.* 1977), its precise meaning remains rather ambiguous. Some of the more sophisticated work carried out under the auspices of the UN (for example, Drewnowski and Scott 1966; UNESCO 1978) has been passed over. This is illustrated in the Brandt Report. There are a number of references to the 'elementary' needs of health, housing and education and the need to eliminate 'absolute' poverty. But the Brandt Committee's treatment of the concept of poverty is as unspecific and ambivalent as that of the ILO. Thus it is argued in some passages that the elimination of absolute poverty and improvements in basic services can be achieved 'only' through economic growth (though growth itself is stated to depend on 'more purposeful collaboration between north and south and much more systematic assistance from the north' — Brandt 1980: 58—9). However, in other passages the needs of the poor are recognised to be more complex and to imply more complex anti-poverty strategies. Thus

> if the poor are to gain directly from growth and participate fully in the development process, new institutions and policies are needed to achieve new distribution of productive resources to the poor, generate rapid expansion in jobs and income-earning opportunities and to provide social and economic services on a mass basis. (1980: 128)

In some respects the World Bank has, in its publications, withdrawn from an ambiguous formulation of 'basic needs' to a more coherent interpretation of subsistence in conceptualising and measuring poverty. National household expenditure surveys have been used as basic sources of information and poverty standards have been developed 'by estimating the minimum income required to provide for adequate nutrition while allowing for a proportion of total expenditure for non-food items' (Hasan 1978). Essentially the method is the one used by the US government within its own territory (see Orshansky 1969; USA 1976.)

If the conceptualisation of 'absolute' poverty through the medium of 'subsistence' or 'basic needs' poses problems then the attempt to define 'relative' poverty poses problems too. Sometimes this has been expressed very crudely in relation to inequality. Countries are compared in respect of the percentage of national disposable personal income commanded by the poorest 10 per cent or 20 per cent (rather like the examples of West Germany and India at the start of this introduction). The OECD went one step further. As a by-product of its work on the reasons for the rapid expansion of public expenditure in most OECD economies during the 1960s and 1970s, the organisation decided to explore the evolution of income maintenance programmes in relation to the objective of reducing poverty. Two contrasting definitions were given:

(1) In terms of some absolute level of minimum needs, below which people are regarded as being poor, for purposes of social and government concern, and which does not change through time;
(2) As some relative level of income (equal, for instance, to a given percentage of average family income), which would rise (though not necessarily in a proportionate way) as national income grows. (OECD 1976: 63).

No country stuck resolutely to the first definition, and either moved haphazardly from one to the other or maintained a historical standard relative to earnings. For Australia, Canada, France, the UK, the USA, Belgium, France and Ireland, the OECD reproduced national estimates of the percentages of the population living below the poverty line. These estimates were derived from the income levels which these countries used as criteria of eligibility for purposes of granting social aid, or were derived from private sources. However, in addition, the OECD worked out a 'standardised' estimate for these countries. Two persons in a household with an income of less than the average disposable income per person in that country were regarded as being in poverty and using this figure as a base, standard percentages of the income required for two people were added or subtracted for households with more than two persons or only one person. 'A household is counted as poor if, given its size, its income falls below these percentages of disposable income per head' (OECD 1976: 66).

In interpreting these approaches it is necessary first of all to appreciate that they are socially and culturally structured: that is, individuals in any society have certain perceptions of 'poverty' and these tend to be determined by the existence and mode of operation of certain social and cultural institutions. Thus empirical studies have shown that different percentages of a population hold different perceptions of poverty, including 'starvation', 'malnutrition', 'subsistence', 'basic needs' and 'relative' poverty (Townsend 1979). Other studies have shown that the percentage of the population in European countries who say that poverty exists and who blame individuals rather than social and economic institutions varied widely (EC 1977; Chapter 2 below). Cultural conceptions of poverty typify the efforts made by a population to explain itself and justify certain conditions in its midst. In some countries the views of ruling elites have been more influential than in others; and in some countries scientific ideas have made more headway than others. Thus there is a striking difference between some members of the EEC in the literature of poverty, as this book will illustrate. In official FRG publications there has been a tendency to treat poverty as a straightforward residual phenomenon applying to a tiny percentage of the population outside employment who are not covered by the provisions of the Federal Social Assistance Act of 1961 (FRG 1981). Conversely, the French government has recognised for some time that the concept is more complex, more subtle and widespread. Thus a recent report of an interdepartmental committee reviewing the nature and distribution of poverty called attention to multiple forms of deprivation, the consequences of low income for social relationships, the problems of aid versus control, and the difficulties of changing deep-rooted structures. The trouble with this 'multiple' approach is that if carried to excess it can mean all things to all men. Thus, 'in short, poverty disturbs, poverty is denied, poverty is exaggerated. It is bad conscience, it is an alibi, it is a means of pressure' (France 1981). (For a historical analysis of the treatment of the concept in France see Sinfield 1980.) Certainly, among EC member-states the difference in the number of studies published about poverty is striking, varying from the Federal Republic of Germany and the Netherlands, where until recently scientific interest was small, to France and the UK — the latter having a burgeoning literature (among recent examples are Townsend 1970 and 1979; Fiegehen *et al.* 1977; Higgins 1978; Holman 1978; Coates and Silburn 1981; Donnison 1981; MacGregor 1981; Sen 1981).

What has to be extracted from any review of meaning is the need to pursue objective or scientific criteria of poverty in order to make sense of varying national applications and submit them to rational and ordered judgement. Locked in many administrative analyses of a national or international kind there is the assumption that certain specific human needs are universal and are basic to any additional needs which may arise relative to membership of a particular society or culture. However, this notion has not been followed through consistently. Traditionally a distinction has come to be made between so-called primary and secondary needs. But this distinction, which has been variously described — as between 'absolute' and 'relative', or 'basic' and 'non-basic' — becomes, upon investigation, extraordinarily difficult and ultimately impossible to justify. The criteria according to which a boundary might be drawn are elusive; and they are elusive because conceptions of absolute need can be invoked only by rejecting individual membership of society. Whether people's needs can be defined or measured, irrespective of that membership of society, is problematic.

A belief has been fostered that if only people can have their needs for food, shelter and clothing met, society has no further obligation towards them. But that is to treat human beings as physical beings rather than social beings. In truth, they are simultaneously physical and social beings, so that even their physical needs are 'filtered' socially. Definitions of food, shelter and clothing vary according to social definition or convention (including local and national availability of goods and services) and it is impossible to lay down a diet, a set of clothing or even a style of housing which will apply to all the peoples of the world.

The social character of human needs must be expressed even more strongly. People are citizens, neighbours, friends, parents and workers in a wide variety of public and private industries or services. As such they have roles, obligations and relationships, which have to be fulfilled — often at monetary expense. These needs can be as pressing as the drive of hunger and acts of self-protection in a punishing climate.

The 'absolute needs' approach tends, therefore, to disintegrate upon close inspection and analysis. Ideologically, the approach carries implications that deserve clarification. A definition of 'absolute' need represents a severe definition of human need. The impression is conveyed that if the need so defined can be fulfilled from the incomes which people receive, then society as a whole has no further responsibility for them. By representing, or purporting to represent, a standard of *physical* subsistence, people's real or full needs in their capacity as members of society, that is, in performing the roles and fulfilling the relationships imposed upon them or expected of them, are ignored or depreciated. In particular, the *financial* responsibilities of husbands and wives, parents and grandparents, neighbours and friends for their spouses, children and friends, other than any exercise on behalf of the *physical* needs of food, shelter and clothing of their immediate household dependants, are ignored. A mean conception of human need is thereby developed and legitimised. By contrast the social definition will take more account of the needs of membership of society and the forms of deprivation that arise when people lack the resources to fulfil their roles and obligations as members. An attempt to express a thorough-going relativist viewpoint will be found in *Poverty in the United Kingdom* (Townsend 1979). Also Ferge (1980) and others (ECSWTR 1979) have adopted a s viewpoint in developing a co-ordinated perspective for poverty research in Europe.

Human and social needs, therefore, may be said to originate in social organisation and relationships. Ideas of 'need', as well as the circumstances in which sections of any population find themselves, are socially conditioned. If people lack or are denied resources to obtain access to diets, amenities, standards, services and activities which are common or customary in society, or to meet the obligations expected of them or imposed upon them in their social roles and relationships and so fulfil membership of society, they may be said to be in poverty. This approach is built upon a conceptualisation of 'relative deprivation' as opposed to 'subsistence'. Deprivation can arise in any or all of the major spheres of life — at work, where the means largely determining one's position in other spheres are earned; at home, in neighbourhood and family; in travel; and in a range of social and individual activities outside work and home or the immediate vicinity of the home. In principle, there could be extreme divergencies in the experience of different kinds of deprivation. In practice, there is a systematic relationship between multiple deprivation and level of resources. Empirical observation also suggests there is a threshold of income, or command of total resources, below which forms of deprivation multiply disproportionately to falling income. As income diminishes it seems that people strive to play their expected roles and conform with the customs of a society, but when their resources are low they will tend to withdraw from participation in relationships and customs — though this can sometimes mean concentrating on certain restricted roles or activities at the expense of others. A great deal of further work is required to confirm this suggestion and show how social groups, families and individuals react to sudden falls in income or reconcile membership of society with low income over very long periods. But, following this alternative approach it would be possible to develop a 'participation' standard as an alternative to the 'subsistence' or 'basic needs' standard of income or command over total resources.

Measurement

For some European countries there has been a long history of the
m~~ ~~   well as general discussion of poverty. Examples will be
apters of this book relating to particular member
t years there have been strenuous attempts to bring
udies into a comparative perspective (see, in particu-
1977; Beckerman *et al.* 1979; EC 1979; ECSWTR
Ferge 1980; George and Lawson 1980; Madge and
number of comparative studies on the theme of

poverty has not been large and it is fair to say that comparison has so far been relatively circumspect rather than precise. On the other hand, a large number of studies indirectly relating to poverty in Europe (many of them dealing with social services or particular minorities) have been published (for example, Shanas *et al.* 1968; Reubens 1970; Titmuss 1971; Castles and Kosack 1973; Kaim Caudle 1973 and 1980; Lawson and Stevens 1974; Lawson and Reed 1975; Maynard 1975 and 1981; Heidenheimer *et al.* 1976; Kahn and Kamerman 1977, 1978 and 1980; Bradshaw and Piachaud 1980).

Illustrations from these studies will be given. An OECD study found that according to national definitions in the early 1970s there were 13.2 per cent of the population in the UK, 14.4 per cent in Belgium, 15–20.0 per cent in France, and 24.0 per cent in Ireland below the poverty line. However, as the OECD went on to point out, these figures 'are based on very heterogeneous concepts and definitions and are therefore far from being strictly comparable' (OECD 1976: 65). Concepts of 'subsistence' or 'basic needs' generally lay behind the definitions but even so they could not be said to have been implemented similarly in practice. Some form of standardised criterion deserved to be adopted. The OECD observed that a number of the national studies took a cut-off point of low income, for single non-retired people, of around two-thirds of the average *per capita* household disposable income. In defining relative poverty they took the figure of 66.7 per cent as a starting point and for each additional person added a diminishing percentage resulting in 100 per cent as the standard percentage for two people, 125 per cent for three people, and so on. In effect, a very crude equivalence scale, making no allowance for the age, marital status, employment status, or level of disability of each individual, was used. Households were counted as poor if they fell below these percentages of disposable income per head.

On this 'standardised' basis, the estimate of the percentage in poverty in the UK was then nearly halved, by comparison with the measure based on the national definition, to 7.5 per cent, but the figure for France remained about the same, at 16 per cent. Standardised measures were not produced for Ireland and Belgium, but the estimate for West Germany was 3 per cent, for Sweden 3.5 per cent and for Norway 5 per cent.

Finally, trends in income distribution for France, West Germany and the UK for periods of up to 10 years during the 1960s and early 1970s were traced. For France and West Germany the proportion in poverty had been reduced. For the UK the proportion had increased. Reservations were expressed about the data available for some of these countries and in general there was disappointingly little discussion of the problems and implications of measurement (OECD 1976).

Others have followed and developed this approach. Wilfred Beckerman provided a much fuller discussion of some of the difficulties in presenting an analysis of developments in Australia, Belgium, Britain and Norway. He estimated that 9.9 per cent of the population of Britain in 1973 were below a standardised poverty line and 6.1 per cent of the population of Belgium. He also found that social security measures had been more effective in Belgium than in Britain in reducing the numbers in poverty (Beckerman *et al.* 1979). An earlier study, based on comparable surveys of old people in Britain and Denmark as well as the USA, produced a more exact picture of the distribution of income (see Wedderburn in Shanas *et al.* 1968).

Although no one can be satisfied with the quality of comparative information about the distribution of living standards in the different European countries, these are among the best examples of the studies that have been carried out. They allow inferences to be drawn about relative conditions in different societies. But, as already noted, there have also been a number of studies of the relative value and importance of different social security programmes, which complement the more direct information about incomes. One of the latest instances is a study of benefits for children in the EC. This went further than previous international comparisons, including not only family allowances and tax allowances but also the principal other ways in which the 'costs' of children are met — through education, health and housing schemes. As a consequence this comparative study is more securely based than some others, though the authors disclaim finality and properly call attention to the lack of 'simple interpretative conclusions'. They point out that it is not true that the richest countries in the EC have the most generous child support. 'Nor is there any association between the dominance of a particular church or political party and the level of child support. This study has failed to find any general explanations for variation in the level of child support' (Bradshaw and Piachaud 1980: 140). When the nine countries are compared in income provision for children by size of family *and* at different levels of income there are varying results. Bradshaw and Piachaud found that Belgium, France and Luxembourg were invariably at the top of the ranks, and Italy and Ireland consistently eighth and ninth. The UK's otherwise low ranking was redeemed partly because its support system was (in the year examined) more generous for small families than some other countries, like West Germany, and partly because (with Denmark) its system was relatively more generous than the systems in some other countries at the lowest levels of income.

Statements about particular benefits or services have to be built up in relation to the total resources committed by different countries to the social services. In general terms, The Netherlands, Luxembourg, West Germany, France, Denmark and Belgium all spend much more (up to half as much again) on social benefits, expressed as a percentage of Gross Domestic Product (GDP), than do the UK and Ireland. (See Chapter 2; EC 1979; there is a discussion of problems of definition and measurement in Keithley 1981.) Through such measures we obtain ideas of what is afforded, and therefore what questions must be confronted in developing explanations of social policies adopted in different European countries. We also get some hint of the alternative policies which might be pursued in certain member-countries.

These two sets of evidence about low income, on the one hand, and the effect of social services and social security in particular, on the other, are obliging us to review the extent of agreement that exists about conceptions and definitions of poverty. Our perceptions of need are at stake. There has been a tendency, especially among economists (examples are Watts 1977 and Kakwani 1980a and 1980b), to play down the significance of choosing any particular income cut-off point in defining the extent of poverty or low incomes. Economists have often recognised that there are more difficulties than they have discussed in specifying a poverty standard but have argued that the choice is illustrative only and assume that it will not make much difference to the discussion of policy strategies, which their illustrations are intended to serve. (See, for example, discussions of negative income tax schemes which have been influential in the past two decades by Friedman 1963; Tobin 1965; Lapman 1966; and Lees 1967.) In point of fact the choice is fundamental. For example, a standard which produces a figure of 3 per cent poor has very different implications from one which produces a figure of 20 per cent poor. Again, a standard which assumes that the income needs of an adolescent dependent child in the home are only half those of an adult has very different implications from one which assumes that their income needs are the same. A poverty standard represents a conception of what people need in modern society. In the last analysis it represents not only what income we think people deserve to have but what we will be prepared to pay them from taxes and other sources.

The scientific study (or translation into measurement) of conceptions of poverty can be approached, first of all in terms of the perceptions of poverty of individuals in a member-country (Townsend 1979) or in all countries of the EC (EC 1977; Chapter 2 below). Secondly, the perceptions of groups and of societies or governments can be elucidated. Members affiliating to particular political parties, members of particular professions, staff of social service agencies and administrative or ruling elites may each adopt perceptions substantially different from those

prevailing among the public at large. Governments institutionalise standards of need in legislation, regulations and modes of administration. We
can all observe that the perception of need institutionalised by a national
government is different from that institutionalised by some other governments. We can also imagine needs or levels of need not so far implemented in the administration, or even represented in the policies, of any
ruling administration known to us. So, for purposes of scientific study
and liberating our perceptions from those tied too closely to precedent
and culture, collective conceptions and definitions of poverty can be
studied and explained, but only if some 'objective' standard of poverty
going beyond the sum of the comparative study of standards in practice
in different countries is conceived.

Such an 'objective' approach involves the observation of material
deprivation —at work, in the home and environment, in fulfilling social
obligations and sharing in social customs and amenities — in relation to
levels of resources. The relative deprivation of some populations or
sections of society is not some intangible expression of disprivilege and
inequality. At its extreme it involves early death. The components of
different forms of material deprivation seem to be correlated with high
mortality (see references in Black 1980).

Explanation
Explanation of the phenomenon of poverty must proceed in conjunction
with sharper observations — and measurement — of the phenomenon
comparatively. If poverty is different from, but closely related to, inequality then we take the first step towards identifying those forces that
govern the establishment of the system of roles, customs and activities
of a nation — or what might be called its style of living — so that we can
understand what it is that people are deprived of and to what extent they
are deprived. This is analytically independent of the task of identifying
those forces that govern the distribution of income (and other resources)
in order to satisfy, or fall short of, that style of living. A principal component of the former is the definition within a society of those who are
eligible to occupy labour-force roles, and what kind of roles. A principal
component of the latter is the construction of the differential wage and
salary system and the complementary social security benefit system. This
approach is therefore different analytically from theoretical explanations
of social inequality or stratification. Both 'social policy' and the indivisi-
bility of social policy and economic management have become of central
importance in explaining poverty (for example, Parkin 1971; Giddens
1973; Scase 1977).

A first step is to comprehend the place taken by each nation-state and by groups of nation-states, like the members of the EEC described in this book, in the world economy. The dominance of European countries is partly a function of their place in colonial history and their opportunity to play a dominant part in setting up, and operating, the world's economic institutions. Once deprived of an equal say in world markets, poor countries find themselves ill-equipped to claim high prices for their products. Some years ago Julius Nyerere gave a vivid example of the relative powerlessness of decolonised nations. 'While as late as 1965 Tanzania could buy a tractor with 5.3 tons of cotton or 17.3 tons of sisal, by early 1972 an equivalent tractor cost 8 tons of cotton or 42 tons of sisal.' (*Third World* November 1972). In studying poverty in Europe in relation to the differences in overall prosperity of member-states the fact that the EC is also engaged in a competitive trading relationship with the Third World, or the countries of what is now called the 'South', must not be forgotten.

It can be seen in Table 1.1 that European countries share a position of privileged status in the ranks of the world's living standards. Six of the EC countries are among the world's 10 wealthiest states and the other member-countries are not far behind. Through NATO and the EC steps have been taken to confirm and maintain this degree of influence in the world's social development. While it is difficult to convey complex modern history in crude outline without distortion it is necessary to point out that the rapid economic expansion of many European countries and their high living standards have been gained in part at the expense of the poor countries of the South. This has been conceded even by those drawing up the Brandt Report, but has been expressed more sharply by advocates of a far more equal conduct of the world's affairs (Hayter 1981). It is perhaps best illustrated in the 'debt trap' created for poor countries in the so-called aid policies of the wealthy powers (see, for example, Payer 1974).

The EC has to be seen as a self-interested organisation seeking to enhance its wealth and power in relation to the rest of the world. The capacity of individual member-nations to control the terms on which they receive imports, including the tariffs to be charged, and how far government aid to industry is legitimate is heavily restricted. The EC is part of a system of global trade and exchange set up by the rich countries to protect their interests. But in exchange for the prosperity believed to be guaranteed by membership each of the governments of the member countries has experienced a drastic reduction of its power to control its national economy. Throughout the post-war years the liberalisation of trade, initially a condition of Marshall Aid, became more of a reality. Britain and other Western European countries had removed virtually all

Table 1.1 *High and low ranking countries[1] according to GNP per capita*

Rank		GNP per capita[2] (1979) ($US)
1	Kuwait	17 100
2	Switzerland	13 920
3	Sweden	11 930
4	Denmark	11 900
5	West Germany	11 730
6	Belgium	10 920
7	Norway	10 700
8	USA	10 630
9	The Netherlands	10 230
10	France	9 950
11	Canada	9 640
12	Australia	9 120
13	Japan	8 810
14	Austria	8 630
15	Libya	8 170
16	Finland	8 160
17	Saudi Arabia	7 280
18	German Democratic Republic	6 430
19	UK	6 320
20	New Zealand	5 930
21	Italy	5 250
22	Ireland	4 210
100	Pakistan	260
109	India	190
114	Burma	160
115	Mali	140
118	Ethiopia	130
120	Bangladesh	90

1 Countries with less than 1 million population are not included in the table. The GNP *per capita* for the following countries was ($US):

Qatar	16 670
United Arab Emirates	15 590
Luxembourg	12 670
Iceland	10 400

2 Converting GNP to a common currency at prevailing exchange rates is a misleading way of comparing real incomes. Estimates have been made of equivalent purchasing power with the following results:

	Exchange rate ($US)	Purchasing power ($US)
Industrial countries	10 660	8 960
Middle-income countries	1 710	2 690
Low-income countries	220	730

Source: World Bank 1981.

licensing of imports by 1960 and had reduced import duties and tariffs to considerably less than 10 per cent by 1970. Western Europe is now a tariff-free region for trade in manufactures. In Britain, and to a lesser extent, the Federal Republic of Germany, France and Italy a large part of the machinery in factories and of goods in the shops has been made elsewhere. The spread of free trade was followed closely by free movement of capital, first according to certain rules to finance trade and investment in new technology and then with little impediment at all. Today, there is a constant flow of money from sterling to dollars, from bank accounts in California to real estate in London, from West German shares to British government securities, and so on. This freedom of trade and capital has allowed multinational companies to grow at a rapid pace and to compete on a global scale.

The power of any government to control the national economy has, as a consequence, diminished. The change from the early post-war years is dramatic. A large part of trade, investment and employment cannot be wholly controlled and governments require the confidence of financial markets to carry out their expenditure plans. This does not mean that control has simply moved to international institutions like the IMF, GATT, OECD and the EC. They have increasingly played the main part in evolving new rules to police the system of finance, investment and trade and enforce market rules.

However, the percentage share of the world resources of the European states, and the growth of that share, cannot be interpreted only in national political or Euro-political terms. Transnational corporations have become of huge influence. Economic conditions have favoured the emergence of both big national and new transnational corporations. Production is being reorganised internationally — with fundamental implications for rich as well as poor countries to control the extent of poverty in their midst. The traditional international division of labour is being superseded. The relocation of manufacturing industry in countries such as Brazil, Taiwan and South Korea, where labour is cheap and where manufacturing processes car be divided into stages that require workers to undergo only short spans of training, is very rapid. As early as 1975, for example, the workforces of foreign subsidiaries of West German manufacturing firms equalled 20 per cent of their workforces in West Germany itself (Fröbel *et al.* 1979). In 1979, one of the first steps of Mrs Thatcher's goverment on attaining office was to relinquish exchange controls, so giving a fillip to overseas investment. Multinational companies based in Britain have thrived in the late 1970s and early 1980s despite the faltering fortunes of national companies. Increasingly, the transnational companies follow policies that transcend the capacities to control them of even the strong nation-states. Measured on annual turn-over, 43 of the 100 wealthiest powers in the world are transnational companies and not nation-states. Exxon and Standard Oil, for example, have larger budgets than do Switzerland, Yugoslavia and Saudi Arabia. Already, a third of all trade is not even between nations — it takes place between different subsidiaries or divisions of General Electric, Unilever, Exxon or Phillips.

The growing profits of transnational companies have been occurring at the expense of millions of people in both the pioneering countries as well as some of the newly-penetrated countries of the manufacturing process. In the former, there has been declining output, short-time work-ing, mass redundancies and abrupt changes of jobs. For many workers there has been a loss not just of job, but trade or skill as well, and many have been forced to sell their labour-power as unskilled or partly skilled workers for lower wages. Cuts in social security benefits and public expenditure have deepened the problems of major recession and have worsened the problems of those outside employment as well as lower paid wage earners.

It could fairly be said that poverty has been compounded in two respects since the formation of the EC. Although in a competitive world economy the EC's preferential arrangements have maintained, and perhaps enhanced, the average position of the member-countries in re-lation to the world economy, and real incomes have increased, this has been at the expense of:

(a) growing regional and class inequalities (including a rising proportion of the total population living on low incomes, many but not all of them because of unemployment);
(b) secondly, a rapidly evolving mass consumer lifestyle which is becom-increasingly inaccessible to those on the low incomes defined histori-cally in terms of a fixed purchasing value of subsistence or basic needs.

It is the absence of anything that could be described as an effective counterbalancing European social policy (including control according to social values or objectives of emerging transnational corporations) and a weakening momentum of some corresponding national welfare state strategies that explain this worsening situation. I will discuss these in turn. At a time of rapid multinational developments in industry, trade and the management of national economies, why were the com-bined attempts of member-states to offset poverty, redress inequalities and harmonise benefits and services so feeble?

European Policies

I will discuss the Community's regional policy, the European Social Fund, and the European Programme of Pilot Schemes to Combat Poverty. From the beginning, favourable postures were struck about regional problems. In its preamble the 1958 Treaty of Rome referred to ensuring harmonious development 'by reducing the differences existing between the various regions and by mitigating the backwardness of the less favoured regions'. Article 2 of that treaty specifically referred, for example, to the eastern border regions of West Germany and the Mezzogiorno of southern Italy. However, many politicians and economists believed that the commitment to regional policies, which could not be differentiated in principle from national subsidy policies like the Regional Employment Premium applied in Britain between 1967 and 1977, necessarily contradicted the over-riding commitment of the EC to the principle of free competition and trade. They believed that attempts to reduce regional disparities would lead to slower economic growth and less efficient production. As a consequence, regional policy emerged as a series of exceptions to the Community's rules (see, for example, Articles 49, 80, 92 and 226 of the Treaty of Rome) and was never built into a major positive programme. Thus the Commission took steps to discourage member-states from pursuing certain kinds of internal regional policy (like the Temporary Employment Subsidy and the Regional Employment Premium in Britain) and has sought to restrict the size of financial inducements offered (Armstrong 1978).

Between 1958 and 1972 there was remarkably little progress towards a systematic regional policy and activity mainly devolved upon four institutions: the European Coal and Steel Community; the European Investment Bank; the European Social Fund and the guidance section of the European Guidance and Guarantee Fund. In 1972 it was decided at the Paris summit to strengthen regional policy. A European Regional Development Fund was set up after lengthy dispute from 1 January 1975. By comparison with national budgets the sums of expenditure involved were not large. Thus, in 1973, when the scope of work of the Fund was still in contention, the Commission proposed to spend £940 million over the three years 1974–6, whereas the eventual regulations provided powers in 1975 to spend only £540 million over the next three years. This was believed to represent 'an extremely limited package of regional policy instruments' which 'compares unfavourably with the huge range of regional policy instruments available to a member state such as the UK'. (Armstrong 1978: 517. See also Chisholm 1976; Holland 1976). In 1977 the Fund was only 4 per cent of EC budget commitments. The agriculture policy (which accounts for nearly three-quarters of the budget) was, and is, the real regional policy and, as one of the European Commissioners, George Thomson, said in 1977, 'the blunt truth about the Community Farm Policy is that it is anti-regional' (*The Times*, 6 January 1977. See also Thomson 1979).

Like the Regional Fund the Social Fund also comprises a very small percentage of the European budget — in 1977 just over 5 per cent. Created originally by the Treaty of Rome the Social Fund was substantially revised in 1971, when powers were taken to act to relieve the difficulties created by the Community's own policies and the other problems of structural unemployment. Most of its funds have been in the form of part-reimbursement of member-state employment policies. In the mid-1970s the Director General for Social Affairs at the European Commission acknowledged the problems of rising unemployment and said that 'the long-term natural growth rate of the community's economies may be too low to provide jobs for all who seek them — unless special measures are taken to create job vacancies' (Shanks 1977: 19). The annual budget of the recast Social Fund grew from around 40 million EUA in 1973 to about 250 million EUA in 1978 (a little over two units being equivalent to a pound sterling). The worsening of unemployment towards the end of the 1970s became of greater concern and in 1980, 909 million Units of Account were authorised for the Social Fund. As much as 395.5 million EUA was allocated for aid to improve the employment situation in specific regions, industries or groups of firms and 358 million for operations to assist young people, 74 million for handicapped workers, and between 20 million and 30 million each for agriculture and textiles, women and migrant workers. Nearly a third of the total was allocated to Italy, and around a fifth to both the UK and France.

In 1974, as part of the Social Action Programme, it was agreed 'to implement in co-operation with the member states specific measures to combat poverty by drawing up pilot schemes'. Ireland played a big part in the original conception of what came to be called the European Programme of Pilot Schemes to Combat Poverty (see Davies 1979; Espoir 1980). As Edward James, the Director of the European Special Programme (Social Policy Observation Information and Research) has said, this programme of pilot schemes to fight poverty, proposed initially by the Irish Labour party, was attractive to a government looking for a timely and dramatic gesture, was cheap and easy to get under way and indicated a commitment to fighting poverty in general, without committing the government to any line of policy in particular (James 1980). This is not to suggest that the commitment was not genuine but that the modest programme recommended could only be a kind of token or prelude for any substantial proposals to deal with poverty, which would mean developing a powerful range of major policies to change existing structures and methods of allocating resources, and also educate if not restrain those representing vested interests on behalf of those sections of the population enjoying a disproportionately large share of available resources. Included in the pilot schemes were projects to bring services to poor people but also mobilise people on their own behalf. The UK projects included seven schemes for family day centres run by voluntary organisations — one project being in Liverpool, one in Croydon and the rest in Greater London. Some cross-national studies were also undertaken. In 1975, 2.5 million EUA were allocated and the total rose year by year, reaching 5.75 million units in 1979.

A measured historical assessment of EC social policies is therefore likely to conclude that, whether in relation to the aggregate income of the member-states or even the Community's budget, very little contribution has been made to meeting the emerging problems of Europe. Indeed, it could be argued that, on the contrary, the EC has helped to sharpen inequality and poverty to a greater extent than anyone might have expected — from having had an acquaintance with the history of national welfare states. Michael Shanks, a former Director General of Social Affairs, pointed out that if the EC's social policy had been based strictly on the Rome Treaty it would necessarily have concentrated on:

(a) measures to ensure the free movement of labour;
(b) equalisation of social costs and constraints on enterprise.

But he went on to argue that harmonisation between member-states was simply not feasible in practice (Shanks in Kapteyn 1977; see also Watson 1977). He recognised that European social policy was more a 'self-contained area of activity' than 'an integrated part of overall strategy, influenced by and influencing other policies' and that much remained to be done 'to humanise the process of economic growth and integration.' (Shanks 1977: 99—101.) Altogether his evaluation smacks of judicious understatement and failed to get to grips with the social preferences and discrimination implicit in any form of economic management. Certainly some of the hopes about the likely importance of social policy cautiously expressed in the early years of the EEC have not materialised (see, for example, Collins 1964, 1972 and 1975).

National Policies

By far the most important attempts to reduce poverty in Europe are therefore represented not by the cross-national measures but by the national policies of member-states. Income maintenance systems and social services in individual European countries have long been acknowledged to be stronger and more extensive than in the USA, for example:

Welfare reform in the United States only occurs when a high crisis threshold is surpassed in the Great Depression or during the 1960s. This reform pattern of pressure politics contrasts sharply with the bureaucratic politics characteristic of West Germany. The greater political importance of social classes and trade unions in West Germany has led to the creation of institutionalisation structures for dealing with political issues that might arouse class antagonisms. Conflicts over welfare policy are handled within this institutional framework and are thereby routinized and depoliticized. (Leibfried 1979: 195–196)

This theoretical interpretation is shared in practice by many observers (usually in social administration) who have sought to compare European with US social services. Thus, in one of a series of comparative studies, two Americans reflected on the frustrations felt by many in their country:

> We apparently consider it legitimate, whether in the interests of the economy or of equality of the sexes, to open broader opportunities for women in the labour force, yet we do not face rapidly and thoughtfully need for a parallel child-care policy, fearing apparently that its outcome will be to 'federalise' the children .... The assignment of general tax revenues for social programmes is morally no different — if the services are in the public interest — from tax revenue for roads, canals, guns or forest-fire fighting. (Kahn and Kamerman, 1977: 171–2)

It is therefore important to establish the point that a number of the European welfare systems are sophisticated and ameliorative relative to those of some other countries in the world which have reached approximately the same stage of economic development. Such a conclusion opens our minds to the possibility of deterioration in the effectiveness of those welfare systems to cope with the changes in the organisation of the world economy and, in particular, to make up for the deficiences in the social policies of the EC. Although those systems may be increasingly less relevant to some of the emerging problems of unemployment, deprivation and poverty, and may be becoming institutionally less redistributive from rich to poor than they were (quite apart from what they were supposed to be), they remain nonetheless substantial. This can be seen from a number of statistical compilations from the EC (as reviewed in Chapter 2). In the late 1970s, total tax receipts averaged nearly 40 per cent of Gross National Product (GNP) and had been growing. During the last 10 years, there have been steady improvements in medical staffing and nursing, for example. And although social protection expenditure grew more slowly in the UK during the 1970s than in the other eight member countries it grew on average in the EC from 22.7 per cent of net national disposable income in 1970 to 30.8 per cent in 1977 (with another 5 or 6 per cent to be added for expenditure on education) (EC 1980).

Many member countries are now preoccupied with high rates of unemployment, the problems of developing public employment schemes at least for large numbers of school leavers, and the payment of unemployment benefits. But this represents more than a late twentieth century crisis in the management of welfare states. For years, a structural problem has been building up. Many of the efforts made by radical groups and parties to improve cash benefits and welfare services have been frustrated by the steady increase in the numbers, and proportion, of the population who are dependants. This is more than a problem of ageing, being compounded by higher school-leaving ages, earlier retirement, an increased number of one-parent families, a small increase in the number of people disabled following accidents and new pressures to persuade married women to withdraw from the labour market.

The traditional assumption of financing the welfare of the poor from taxes is being questioned vigorously. For much of the post-war period the politics of welfare have been concerned in practice with the surplus, or with economic growth. The welfare state has been concerned more with redistribution than distribution. But the financial equation has now become strained and in different contexts the interests of the poor seem to be clashing more openly with those of taxpayers. The worsening economy, together with forces making for greater inequality and disproportionate increases in dependency, have made it more and more difficult to maintain, still less improve, levels of benefit.

These trends are calling attention to the need to transform the nature of social policy — by insisting on the inseparability of social and economic management and by making the allocation of resources in the first place, rather than their reallocation once received, the central concern of policies to attack poverty. This involves large-scale interventionist employment programmes for both industry and services, legislation on accumulated wealth, and policies to reduce the span of wages and salaries (for example, by introducing maxima as well as minima) (see Townsend 1979, Cripps *et al.* 1981). A group of German social scientists, for example, made an analysis of the redistribution system which

> uncovers deficiencies in state policies intended to modify deprived market situations which emanate from their construction principles. To counteract these deficiencies, it is necessary to devise preventive policies that intervene in the allocation rules of the market itself. Moreover, an indispensable complementary strategy seems to be a reconstruction of the systems of secondary distribution including decoupling the status in the labour market from benefits actually meeting needs. (Heinze, *et al*. 1981: 219)

There remains a formidable task — to make the analysis of poverty more international and more scientific; to insist on adopting a wide range of criteria of deprivation in studies of poverty and the strategies to mitigate the phenomenon; to interrelate explanations depending on multinational and not only national causal factors; and to show the greater importance of strategies of prevention than of casualty treatment. We hope that this book makes some contribution to this task.

References

Armstrong, H. W. 1978, 'Community regional policy: a survey and critique', *Regional Studies*, vol. 12.

Australia 1975, *Poverty in Australia*, First main Report of the Commission of Inquiry into Poverty, Canberra, APGS.

Batson, E. 1941−4, *Social survey of Cape Town*, Reports of the School of Social Science and Social Administration, University of Cape Town.

Batson, E. 1945, *The poverty line in Salisbury*, University of Cape Town.

Beckerman, E. *et al.* 1969, *Poverty and the impact of income maintenance programmes*, Geneva, ILO.

Bettison, D. S. 1960, 'The poverty datum line in central Africa', *Rhodes Livingstone Journal*, no. 27.

Black, D. (Chairman) 1980, *Inequalities in health*, London, DHSS.

Booth, C. 1903, *Life and labour of the people in London*, London, Macmillan (17 vol. edition). (Original volume on East London published in 1889 by Williams and Norgate.)

Bowley, A. L. and Burnett-Hurst, A. R. 1915, *Livelihood and poverty, a study in the economic and social conditions of working class households in Northampton, Warrington, Stanley, Reading and Bolton*, London, King.

Bradshaw, J. and Piachaud, D. 1980, *Child support in the European Community*, LSE Occasional Papers on Social Administration no. 66, London, Bedford Square Press.

Brandt, W. (Chairman) 1980, *North-South: A Programme for Survival*, London, Pan Books.

Castles, S. and Kosack, G. 1973, *Immigrant workers and the class structure in Western Europe*, 1973, Oxford, OUP.

Chisholm, M. 1976, 'Regional policies in an era of slow population growth and higher unemployment', *Regional Studies*, vol. 10, no. 2.

Coates, K. and Silburn, R. 1981, *Poverty: the forgotten Englishmen*, Harmondsworth, Penguin Books. (Reprinted with new introduction and epilogue.)

Collins, D. 1964, 'Towards a European social policy', *Journal of Common Market Studies*.

Collins, D. 1972, 'First thoughts on social policy in the Common Market' in K. Jones (ed.), *Year book of social policy 1971*, London, Routledge & Kegan Paul.

Collins, D. 1975, *The European Coal and Steel Community*, 1951−70, London, Martin Robertson.

Cripps, F., Griffith, J., Morrell, F., Reid, J., Townsend, P. and Weir, S. 1981, *Manifesto*, London, Pan Books.

Davies, L. 1979, 'Fighting poverty EEC style', *Community care*, 7 June.

Department of Economic and Social Affairs, United Nations, 1971, *Industrial Social Welfare*, New York.

Donnison, D. 1981, *The politics of poverty*, London, Martin Robertson.

Drewnowski, J. and Scott, W. 1966, *The level of living index*, United Nations, Research Institute for Social Development, Report no. 4, Geneva, September.

EC 1977, *The perception of poverty in Europe*, Brussels, Commission of the European Communities.

EC 1979, *The European social budget 1980–1975–1970*, Brussels, Commission of the European Communities.

EC 1980, *Social indicators for the European Community 1960–1978*, Luxembourg, Eurostat.

EC 1981, *Report on Social developments, 1980*, Brussels, Commission of the European Communities.

ECSWTR (European Centre for Social Welfare Training and Research) 1979, *Anit-poverty measures in European countries*, Eurosocial Reports no. 14, Vienna.

Espoir 1980, *Europe against poverty, evaluation report of the European programme of pilot schemes and studies to combat poverty*, Canterbury, Espoir.

Ferge, Z. 1979, *A society in the making: Hungarian social and societal policy, 1945–75*, Harmondsworth, Penguin Books.

Ferge, Z. 1980, *The social reproduction of socially disadvantaged situations of poverty or deprivation*, Vienna, ECSWTR.

Fiegehen, G. C., Lansley, P. S. and Smith, A. D. 1977, *Poverty and progress in Britain, 1953–1973*, London, National Institute of Economic and Social Research.

France 1981 *Contre la Précarité et la Pauvreté*, Report to the President of an inter-department Working Party, Paris.

FRG 1981, *Poverty study for the European Commission*, Interim Report EEC.

Friedman, M. 1963, *Capitalism and freedom*, University of Chicago Press.

Fröbel, F., Heinrichs, J. and Kreye, O. 1979, *The new international division of labour*, Cambridge, CUP.

George, V. and Lawson, R. 1980, *Poverty and inequality in common market countries*, London, Routledge & Kegan Paul.

Ghai, D. P. et al. 1977, *The basic needs approach to development: some issues regarding concepts and methodology*, Geneva, ILO.

Giddens, A. 1973, *The class structure of the advanced societies*, London, Hutchinson.

Halliday, A. 1965, 'The significance of poverty definition to Australians', *Australian Journal of Social Issues*, vol. 10.

Harrington, M. 1962, *The other America*, Harmondsworth, Penguin Books.

Hasan, P. 1978, 'Growth and equity in East Asia', *Finance and Development*, June.

Hayter, T. 1981, *Creation of world poverty*, London, Pluto.

Heidenheimer, A. J., Helco, H. and Adams, C. T. 1976, *Comparative public policy*, London, Macmillan.

Heinze, R. G., Hinrichs, K., Willy Hohn, H. and Olk, T. 1981, 'Armut und Arbeitsmarkt: zum Zusammenhang von Klassenlagen und Verarmungsrisiken im Sozialstaat', *Zeitschrift für Soziologie*, July.

Henderson, R. F. 1980, 'Poverty in Britain and Australia: reflection on poverty in the United Kingdom by Peter Townsend', *The Australian Quarterly*.

Henderson, R. F., Harcourt, A. and Harper, R. J. A. 1970, *People in poverty, a Melbourne survey*, Melbourne, Cheshire.

Higgins, J. 1978, *The poverty business, Britain and America*, Blackwell.

Holland, S. 1976, *The regional problem*, London, Macmillan.

Holman, R. 1978, *Poverty: explanations of social deprivation*, Oxford, Martin Robertson.

ILO 1976, *Employment growth and basic needs: a one-world problem*, Report of the Director General of the ILO, Geneva, ILO.

ILO 1977, *Meeting basic needs: strategies for eradicating mass poverty and unemployment*, Conclusions of the World Employment Conference 1976, Geneva, ILO.

India 1978 *Five year plan, 1978—83*; Planning Commission, Delhi, Government of India.

James, E. and Laurent, A. 1975, 'Social security: the European experiment', *Social trends*, London, HMSO.

James, E. 1980, '*A role for Europe*', Papers to a conference on responses to poverty in European countries', Civil Service College, Sunningdale.

Kahn, A. J. and Kamerman, S. B. 1977, *Not for the poor alone: European social services*, New York, Harper.

Kahn, A. and Kamerman, S. (eds) 1978, *Family policy: government and families in fourteen countries*, New York, Columbia University Press.

Kahn, A. J. and Kamerman, S. B. 1980, *Social services in international perspective*, New Brunswick and London Transaction books.

Kaim-Caudle, P. R. 1973, *Comparative social policy and social security*, London, Martin Robertson.

Kaim-Caudle, P. 1980, 'A cross-national evaluation of post-war European social policies', University of Durham (publication forthcoming).

Kakwani, N. 1980a, *Income inequality and poverty*, Oxford, OUP.

Kakwani, N. 1980b, 'Issues in measuring poverty' in Social Welfare Research Centre, *The poverty line: Methodology and Measurement*, University of New South Wales, Australia.

Kapteyn, P. J. G. (ed.) 1977, *The social policy of the European communities*, Sitjthoff.

Keithley, J. 1981, 'The European social budget', *Social Policy and Administration*, vol. 15, no. 2.

Lampman, R. 1966, in Klein, W. A., 'Some problems of negative income taxation', *Wisconsin law review*.

Lawson, R. and Reed, B. 1975, *Social security in the European Community*, London, Chatham House, PEP.

Lawson, R. and Stevens, C. 1974, 'Housing allowances in West Germany and France', *Journal of Social Policy*, vol. 3.

Lees, D. 1967, 'Poor families and fiscal reform', *Lloyds Bank Review*.

Leibfreid, S. 1979, 'The United States and West German Welfare Systems: a comparative analysis', *Cornell International Law Journal*, vol. 12.

Maasdorp, G. and Humphreys, A. S. V. (eds) 1975, *From shanty town to township: an economic study of African poverty and rehousing in a South African city*, Cape Town, Juta.

Madge, C. and Willmott, P. 1981, *Inner city poverty in Paris and London*, London, Routledge & Kegan Paul.

MacGregor, S. 1981, *The politics of poverty*, London, Longmans.

Malaysia 1976, *Third Malaysian plan*, 1976—80, Kuala Lumpur, Government Press.

Maynard, A. 1975, *Health care in the European community*, London, Croom Helm.

Maynard, A. 1981, 'The inefficiency and inequalitites of the health care systems of Western Europe', *Social Policy and Administration*, vol. 15, no. 2.

OECD 1976, *Public expenditure on income maintenance and programmes*, Studies in Resource Allocation no. 3, Paris.

Orshansky, M. 1969, 'How poverty is measured', *Monthly Labour Review*, February.

Parkin, F. 1971, *Class, inequality and political order*, London, MacGibbon and Kee.

Payer, C. 1974, *The debt trap: the IMF and the third world*, Harmondsworth, Pelican.

Pillay, P. N. 1973, *A poverty datum line study among Africans in Durban*, Occ. Paper no. 3, Department of Economics, University of Nepal.

Plotnick, R. D. and Skidmore, F. 1975, *Progress against poverty: a review of the 1964—1974 decade*, Institute for Research on Poverty. University of Wisconsin-Madison, New York, Academic Press.

Reubens, B. G. 1970, *The hard-to-employ: European programmes*, New York, Columbia University Press.

Roberti, P. 1979, 'Counting the poor: a review of the situation existing in six industrialised nations' in DHSS Social Security Research, *The definition and measurement of poverty*, London, HMSO.

Rose, M. E. 1972, *The relief of poverty, 1834—1914*, London, Macmillan.

Rowntree, B. S. 1901, *Poverty: a study of town life*, London, Macmillan.

Russett, B. M. *et al*. 1965, *World handbook of political and social indicators*, Yale University Press.

Sawyer, M. and Wasserman, M. 1976, *Income distribution in OECD countries*, Paris.

Scase, R. (ed.) 1977, *Industrial society: class, cleavage and control*, London, Allen & Unwin.

Sen, A. 1981, *Poverty and famines*, Oxford, OUP.

Shanas, E. *et al*. 1968, *Old people in three industrial societies*, London, Routledge & Kegan Paul.

Shanks, M. 1977, *European social policy, today and tomorrow*, Oxford, Pergamon Press.

Sinfield, A. 1980, 'Poverty and inequality in France' in V. George and R. Lawson, (eds), *Poverty and inequality in Common Market countries*, London, Routledge & Kegan Paul.

SWRC 1980, *The poverty line: methodology and measurement*, Kensington, Social Welfare Research Centre, University of New South Wales.

Thomson, G. 1979, 'Europe — the issues that matter', *New Europe*, vol. 7, no. 1, Winter.

Titmuss, R. M. 1971, 'Social security and the six', *New Society*, 11 November.

Tobin, J. 1965, 'Improving the economic status of the negro', *Daedalus.*

Townsend, P. (ed.) 1970, *The concept of poverty*, London, Heinemann.

Townsend, P. 1979, *Poverty in the United Kingdom*, London, Allen Lane and Penguin Books.

Townsend, P. 1981, *An alternative concept of poverty*, Division for the Study of Development, UNESCO, Paris.

UNESCO 1978, *Study in depth on the concept of basic human needs in relation to various ways of life and its possible implications for the action of the organisation*, Paris, UNESCO.

USA 1976, *The measure of poverty*, Washington, DC, United States Department of Health Education and Welfare.

Watson, P. 1977, 'Harmonisation of Social Security within the European community — the history of a changing concept', *Social and Economic Administration*, vol. 11, no. 1.

Watts, H. W. 1977, 'An economic definition of poverty' in M. Moon and E. Smolensky, (eds), *Improving measures of economic wellbeing*, New York, Academic Press.

World Bank 1981, World Development Report, London, OUP, 1981.

2 Resources, Welfare Expenditure and Poverty in European Countries
*Robert Walker**

This chapter contains comparative information about the nature and extent of poverty in Europe and about the national policy environments. The first part investigates the variation in national resources between the countries of the European Community (EC) and shows how these are marshalled to meet the demands for social welfare. The second part serves to complement the previous chapter by examining national conceptions of poverty as revealed in response to a cross-national survey of social attitudes and by a brief examination of the function of social assistance. Finally, a preliminary attempt is made to order the existing information on European poverty.

Unfortunately study of these issues is in its infancy and the data is generally inadequate although the national reports on poverty commissioned in the late 1970s by the European Commission mark a significant advance (see: EC 1981a). Information is also available on social welfare expenditure as a result of the heroic efforts of Eurostat to publish data in accordance with the European System of Integrated Social Protection. This latter information is highly aggregated and does not lend itself to breakdown into the main constituent elements. Nevertheless, despite the limitations of data, we will try to establish a broad context against which to set the chapters that follow. However, first it is necessary to report the definitions of poverty used in this chapter and elsewhere in the book.

The three principal measures of poverty are, in essence, indices of relative poverty and all seek to establish levels of disposable income below which households — of varying composition — may be considered to be poor. The first measure equates the poverty line in each country with the income received by social assistance claimants. However, this measure has a number of weaknesses. First, relative to average earnings, the levels vary from country to country, which prevents direct international comparison. Social assistance rates also vary markedly within certain countries where administration is localised and in Denmark a

*My special thanks to staff in the International Relations Branch Library of the Department of Health and Social Security and the Statistics and Market Intelligence Library of the Department of Trade.

unique poverty level is effectively set for each individual on the basis of their previous income (see Chapter 6). Again social assistance payments are widely believed to be unduly low in relation to what most people regard as acceptable minimum standards (Beckerman 1979). Nevertheless, national poverty levels are useful in providing a measure of a country's success with respect to its own objectives.

The other two measures are closely related. Neither can be used for assessing the performance of countries with respect to national objectives, but both establish a uniform benchmark which makes possible estimation of the extent of relative income poverty in each country. The first index is the international standard poverty line devised by Professor Wilfred Beckerman from an earlier OECD study (Beckerman 1979; OECD 1976). It equates the poverty line for a couple without children with *per capita* disposable income for the country concerned. This figure is multiplied by ratios derived from the British official supplementary benefit scale rates to yield poverty lines for households of different composition (see Annex A). Personal disposable income is taken to equal income net of taxes and social security contributions and after receipt of all social security and allied benefits. National estimates of personal disposable income may be derived from the annual OECD publication *National Accounts of OECD Countries*. However, the most recent statistics relate to 1978 and for later years disposable income is established as an empirically derived proportion of Gross Domestic Product (GDP) (see Annex B).

The Beckerman index is also imperfect. The choice of poverty level is essentially arbitrary; it approximates to the average of social assistance limits for the countries included in the original OECD study. Also the adoption of the equivalence ratios implicit in the UK supplementary benefit scheme is questionable since these are not based on any systematic survey of needs.

The final measure is that used in the national studies of poverty, recently commissioned by the European Commission (EC 1981a). With this measure a household's disposable income, adjusted for household composition according to an equivalence scale akin to that used by Beckerman, is related to the national average of all household disposable income when similarly adjusted for composition. The household is then defined as being in poverty if its disposable income is less than a given proportion of the national average. In this way poverty lines of varying severity may be set and two are reported below (equating to 40 and 60 per cent of disposable income respectively).

Although the poverty lines adopted here are arbitrary, they have established 'pedigrees' in that they derive from work sponsored respectively by the OECD, ILO and the European Commission. Beckerman's poverty standard equates closely with the '60 per cent disposable income' line and both indices are somewhat higher than social assistance levels in most countries. The '40 per cent disposable income' level is generally more similar to social assistance rates.

Resources and Expenditure

National income

The extent of income poverty in a society is a function of the total national income, its distribution, and the precise measure of poverty adopted. This section focuses on national income, while measures of poverty are discussed below. First, the nine EC countries are compared with respect to their national income, here expressed in terms of *per capita* GDP. Next, since the initial income distribution in most advanced industrial countries is largely achieved through the labour market, the number excluded from it in each country is assessed. (The command of income exerted by the holders of wealth should not of course be overlooked.) People excluded from the labour market — here termed dependants or dependent groups — are likely to be the main recipients of the secondary transfers of income that arise from government intervention through taxation and welfare expenditure. To the extent that these transfers are more or less generous, the dependent groups will run a greater or lesser risk of income poverty. Finally, therefore, this section examines the distribution of welfare expenditures in the European countries.

A common measure of national income is GDP, which corresponds to the value of goods and services produced by a country, plus taxes linked to imports and less intermediate consumption. In comparisons between countries and over time, GDP is usually expressed on a *per capita* basis to allow for differences in population size. In the same way between-country comparisons necessitate that the value of GDP be expressed in terms of common metric. (This metric is often US dollars or, in the case of Eurostat publications, the European Unit of Account, ECU.) Where conversion to a common metric involves the use of market exchange rates — as in both the examples — there is no guarantee that a unit of the common metric would purchase the same volume of goods and services in each country. Recently, national account statistics for European countries have become available expressed in terms of a metric — the 'Purchasing Power Standard' (PPS) — which in some measure overcomes this problem. Under this system purchasing power parities — derived from data on the prices of around one thousand products in each European country — are used instead of monetary exchange rates to convert a value in one national currency into a value in another country's currency. The result is that one unit of the PPS would theoretically 'purchase' an equivalent volume of goods and services in any European country.

Table 2.1 reveals that the choice of metric is of more than academic significance. When GDP for 1980 is expressed in terms of US dollars at current rates, *per capita* GDP appears highest in West Germany followed by Denmark, Luxembourg and France. Moreover, *per capita* GDP in West Germany is more than two and a half times that of the poorest country, Ireland (exactly the same ratios would obtain if GDP were expressed in ECUs). However, when account is taken of purchasing power, *per capita* GDP in Luxembourg equates with a larger volume of goods and services than in West Germany and Denmark. Expressing GDP according to PPSs also greatly reduces the dispersion between countries so that *per capita* GDP in the richest country (Luxembourg) falls to less than twice that in the poorest (Ireland). The UK ranks seventh according to both measures but appears more similar to Italy than to The Netherlands when using PPSs.

From the perspective of social policy, increments to national income are frequently of more interest than absolute levels. This is because governments have generally found it less difficult to introduce new welfare programmes funded from newly created wealth rather than from a redistribution of existing wealth. Growth rates in Europe as a whole declined over the period 1965 to 1980 although with significant year-to-year variations (Table 2.2). However, if the year 1974/5 is excluded, when negative growth was recorded in all countries as a consequence of the marked rise in oil prices, the decline in growth between the two halves of the 1970s is much reduced.

During the 1960s growth was highest in Italy, France and Denmark. But the 1970s saw the eclipse of the Italian economic miracle, while Denmark slipped to the bottom of the growth league in the early 1970s only to recover somewhat between 1974 and 1979. France alone retained a position in the top three throughout the 15-year period. West Germany was relatively less affected than her European partners by the economic slow-down of the late 1970s and consequently, almost by default, moved to the top of the growth league for the period 1974 to 1979. During this period, West Germany also took over from Denmark as the country with the second highest *per capita* GDP behind Luxembourg which boasted the highest *per capita* GDP throughout the entire period. The UK achieved below average growth in all but three of the 16 years considered and between 1965 and 1969 was overtaken first by France and the Netherlands and finally by Belgium in terms of *per capita* GDP.

Per capita GDP is a measure of average living standards as well as of

Table 2.1   Per capita GDP at market prices, European countries, 1980

	Per capita PPS[1] (1)	GDP $US[2] (2)	Ratio to poorest country Col. (1)	Ratio to poorest country Col. (2)	Ratio to UK Col. (1)	Ratio to UK Col. (2)	Total Population (000s)
Luxembourg	9206	12 570	1.94	2.42	1.29	1.35	364
West Germany	8837	13 305	1.86	2.56	1.24	1.42	61 566
Denmark	8517	12.952	1.79	2.49	1.19	1.39	5 123
France	8473	12 136	1.78	2.34	1.18	1.30	53 713
Belgium	8175	11 816	1.72	2.27	1.14	1.27	9 859
The Netherlands	8071	11 851	1.70	2.28	1.13	1.27	14 150
UK	7150	9 335	1.50	1.80	1.00	1.00	55 945
Italy	6747	6 906	1.42	1.33	0.94	0.74	57 070
Ireland	4748	5 193	1.00	1.00	0.66	0.56	3 401

1 Source: EC 1982a.

2 At current prices and exchange rates. Source: OECD 1982.

Table 2.2   Growth in real GDP, European Countries, 1965–80

	Average annual rate of growth of real GDP per capita[1]				
	1965–9 (%)	1969–74 (%)	1974–9 (%)	1975–9 (%)	1979–80 (%)
West Germany	3.6	3.2	3.2	4.4	1.7
Denmark	4.1[2]	2.1	2.2	3.1	−0.4
France	4.8	4.6	2.7	3.4	0.8
Luxembourg	3.1	4.8	0.5	2.6	0.4
Belgium	3.2	5.3	1.9	2.9	2.3
The Netherlands	3.4	3.9	2.6	3.8	−0.3
UK	1.7	2.6	1.9	2.5	−1.5
Italy	5.0	3.7	1.8	3.5	3.7
Ireland	–	3.4[3]	2.6	3.1	0.1
EEC[4]	4.1	3.6	2.4	3.5	0.9

1 1975 prices and purchasing power parities; simple average over period.

2 1966–9.

3 1970–74.

4 Includes Greece.

Source: EC 1982a; own calculations.

national resources and is compared with other measures of living standards in Table 2.3. Whereas *per capita* GDP reveals nothing about the dispersion of income, measures relating to the ownership of consumer durables reveal somewhat more since the number of durables owned by most individuals is likely to be strictly limited. On the other hand, ownership of certain durables may not be as desirable in some cultures as in others — even where purchasing power is approximately equal. Personal disposable income and *per capita* private consumption are net of direct taxation and expenditure by governments and by private profit-making institutions, thereby giving an indication of the money individual citizens have to spend (the latter measure excludes personal savings). In contradistinction, infant mortality and the level of school enrolment may be interpreted, in part at least, as output measures related to government expenditure. The price-earnings index represents an attempt to relate wages to prices and may be viewed as a measure of the average number of hours of paid work necessary to purchase a given basket of goods (the higher the index, the larger is the number of hours).

Table 2.4 shows that a different ranking of countries emerges with respect to each of the indices of living standards. In part these variations are artefacts of the measure chosen. West Germany, for example, is ranked eighth in terms of full-time enrolment of 15—19-year-olds but has a very large part-time education programme for this age group (see Chapter 5). Other discrepancies are more significant. For example, the disparity between Denmark's rankings on *per capita* GDP and on *per capita* private consumption reflects the high rate of both direct taxation and public sector spending.

The mean rankings of living standard should be treated with care since the choice of measures is arbitrary, may not necessarily be additive, and possibly gives excessive weight to certain components of the concept of the living standard. Nevertheless, they do point to a rough similarity of living standards, at least between Luxembourg, The Netherlands and Denmark, with a marked distinction between the three poorest countries — Ireland, Italy and the UK — and the other members of the EC.

Dependency groups and low wage earners

It may be valuable briefly to consider the comparative burden of dependency in the European countries (later parts of the book deal with details for particular countries). Unless they are to be left destitute, individuals with no productive capacity — in a purely economic sense — place a 'burden' on those who are engaged in the economic process. In traditional societies this burden was borne directly by kin or, from quite early on, by the local community through embryonic schemes of social assistance.

Table 2.3   Indicators of living standards in European countries

	Year	Luxembourg	West Germany	Denmark	France	Belgium	The Netherlands	UK	Italy	Ireland
Per capita GDP[1] (PPSs)	1980	9206	8837	8517	8473	8175	8071	7150	6747	4748
Per capita private consumption[1] (PPSs)	1980	5495	5319	4802	5395	5143	4792	4343	4288	3029
Per capita personal disposable income[2] (PPSs)	1980	–	5661	4878	6044	6202	5490	4698	5378	–
Passenger cars[3] (per 000)	1978	423	346	219	327	302	288	256	300	194
Telephones[3] (per 000)	1979	547	434	609	415	352	486	480	318	174
Full-time school enrolment[3] (% of children aged 15–19)	1977	33.5	41.5	57.4	33.5	61.3	62.7	44.6	43.9	50.0
Infant mortality[3] (per 000 – 6 months)	1979	13.0	13.5	8.8	9.8	11.2	8.7	11.8	15.3	12.4
Price/earnings index[4]	1977	81	76	90	145	98	81	131	–	–

1 Source: EC 1982a.
2 Estimate.
3 Source: OECD 1982.
4 Interpreted as the hours of work necessary to earn sufficient to purchase a specific basket of goods, standardised to the seven-country mean. The basket consists of all non-duplicated items for which information is given for all seven countries (EC 1980a). Non-consumer durables are weighted by 10.

Table 2.4   Relative living standards in European countries

	Luxembourg	West Germany	Denmark	France	Belgium	The Netherlands	UK	Italy	Ireland
Per capita GDP[1]	1	2	3	4	5	6	7	8	9
Per capita private consumption[1]	1	3	5	2	4	6	7	8	9
Passenger cars[1]	1	2	8	3	4	6	7	5	9
Telephones[1]	2	5	1	6	7	3	4	8	9
Full-time school enrolment[1]	9	8	3	4	2	1	6	7	9
Infant mortality[1]	7	8	2	3	4	1	5	9	6
Price/earnings index[1]	2.5	1	4	7	5	2.5	6	–	–
Mean rank (rank)	3.4(1)	4.1(5)	3.7(3)	3.9(4)	4.4(6)	3.6(2)	6.0(7)	7.5(8)	8.5(9)

1 As for Table 3.3.

In modern societies the burden is shared more widely through private and national insurance schemes and by provisions funded from general government revenue. (This is not to ignore the responsibility still carried by kin, especially with respect to children but also in regard to the elderly and infirm.)

Accurate measures of dependency are difficult to construct. The precise age of retirement, for example, depends on the minimum age at which pensions may be claimed, the size of pension in relation to wages, the possibility of working beyond retirement age, the state of health, etc. All these differ both between countries and between individuals within a country. Nevertheless, an approximate indication of age dependency is given by Table 2.5 which shows, for each country, the number of people aged 65 years and over as a percentage of those aged between 15 and 64 years. This ratio increased in all countries except Ireland between 1960 and 1979, most notably in West Germany where it increased from 16.4 per cent to 23.6 per cent. While in West Germany and in the UK the increase was evenly distributed between the two decades, a marked increase was noticeable during the 1970s in Italy and Denmark, while in France, The Netherlands and Belgium the position stabilised between 1975 and 1979 and did so even earlier in Luxembourg. The UK changed from being ranked fourth in 1960 to second in 1979.

The corresponding measure of child dependency is given in Table 2.6, which shows, for each country, the number of children aged under 15 years as a percentage of the population aged between 15 and 64 years. This measure shows a much greater between-country variation than that for age dependency and ranged, in 1979, from 52.1 per cent in Ireland to 27.3 per cent in Luxembourg. Nevertheless, the period 1960– 79 marked a convergence between all countries except Ireland, with the dependency ratio lower in each country in 1979 than in either 1960 or 1970 (although a steady decline occurred only in the Netherlands). The UK's relative position was virtually unchanged. During the 1970s, the falling numbers of children more than compensated for the increased numbers of elderly in most countries when measured in terms of a composite index of dependency (e.g. see EC 1980a). The only exceptions were Denmark and Italy which both experienced very large increases in the numbers of elderly.

However, when comparing levels of child poverty, concentrations of children in large families and in incomplete ones may be more significant than differences in the child dependency ratio. Table 2.7 indicates that in the early 1970s, families with many children were common in Ireland and, to a lesser extent, in the Netherlands and France. (Comparable data would probably show a prevalence of large families in Italy.)

Table 2.5   Age dependency in European countries, 1960–2000

	1960	1965	1970	1975	1979	1990	2000
West Germany	16.4	18.2	20.3	21.8	23.6	20.0	21.7
France	19.4	19.0	21.0	22.2	22.0	20.0	21.8
Italy	15.2	15.2	16.9	18.7	20.4	19.7	–
The Netherlands	14.8	16.1	15.9	17.2	17.3	18.6	20.3
Belgium	18.8	20.6	20.6	21.8	21.9	18.6	19.7
Luxembourg	16.2	18.2	20.0	19.4	20.0	18.8	20.5
UK	18.5	18.5	20.6	22.2	23.0	23.1	21.8
Ireland	19.0	19.0	19.0	19.0	18.3	–	–
Denmark	17.2	16.9	18.8	20.3	22.0	23.1	21.2

Note: Age dependency = $\dfrac{\text{(persons aged 65 or more)}}{\text{(persons aged between 15 and 64)}} \times 100$

Source: EC 1981b.

Table 2.6   Child dependency in European countries, 1960–2000

	1960	1965	1970	1975	1979	1990	2000
West Germany	32.8	34.8	35.9	34.3	29.4	22.8	23.3
France	43.5	39.7	40.3	38.1	35.9	33.8	34.4
Italy	36.4	36.4	36.9	37.5	35.7	31.8	34.4
The Netherlands	49.2	45.2	42.9	39.1	35.5	24.3	24.6
Belgium	37.5	38.1	38.1	34.3	31.9	24.3	21.1
Luxembourg	30.9	34.8	33.8	29.9	27.3	26.1	26.5
UK	35.4	35.4	38.1	36.5	34.2	30.8	34.4
Ireland	53.4	53.4	53.4	53.4	52.1	–	–
Denmark	39.0	36.9	35.9	35.9	33.6	30.8	30.3

Note: Child dependency = $\dfrac{\text{(children aged under 15)}}{\text{(persons aged between 15 and 64)}} \times 100$

Source: EC 1981b

Table 2.7   The distribution of children in European countries

	Ireland (1966)	The Netherlands (1971)	France (1962)	Belgium (1970)	West Germany (1970)	UK (1971)	Denmark (1976)
Proportion of married couples with							
0	25.0	30.8	36.0	38.2	36.1	51.0	47.1
1	19.7	21.7	24.7	25.5	27.0	18.6	19.6
2	17.8	23.9	19.0	18.4	22.0	18.3	22.9
3	14.3	12.6	10.5	9.2	9.3	7.8	8.1
4	10.0	5.9	9.7	8.5	3.4	2.7	2.2
5	27.1	5.1			2.7	1.5	
children							
Proportion of families with children that are:							
married couples	91.9	90.6	86.6	86.5	85.7	90.5	90.1
lone mother	8.1	7.7	10.9	10.3	12.2	7.7	8.9
lone father	1.7	1.7	2.5	3.2	2.1	1.7	1.0

Sources: OECD 1979; the Netherlands 1976; Denmark 1981.

Table 2.8   Divorce and illegitimacy in European countries, 1960—79

	1960	1970	1975	1979
(a) Divorces per 1000 existing marriages				
Denmark	5.9	7.6	10.6	10.7
West Germany	3.6	5.1	6.7	2.1[1]
France	2.9	3.4	4.9	5.8[1]
Netherlands	2.2	3.3	6.0	6.9
UK	2.0	4.7	9.6	11.2
Belgium	2.0	2.4	4.4	5.4[1]
Luxembourg	—	—	—	—
Italy[2]	0	0	0.8	0.8
Ireland[3]	0	0	0	0
(b) Illegitimate births per 1000 live and still births				
Denmark	78.2	110.3	217.3	307.1
West Germany	63.3	54.6	61.2	71.3
France	60.7	68.4	85.1	93.9[4]
UK	52.0	80.0	90.0	106.0
Luxembourg	31.7	40.1	42.2	55.9
Italy	24.2	21.8	25.9	38.1
Belgium	20.7	27.7	31.2	30.9[5]
Ireland	15.9	26.5	37.4	46.0
Netherlands	13.6	20.9	21.6	34.5

Notes: [1] 1978 [2] Divorce legalised 1971 [3] No legal divorce [4] 1978 [5] 1977

Source: EC 1981b

The proportion of large families was lowest in Denmark and the UK reflecting larger numbers of childless couples.

Table 2.7 also reveals that in the early 1970s incomplete families were most numerous in West Germany, Belgium and France. Since then it is likely that the numbers of incomplete families have increased markedly in all countries on account of higher divorce rates and greater numbers of illegitimate births (see Table 2.8).

An important group with restricted access to employment comprises those people with physical or mental disability. Later chapters indicate that financial and other provisions for the disabled are frequently inadequate but, for the most part, space prohibits detailed consideration of their circumstances. Comparative information on the numbers of disabled is not available.

Unemployment is a form of dependency with special political significance. Part of this significance stems from the widely held belief — frequently encouraged by politicians — that the level of unemployment is sensitive to the actions of governments. Although the numbers experiencing unemployment are small in relation to, for example, retirement, the rapid flows in and out of employment cause cross-sectional statistics to understate the numbers actually affected. The unpredictability of unemployment and the abrupt and frequently drastic loss of income — which often coincides with peak demands of dependants, especially young children, on family budgets — makes unemployment a particularly pernicious social phenomenon.

Table 2.9 records a marked increase in unemployment during the 1970s in every country in Europe. Also apparent in all countries, though less marked in Italy and the UK, is the abrupt increase in unemployment which occurred between 1974 and 1975 as a consequence of the OPEC-induced recession and from which the unemployment in no country has recovered. Even in West Germany the 1980 level of unemployment, which was lower than any other country for which comparable information is available and which had fallen inexorably from its 1975 peak, was almost twice that of 1974.

The causes of unemployment are discussed more fully in the next part of this volume. However, orthodox economists believe that most of the unemployment suffered in the 1970s was demand deficient and linked to the continuing slow-down in worldwide economic growth and to the sensitivity of governments to the need to control inflation. Nevertheless demographic factors have also contributed to the growth and pattern of unemployment. For example, increased numbers attaining the age of 16, and in many cases therefore joining the labour market, coincided with the depressed post-1974 economies in all countries except Denmark, France and Luxembourg.

Given the theme of this volume, low wage earners warrant attention. Therefore, in Figure 2.1 the 1972 earnings of selected occupational groups are compared with average earnings and with international standard poverty lines. Equally detailed information is not available for the period since 1972 although it appears that skill differentials narrowed up to 1975 since when they have remained relatively stable (see Saunders 1980 and the next section of this volume). (For discussions of the causes of wage differentials in general or of low pay in particular, see Blackaby 1980; UK 1979; Field 1977. Table 2.9 limits consideration to sex and skill differentials.)

Figure 2.1 confirms the protection against poverty afforded by regular employment, although direct comparison of earnings with the international poverty standards may be somewhat misleading in that the latter are defined net of direct taxation. Moreover, average figures conceal within-group variation in earnings and around half of each group will receive lower than average wages depending on the precise form of the

Table 2.9 Standardised[1] unemployment rates 1970–80 (% of total labour force)

	1970	1971	1972	1973	1974	1975	1976	1977	1978	1979	1980
Italy	5.3	5.3	6.3	6.2	5.3	5.8	6.6	7.0	7.1	7.5	7.4
UK	3.1	3.7	4.1	3.0	2.9	3.9	5.5	6.2	6.1	5.7	7.4
France	2.4	2.6	2.7	2.6	2.8	4.1	4.4	4.7	5.2	5.9	6.3
Belgium	2.1	2.2	2.7	2.8	3.1	5.1	6.6	7.5	8.1	8.4	9.0
Netherlands	0.9	1.3	2.3	2.3	2.8	4.0	4.3	4.2	4.2	4.2	4.9
West Germany	0.8	0.9	0.8	0.9	1.6	3.7	3.7	3.7	3.5	3.2	3.1
Denmark[2]	1.0	1.2	1.2	0.7	2.0	4.6	4.7	5.8	6.5	5.3	6.2
Luxembourg[2]	0.0	0.0	0.0	0.0	0.0	0.2	0.3	0.5	0.7	0.7	0.7
Ireland[2]	5.8	5.6	6.5	6.0	6.3	8.7	9.8	9.2	8.4	7.5	8.3

[1] Adjusted to preserve comparability over time and to conform with ILO definition. Adjustments made to 'registered' unemployment to include unemployed not covered by register and to exclude employed persons still carried on the register.
[2] Registered unemployment, not standardised.

Source: OECD 1981a.

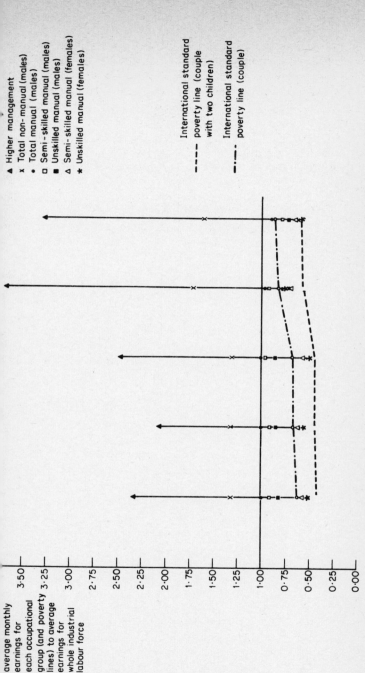

Figure 2.1 *Earnings in relation to international standard poverty lines for selected European countries, 1972*

Note: For the UK, higher management includes all salaries. For other countries certain staff with incomes above a ceiling are excluded.

Source: Adapted from Saunders and Marsden (1979) and own calculations.

▲ Higher management
✗ Total non-manual (males)
• Total manual (males)
□ Semi-skilled manual (males)
■ Unskilled manual (males)
△ Semi-skilled manual (females)
★ Unskilled manual (females)

–––– International standard
      poverty line (couple
      with two children)

–·–·– International standard
       poverty line (couple)

average monthly
earnings for
each occupational
group (and poverty
lines) to average
earnings for
whole industrial
labour force

3·50
3·25
3·00
2·75
2·50
2·25
2·00
1·75
1·50
1·25
1·00
0·75
0·50
0·25
0·00

earnings' distribution. Figure 2.1 also shows that, although probably relatively few in number, unsupported mothers working in semi-skilled or unskilled jobs would on average find it impossible to earn in excess of the poverty standard. In Italy this would also be true for the average unskilled male worker, and in France for the average semi-skilled worker as well.

Social Protection Expenditure

Statistics on social protection expenditure compiled by the Commission of the EC relate to:

> Any expenditure involved in meeting expenses by households incurred as a result of the materialisation or existence of certain risks or needs, insofar as this expenditure gives rise to the intervention of a 'third party', namely a unit other than the households themselves — a public or private administration or undertaking — without there being any simultaneous equivalent counterpart by the beneficiary. (1979: 3)

The European statistics therefore cover certain of the needs of the dependent groups identified above and additional risks or needs associated with sickness, invalidity, disability, occupational accidents and diseases, placement, vocational guidance, resettlement and — in part — housing. In practice the chief component is social security expenditure and there are notable omissions including education, social work, the effects of tax allowances, subsidies and other methods of intervention. Also only current expenditure is assessed.

Nevertheless, the social protection statistics provide the best available basis for comparing the social expenditure of European countries. Table 2.10 relates *per capita* expenditure on social protection to *per capita* GDP, both expressed in PPSs. It should be noted that between-country comparisons of the ratio of social expenditure to GDP may be misleading where countries differ significantly in terms of the proportion of benefits which are paid in cash or kind. This is because cash transfers are included in social expenditure but not in GDP, while benefits in kind constitute the use of resources and are included in GDP as well as under social expenditure. Table 2.11 shows the split between benefits in cash and in kind for each country in 1980.

Table 2.10 shows that the three countries with lowest *per capita* GDP, namely the UK, Italy and Ireland, also spend a significantly smaller proportion of their GDP on social protection than do the richer countries. Consequently, the between-country dispersion in *per capita* social expenditure markedly exceeds the dispersion in GDP with the average citizen in the most 'generous' country — i.e. West Germany — receiving 1.6 and 2.4 times more than in Italy and Ireland respectively. *Per capita* social expenditure in The Netherlands, while marginally less than in West

Table 2.10 Social protection expenditure in European countries, 1980

	Luxembourg	West Germany	Denmark	France	Belgium	The Netherlands	UK	Italy	Ireland
Per capita social protection expenditure (PPs)	2435	2498	2385	2187	2264	2476	1575	1539	1056
Per capita GDP (PPSs)	9196	8826	8521	8478	8175	8066	7361	6749	4799
Social protection expenditure as a % of GDP	26.5	28.3	28.0	25.8	27.7	30.7	21.4	22.8	22.0

Source: EC 1982b and previous years; own calculations.

Table 2.11 The nature of social benefits in European countries, 1980

	The Netherlands (%)	Belgium (%)	Luxembourg (%)	Italy (%)	UK (%)	France (%)	West Germany (%)	Denmark (%)	Ireland (%)
Benefits in cash	78.6	78.5	76.8	73.5	68.3	67.7	67.1	60.9	59.1
Benefits in kind	21.4	21.5	23.2	26.5	31.7	32.3	32.9	39.1	40.9
Total[1]	100.0	100.0	100.0	100.0	100.0	100.0	100.0	100.0	100.0

1 Rounding errors.

Source: EC 1982b.

Germany, represents a significantly larger proportion of GDP (31 per cent as against 28 per cent).

Table 2.12, which records the growth in social expenditure between 1970 and 1980, shows that throughout the period The Netherlands was spending a relatively high proportion of GDP on social welfare but that in 1970 and 1977 the proportion was exceeded by that of Germany. The juxtapositioning of The Netherlands with West Germany may relate as much to their differing economic performance as to policy intentions. Certainly until 1974 the Dutch economy was growing faster than Germany's but was more affected by the oil price rises of that year. Moreover, the relative fall in Dutch social protection expenditure in 1977 was associated with a short spell of unprecedented economic growth. The continued expansion of social spending in the Netherlands also reflects the linking of social security benefits to wage inflation (higher in the Netherlands than in Germany) via their indexation to the minimum wage.

Social protection expenditure in the other two Benelux countries also increased faster than elsewhere in Europe and again falls in real output, which followed the oil price rise of 1974, resulted in an artificially large increase in the proportion of GDP spent on social protection. The latter phenomenon is apparent in all countries to a varying degree and, moreover, although every country spent a higher proportion of GDP on social protection in 1980 than in 1970, Table 2.12 reveals that the latter half of the decade saw a significant slowing in the rate of increase. Indeed between 1975 and 1980 social expenditure in Italy, West Germany and the UK grew only at the same rate as GDP, and in 1980 the UK slipped below Ireland to the bottom of the social protection league.

Cursory comparison of Tables 2.5, 2.6 and 2.9 with Table 2.12 reveals no systematic relationship between aggregate expenditure and the changing pattern of dependency. However, more sophisticated analysis is undoubtedly needed.

A recurring theme later in the book concerns the significance of differing methods of financing social expenditure. Is there less taxpayer resistance to high social insurance contributions than to high direct taxation, for example? Table 2.13 gives the source of receipts for 1980, differentiating general taxation from contributions made by employers and by protected persons. The term 'contributions' covers a range from hypothecated taxes to payments made into fully funded insurance schemes. Social protection is predominantly funded through taxation in Denmark, and in Ireland and the UK taxation constitutes the largest source of funds. Contributions are more important elsewhere with employers contributing more than employees in France and Italy, where the former account for over 50 per cent of total funding, and also in Belgium and West Germany. Direct contributions by individuals are more

Table 2.12 Social welfare expenditure as a percentage of GDP, 1978–80

	1970	1971	1972	1973	1974	1975	1976	1977	1978	1979	1980
West Germany	21.4	21.8	22.6	23.1	24.6	27.8	27.4	29.1	28.8	28.2	28.3
Netherlands	20.8	22.0	23.2	23.3	25.2	28.1	28.5	28.1	28.9	29.9	30.7
Italy	18.4	20.2	21.2	20.8	21.6	22.6[1]	22.6	22.1	23.2	23.1	22.8
Denmark	19.5	20.7	20.9	21.1	24.0	25.9	25.3	25.1	26.0	27.1	28.0
France	19.2	19.3	19.4	19.8	20.5	22.9	23.1	24.0	25.0	25.3	25.8
Belgium	18.5	18.9	19.8	20.4	21.5	24.6	25.1	26.2	26.4	27.0	27.6
Luxembourg	16.6	18.0	18.4	17.0	16.6	23.0	23.7	25.9	26.0	25.3	26.5
UK	16.3	16.7	17.3	17.0	19.4	20.8	19.9	20.4	20.4	19.9	21.4
Ireland	13.2	13.6	13.4	15.6	17.7	19.7	19.3	18.6	17.5	19.2	21.9

1 Change in statistical series
2 Derived from aggregate statistics
3 Welfare expenditure estimated according to increase in price index

Source: EC 1980b, 1982b

Table 2.13   Financing social protection in European countries, 1980

Types of Current receipts	Denmark	Ireland	UK	Luxembourg	The Netherlands	Belgium	West Germany	France	Italy
Employer's social contributions	9.6	25.1	33.3	36.2	37.1	40.9	42.7	56.0	58.8
Social contributions paid by the protected persons	1.8	11.3	14.6	22.9	31.0	20.2	27.5	23.7	13.6
Current general government contributions (taxes)	85.0	62.5	43.6	31.6	20.4	34.7	26.7	17.7	24.9
Other current receipts	3.5	1.0	8.5	9.4	11.5	4.2	3.1	2.6	2.7
Total[1]	100.0	100.0	100.0	100.0	100.0	100.0	100.0	100.0	100.0

[1] Rounding errors.

Source: EC 1982b.

significant in the Netherlands but even so account for only a little over a third of the total bill. No simple relationship is apparent between the volume of aggregate expenditure and the source of funds.

Tables 2.14—2.16 present a comparison of expenditure levels on benefits pertinent to the three dependency groups previously identified and relate expenditure to national resources. The analysis is similar to that conducted in the European Social Budget (EC 1979) but is less sophisticated in that no attempt is made to assess the numbers entitled to benefit. Instead the demographic groups used in the European Commission's Social Protection Statistics (EC 1980b) are employed and therefore the results are not directly comparable with the Social Budget. The tables do, however, present factual information for 1979 whereas the latest year covered by the Social Budget is 1975.

Table 2.14 allocates 1979 expenditure on old-age and survivors' benefits included in the EC social protection accounts on a *per capita* basis for all persons aged 60 or over in each country. Since retirement ages vary between countries and receipt of benefit may be conditional on other factors, the figures may not be interpreted strictly as average benefit rates received. Rather, they give an indication of the resources directed towards the 'over 60s', controlling for the numbers involved. The value of benefits is lowest in the three poorest countries — Ireland, Italy and the UK — but is also relatively low in prosperous Denmark partly on account of the high retirement age of 67. Benefits are highest in Luxembourg and roughly comparable between West Germany, The Netherlands and France. Between 1970 and 1979 levels increased in real terms in all countries but increases were most marked in Belgium (a 101 per cent increase) and France (a 93 per cent increase). (See also Chapter 10 on the changing emphasis of French policy towards the aged.)

Relating benefit per person aged 60 or over to GDP per economically occupied person (as defined in EC 1982a) provides a measure which takes account of the economic base of a country and thereby 'what it can afford'. One might have related GDP to total population rather than to the economically occupied population but the latter seems more relevant when considering social transfers (see also EC 1979). Assuming that social expenditure is in fact influenced by the strength of a country's economic base, between-country variations on this measure should be less than that obtaining for average levels of benefits. This is in fact the case although Luxembourg remains conspicuous by its relative generosity while Ireland lags some way behind (Table 2.14).

The symmetry between national income and resources means that the relative measure presented in Table 2.14 may also be interpreted as a measure of the value of benefits paid to the elderly in relation to the

Table 2.14 *Value of old age and survivors' benefits in European countries, 1970–9*

	Year	Luxembourg	West Germany	The Netherlands	France	Belgium	Denmark	Italy	UK	Ireland
Benefits per person aged 60 years or over (PPSs)	1979	5350	4505	4374	4357	3768	3588	2863	2775[1]	1515[1]
Real increase in benefit per person aged 60 years or over (%)	1970–91	53	53	44	93	101	101	–	38[2]	49[2]
Benefits per person aged 60 years or over as a % of GDP per economically occupied	1979	28.5	23.7	21.4	23.5	19.1	21.5	19.7	20.5[3]	12.5[3]
	1976	28.0	22.9	21.8	21.1	18.1	19.7	16.5	20.3	12.9
	1974	20.6	21.8	20.9	18.2	19.2	19.8	17.2	20.0	12.8
	1971	22.1	21.3	20.1	16.5	13.1	18.1	–	17.5	10.6

1 1978 figures adjusted according to consumer price index.
2 1971–8.
3 1978.

Source: EC 1980b; own calculations.

Table 2.15 Value of family benefits in European countries 1970—9

	Year	Belgium	France	West Germany	Denmark	The Netherlands	Luxembourg	UK	Italy	Ireland
Benefits per child under 15 years (PPSs)	1979	1058	1005	960	919	832	790	603[1]	340	210[1]
Real increase in Benefits per child under 15 years (%)	1970—9	42	42	95	19	55	52	107[2]	—	15[2]
Benefits per child under 15 years as a % of GDP per economically occupied person	1979	5.8	5.4	5.1	5.5	4.1	4.2	4.4[3]	2.3	1.7[3]
	1976	5.7	4.9	4.4	5.8	3.8	4.3	3.2	3.1	2.1
	1974	5.1	5.0	3.2	6.4	3.7	3.2	3.0	3.7	2.9
	1971	5.2	5.2	3.6	5.7	3.6	3.3	2.5	—	2.2

1 1978 figures adjusted according to consumer price index.
2 1971–78.
3 1978.

Source: EC 1980b; own calculations.

Table 2.16 Value of unemployment benefit in European countries, 1977–9

	Year	Luxembourg	The Netherlands	Denmark	Belgium	France	West Germany	UK	Ireland	Italy
Benefits per registered un-employed person (PPSs)	1979	12280	9506	8958	4978	3957	2899	2339[1]	1967[1]	862
Benefits per registered unemployed person as a % of GDP per economically active person	1979	65	47	54	26	21	15	17[2]	16[2]	6
	1977	16	39	49	24	21	16	18	17	6

1 1978 figures adjusted to consumer price index.
2 1978.

Source: EC 1980b; own calculations.

income of the economically occupied. This gives one a first hint of the degree of protection afforded to the elderly against the threat of relative poverty. On this basis, therefore, protection appears to be much greater in Luxembourg than elsewhere and least in Ireland. Table 2.14 also shows that while the level of benefits relative to GDP per occupied person increased in all countries during the 1970s, progress was highly variable. In some countries 'great leaps forward' were followed by periods of stability (e.g. Luxembourg and the UK) and even relative decline (e.g. Belgium). In other countries progress was steady (e.g. West Germany and France) or sometimes haphazard (e.g. The Netherlands and Italy).

Table 2.15 presents a corresponding analysis for family benefits and here similar reservations hold. Not all children under 15 (especially first children) receive benefits, while in some countries benefits are paid to 'children' in tertiary education. Moreover, the statistics do not take account of provisions through the tax system although the impact of fiscal changes is evident in, for example, the large increase in the real value of benefits recorded in the UK as a consequence of the replacement of tax allowances by child benefit. Similar changes took place in The Netherlands up to 1979 and in West Germany in 1975 (see Chapters 8 and 9). The very limited growth in benefit levels in Denmark reflects a shift away from universal child benefit toward selective measures to benefit lower income families. The decline in the value of child allowance in Ireland since 1974 accords with other studies (e.g. Fitzgerald n.d.) and occurred at the same time as the fall in the rate of child tax relief (Bradshaw and Piachaud 1980).

Family benefits have greatest purchasing power in Belgium and least in Italy and Ireland. Relative to GDP per occupied person, benefits are most generous in Belgium, Denmark, France and West Germany (i.e. above 5 per cent). They are lower in The Netherlands, Luxembourg and the UK (between 4.1 and 4.4 per cent) and fall some way behind in Italy and Ireland 2.3 and 1.7 per cent respectively. (Luxembourg emerges as more generous and Denmark as less so in a more comprehensive analysis of child support: e.g. see Bradshaw and Piachaud 1980.)

The value of unemployment benefits — defined to include social assistance payments to the unemployed — are compared in Table 2.16. Although information is only available for two years, the radically changed circumstances of the unemployed in Luxembourg are evident and reflect the effective introduction of an unemployment benefits scheme. However, the most significant feature of Table 2.16 is the marked variation in benefit levels from one country to another both in relative and absolute terms. While benefit levels in Luxembourg in 1979 may be artificially high due to statistical manipulation of a very small absolute number of unemployed, the regulations which allow for an 80 per cent replacement of loss of earnings would in any case place Luxembourg on a par with The Netherlands and Denmark. In these three countries benefits are more than twice as generous — relative to GDP per occupied person — as in the next highest country, Belgium. Moreover, in marked contrast with old age and family benefits, unemployment benefit in West Germany, relative to GDP, is lower than in either the UK or Ireland and only higher than in Italy.

Differences recorded in Table 2.16 reflect the time for which benefits are payable as well as the actual level of payment. Unemployment benefit is paid indefinitely in Belgium and for three years in Denmark (after which transfer to social assistance may entail no loss of income — see Chapter 6). Elsewhere primary benefits are replaced by secondary schemes: in The Netherlands after six months; West Germany after 4–12 months; and in France normally after one year. In the UK and Ireland earnings-related supplements are lost after six months. Secondary benefits are also paid for varying lengths of time (see DHSS 1980).

By way of summary, Table 2.17 relates total *per capita* expenditure on unemployment and the old-age benefits to the international standard poverty line for each of the five countries featured in this volume. This analysis must be considered tentative for many of the reasons already

Table 2.17   Expenditure on unemployment and old-age benefits and the international standard poverty line for selected countries, 1978

	Denmark[1]	The Netherlands	West Germany	France	UK
Benefits per registered unemployed person as:					
(a) % of the international standard poverty line[2] for a single person	278	275	95	121	94
(b) % of the international standard poverty line[2] for a couple and two children	120	119	41	52	41
Benefits per person over retirement age as a % of the international standard poverty line[2] for a single retired person	194	174	159	110	108

1 1976
2 Defined according to Beckerman 1979; source of income figures: OECD 1981b.

covered. In addition, the aggregate nature of the financial statistics — in including administrative costs and a range of different benefits for varying circumstances — attain greater significance. Moreover, the nature of the international poverty line is itself arbitrary as explained above. Nevertheless, what Table 2.17 succeeds in showing is that there is a more significant risk of poverty — according to the international standard — among the elderly in France and in the UK than in the other three countries. The picture is somewhat different with respect to unemployment. In this case the situation in West Germany is more akin to that in France and in the UK where the risk of poverty is substantial even for an unemployed single person. More importantly, however, the unemployed family man with two children is close to the international poverty line in all countries. Therefore only with the assistance of other benefits — most notably provisons for the family — can the unemployed person hope to escape severe deprivation.

Conceptions of Poverty

Individual perceptions of poverty

In 1976 the European Commission appended a series of questions concerned with the perception of poverty to the summer 'Eurobarometer' — a regular six-monthly public opinion survey conducted in the nine member-states of the Community. The methodology used was akin to market research with predominantly closed questions being asked of quota samples (in four countries) and stratified random samples (elsewhere). Approximately 1000 people were interviewed in each country except Luxembourg where the sample was 268. The survey afforded little scope to explore individuals' own conceptions of poverty but solicited responses about the perceived extent of the problem according to a given definition. Although analysis of the survey has been severely criticised for being over ambitious, responses to individual questions are judged to be relatively sound (Golding 1980). However, one qualification is necessary. There is a major problem in standardizing questions used in different countries because of variations in the interpretation of concepts as well as in the precise meaning of words which are translated (see also Chapter 1). This qualification applies particularly to attitude surveys which cannot be checked carefully in relation to the material conditions, incomes and socio-economic status of respondents.

Table 2.18 records responses to the question:

> Are there at the present time in your town, part of town or village, people whose general standard of living you consider to be very bad compared with that of other people, that is people really in poverty?

It is worth noting that the question first defines poverty and then labels it. It adopts an overtly relative, or comparative, notion of poverty, places emphasis on standard of living as opposed to simple lack of finance, and stresses that only extreme instances should be considered. It also focuses the respondents' attention on poverty occurring in their locality although, unfortunately, with variable meaning attached to the latter.

Although the majority of Europeans are clearly unaware of any poverty existing in their neighbourhood, the picture revealed by the survey is a complex one. The grouping of countries in Table 2.18 shows that a majority of people in Italy and Luxembourg acknowledge the existence of poverty and that in West Germany and France more people accept that poverty exists than reject its existence. However in Ireland, Belgium, the UK and The Netherlands the opposite is true and, indeed, only in Denmark does a clear majority deny that poverty exists.

Table 2.18   The perception of poverty in European countries, 1976

| | % of respondents reporting:[1] | | | |
	That there are people really in poverty	That there are not people really in poverty	Don't know	Total
Denmark	16	66	18	100
The Netherlands	22	49	29	100
UK	36	49	15	100
Belgium	37	47	16	100
Ireland	43	49	8	100
France	47	44	9	100
West Germany	48	22	30	100
Luxembourg	53	22	25	100
Italy	68	17	15	100

[1] See text for precise question.

Source: EC 1977.

An additional distinction is apparent within the first three groups between countries where a high proportion were uncertain about how to reply (Luxembourg, West Germany and The Netherlands) and those where few people had difficulty replying to the question. The variation in response may reflect differing degrees of uncertainty as to the meaning of poverty used in the question. Interestingly, the proportion recognising poverty in each country only mirror, in a partial and distorted way, the variations in the extent of measured relative poverty (see below).

The entire sample was also asked: 'Why, in your opinion, are there people who live in need?' and presented with the alternative responses listed in Table 2.19. Again the range of response was considerable. The

Table 2.19 Perceived causes of poverty

Response[1]	Italy (%)	France (%)	West Germany (%)	UK (%)	Luxembourg (%)	Ireland (%)	Belgium (%)	Denmark (%)	The Netherlands (%)
Because there is much injustice in our society	40	35	23	16	16	19	17	14	11
Because of laziness and lack of willpower	20	16	23	43	31	30	22	11	12
Because they have been unlucky	14	18	18	10	20	25	21	17	20
It's an inevitable part of progress in the modern world	10	18	10	17	6	16	15	28	16
None of these	4	7	8	4	6	4	9	8	11
Don't know	12	6	18	10	21	6	16	22	30
Total	100	100	100	100	100	100	100	100	100

[1] See text for precise question asked.

Source: EC 1977.

Table 2.20   Perception of policy effectiveness in European countries, 1976

| | % of respondents who think that what the authorities are doing for people in poverty is | | | | |
	Too much	About what they should do	Too little	Don't know	Perception of poverty[1]
Denmark	10	48	31	11	Low
The Netherlands	7	34	40	19	Low to Moderate
UK	20	35	36	9	
Belgium	2	25	55	18	
Ireland	7	39	50	4	
France	2	23	68	7	Moderate to high
West Germany	6	40	46	8	
Luxembourg	10	34	39	17	High
Italy	2	12	75	11	

[1] See Table 2.18.

Source: EC 1977.

most common answer in Italy and France related to social injustice as a cause of poverty and the temptation is to view this as a manifestation of the strength of the communist and left-wing vote in both countries. In West Germany, belief in injustice was tempered by significant numbers who laid blame on personal failings such as laziness and lack of will-power, and, in the UK, 43 per cent (i.e. half of those who expressed an opinion) echoed this second theme. 'Laziness and lack of willpower' was also the most commonly perceived factor in Luxembourg, Ireland and Belgium but in each country almost equal numbers saw 'luck' as being important. In Denmark the most popular reply was 'modern progress' while a very high proportion of the Dutch (41 per cent) refused to express an opinion. Four of the five countries exhibiting the highest perception of poverty also had the highest proportions viewing injustice as a cause of poverty. (The exception was Luxembourg.)

Respondents' opinions as to how well the authorities are coping with the problem of poverty may be affected by their beliefs about the extent of poverty and its causes. This supposition is examined in Table 2.20, although it must be stressed that the analysis is prone to the ecological fallacy and could be substantiated only by correlation of responses at the level of the individual.

In Denmark — where just 16 per cent believe poverty to exist — and in the UK — where very large numbers blame poverty on individual failings — the majority of people are content with goverment policies or indeed believe that government is doing too much to help the poor. Else-where, respondents were much less contented with the authorities' response to poverty and, interestingly, the degree of contentment ex-pressed in a country does not appear to be related solely to a low per-ception of the problem. For example, although perception of poverty was high in both Italy and Luxembourg, dissatisfaction with government policies was much greater in Italy. In part this may relate to the greater propensity among Italian respondents to point to structural causes of poverty which may also be thought of as more amenable to government action than are other factors. Similar considerations might also help explain the differences between France and West Germany. It is more difficult to speculate about the differences among countries with low to moderate perception of poverty. However, it may be significant that Belgium and Ireland, the two countries exhibiting most dissatisfaction with government policies, do have similar response profiles with respect to the question on 'causes' (See Table 2.19.).

National institutional definitions of poverty

Insight into official conceptions of poverty may be gained through con-sideration of the social assistance schemes in different countries. Such a task of comparison is fraught with difficulties. Social assistance is usually taken to relate to statutory provisions provided subject to a means-test but the scope and functions of means-tested benefits vary widely both within and between countries. Moreover, social assistance schemes are inevitably forged in particular social and economic climates and are con-tinually subject to remodelling. Without an understanding of the ante-cedents of a particular system, or of an individual provision, the risks of comparative analysis are enormous. These difficulties no doubt help explain why no comparative analysis of social assistance in Europe has been published to date although some of the basic data is becoming available (Lawson 1979).

Prior to risking comparison, certain important distinctions need to be drawn (following, in part, Lawson, 1980a). The first is between assistance schemes which offer primarily financial assistance — as in the UK, The Netherlands and Ireland — and those which in addition provide other forms of support — e.g. benefits in kind, medical care, domiciliary aid, counselling and social work. Social work services are particularly important in France, Belgium, Luxembourg and West Germany and more recently in Denmark, which has been embarking upon an integration of financial aid with employment services and practical social work and counselling.

A related distinction is apparent between centrally and locally organised schemes. The UK and Irish schemes fit into the former category, so may that of The Netherlands which, although still administered by local authorities, is very uniform with rates equating to the national minimum wage. Similarly, Danish social assistance is run locally but the short-term 'temporary assistance' benefit is dependent on claimants' former living standards while 'continuing assistance' — for those permanently outside the labour force — is subject to national rates. Elsewhere, schemes vary markedly at the level of the administering local authority although there have been moves — most noticeably in West Germany — towards more national and uniform policies.

The local multifaceted approach to national assistance may be viewed as a response to the personal problems of the very poor and often inadequate who either fall outside the scope of insurance-based social security cover or have failed to meet their obligations under it. The policy emphasis in these countries may have been on the provision of generous and increasingly comprehensive insurance schemes with social assistance provisions representing a response to a marginal problem of poverty that is not seen as being amenable to a response at national level. The poor may thereby be viewed as social outsiders and it is significant that wide-ranging financial obligations on family members have tended to be retained under the local-based assistance schemes in France, West Germany and Belgium. Nevertheless, social assistance policies at local level will vary greatly according to local social and political conditions so that family obligations may or may not be enforced and benefit levels themselves may vary widely.

Research since the 1960s (e.g. NAB 1967; Graffar *et al.* 1967; de la Gorce 1965; Mercier 1974), which has indicated that poverty is less marginal than previously thought, has been an element in the state, particularly at the centre, assuming greater responsibility for policies to combat poverty. One aspect of this has been a tendency towards the standardisation of social assistance regulations. Another has been the growth of categorical assistance schemes aimed at specific groups — often constituted within a tight legal framework — to complement general schemes. Examples include the French national 'social minimum provisions' for the elderly, disabled and single parents (introduced in 1956, 1971 and 1975, and 1976, respectively); National Solitary Fund allowances for the elderly, disabled and lone parents in Luxembourg; national social pensions in Italy for those over 75 (1969); and 'guaranteed income for the elderly' in Belgium (1969). Belgium also introduced, in 1974, a national general assistance scheme — 'right to subsistence income' to complement local social aid. In West Germany schemes for specific groups have tended to be accommodated — often incongruously — within the insurance system (see Chapter 5). Categorical assistance is generally less important within the centrally organised systems (e.g. the UK, The Netherlands and Denmark), although Ireland is a notable exception where many benefits establish different assistance levels for different groups (Ó Cinnéide 1980).

A final distinction of relevance relates to the role which social assistance levels have played in national debates on poverty. Standardised national schemes facilitate the equating of social assistance levels with 'national poverty lines' as has happened in the UK and, to a much lesser extent, in The Netherlands where since 1978 assistance rates have equalled the minimum wage (Le Blanc 1975; Deleeck 1979). However, the plethora of categorical schemes has inhibited agreement on appropriate levels in Ireland, and in Denmark the debate on poverty has been muted. National average rates have assumed the status of a national poverty line in West Germany but there has been considerable disagreement about the precise level of assistance (see Geissler 1975; Kögler 1976); Klanberg 1979; Kortmann 1978; Lawson 1980b). In France, the absence of national assistance rates has caused the minimum wage to be adopted as the poverty standard, despite its significant deficiences for this purpose (See Chapter 3).

Despite marked differences in the nature of social assistance, instructive if limited comparison is still possible provided individual schemes are selected such that as far as possible they fulfil similar functions. This is attempted in Table 2.21, which shows the value of social aid benefits for married couples in relation to average manual wages and to the international poverty line. The benefits chosen have national applicability (except that West German values relate to Federal averages) and all but those for France, Luxembourg and Italy are of a general rather than a categorical type. (The exceptions in each case relate to benefits available to the retired.) Two benefit levels are reported for Denmark, the UK and three for France. In Denmark, the maximum daily cash benefit (*Dagpengemaksimum*) is the maximum payable to those on social security and social assistance schemes who are returning to the labour force; continuing assistance is for those without prospects of returning to work. The long-term rate in the UK is available to supplementary pensioners and those − with the exception of the unemployed − who have received benefit continuously for one year or more. In France, most social aid payments are supplementary but *Aide aux Personnes Agées* is a primary benefit paid to elderly foreigners without insurance cover. It is equal to the monthly allowance paid after three months dependence on *L'Aide Médicale* and to the supplementary allowance of the *Fonds National de Solidarité* (*FNS*) paid in addition to the *Allocation aux Travaillers Salaries*

Table 2.21 Social minima in European countries, 1980

	Annual value 1980 (PPSs)[1]	1980 Value as % of:		Annual value 1977 as a % of the international poverty standard (1977)[2]
		(a) Average gross earnings of male manual workers in manufacturing	(b) International poverty standard[2]	
Denmark				
(a)	9296	79	195	202[3]
(b)	6091	54	128	111
The Netherlands	5581	57	124	91
France				
(a)	5140	64	86	80
(b)	2537	31	42	38
Luxembourg	3672[4]	32[4]	—	—
UK				
(a)	3586	37	75	78
(b)	2829	29	59	65
Belgium	2849[4]	32[4]	53[4]	54[3]
West Germany	2308	22	43	49
Ireland	2062[4]	26[4]	—	—
Italy	1041[4]	—	25[4]	27[5]

1 1980 values expressed in 1979 PPSs.
2 As defined by Beckerman (1979).
3 1976.
4 1979.
5 1978.

Table 2.21 (continued)

Notes:

Denmark:	(a)	Maximum daily cash benefit (temporary assistance)
	(b)	Continuing assistance (includes a pension contribution)
The Netherlands:		General regular assistance
France:	(a)	National social minimum pensions — *Le Minimum Vieillesse* (*AVTS, Retraite minimum, allocation speciale plus allocation supplémentaire (NFS)*)
	(b)	Social aid: *Aide aux Personnes Agées*
UK:	(a)	Supplementary benefit (long-term rate)
	(b)	Supplementary benefit (ordinary rate)
Luxembourg:		National solidarity fund allowances
Belgium:		Right to a subsistence minimum
West Germany:		Federal average scale rates for subsistence aid (*Hilfe zum Lebensunterbalt*)
Ireland:		Supplementary welfare allowance
Italy:		National social pension

to guarantee national social minimum pension (see Chapter 10). Additional elements or benefits to cover housing expenses are available except in The Netherlands and Luxembourg. (The maximum daily cash benefit in Denmark also includes full housing allowance).

A remaining difficulty is the extent of discretionary additional payments about which little information exists but which may vary widely both within and between countries. Additions may be unusually important in West Germany and were so, in 1980, in the UK.

The social minima included in Table 2.21 vary dramatically in purchasing power. A couple on social assistance in Denmark are between six and nine times better off than their Italian counterparts and — significant as evidence of distinct national priorities — three to four times more prosperous than West German claimants. Benefit levels in The Netherlands are also high (although they include housing costs) as are national social minimum pension levels in France. (In 1981 the latter were increased still further by President Mitterrand.) However, French social aid payments which are usually taken as a base level (e.g. van Ginneken 1981) are on a par with those in West Germany and with ordinary-rate supplementary benefit in the UK.

Significant differences remain when social assistance levels are expressed in relation to average earnings and to the international poverty line standard. Social assistance rates in Denmark equal at least half average earnings and can approach 80 per cent for previously highly paid earners; in West Germany they are less than a quarter. In fact, in 1977 Denmark was the only country where social assistance payments guaranteed incomes above the international poverty line, but by 1980 this was also true of the Netherlands. The addition of housing allowances in the UK would probably increase assistance levels to close to the poverty threshold. Except in these three countries — and minimum pensions in France — social assistance appears from this analysis to be grossly inadequate as a protection against relative poverty.

Table 2.22 gives an indication of the proportion of people receiving social assistance payments in six European countries. (The question of non take-up of benefit is ignored.) Many of the same problems apply when interpreting Table 2.22 as applied in relation to Table 2.21. Moreover, the figures in Table 2.22 concern 1975 and the trends discussed earlier in this chapter will significantly have increased the numbers entitled to benefit.

The small number of recipients in West Germany is partly a virtue (or otherwise) of relatively low social assistance levels but equally the existence of comprehensive insurance schemes is important. On the other hand, The Netherlands and Denmark — though to a noticeably lesser

Table 2.22   Proportions receiving social assistance in selected
European countries, 1975

| | Recipients as a % of population | | |
	Aged 15 to retirement age	Above retire- ment age	Aged over 15 years
West Germany[1]	1.1	2.5	1.3
The Netherlands[2]	2.4	5.2	2.8
France			
(a) *Aide Sociale a l'Enfance* (1978)	1.3	–	–
(b) *Minimum Vieillesse* (1979)	–	20.6	–
(c) *Aide Medicale* (1978)	–	–	4.4
Denmark[3]	–	–	5.2
UK[4]	3.4	19.8	6.7
Ireland[5]	5.2	37.5	20.4

1 Subsistence aid outside institutions.
2 Recipients living at home.
3 Includes special assistance grants and benefits as well as regular financial aid.
4 Includes family income supplement in addition to supplementary benefit.
5 Excludes home assistance.

Source: Adapted from Lawson 1980.

extent — have managed to achieve both high social minima and low numbers of claimants. One must therefore expect to find that both countries have generous and comprehensive schemes of protection which obviate the need for recourse to social assistance.

The relatively high social minima in the UK are accompanied by sizeable numbers of claimants which suggests that alternative measures of social protection are much less effective. Likewise in France, when minimum levels are high — as with the *Minimum Vieillesse* — so too are the number of recipients. Finally, Ireland is in an unenviable class of its own with very low social minima — both in absolute and relative terms — coinciding with very large numbers of claimants.

Some tentative conclusions — or more properly hypotheses — about national approaches to social protection may be drawn by cross-referencing Tables 2.21 and 2.22 with Table 2.10. The Netherlands is a country which by European standards has only moderate *per capita* GDP but which has chosen to spend more on social protection — in relative terms — than any other country in Europe. As a consequence, its social protection is generous and comprehensive and social assistance is available at a relatively high level for the comparatively few people who require it.

West Germany and Denmark are similar to each other in terms of the amount spent on social protection but, whereas West Germany has opted for expenditure on a generous and comprehensive social insurance system at the expense of relatively low social minima for those falling outside the scheme, Denmark has opted for a more egalitarian road. Danish provisions guarantee high social minima for everyone and the analysis suggests that benefits provided under the tax-financed social security system are only marginally better than social assistance but also that the system may not be overly comprehensive.

French expenditure on social protection — during the 'pre-Mitterrand' period — was relatively low, in relation to its *per capita* GDP. In fact, France comes sixth with respect to *per capita* expenditure on social protection and as a consequence, with important exceptions, preventive social security is not comprehensive and social minima are low.

Social welfare expenditure in the UK is not exceptional: it is low in *per capita* terms, but then *per capita* GDP is also low. It should be noted, though, that UK expenditure is generally closer to that of Italy and Ireland — both poorer than the UK — than it is to that of The Netherlands or Belgium, which are a little more prosperous. What is unusual about the UK is that the social assistance minima — particularly long-term rates — appear to be set at a comparatively high level. However, the sizeable number who are actually dependent on social assistance suggests that preventive schemes are less than adequate. In both these respects, therefore, the UK resembles a poorer Denmark.

Finally, it is worth noting that three of the four countries with the highest social minima (relative to the international poverty standard) coincide with those where fewest people reported the existence of poverty in the perception of poverty study (Table 2.18). Likewise, countries where people were less satisfied with government action on poverty coincide — though in different order — with those with the lowest social minima (Table 2.20). This may, of course, be no more than coincidence. Why, for instance, do so few Irish recognise the existence of poverty despite low levels of social assistance and high numbers of recipients? On the other hand, it may serve to emphasise the interdependence of institutional and individual perceptions of poverty and point to a common understanding of poverty among the people of Europe.

Patterns of Poverty

Household income distribution

Although students (and perhaps societies, e.g. Denmark) may be concerned with inequality and yet pay no attention to poverty, study of relative poverty necessitates consideration of inequality for at least two reasons. Firstly, poverty has to be defined relative to some point or group within society and the choice of an appropriate reference point necessitates consideration of the shape of, for example, the income distribution and of the 'distance' — in income terms — between the poverty line and the reference point. Secondly, policy responses that attempt to reduce the numbers in poverty (other than those which alter the reference point) necessarily entail an allocation of new or existing resources which alters the pattern of inequality.

Unfortunately, there is very little information on inequality which facilitates international comparison and what is available is generally limited to income inequalities. Lawson and George (1980) have compared the pre-tax income shares of rich and poor households in eight European countries, but stress the limitations of their data (see Table 2.23). A more systematic study — used in part by Lawson and George — is that conducted by Sawyer for the OECD (Sawyer 1976). Again, the data relates to income in the early 1970s and moreover comprehensive statistics are provided for just four European countries. Also, significant differences in the sources of income data mean that international comparison must be tentative.

Cumulative post-tax household income derived from the Sawyer study is presented for France, Germany, The Netherlands and the UK in Figure 2.2 and the Gini measure of inequality is given in Table 2.24 for incomes before and after tax and standardised for variations in household size. Pre-tax income includes wages, salaries, entrepreneurial income, property income and current transfers. Post-tax income covers the same items but deducts direct taxes and social security contributions. (The Gini coefficient relates an area between the Lorenz curve of cumulative income and the diagonal to the area beneath the diagonal and ranges from 0.0 (i.e. total equality) to 1.0; an important characteristic of the Gini coefficient is that it

> assumes that the transfer of a given amount of income from the very richest equally to everyone . . . would have the same impact as a transfer of an equal amount from everyone to the poorest, even though the change in income will add proportionally much more to the poor than it subtracts from the rich. (OECD 1976).

There is a remarkable degree of similarity between countries in terms of the distribution of their household income. Nevertheless, interesting differences are apparent, most of which seem generally consistent with the findings of the previous section. France emerges as particularly inequitable in terms of household income with the rich appearing proportionately richer, and the poor relatively poorer, than in the other countries. Moreover, the French tax system is more or less neutral in

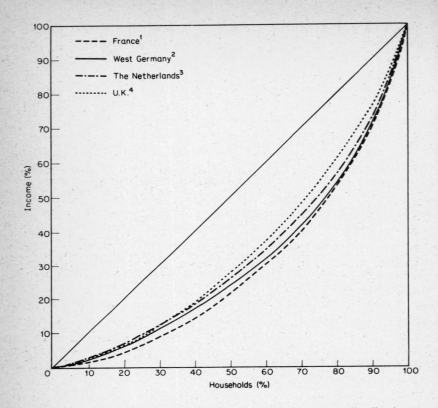

Figure 2.2   *Lorenz curves for post-tax household income distribution in France, the Netherlands, West Germany and the UK, early 1970s*

Notes: [1] 1970 [2] 1973 [3] 1967 [4] 1973
Source: OECD 1976

its impact whereas the British and Dutch systems, for example, appear quite progressive although no definitive judgements are possible because of the different ways in which the changes resulting from direct taxation have been calculated by the OECD. (The validity of comparison with the French data has been questioned — e.g. Bégué 1976 — but on balance it seems to be fair (see Sinfield 1980).) Pre-tax incomes in Italy and Ireland are only marginally more equitable than in France.

By way of contrast, The Netherlands and the UK appear most equitable, at least according to the Gini coefficient and after adjustment for household size which compensates for the large number of single-person households in The Netherlands. The pre-tax income distribution in

Table 2.23 Shares of selected deciles and quintiles in post-tax household income distribution for selected European countries

	West Germany (1973) (%)	Belgium[1] (1968) (%)	UK (1971–4) (%)	The Netherlands (1967) (%)	Denmark (1966) (%)	Italy (1971–2) (%)	France[1] (1970) (%)	Ireland (1973) (%)
First decile	31.1	32.6	24.2	30.5	26	28.8	31	–
First quintile	46.8	46.8	39.9	46.4	42	45.4	47	44.5
Fifth quintile	5.9	5.7	5.6	5.5	5	4.5	4.3	4.1

1 Tax units

Source: Adapted from Lawson and George 1980.

Table 2.24 Gini coefficients of income inequality in selected European countries

	Year	Pre-tax income	Post-tax income (a.)	'Standardised' household size[1] (b.)
UK	1973	0.334	0.318	0.327
The Netherlands	1967	0.385	0.354	0.264
West Germany	1973	0.396	0.016	0.386
Italy	1969	–	0.383	–
France	1970	0.416	0.414	0.417

1 Assumes countries have identical distributions of household size.

Adapted from Sawyer 1976.

Denmark is comparable with that of the UK (at a significantly later date) and one can only guess that similarly egalitarian distribution would remain after tax (see e.g. Brodersen 1981).

The income distribution in West Germany is distinctive but to some extent resembles that in Belgium. The rich are no less afluent — in relative terms — in West Germany than those in France or Italy but, on the other hand, those in the lowest two deciles are relatively less poor than elsewhere, presumably reflecting the generosity of insurance-based transfers. Those in the middle-income groups, comprising the majority of wage-earners and lower paid salary employees, receive a relatively smaller share of total household income than in other countries.

The preceding statistics relate to the early 1970s and, while patterns of income inequality are surprisingly resistant to change, the economic vicissitudes suffered by all countries since then may have had significant effects. For example, Brodersen (1981) has reported quite substantial gains in the relevant incomes of the lowest income groups in Denmark over the period 1971—6 on account of net transfers to the increased numbers of unemployed. Likewise, the long established trend towards reduced income dispersion has continued in The Netherlands with the relative position of the ninth decile increasing significantly between 1967 and 1977 (e.g. Odink 1978). Important factors in this change were increases in the levels of social transfers and in the numbers of people who were dependent on them. Income ceilings and contribution rates resulted in vertical transfers between middle and lower incomes (Le Blanc 1978).

The extent and risk of poverty

To conclude this introductory review, Tables 2.25 and 2.26 provide the latest information on the prevalence and risk of poverty in the countries featured in this volume. To focus on poverty is in effect to superimpose 'thresholds' on the income distribution described in the previous section and to count the number of households which fall beneath them. In this instance, the thresholds are set at 40 and 60 per cent of average household equivalent income.

The comparative information in Tables 2.25 and 2.26 is taken from the national studies of poverty commissioned by the European Commission and is the most comprehensive available. Nevertheless, the data are still far from perfect. The information on income is derived from national surveys which used different definitions and varied in their coverage and biases. Equally important, the equivalence scales used in each country were not standardised. The Dutch study employed Beckerman's schedule (reproduced in Annex 2A); the British study used a mixture of short- and long-term supplementary benefit rates; the West German ratios derive

Table 2.25   The prevalence of poverty in selected European countries, mid-1970s

	Year	Poverty lines for a childless couple (1975 value in PPSs)			% of households with incomes less than	
		40% average equivalent disposable income	60% average equivalent disposable income	Social assistance	40% average equivalent disposable income	60% average equivalent disposable income
Denmark[1]	–	–	–	5873	–	–
The Netherlands	1977	2990[2]	4485[2]	4618[3]	3.1	9.1[4]
UK[5]	1975	1827	2749	2649[6]	0.9	14.4
West Germany	1973	2379	3571	2515[7]	2.3	16.5
France	1975	2187	3281	1274[8]	8.5	28.2

1 Estimates of poverty in the Danish national report (Friis 1981) are unavoidably based on inadequate income data. Moreover, the interpretation of the concept of equivalent income is unusual. Social assistance figure equates with (b) in Table 2.21; (a) equals approximately 3880 PPSs including pension contribution.

2 Estimates.

3 Assuming low rent.

4 If the higher equivalences for the elderly proposed by Beckerman are employed the figure rises to 11.6.

5 Great Britain; the proportion of households below the 60% level in the UK may be 14.6%.

6 Including average rent of £4.93 per week.

7 Assuming 10% non-recurrent benefits, average rent and heating.

8 (b) In Table 2.21; (a) Equals 2444 PPSs.

Sources: FRS 1980: Nauta 1980; Hauser, Cremer-Schäfer and Nouvertne 1980; Berthoud, Brown and Cooper 1980; and own calculations 1980:

Table 2.26 The risk of poverty in selected European countries, mid-1970s

Household type	France (a) % of households with less than 60% equivalent disposable income	(b) Ratio to risk for all households	West Germany (a)	(b)	UK (a)	(b)	The Netherlands[1] (a)	(b)
Married couples with:								
1 child	13.5[2]	0.5[2]	6.5	0.4	4.8	0.3	7.3	0.6
2 children	19.5[2]	0.7[2]	16.4	1.0	8.3	0.6	8.2	0.7
3 children	32.5[2]	1.2[2]	30.9	1.9	17.0	1.2	25.1[3]	2.0[3]
4 or more children	54.4[2]	1.9[2]	52.6	3.2	43.0	3.0	–	–
Lone parent	–		28.1	1.7	51.9	3.6	37.1	3.0
Head aged over 65	42.3	1.5	24.3[4]	1.5[4]	26.9	1.9	7.5[5]	0.6[5]
Head economically inactive	43.0	1.5	24.2	1.5	31.9	2.2	15.4[6]	1.2[6]
All households	28.2	1.0	16.5	1.0	14.4	1.0	12.4	1.0

1 Social assistance level (11.6% of households have income less than 60% equivalent disposable income).
2 All households.
3 3 or more children.
4 Head aged over 60.
5 (a) 26.4; (b) 2.1 when the higher equivalences proposed by Beckerman (1979) are employed.
6 Households in receipt of benefit.

Sources: as for Table 2.19.

from national assistance rates and the French adopted a simple three-point scale. Moreover, no comparable information is available for Denmark which may be significant in view of the apparent invisibility of poverty as an issue among the Danes (see Chapter 6). Sadly, the information relates only to the mid-1970s. Finally, the poverty thresholds employed in the studies are arbitrary although, as explained above, they are not inconsistent with definitions used elsewhere in this volume.

Even bearing these reservations in mind, Table 2.25 remains of seminal interest. It shows substantial numbers of households with incomes below the 60 per cent disposable income poverty line in every country but also marked variation between them. In The Netherlands, only one household in eleven is in poverty according to this definition compared with one in four in France. West Germany and the UK fall roughly in the middle of this range. As is to be expected, fewer households have incomes below the 40 per cent disposable income level, although one household in twelve in France falls into this category. However, whereas The Netherlands has least poverty with respect to the more generous '60' per cent level, the UK takes this honour when the more stringent 40 per cent line is adopted. In part, these national variations are due to differences in the value of social assistance relative to the international poverty standard. Dutch social assistance payments are above both the 40 and 60 per cent disposable income lines, the British a little below the 60 per cent level, the West German just above the 40 per cent level and the French (in 1975) beneath both levels. The differences between The Netherlands and the UK in Table 2.25 suggest that the latter may operate a more effective safety net.

While the position of the UK is relatively favourable with respect to the numbers of people falling beneath the '40' per cent disposable income line it should be remembered that the absolute purchasing power of this income is much lower in the UK than in the other three countries. Indeed the '40 per cent disposable income' level in The Netherlands exceeds the '60 per cent disposable income' level in the UK in terms of purchasing power.

Table 2.26 compares the risks of poverty faced by demographic groups within and between countries. The '60 per cent disposable income' poverty line is adopted for each country except The Netherlands where the very similar social assistance level is taken. The demographic groups are chosen to coincide with the dependency groups analysed above, although the match is not perfect and no analysis of the unemployed is possible. It is clear that in all countries the economically inactive, the elderly, large families and lone-parent households run substantially enhanced risks of poverty. However, the risks are not uniform. The elderly, for example, are much less likely to experiencee poverty than are lone parents or larger families (i.e. those with more than three children) in all countries.

Moreover, after standardising for differences in the extent of poverty, certain groups appear to be 'better protected' in some countries than in others. This applies to the elderly in The Netherlands, to single parents in West Germany and to large families in France (and perhaps also in The Netherlands). On the other hand, West Germany is notable in that a second child effectively doubles the risk of poverty and that households with three children are almost twice as likely to be in poverty as the average for all households. The generally higher risk ratios given in Table 2.26 for the UK imply that poverty in the UK is more concentrated among the groups covered by the table than is the case in other countries.

Of the groups featured in Table 2.26 those with the highest absolute risk of poverty include French and West German families with four or more children, and lone-parent households in the UK. In each case more than one household in two has an income below the '60 per cent disposable income' level. Almost as disadvantaged are large families in the UK and the elderly in France (with 1.7 million out of a total of 4.1 million elderly households 'in poverty' the latter constitute the largest group at risk; but see Chapter 10). However, perhaps the most surprising of all — given the generosity of social provision in The Netherlands — is the precarious position of lone-parent households in that country.

Tables 2.25 and 2.26 refer to the situation in the mid-1970s. The changed circumstances since then will in most cases have increased the risk of poverty although certain policy changes may have improved the circumstances of particular groups. Nevertheless, the statistics provide a guide to the context in which recent policies have been formed and give a basis for assessing the success of earlier ones.

References

Beckerman, W. 1979, *Poverty and the impact of income maintenance programmes*, Geneva, ILO.

Bégué, J. 1976, 'Remarques sur une étude de L'OCDE concernant la répartition des revenus dans divers pays', *Economie et Statistique*, 84, pp. 97–104.

Berthoud, R., Brown, J. C. and Cooper, S. 1980, *Poverty and development of anti-poverty policy in the United Kingdom*, London, Policy Studies Institute (published in 1981 in revised form by Heinemann Educational Books).

Blackaby, F. T. 1980, *The future of pay bargaining*, London, Heinemann Educational Books.

Bradshaw, J. and Piachaud, D. 1980, *Child Support in the European Community*, London, Bedford Square Press.

Brodersen, S. 1981, *Unit of analysis and income concepts in income distribution and redistribution studies with an application to Danish household budget survey data*, Mimeo, Department of Applied Economics, Cambridge.

Deleeck, H. 1979, 'Bestaanszekerheid en sociale zekerheid', *Begisch Tijdschrift voor Sociale Zekerheid*, 6.

DHSS 1980, *Social benefit tables for member states of the European communities, position at 1 January 1980*, London, DHSS.

Denmark 1981, *Statistisk Årbog 1981*, Copenhagen, Danmark Statistisk.

EC 1977, *The perception of poverty in Europe*, Brussels, Commission of the European Communities.

EC 1979, *The European social budget 1980–1975–1970*, Brussels, Commission of the European Communities.

EC 1980a, *Social indicators 1967–78*, Luxembourg, Eurostat.

EC 1980b, *Social protection statistics: receipts and expenditures 1970–1979*, Luxembourg, Eurostat.

EC 1981a, *Final report from the Commission to the Council on the First Programme of Pilot Schemes and Studies to Combat Poverty*, Brussels, Commission of the European Communities.

EC 1981b, *Demographic Statistics 1979*, Luxembourg, Eurostat.

EC 1982a, *National accounts ESA — aggregates 1960–1980*, Luxembourg, Eurostat.

EC 1982b, *Social Protection Statistics: expenditures and receipts 1970–1980*, Luxembourg, Eurostat.

Field, F. (ed.) 1977, *Are Low Wages Inevitable?*, Nottingham, Spokesman Books.

Fitzgerald, E. n.d., *Alternative Strategies for family income support*, National Economic and Social Council.

Friis, H. 1981, *Poverty and poverty policy in Denmark*, Copenhagen, Socialforskningsinstituttet.

FRS 1981, *La Pauvrété et la lutte contre la pauvrété*, Paris, Fondation pour la Recherche Sociale.

Geissler, H. 1975, Dokumentation 'Neve Soziale Frage' — Zahlen, Daten, Fakten, Mimeo, 5 November.

George, V. and Lawson, R. (eds) 1980, *Poverty and inequality in Common Market countries*, London, Routledge & Kegan Paul.

Ginneken, van W. 1981, 'Unemployment: some trends, causes and policy implications', *International Labour Review*, vol. 120, no. 2, pp. 165–81.

Golding, P. 1980, 'In the eye of the beholder: An evaluation of the European Commission Study "The perception of poverty in Europe" in ESPOIR', *Europe against poverty, vol. II*, Canterbury, ESPOIR.

Gorce, de la, P-M. 1965, *La France pauvre*, Paris, Bernard Grasset.

Graffar, M. *et al.* 1967, 'Etude de la consommation de soixante familles assistées par le bureau de secours de la CAP de Bruxelles', *Revue de l'institut de Sociologie*, 1, pp. 115–72.

Hauser, R., Cremer-Schäfer, H. and Nouvertnê, U. 1980, *National report on poverty in the Federal Republic of Germany*, Frankfurt, Arbeitsgruppe Armutsforschung.

Keithley, J. 1981, 'The European social budget', *Social Policy and Administration*, vol. 15, no. 2.

Klanberg, F. 1979, 'Einkommensarmut 1969 und 1973 bei Anlegung verschiedener standards', *Sozialer Fortschritt*, 6.

Kögler, A. 1976, *Die Entwicklung von Randgruppen in der Bundesrepublik: Literaturstudie zur Entwicklung, randständiger Bevölkerungsgruppen*, Schriften der Kommission für wirtschaftlichen und sozialen Wandel, Band 87.

Kortmann, K. 1978, 'Probleme der armut im sozialstaat' in M. V. Pfaff and H. Voigtlander (eds), *Sozialpolitik im Wandel*, Bonn.

Lawson, R. 1979, *The structure of social assistance in 1979*, Prepared for the European Commission, University of Southampton, Mimeo.

Lawson, R. 1980a, *Social assistance*. Talk given to the Comparative Social Policy Study Group, Joint University Council, London, 1 February.

Lawson, R. 1980b, 'Poverty and inequality in West Germany' in V. George and R. Lawson (eds) 1980, pp. 124–60.

Lawson, R. and George, V. 1980, 'An assessment' in V. George and R. Lawson (eds) 1980, pp. 233–42.

Le Blanc, B. 1975, 'Het sociaal aanvaardbare minimum', *Socialisme en Democratie*, April, p. 147.

Le Blanc, B. 1978, 'Op weg naar een economische theorie van de sociale zekerheid', *Deventer* p. 76.

Mercier, P-A. 1974, *Les inégalités en France*, Paris, CREDOC.

NAB (Nationale Aktie voor Bestaanzkerheid) 1967, *Manifest der meest onterfden*, Brussels.

Nauta, A. P. N. 1980, *Poverty in the Netherlands — A report to the Commission of the European Communities*, Rijswijk, Sociaal en Cultureel Planbureau.

Netherlands 1976, *Statistical Yearbook of The Netherlands 1975*, The Hague, Netherlands Central Bureau of Statistics.

Ó Cinnéide, S. 1980, 'Poverty and inequality in Ireland' in V. George and R. Lawson (eds), *Poverty and Inequality in Common Market Countries*, London, Routledge & Kegan Paul, pp. 124–60.

Odink, J. T. 1978, 'De nieuwste ontwikkelingen in de nederlandse personele inkomensverdeling', *ESB*, vol. 5, no. 4, pp. 320–4.

OECD 1976, *Public expenditure on income maintenance programmes*, Studies in resource allocation, 3, Paris.

OECD 1979, *Child and family*, Paris, Centre for Education Research and Innovation.

OECD 1981a, *Economic outlook*, 29, Paris, OECD.

OECD 1981b, *National accounts of OECD countries 1950–1979*, vol. II, Paris, OECD.

OECD 1982, *Germany*, OECD Economic Surveys, Paris.

Saunders, C. 1980, 'Changes in relative pay in the 1970s', in F. Blackaby (ed.), *The future of pay bargaining*, London, Heinemann Educational Books.

Saunders, C. and Marsden, D. 1979, *A six-country comparison of the distribution of industrial earnings in the 1970s*. Background Paper no. 8, Royal Commission on the Distribution of Income and Wealth, London, HMSO.

Sawyer, M. 1976, 'Income distribution in OECD Countries', *OECD Economic Outlook, Occasional Studies*, July, pp. 3—36.

Sinfield, A. 1980, 'Poverty and inequality in France, in V. George and R. Lawson (eds) 1980.

UK 1979, *Report No 8*, Royal Commission on the Distribution of Income and Wealth, London, HMSO, Cmnd 7679.

Annex 2.A: International standard poverty line: ratio between poverty lines of various household types and benchmark household

Household type	ratio
Over pension age:	
Single persons	0.73
Couples	1.15
Under pension age:	
Single adults without children	0.62
Single adults with children	1.12
Couples without children	1.00
Couples with 1 child	1.22
Couples with 2 children	1.43
Couples with 3 children	1.65
Couples with 4 or more children	1.98

Source: Beckerman 1979.

Annex 2.B: Estimate of total household disposable income

Estimate of total household disposable income = GDP × C

	Estimation of C	
	3 year mean (1976–8)	Range (1976–8)
Italy	0.7972	0.0078
Belgium	0.7586	0.0040
France	0.7133	0.0040
The Netherlands	0.6803	0.0080
UK	0.6570	0.0106
West Germany	0.6406	0.0050
Denmark[1]	0.5726	0.0160

1 1974–6.

Part II Poverty, Unemployment and Low Pay
Editorial Overview

Despite the enormous growth of government welfare expenditure detailed in Chapter 2, the majority of income received by individual households in Europe is still allocated through the labour market (OECD 1981). It follows that persons who occupy relatively weak competitive positions within the labour market, or are excluded from it, are likely to run a considerably increased risk of poverty.

Measures to protect those excluded — the old, sick and unemployed — were often adopted very early in the development of social welfare. Frequently, the initiative was taken by church-based voluntary organisations, trade unions and self-protection societies and taken over or regulated by the State only at a much later date. Benefits tended to be restricted to employees, or former employees, and may not have been extended to other groups until very recently, if indeed at all. Occasionally, measures were introduced explicitly with a view to enhanced social control, as in West Germany and to an extent in France (see especially Chapter 5). Later still the State began to play an active role in protecting those clinging precariously to the periphery of the labour market by means of minimum wages, wage policies calculated to improve the position of the low paid and legislation to protect or enhance the employment opportunities of women and the chronically disabled.

The chapters in this section examine some of the policies which have been adopted by European countries to protect those in relatively weak positions *vis-à-vis* the labour market. Reflecting the higher levels of unemployment which characterised the late 1970s and early 1980s, each chapter focuses on the issue of unemployment and on the preventive and ameliorative measures which have been adopted — with varying degrees of success — to limit the extent and degree of poverty suffered by the unemployed. Each chapter also considers the relative position of the low paid, and where appropriate, examines policies which have been enacted to protect them.

The Problem of Unemployment

All four countries experienced much higher levels of unemployment during the latter half of the 1970s than had been suffered at any time in the previous 20 years. By the end of the decade recorded unemployment ranged between two and five times what it had been at the beginning (see Figure 2.5). Moreover, unemployment rose still further in 1981 and began to affect West Germany, which had managed to reverse the upward trend between 1977 and early 1980. In all countries the average duration of unemployment increased throughout the decade.

While there is debate about the relative importance of the various precursors of unemployment, certain factors are clear. Sluggish economic growth throughout the latter half of the 1970s was accompanied by an increased sensitivity of western economies to inflationary pressures — arguably the result in part of greater legislative and institutional rigidities in the labour market (Haveman 1980). The impact of the oil price rises in 1974/5 and 1978/9 was to shift substantially the terms of trade and immediately to limit or actually reduce the incomes of OECD countries. Moreover, the response of governments in France, Denmark, The Netherlands and, particularly, in the UK was to meet the oil price rises by restrictive fiscal and monetary policies in order to prevent inflationary effects being translated into a domestic wage-price formation process. Such measures have tended to exacerbate the problem of restricted growth (OECD 1980b).

Countries have at the same time experienced structural shifts in employment away from agriculture and manufacturing towards the tertiary sector where occupational demands have been focused on service workers, who exhibit high labour force elasticity, and on professional/technical workers who are comparatively few in number. In addition labour supply has expanded, first due to the post-war 'baby boom' cohort entering the labour market and latterly due to the birth cohorts of the 1950s and early 1960s. Female activity rates have also increased.

The young have suffered comparatively high unemployment reflecting the fact that, unlike older workers, they are not protected by job security legislation, collective bargaining agreements and conventional patterns of personnel recruitment (see Figure II.1). Largely for demographic reasons youth unemployment has peaked at different times in various countries but, except in France, the relative position of the young has not deteriorated since 1977 and has improved significantly in West Germany. As the following chapters indicate this is partly the result of government programmes although these are invariably of a holding nature.

While unemployment amongst young people has stabilised, the unemployment rate for women relative to men has continued to worsen in

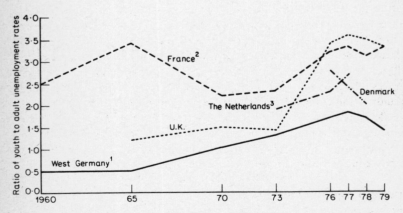

Figure II.1   *Ratio of youth to adult unemployment rates in selected European countries, 1960—79*

Notes: [1] 1958 for 1960 [2] 1962 for 1960 [3] 1975 for 1976
Source: OECD 1980a

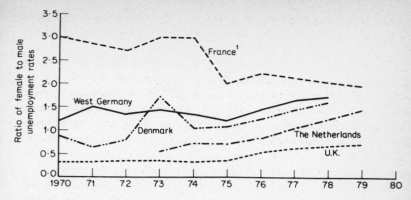

Figure II.2   *Ratio of female to male unemployment rates in selected European countries, 1970—79*

Note: [1] March 1979
Source: OECD 1980c

each country except France where in 1979 women were still more disadvantaged than elsewhere (see Figure II.2). This deterioration may reflect differential lay-off rates since women tend to be less skilled and to have less seniority. Women may also be less geographically mobile and perhaps more discriminating in their job search because they are less frequently the sole breadwinner. Nevertheless it is important to note that during the 1970s total female employment increased in each country, primarily as a consequence of the substantial growth of the tertiary sector. The situation in the UK appears very different. Although the relative position of women has worsened, female unemployment rates are still lower than for men. In part this reflects the fact that unemployment returns relate to registered unemployment — as is also the case in The Netherlands — and women are much less likely to register. Moreover, although female employment rose overall during the 1970s, female employment in industry fell by more than male unemployment (OECD 1980c).

Significantly, both among women and the young, the unskilled and poorly educated bear the brunt of unemployment.

Special Employment Measures

The governments of each country have stressed that the creation of new employment through economic growth must be the main strategy against unemployment. It follows, therefore, that in varying degrees all have been unsuccessful. Moreover, as in the UK, contractionist monetary and financial policies have contributed to the growth of unemployment in France, Denmark and The Netherlands. Even in West Germany where moderately expansionist Keynesian policies have generally been followed, unemployment remains at historically high levels.

Unable to stimulate employment through expansion of general demand, goverments have resorted in varying degrees to specific measures designed to increase the employment potential of specific groups. In the main these measures have sought to increase the attractiveness of certain types of labour by reducing its cost — through subsidies to employers — or by training to improve its quality. However, public sector job-creation measures have also been tried and, in Denmark in particular, explicit attempts have been made to redistribute employment towards the more disadvantaged.

It is inappropriate here to attempt to summarise the special employment measures which have been adopted and which are generally discussed in some detail in the following chapters. However, one or two differences in emphasis warrant mentioning.

First, France and West Germany seem to differ in that the former has targeted employment projects on the young and the latter on the long-term unemployed. The ratio of youth to adult unemployment is much higher in France (3.3) than in West Germany (1.4) but long-term unemployment is also greater (OECD 1980b). In large measure West Germany has responded to the threat of youth unemployment by developing a pre-existing system whereby the last three years of formal education include a significant element of vocational training, usually a blend of employment and training. In Denmark and in The Netherlands there are separate schemes tailored to the needs of both the young and the long-term unemployed. Despite high levels of female unemployment, only in France do any provisions appear to aim differentially at women and little precise information is available on the take-up of general schemes by women.

Secondly, countries have placed different weight on attempts to influence labour supply, increase labour demand or redistribute existing employment. West Germany has emphasised measures to increase labour skills and flexibility whereas The Netherlands has concentrated on improving the system of placement. France and Denmark have been more concerned to stimulate new employment by means of selective subsidies to employers. Denmark and The Netherlands have also adopted early retirement schemes in an explicit attempt to redistribute labour in favour of the young. (The more limited early retirement scheme in France, which pre-dated President Mitterrand's initiatives was designed to ease unemployment in declining areas by permanently reducing labour supply rather than to redistribute existing employment.) With a similar objective, holidays are to be increased in Denmark and overtime may be curtailed.

The differences in emphasis are apparent in Table II.1 which shows the scale of measures adopted but which must be interpreted with care as it summarises much heterogeneous material collated for the OECD. High Dutch spending on labour demand measures is largely due to the cost of sheltered workshops but is also affected by the special 1980 scheme of job creation and by early retirement in the public services. In 1977/8 UK expenditure was similarly concentrated on demand measures although, especially through the Temporary Employment Subsidy and Regional Development Grants, it was distributed among greater numbers of beneficiaries. More is spent on measures to influence labour supply and the balance between demand and supply in both West Germany and Denmark. Exclusion from Table II.1 of expenditure on the West German dual system of initial vocational training is clearly important while the budget of the *Bundesanstalt für Arbeit* (see Chapter 5) constitutes most expenditure under the third column. Training in Denmark is included and significantly affects the number of beneficiaries of labour supply measures although most of the cost is attributed to the early retirement wage and the job offer scheme. The special employment plan B11 is the major component of Danish spending on supply and demand adjustment (see Chapter 6.).

Thirdly, in attempting to create new jobs Denmark and The Netherlands have tended to rely more on the public sector than has West Germany, France, or the UK. In part this reflects the large size of public and semi-public sectors in Denmark and The Netherlands but equally the private sector in Denmark has also been reluctant in its response to government subsidies. Unlike the other countries, France has attempted to stimulate private sector jobs by reducing employers' social security contributions rather than offering wage subsidies.

Finally, it is noticeable that the emphasis of West German policy has enabled it to use the force of sanction rather than to rely on the goodwill of employers. One example was the legislation to ensure sufficient apprenticeships to meet the demographic bulge of the 1970s (see Chapter 5).

It is difficult to establish the relative effectiveness of the different economic and labour market strategies although the performance of the German economy — at least until the early 1980s — seems to establish a prima facie case in favour of the approach adopted there. Likewise it is difficult to evaluate individual measures even though the following chapters report output measures wherever possible. Evaluation of job-creation schemes based on numbers of direct beneficiaries and gross exchequer costs (as presented in Table II.1) may be misleading. Some beneficiaries would have been recruited in the absence of special schemes in which

Table II.1 Special employment measures in selected European countries, late 1970s

| | Measures to affect: | | | | | |
| | (1) Labour demand | | (2) Labour supply | | (3) Adjustment of supply and demand | |
	(a) Cost[1]/head in civilian employment (EUA)	(b) Places/1000 in civilian employment	(a)	(b)	(a)	(b)[2]
Denmark (1979)	16	10	109	53	191	—
France[3]	—	—	—	—	—	—
The Netherlands (1980)	253	28	17	5	8	—
West Germany (1976)	73	24	37[4]	14[4]	587	—
UK (1977/8)	81	89	26[5]	11[6]	37	—

1 Costs are expressed in 1980 EUA.
2 This column is omitted since available information differs in kind.
3 No information is available for France.
4 Excludes dual system of initial vocational training.
5 Includes disabled persons' employment.
6 Excludes 540 000 registered disabled persons.

Source: OECD, unpublished papers; authors' calculations.

case the subsidy represents a simple reduction in labour costs. Similarly, employers might be tempted to substitute temporary labour under a scheme for permanent staff, or, if the scheme results in one employer enjoying a cost advantage over another, new employment may result in a displacement of employment elsewhere in the economy. (It has been estimated that net jobs created by marginal targeted employment subsidies are likely to range from 20 to 50 per cent of the gross employment effect. See Haveman and Christiansen 1978.) Gross exchequer costs by definition exclude savings in unemployment benefit and increased tax yields. They also exclude receipts from the EC's Social Fund which is relevant with respect to measures aimed at young persons. Finally, an exhaustive evaluation should assess net resource costs, though this raises inordinate methodological difficulties (MSC 1981).

However, there do seem to be strong theoretical arguments in favour of the selective employment subsidies which are increasingly replacing general subsidies and relief projects. Selective subsidies are generally paid to concerns that increase their labour force by employing workers from target categories. (Subsidies may also be targeted on types of firm.) Such schemes not only provide additional jobs but effect a shift in employment towards the most disadvantaged, thereby reducing income poverty. Because the target groups would by definition have limited industrial muscle the employment can be achieved with marginal inflationary pressure and with a beneficial impact on the balance of payments since the employment subsidies are, in effect, export subsidies. Moreover, to the extent that the shift is towards mass productive labour, this encourages an increase in total employment albeit at the cost of short-term reductions in productivity (Haveman 1980).

Special employment measures, as their name suggests, generally constitute a short (though increasingly medium) term response to unemployment. The assumption of governments is that high levels of unemployment will themselves be short-lived. If, in fact, they are symptomatic of a secular readjustment of the global economy more radical responses will become inevitable. Moreover, short-term measures have themselves long-term consequences. Subsidies, for example, may preserve outmoded industrial structures and further inhibit future change. Early retirement schemes may confound the problems of funding pensions (see Part IV). Finally, preserving high-paid employment in Europe may serve to exacerbate the global inequalities discussed by Peter Townsend in Chapter 1.

Social Security Provisions
The extent to which the unemployed are protected financially varies

markedly between the four countries (see Table II.2). This variation occurs despite the fact that the main social security provision is, in each case, an insurance-based scheme with benefits and contributions related to earnings. (The UK, in supplementing flat-rate benefits with additions for dependants and in 1982, abolishing earnings-related benefits, is clearly out of step.) Table II.2 shows that income replacement ratios and the time for which initial replacement ratios are maintained are much higher in Denmark and The Netherlands than in West Germany, France or the UK.

Table II.2   Unemployment benefit levels according to length of unemployment in selected European countries, 1980

	Net unemployment benefit[1] as a % of former (average) net earnings[1] after unemployment of:				
	1 month	*7 months*	*13 months*	*25 months*	*31 months*
Denmark	87	87	87	87	87
The Netherlands	85	82	82	82	(85)
West Germany	68	68	$(58)^{2,3}$	$(58)^{2,3}$	$(58)^{2,3}$
France	61	61	$13(36)^2$	$(36)^2$	$(36)^2$
UK	68	49	$(46)^2$	$(46)^2$	$(46)^2$

1 After income tax as appropriate (see OECD 1980d).
2 Bracketed figures relate to social assistance payments, excluding housing additions.
3 *Arbeitslosenhilfe* is an assistance benefit paid under the insurance scheme (see Chapter 5).
4 Assumes couple with two children (benefit includes child allowance in excess of child benefit).

Source: UK 1980; EC 1981b; editor's calculations.

Variations in the length of time for which income replacement ratios are sustained reflect different objectives ascribed to unemployemnt bene-fit. The high and sustained levels of benefit in Denmark and The Nether-lands are seen as enabling the unemployed to make reasoned choices as to how best to re-enter the labour market. On the contrary, in West Germany the incentive to minimise financial outlay from the insurance fund is supported by a strong philosophical emphasis on rehabilitation and on the need to encourage workers to return to the labour force, thereby facilitating their full participation as members of West German society. Traditionally, the French have also been concerned to minimise financial outlays but, by May 1980, 30 per cent of the unemployed had exhausted any entitlement to insurance benefits. Unemployment was a key element in the 1981 socialist victories and one of President Mitter-rand's first acts in office was to increase unemployment benefit. He later announced a special national solidarity unemployment levy on personal incomes in excess of £1500 per month to pay for the improvements.

While provision for income-related benefits and contributions is common to all four countries, the actuarial principle of linking premiums to risk has been dispensed with in all countries except The Netherlands. Instead, income-related benefits are viewed as expressions of community solidarity and related to the economic value of previous work. Relating benefits to former earnings also means that income loss resulting from unemployment is proportionately the same for all income groups, so that accustomed living standards are equally protected. A corollary is that vertical transfers of income in favour of the low-paid are minimised and that the inequalities of the labour market are translated directly into the social security system with the result that the low-wage earner runs a substantial risk of financial hardship in the event of unemployment. This effect can be seen from Table II.3 which shows the net unemployment benefit payable to a person formerly earning average, and two-thirds average, earnings in relation to the international poverty standard and national social assistance levels assuming a two-parent, two-child family. (In the case of The Netherlands a relatively high 'minimum benefit level' serves to protect the low-paid.)

It is also clear from Table II.3 that unemployment benefit in France and West Germany — including family allowances -- is insufficient to lift the family of a worker previously earning average wages above the international poverty standard. It does, however, place them out of reach of social assistance. Moreover, the living standards of the *long-term* unemployed in West Germany, and particularly in France, are much lower than shown in Table II.3. The UK is similar to France and West Germany in both respects. Inclusion of housing costs and allowances would not substantively alter this picture for the person formerly earning average wages although the amount by which his family fell short of the poverty standard would be reduced. However, formerly low-paid workers would be more likely to qualify for supplementary social assistance during the first months of unemployment.

Continuing raised levels of unemployment have strained the finances and administration of benefit schemes. Expenditure on unemployment benefits increased both absolutely and relatively in each country between 1970 and 1979 (See Chapter 2). In 1975, the West German unemployment insurance fund ran into serious deficit and contributions had to be raised. More radical changes were precipitated in the French system that brought about the financial involvement of central government for the first time, ended the role of *Départements* in paying benefits, markedly reduced benefit levels for those who had been made redundant and

Table II.3 Unemployment benefit levels in selected European countries in relation to the international poverty standard and national social assistance levels, 1980

Percentages

	Former gross earnings as a % of average gross male earnings	Net unemployment benefit[1] payable after one month's unemployment as a % of:	
		(a) International poverty standard[2] (couple with 2 children)	(b) Social assistance (national scale rates for a couple with 2 children)
	66	100	66 100
Denmark	91 (92)[3]	105	100 (100)[3,4] 100[4]
The Netherlands	99 (99)[3]	99	99 (99)[3,5] 99[5]
West Germany	61	78	105[5] 135[5]
France[6]			
(a)	53	66	70[7] 88[7]
(b)	–	–	117[8] 147[8]
UK	77	84	126 138

1 Including family allowances, less income tax as appropriate.
2 Defined according to Beckerman (1979).
3 Bracketed figures refer to the minimum wage where it exceeds 66 per cent of average earnings.
4 Temporary assistance; see Table 2.15.
5 See Table 2.15 for definition.
6 Family allowances include means-tested *Complément Familial* payable to 87 per cent of families.
7 National Social Minimum Pension; see Table 2.15.
8 Social aid, see Table 2.15.
9 Supplementary benefit, normal rate, see Table 2.15.

limited for all groups the length of time for which benefit was payable. (A major consequence of this reform was to worsen the position of the long-term unemployed.)

An additional problem has been that large numbers of unemployed have exhausted their entitlement to first-line insurance benefits so that, contrary to design, second and third-line benefits have come to play the role of main income support systems. In The Netherlands, insurance benefits now support only 21 per cent of the registered unemployed. In France, prior to the 1979 reforms, unemployment assistance was increasingly being claimed simultaneously with insurance benefits and, even in West Germany, beneficiaries of social assistance approximately doubled during the 1970s not least as a consequence of unemployment. This problem is exacerbated by the insurance-based nature of main-line systems which fail to meet the needs of the uninsured, especially school leavers and the many women who have spent time outside the labour market.

At the same time concern about faltering national economies brought into question the relationship between insurance benefits and the working of the economy. The reduction in France of the benefit levels for those made redundant must be seen in the context of criticism about the disincentive effects of benefits, although the government never acknowledged the validity of such criticism. In Denmark, the so-called 'paradox problem' of vacancies co-existing with historically high levels of unemployment is taxing policy makers and the OECD has laid the blame firmly on high benefit levels. Likewise, with regard to similar problems in The Netherlands, the OECD have concluded that 'generous benefits probably help prolong the "search period" for jobs' (OECD 1980e). (Indeed, many Dutch economists seem to blame high benefits for a large number of the failings of the Dutch economy: see Wyles 1981.)

The cost of benefits to the taxpayer also emerged as an issue in the 1970s and in Denmark fuelled the spectacular success of the Progressive Party in the mid-1970s. Similar, though electorally less successful, movements have been found in the other countries. A related, more sophisticated, concern relates to the social security contributions paid by employers. These, it is argued, not only reduce profitability and thereby investment potential but also act as a tax on labour which may exacerbate unemployment (e.g. see Tuinier 1979).

However, the political significance of these arguments should not be exaggerated. Unemployment benefits constitute only a small item in the social wage (see EC 1979) and moreover formal and traditonal linkages between benefit levels conspire to make it difficult radically to re-adjust the level of individual benefits. Also social democratic traditions run deep in West Germany, Denmark and The Netherlands

(Naschold 1981) and in France the downward adjustments to unemployment benefits may have contributed to the 1981 socialist victory. Again, the involvement of the trades union movement both in policy relating to unemployment benefits and administration in all four countries must be a significant factor protecting existing benefit levels. Finally, as Karl Furmaniak argues in Chapter 5, it is possible that the clear insurance basis of unemployment benefit schemes inhibits development of significant taxpayer resentment. Certainly policy responses have generally focused on methods of ensuring rapid and effective job replacement through administrative reform and on improved training rather than on the erosion of the living standards of the unemployed, although this conclusion has less applicability to the UK. Additional training funds have been made available (in Denmark, West Germany and in The Netherlands); grants introduced to encourage geographic mobility and special benefits paid to top up incomes if low wage jobs are taken (West Germany); new measures implemented to improve communication between industry and government placing services (Denmark); and reorganisation undertaken of the unemployment and employment services (in Denmark and planned for The Netherlands).

Low Pay and Wage Differentials

Each chapter also addresses the question of the working poor who, as Antoine Lion emphasises, all too frequently change places with the unemployed in what might be likened to a *danse macabre*. Other linkages between unemployment and low pay are also discussed in the individual chapters, for example, the significance of benefit levels for work incentives (Denmark); the impact of minimum wage levels on employment opportunities (France, Denmark); differentials and inflation (France, The Netherlands); and methods of dynamising benefits to wage increases (each of the countries).

However, the countries differ markedly in the emphasis placed on low wages within the overall approach to setting wage levels. Both Denmark and The Netherlands have highly centralised pay bargaining systems involving representatives of unions and employers which lead to wage agreements that are enforceable by law and which in both cases contain indexation clauses. In principle, collective agreements are reached by the unions and employers with the government acting as the final arbitrator (tripartite arrangements existed in The Netherlands until the late 1960s). However, in practice, throughout the 1970s both governments have imposed a series of wage policies usually accompanied by wage control. In Denmark, these policies have included proportionately larger increases for the poorest paid and in 1977, a minimum wage was introduced into the statutory collective agreements.[1] Moreover, the system of indexing which involves flat rate increases also benefits the lower paid. In The Netherlands, the minimum wage (and benefit levels which are equated to it) moved ahead of increases in average wages during the 1970s. Furthermore the progressive tax system, allied to incomplete indexation, has also made for a narrowing of differentials in net income (OECD 1980e). However, in contrast with Denmark, recent attempts by the Dutch government to weaken indexation have not harmed the position of low wage-earners nor has wage-drift been sufficient to restore differentials.

In France, a minimum wage was adopted after the Second World War and plays an important symbolic role. After the 1968 troubles, the minimum wage was increased substantially and reconstituted so as to make it a mechanism in the reduction of wage inequalities. In 1981, one of President Mitterrand's first acts was to increase the level of the minimum wage. Furthermore, the minimum wage has also been used as a poverty standard in much of recent French research. In other respects, however, wage bargaining is much less centralised than in either Denmark or The Netherlands and the involvement of trade unions, who represent only a little over 20 per cent of workers, is limited to industry-wide bargaining. French governments have tended to rely heavily on wage control in order to encourage wage restraint rather than to attempt centralised discussions on incomes policy.

In West Germany, no specific measures are taken to enhance the relative position of the lower paid. Moreover, in spite of there being only a few large industrial unions and, until recently, tripartite discussions on the feasible growth of incomes, the autonomy of employers and trade unions in negotiations is sacrosanct. Nevertheless, national collective agreements are legal contracts and, moreover, the government has power to extend their provision to all businesses within an industry regardless of whether the employers were a party to that agreement (Dean 1980).

Table II.4 shows national minimum wage rates and average wages in low-pay industries, both expressed as a percentage of average wages and of the international poverty line. Pay in low-wage industries appears higher, relative to average wages, in those countries with a statutory minimum wage but equally, by the same criterion, the minimum wage in France is relatively much lower than in The Netherlands or Denmark. Indeed, whereas the net minimum wage in Denmark and The Netherlands

---

[1] The 1981 collective agreements were successfully concluded without government intervention so that, although minimum wage provisions were generally retained in industry-based agreements, no statutory minimum wage now exists in Denmark.

Table II.4   Minimum wage levels in relation to average male manual earnings and the international poverty standard in selected European countries, 1980

	Gross minimum wage as a % of:		Net[3] minimum wage as a % of:
	(a) Average gross male manual earnings	(b) International poverty standard (couple with 2 children)[1,2]	(c) International poverty standard (couple with 2 children)[1,2]
Denmark	72	131	98
The Netherlands	72	124	97
France	64	76[4]	68

	Gross average wage in the lowest paid industry[5] as a % of:		Net[3] average wage in the lowest paid industry as a % of:
	(a)	(b)[6]	(c)
Denmark	83	150	116
The Netherlands[7]	76	131	104
France	72	84[4]	75
West Germany	65	99	78
UK	60	96	81

1 Gross minimum wage given in this column includes family allowances.
2 International poverty standard defined according to Beckerman (1979).
3 Net of income tax and social security contributions assuming two-thirds average male manual earnings (see Bradshaw and Piachaud 1980).
4 Family allowances include means-tested *Complément Familial* which is paid to 87 per cent of families.
5 In each case average earnings of male manual workers in clothing and footwear manufacturing (source: EC 1981a).
6 Gross average wage including family allowances.
7 Estimate of earnings.

roughly equates with the International Poverty Standard for a two-child family, the corresponding figure in France is only two-thirds. The fact that low wage industries in France, West Germany and the UK pay wages considerably below the International Poverty Standard, though above national social assistance levels, demonstrates that even steady employment cannot guarantee protection from financial hardship.

Table II.5 shows the movement in skill differentials in male wage rates over the 15 or so years to 1979. Between country comparisons of the actual ratios is hazardous because of differing definitions but differentials do appear to be narrowest in Denmark and perhaps widest in France (where the figures relate only to selected industries). Differentials

Table II.5   Ratio of unskilled to skilled hourly male manual
earnings for selected European countries, 1966—79

	1966	1969	1972	1973	1975	1977	1979
Denmark[1]							
(a) Copenhagen	83[2]	84[3]	—	86	86[4]	—	86
(b) Other areas	83[2]	85[3]	—	87	89[4]	—	88
West Germany							
(a) Engineering	78	80	80	—	79	80	—
(b) Low-wage industries	83	85	82	—	81	81	—
The Netherlands[5]	—	—	77	—	—	—	—
France[6]							
(a) Engineering	59	59	57	58	60	59	—
(b) Low-wage industries	59	60	61	69	71	70	—
UK							
(a) Engineering	71	71	73	—	76	79[4]	78[7]

1 Adapted from OECD 1980f.
2 1965.
3 1970.
4 1976.
5 Adapted from Ginneken 1981.
6 Ratio of *Manoeuvre ordinaire* to *Ouvrier hautement qualifié* earnings.
7 1978.

Source: adapted from Marsden 1980.

narrowed in every country except West Germany although since 1975 they may have stabilised in the other countries. (Wage differentials between industries also lessened in every country except West Germany (Saunders 1980), while sex differentials decreased in all countries except France, which nevertheless retains the most equitable distribution (OECD 1980b).)

While it is notoriously difficult to disentangle the pressures on wage differentials it has been suggested that movements in the minimum wage and policies to compensate for rising costs of living (especially in The Netherlands and Denmark) may both have been important. With regard to the operation of minimum wages the French figures reveal that the impact of adjustments to the minimum wage are greatest when it is close to actual wages. Consequently, the 1972 rise in the French minimum wage had more effect than the larger increase in 1968 and the effect of both was more marked within low income industries than within high ones.

Another consideration must be the relative bargaining strength of groups within the labour force. The advance in a relative position of the unskilled coincided in Denmark with conditions unfavourable to wage-drift and to the bargaining power of the skilled; and in France and the UK with a movement of power away from the union structure to the shop floor where less skilled workers have more voice. Latterly, both these trends may have weakened to stem the erosion of differentials. Moreover, neither factor has been important in West Germany during the last 15 years where, in addition, the already relatively egalitarian wage distribution may have lessened pressures towards additional equality.

References

Beckerman, W. 1979, *Poverty and the impact of income maintenance programmes*, Geneva, ILO.

Bradshaw, J., Piachaud, D. 1980, *Child Support in the European Community*, London, Bedford Square Press.

Dean, A. J. H. 1980, 'Roles of government and institutions in OECD countries' in F. T. Blackaby (ed.) *The future of pay bargaining*. London, Heinemann.

EC 1979, *The European social budget 1980–1975–1970*, Brussels, Commission of the European Communities.

EC 1981a, 'Earnings in industry', *Wages and incomes: rapid information*, 23 April, Luxembourg, Eurostat.

EC 1981b, *Social protection statistics: receipts and expenditures 1970–1979*, Luxembourg, Eurostat.

Ginneken van, W. 1981, 'Unemployment: some trends, causes and policy implications', *International Labour Review*, vol. 120, no. 2, pp. 165–81.

Haveman, R. 1980, *The potential of targeted marginal employment subsidies: economic and institutional issues*, Paper prepared for OECD Working Party on Employment, Mimeo.

Haveman, R. H. and Christiansen, G. B. 1978. 'Public employment and wage subsidies in western Europe and the US: What we're doing and what we know' in US National Commission on Manpower Policy, *European Manpower Policies*.

Marsden, D. 1980, *Study of changes in the wage structure of manual workers in industry in six community countries since 1966, and proposals for the development of future community surveys*, Brussels, Eurostat.

MSC 1981, *Manpower review 1981*, London, Manpower Services Commission.

Naschold, F. 1981, 'The future of the welfare state' in W. J. Mommsen (ed.), *The emergence of the welfare state in Britain and Germany*, London, Croom Helm, pp. 395–407.

OECD 1980a, *Youth unemployment*, Paris.

OECD 1980b, *OECD economic outlook 28 (December)*, Paris.

OECD 1980c, *Women and employment*, Paris.

OECD 1980d, *The tax/benefit position of selected income groups in OECD member countries, 1974–1979*, Paris.

OECD 1980e, *Netherlands*, OECD Economic Surveys, Paris.

OECD 1980f, *Denmark*, OECD Economic Surveys, Paris.

OECD 1981, *National accounts of OECD countries 1950–1979*, vol. II, Paris.

Saunders, C.T. 1980, 'Changes in relative pay in the 1970s' in F. T. Blackaby (ed.), *The Future of Pay Bargaining*, London, Heinemann.

Tuinier, G. 1979, 'The relationship between social security and taxation in The Netherlands' in *Social Security and Taxation*, Geneva, International Social Security Association, Studies and Research, 13, pp. 109–12.

UK 1980, *Social benefit tables for member states of the European Communities position at 1 January 1980*, London, DHSS.

Williams, S. 1981, 'The broader economic and social questions relating to youth employment', *Policy Studies*, vol. 1 no. 4, pp. 200–12.

Wyles, J. 1981, 'A brooding sense of missed opportunities' in *Financial Times Survey (The Netherlands)*.

3 France: Poverty and Work
*Antoine Lion**

Introduction

To understand fully the nature of poverty in France it is necessary to examine the relationship between poverty and work. Low income, poor housing and limited education are probably less important to the experience of poverty, and to our understanding of it, than the fact of being without paid employment. To be excluded from the labour market — for whatever reason — is to run the risk of poverty. Indeed, the single most important cause of poverty in France is exclusion from the labour market.

The term 'exclusion' has acquired at least two meanings in the French debate on poverty. (For a further discussion of social exclusion, see France 1979a.) The first is typically expounded by the movement *Aide à Toute Détresse — Quart Monde* (see Chapter 7) and states that certain groups were excluded from the labour market at an earlier stage in the economic development of society and have remained excluded by a process which is transmitted from one generation to the next. Such groups are excluded not only from the labour market but also from most other socially acceptable areas of modern life.

The second use of the term 'exclusion' relates to a new process by which previously secure groups are losing their place in the labour market or, because they are employed in what, in France, are called *les formes précaires du travail* (precarious work roles — see below) are in continual danger of doing so. Another aspect of the same process is that certain groups are finding it increasingly difficult to make an initial entry into the labour market.

Most of this chapter is devoted to a consideration of the second process of exclusion which raises new and disturbing policy issues. We shall first examine the growth of unemployment and the associated phenomena of *paupérisation* (impoverishment); then consider the extent to which this is alleviated, or indeed exacerbated, by the French insurance and assistance systems; and, finally, explore the solutions presented by job

*Adapted by Robert Walker from the original seminar paper given in May 1980.

creation. The last part of the chapter focuses on another aspect of the relationship between poverty and work: low pay. In particular, we shall examine the working of the French minimum wage (*Salaire Minimum Interprofessionnel de Croissance — SMIC*).

Unemployment and Pauperisation

The source of official statistics on unemployment is the *Agence Nationale Pour l'Emploi* (*ANPE*). The main function of ANPE is to find new employment for the unemployed and registration with ANPE is a necessary condition for the receipt of unemployment benefit. According to ANPE, unemployment at the end of April 1980 stood at 1 438 000 which equated to a little more than 6.5 per cent of the economically active population (*population active*). Table 3.1 shows that estimates of unemployment made by the OECD (using the slightly different ILO definition) have increased steadily throughout the 1970s.

Inevitably, the official estimates are incomplete. Most significantly, they relate only to registered job seekers and consequently exclude many persons who are '*pas même chômeurs*', that is who through social

Table 3.1   *Labour market changes in France 1973—7*

	1977 (000s)	Changes from previous year				
		1973	1974	1975	1976	1977
Resident labour force[1]	22 365	1.2	0.8	0.0	0.6	0.7
Registered unemployed	1 135	−3.2	6.7	44.6	11.4	14.3
Employed labour force[2]	21 230	1.1	0.4	−0.6	0.4	0.7
Wage earners in the market sector (not including agriculture)	13 785	2.7	−0.1	−0.5	2.0	0.2
Agricultural and food industries	511	0.8	−0.7	−0.8	−0.3	0.8
Energy	296	−2.3	−0.8	−0.3	−0.9	−1.4
Intermediate goods industry	1 615	3.1	0.5	−4.0	0.3	−2.7
Capital goods industry	1 905	0.3	−2.9	−4.6	−0.3	−2.3
Consumer goods industry	1 428	4.7	0.3	−2.0	1.6	−1.4
Industry	5 755	2.4	−0.6	−3.0	0.5	−1.8
Building and civil engineering	1 577	−	−3.1	−3.0	0.2	−2.0
Industries (including BCE)	7 332	1.8	−1.2	−3.0	0.4	−1.9
Tertiary market sector	6 453	3.9	1.4	2.7	3.8	2.6
Wage earners and salaried employees in agriculture, forestry, fishing	415	−5.3	−5.3	−5.0	−4.4	−4.2
Non-marketable services	3 761	2.2	1.2	1.2	0.7	0.3

1 Estimates.
2 In 1977 there were about 3.6 million non-wage earners (of whom 1.6 million were in agriculture).

Source: OECD 1977.

circumstances or physical or mental handicap are prevented from finding a job. A significant number are prevented from registration because they do not fulfil certain bureaucratic conditions. For example, at present the unemployed have to report to their local ANPE agency each fortnight and are struck off the unemployment register if they fail to do so on two consecutive occasions without presenting a medical note. This regulation is under review, but in the past it has excluded considerable numbers — frequently the poor and unfit — for long periods at a time. Finally, other people may not register because they perceive little benefit from doing so or because they are unaware of the necessity. The net result is that official figures understate the true number of unemployed to a considerable extent.

The consistent upward trend in unemployment has many causes. Economic growth since 1973 has been sluggish (averaging 3 per cent per annum; OECD 1979) reflecting a slow-down in foreign and domestic demand, while at the same time continuing inflation has caused the government to adopt a tight monetary policy. Significant structural changes have also been under way with falls in employment in building and industry — notably in consumer and intermediate goods and, to a lesser extent, in capital goods — which have been partially offset by rapid rises in employment in the tertiary market sector (see Table 3.1). Growth in industrial production has been concentrated in efficient sectors and firms and has been associated with large gains in productivity — and thereby disproportionately small increases in new employment — or with mergers that have resulted in a shedding of jobs. Throughout the period the government has largely refused to finance firms or industries that have encountered difficulties as a result of structural changes, arguing instead that the limited resources available should be concentrated on growth sectors, particularly high technology industry, which might in time produce the economic conditions necessary for the reabsorption of large numbers of unemployed. The net result has been a decline in total employment of 120 000 between 1973 and 1978 and a growing regional imbalance of unemployment.

While the demand for labour contracted in the 1970s, the supply increased by an average of over 100 000 per annum. The growth in supply was maintained despite a sevenfold decrease in arrivals of immigrant workers between 1973 and 1978 and a probable fall in the percentage of foreign workers in the labour market (OECD 1979). As elsewhere in Europe, the increase in labour supply was due primarily to two factors: first, to a rise in the number of school leavers reflecting the high birth rates which occurred in the late 1950s and early 1960s and secondly, to an increased propensity for married women to return to the labour market. The former trend has eased but will reassert itself in the mid-1980s; the latter is more uncertain. At present the economic activity rate of females in France is a little less than 50 per cent which is considerably lower than in the other countries covered in this volume. However, the strong traditional emphasis given to the family in France, the relatively generous level of family support and the continuing importance of rural communities may impose a ceiling on female activity rates that is lower than in other countries.

An additional factor has been the significant development of *les formes précaires de travail* in recent years. There are two principal forms of *travail précaire: le travail temporaire* (or *le travail intérimaire*) — essentially an extension of the traditional bargaining for employment conducted between employers and prospective employees — which has increased markedly since the law of 3 January 1972; and *le travail à durée déterminée* (i.e. fixed-term contracts). Both forms of *le travail précaire* are commonest among unskilled workers but men predominate in *le travail temporaire* and women in *le travail à durée déterminée*. Between 1976 and 1979 the proportion of job seekers whose unemployment arose from the loss of *travail précaire* increased from 30.8 to 43.5 per cent with *le travail à durée déterminée* contributing 35 per cent to the latter figure and *le travail temporaire* about 8 per cent (France 1981b).

The increase in unemployment has been accompanied by a disproportionately rapid growth in long-term unemployment (see Table 3.2). The group which has been most affected by this rise consists of persons aged over 45 who suffer some mental or physical disability. Although the

Table 3.2   *Persons available for work and seeking paid employment by length of search, France 1970—9.*

Have been seeking work for:	1970 (%)[1]	1974 (%)[1]	1977 (%)[1]	1979 (October) (%)[1]
Less than 1 month	16.7	15.7	8.5	13.1
1 month, but less than 3 months	25.2	23.0	17.8	19.4
3 months, but less than 6 months	15.0	17.7	18.5	16.1
6 months, but less than 1 year	14.9	17.0	24.4	15.9
1 year, but less than 2 years	9.9	11.1	16.3	17.4
2 years and over	10.3	8.2	9.5	13.4
Number	309 359	427 355	982 214	1 468 823

1 Column totals sum to less than 100 per cent on account of missing returns.

Source: Employment Surveys, INSEE, FRS 1980.

disability may frequently be so slight as to cause no problem in ordinary life, it nevertheless acts as a considerable hindrance when seeking work. Indeed, a study recently commissioned by ANPE has revealed that this group accounted for 35 per cent of persons who had been unemployed for more than 12 months (Merle 1979).

Women aged under 40 constituted the second largest group identified in the ANPE study and accounted for 30 per cent of the long-term unemployed. Since such women represent only 26 per cent of the workforce it is clear that they are disproportionately at risk of long-term unemployment. Two other smaller groups identified by ANPE were unqualified youths seeking their first employment and, at the other end of the age range, persons aged over 54 who while perfectly fit had little hope of further employment before retirement (when, in many cases, their pension entitlement would be very limited; see Chapter 10). In each case the problem of finding work was found to be exacerbated by an absence of educational qualifications.

Associated with the rise in long-term unemployment has been an emergence of a new social problem of considerable magnitude: the process of *paupérisation* (impoverishment). This problem has been recognised only recently. A report *'Paupérisation et Personnes Isolées'* prepared for the new quinquennial national plan showed that large numbers of people who had not previously claimed supplementary benefit or national assistance have been forced to enter the welfare system (France 1981a). This situation is very disturbing because there is considerable evidence that once such a state of dependency has been created, it proves very difficult to break (e.g. Pitrou 1978). The real danger, therefore, is that the process of *paupérisation* is creating new groups who will be excluded from the labour force and from society in perpetuity and who in future generations will suffer the same deprivations as those detailed by *Aide à Toute Détresse — Quart Monde*. Uncertainty of employment and of income associated with *les formes précaires de travail* may also contribute to transmitted *paupérisation*. Unable to plan and to put aside money for future expenses, families are forced to face the future on a day-by-day basis which may engender in them a deep and incapacitating fatalism (France 1981b).

Another facet of *paupérisation* is the prospect of greater cohesion among the groups affected. With large numbers of unemployed, often concentrated in relatively small regions of industrial decline, there must be a growing awareness that unemployment cannot be attributed to individual failure and that it is not just an individual accident or personal catastrophe but a collective social phenomenon with social and political causes. The political impact of this growing awareness remains slight at the national level but already the major unions have been able to mobilise the jobless and, more especially, those whose jobs are in jeopardy because of impending redundancy. However, one factor which militates against a growing cohesion is the possible development of tensions within the working class caused by unemployment itself. As the standard of living within a town or region declines, the interests of those remaining in work diverge from those who have already lost their jobs and therefore any vestige of solidarity dissolves in the competition for work. The effects of this process have already been recognised by Maclouf (1980).

While the causes of *paupérisation* lie deep in the workings of the economy and the main battle against it must be waged by means of employment policy, improvements in social security are more easily obtained in the shorter term. It is important therefore to examine the extent to which the existing system of social benefits protects individuals from *paupérisation* and to what extent it may exacerbate the problem.

The Reform of Unemployment Benefit

Two separate unemployment benefit schemes coexisted in France until 1979. One was an insurance-based benefit and the other was provided through social assistance (*l'aide publique*). The insurance scheme originated in a national agreement of 31 August 1958 following which 46 independent regional organisations, ASSEDICs (*Association pour l'Emploi dans l'Industrie et le Commerce*) were created to administer the scheme. The amount payable was generally fixed at 35 per cent of previous earnings but with a 15 per cent supplement during the first three months. In the case of redundancy benefits equivalent to 90 per cent of former earnings were payable for up to one year (*licenciements pour cause économique*). Eligibility was conditional upon 91 days' membership of the scheme or 520 hours' paid work during the 12-month period preceding unemployment. The scheme was jointly funded by employer and employee contributions of 1.76 and 0.44 per cent of wages respectively (EC 1978). Unemployment assistance was available in cases where insurance benefits were less than the social minimum (see Chapter 2). Assistance was funded by central government and payable through the local authority for employment (*Direction Départementale du Travail*).

The system was unduly complex and inconvenient for claimants. Not only were two benefits frequently payable simultaneously by different authorities but the claimant had first to register with ANPE prior to receipt of benefit and then to return fortnightly in order to register for work. There were other serious weaknesses. The conditions of entitlement excluded school leavers and persons, notably housewives, attempting to return to the labour market. The generous conditions for redundancy — which had been devised in order to facilitate industrial change at a time when redundancy was rare — proved increasingly expensive. Furthermore, the disparity between those who had been made redundant and those who had been dismissed and who were entitled to benefit equal to only 35 per cent of their former wages became ever more pernicious as economic difficulties made the distinction largely academic. High redundancy payments were also considered, in certain quarters at least, to have strong disincentive effects. (The government view was that this was only a marginal factor and probably limited to young single people. Although the average duration of unemployment for those made redundant exceeded that for other groups, redundancies were inevitably concentrated in sectors of the economy which were in decline and in which fewer vacancies occurred.) However, perhaps the most important factor precipitating reform was the increasing cost of the insurance — due in part to higher unemployment — which was borne largely by employers. (Although the state fully funded unemployment assistance, it made no contributions towards the insurance scheme.)

1979 saw the implementation of a restructured scheme which was proposed by the ASSEDICs through their national union, UNEDIC (*Union Nationale Interprofessionelle pour l'Emploi dans l'Industrie et le Commerce*). The UNEDIC which, like the ASSEDICs themselves, is composed of representatives from both sides of industry is largely instrumental in the development of French policy on unemployment benefits although its recommendations require government approval before implementation. The net outcome of the change was the replacement of exisiting schemes by five new ones, each tailored to meet different circumstances but all payable through the ASSEDICs and financed jointly by employers, employees and the government. Perhaps the most significant change was the abolition of unemployment assistance, and with it, the role of *départements* in providing the basic minimum subsistence level for the unemployed.

Present System of Unemployment Benefits

The new system of unemployment benefits is summarised in Table 3.3. Cover under the scheme is available to all employees except those in government and in certain parts of the public sector where full job security is normally assured. All benefits are paid monthly and are taxable. The basic benefit, payable (in May 1980) to a third of job seekers, is the *Allocation de Base* which is available to full-time workers who lose their jobs for reasons other than redundancy. The benefit consists of two elements: a flat-rate amount of 22 FFr per day (which,

Table 3.3   Unemployment benefits in France (end of May 1980)

Benefit	Amount of benefit	Period of entitlement	Number of claimants	% of all job seekers[1]
Allocation de Base (AB) (ordinary allowance)	23.50 FFr/day plus 42% of previous wages	365 days if aged under 50 yrs	445,812	33.3
Allocation Spéciale (ASP) (redundant workers' allowance)	23.50 FFr/day plus 65%, 60%, 55% or 50%	365 days	122,711	9.2
Allocation Forfaitaire (AF) (flat-rate allowance)	46 FFr/day, 34.50 FFr/day or 23.50 FFr/day dependent on category[2]	365 days	79,517	5.9
Allocation de Fin de Droits (FD) (end of entitlement allowance)	23.5 FFr/day	274 days if aged under 50 yrs; 365 days if aged 50–5 yrs; 456 days if aged over 55 yrs	84,834	6.3
Total (AB + ASP + AF + FD)			732,514	54.8
Garantie de Ressources (GR) (resources guarantee reports)	70% of previous earnings	Until aged 65 yrs 3 months or receives retirement pension	175,010	13.1
Fonds National de l'Emploi (FNE) (national employment fund)	Dependent on circumstance		1,804	0.1
Idemnités de Formation (IF) (retraining funds)	100% of previous earnings	1 year	15,716	1.2
Total claimants			925,044	69.2
Job seekers not receiving benefit			412,307	30.8

1 Although recipients of GR, FNE and IF are not usually considered to be seeking work they are included.
2 See text.
Source: Liaisons sociales.

incidentally, is considered to be too small to have a significant redistributive effect) and an additional payment equivalent to 42 per cent of the recipient's insurable earnings averaged over the last three months of employment. The resultant benefit has upper and lower limits equivalent to 90 per cent of previous earnings and 57 FFr per day respectively (January 1980) with most claimants receiving in the order of 60 per cent of previous earnings (CSC 1980). In order to qualify for benefit, persons must be aged under 65, be registered for work and must also have worked for at least 91 days in the 12 months preceding application. Benefit is normally paid for a maximum of 12 months but this limit is increased to about 26 months for persons aged between 50 and 55 and to around 2½ years for older claimants.

Benefits payable under the *Allocation Spéciale*, the redundant workers' allowance, are much less generous than under the previous system. Instead of receiving 90 per cent of previous insured earnings for up to 12 months, the recipient is guaranteed 75, 70, 65 and 60 per cent respectively for the first four quarters of unemployment. Generally the benefit consists of the same flat-rate elements as for *Allocation de Base* with an additional amount equivalent to 65 per cent of previous insured earnings for the first three months, declining by 5 per cent quarterly to 50 per cent in the fourth quarter. If this compilation does not sum to the guaranteed amount a supplement is payable.

The conditions for payment of *Allocation Spéciale* are stringent. The applicant must have worked for at least 6 of the 12 months preceding redundancy and the redundancy must be proven. The latter condition entails a negotiated agreement between employer and trade union which is confirmed by an inspector from the *Direction Départementale du Travail*.

Allocation Spéciale is payable for 12 months in the same way as *Allocation de Base*. Thereafter an end of entitlement allowance (*Allocation de Fin de Droits*) is available at the very low rate of 22 FFr per day — an amount equivalent to only a fifth of the minimum wage (SMIC). The length of time for which *Allocation de Fin de Droits* is payable varies according to age and ranges from 9 months for people under 50 years, to 15 months for those aged between 55 and 64.

The two other schemes, *Allocation Forfaitaire* and *Garantie de Ressources*, are tailored to the needs of discrete groups. The former goes some way towards alleviating the problems of the young unemployed, who were excluded from benefit under the previous scheme, by providing 12 months' flat-rate benefit irrespective of contribution record. The precise rate of benefit is determined by the category of claimant. The highest benefit (43 FFr per day, January 1980) is payable to young job-seekers who have undertaken technical training or who have completed an apprenticeship, to lone women with dependants and to other women who have completed an approved training course of at least 500 hours. An intermediate rate (32 FFr) is payable to young men within the year following completion of national service and a limited benefit of 22 FFr is available to academically well-qualified young people, to family bread-winners who are aged between 16 and 25, regardless of qualification, and to certain categories of discharged prisoner. As is evident from the preceding categories of claimant, entitlement is usually dependent upon the completion of some form of vocational training. So, for example, in order for a lone woman to receive *Allocation Forfaitaire* she would need to hold a technical diploma, or to have completed an approved training scheme or a four-month period of on-the-job training (*Stage Pratique*).

Garantie de Ressources is a retirement wage available to certain workers who lose their jobs after their 60th or, occasionally, their 55th birthday. It provides for benefits equivalent to 70 per cent of previous pay and lasts until the recipient reaches the age of 65 years 3 months or until he or she claims his or her retirement pension. However, the *Garantie de Ressources* is not universally available but is restricted to employees in declining industries. One consequence of this policy is that few, if any, jobs are released for the benefit of younger job-seekers.

The 1979 reforms have lessened some of the deficiencies of the previous system but have done little to slow the destructive process of *paupérisation*. With all benefits paid through the ASSEDICs the system is administratively much simpler and the financial management of the government means that the scheme is more secure. (In 1979 out of a total expenditure of 90 000 million FFr, the government contributed 7000 million FFr and has promised to meet a third of all incremental costs.) Furthermore, by bringing a number of 'at-risk' groups, especially the young and certain categories of women, within the scope of the scheme and by raising the general level of benefit the reforms have succeeded in raising the relative living standards of some of the poorest people in France.

However, certain groups remain disadvantaged. Access to *Allocation Forfaitaire* remains quite restricted for single women and for the badly educated or handicapped. Workers in temporary employment (*le travail intérimaire*) are required to have done 1000 hours' work in the preceding year, compared with 520 hours for full-time workers, and consequently find it harder to qualify for benefit. Self-employed persons are also excluded from the scheme. Indeed, in May 1980 almost a third of job-seekers were not receiving benefit (Table 3.3).

While the reforms did increase levels of benefit, in common with

French policy generally they did not create a social minimum. Instead, workers previously employed in low-wage industries, particularly in agriculture and the tertiary sector, still stand to receive very low levels of benefit. A person previously earning the minimum wage (SMIC) might typically receive 1459 FFr per month in *Allocation de Base* which is equivalent to 31 per cent of the national average wage (July 1980). Such a person might well be entitled to *Aide Sociale* in addition to *Allocation de Base*. However, since the low-paid are typically female (see below) they might find themselves excluded from assistance on account of their husband's earnings with the result that the household suffers a significant drop in income.

Most significant of all, the 1979 reforms gave nothing to the long-term unemployed whose situation was actually exacerbated by the abolition of unemployment assistance which had previously been payable indefinitely. Under the present system, once a person has exhausted entitlement to *Allocation de Fin de Droits* — after a maximum of 21 months' unemployment — only means-tested *Aide Sociale* is available subject, in theory at least, to imposition of the *obligation alimentaire* which places an obligation on members of the extended family to support the claimant financially.

The deprivations suffered by the long-term unemployed are considerable. They inevitably experience a very marked drop in income such that they are totally unable to retain their previous standard of living. At the same time many will find it impossible to cancel outstanding mortgage and hire-purchase commitments and will thereby face legal sanctions that place them in an impossible position. Again, once the unemployed are forced to rely on the *Bureau d'Aide Sociale* they fall outside the established system of social security. Entitlement to benefit is no longer a question of right but is dependent upon an assessment made by social workers against which there is no formal system of appeal. Frequently, too, the social services are unable to cope with the demands placed upon them especially as more and more persons are forced to turn to *Aide Sociale* for financial help. Another problem faced by the unemployed is the frequent lack of congruence between the principle of entitlement, which governs the operation of the bureaucracies that provide benefits, and the principle of need, which determines the behaviour of claimants (Outin 1979). The difficult position of the long-term unemployed is now officially recognised. As has been mentioned already, the problem of *paupérisation* is addressed in the Eighth Economic Plan. Also, in February 1981 a report of an interdepartmental working party suggested a number of reforms to assist the long-term unemployed. (France 1981b). These included an extension of the period of entitlement to benefit on a means-tested basis — either by amending the *Allocation de Fin de Droits* or by introducing a specific benefit — and a relaxation in the conditions of entitlement for certain groups, notably unsupported mothers and disabled. The report also stressed the need for bodies paying out benefits to regularise as much as possible the flow of resources of those with uncertain incomes. Delays in benefit payment may have severe consequences for those with limited resources. Moreover, benefit systems have in the past been designed to meet the circumstances of those whose income has arisen from regular, full-time employment.

Measures to improve job placement

In response to the problems of unemployment and *'travail précaire'* the interdepartmental working party, cited above, argued for co-ordinated action on three levels. In addition to income substitution (see above) it proposed a series of measures to improve job placement and job adaptation. Its recommendations with respect to the latter two objectives were based on two propositions (France 1981b; pp. 68—9):

> — To secure, in the job-placement service, more active and individualised assistance to job seekers who are likely to suffer from long periods of unemployment or repeated unemployment;
> — To favour a policy which fits workers into new jobs, rather than one which simply pays out assistance, by making young people and women without insurance cover and the long-term unemployed priorities in employment policy.

The committee proposed that ANPE be mobilised on behalf of the long-term unemployed by instigating better monitoring and by appointing, in certain areas, specialised job counsellors to identify those in greatest danger of long-term unemployment and to provide individual assessments of their employment and training needs.

The committee also urged a switch in job-placement priorities away from young people in favour of the long-term unemployed and indicated means of adjusting ANPE initiatives to meet their specific needs. Moreover, it also recommended replacement of the current system of subsidies to firms to encourage them to employ or train additional staff by one based on aid tied to the needs of the individual. Specifically, this would mean that the subsidy given to a firm to employ a particular individual would be related to the difficulty of finding that person another job. (This would also mean that the level of subsidy would be determined by the local employment service office and reflect local conditions.)

Finally, the committee stressed the need for greater co-ordination between the institutions involved, suggesting, among other things, that the ASSEDICs should warn the ALE (*Agence Locale pour l'Emploi*) when recipients come to the end of their benefit.

Policies to stimulate employment

Given that unemployment is the main cause of *paupérisation*, the best way to combat this form of poverty is to create new employment. However, it should be made clear that French policy in this regard has traditionally emphasised economic considerations rather than social ones. This is most evident in the three National Employment Pacts of 1977, 1978 and 1979. The First Employment Pact consisted essentially of the State taking over, for one year and on certain conditions, employers' contributions for new employees under 25 years of age. In addition, it extended to certain restricted categories of women the existing scheme under which the State can fund the cost of staff training and meet, in part, the wage costs of trainees (see OECD 1977 for details).

These measures were largely renewed in the Second Pact in 1978 and supplemented with a range of measures designed to stimulate female employment. The latter exempted employers from 50 per cent of the first year's social security contributions for each woman recruited who had at least one dependent child and who was also unmarried or had been widowed or divorced in the preceding two years. The measures also opened, to the same categories of women, training schemes which had previously been reserved for young persons.

The Third National Employment Pact, instigated in July 1979 and due to expire in December 1981, has three major components. The first is virtually identical to the provision for exempting employers from social security contributions included in the Second Pact. Again provisions are made for certain categories of women although in practice they have not been widely implemented. The second component is a temporary work experience scheme for young persons under which a large part of the wage costs is met by the State. This in turn includes provision for the on-the-job training with a guarantee of employment from the employer. The third component also involves training but in this case the young person is not actually employed by the firm which provides training and there is no formal guarantee of employment.

3.5 billion FFr (30 June 1980) were allocated to be spent by the government during the two-and-a-half years currency of the Pact and it is anticipated that 250 000 new jobs will result each year as a consequence of the employers' exemption from social security contributions, and 150 000 from the work experience and training schemes.

Early assessment of the Third Employment Pact has indicated that the main beneficiaries of the training and work experience schemes have been relatively well-qualified young people and that the proportion of less qualified candidates has actually declined. As a consequence, therefore, it may be that the latest Pact is simply creating a new elite at the expense of the most needy.

The first two Pacts have been more comprehensively evaluated. The OECD concluded that the Pacts had served to curb the trend towards high unemployment among the under-25s — reducing the proportion of job applicants in this age group from 44.5 to 42.5 per cent between 1976 and 1978. However, the OECD found that the impact of the Second Pact was noticeably less than the First and that the main contribution of both was to reduce the traditional end of summer unemployment peak rather than the total number of jobless (OECD 1979).

A strategy for redistributing existing employment which has at various times attracted the attention of trade unions, employers and government is a reduction of the working week. Table 3.4 shows that the length of the working week is already declining steadily in France and that the trend has been particularly strong in sectors which have faced the severest economic difficulties.

Table 3.4   Length of working week for all persons in dependent employment in France 1973—8 (hours)

	1973	1975	1977	October 1978
Industry	43.2	41.6	41.2	41.1
Energy	40.4	39.8	39.8	39.8
Building and civil engineering	47.1	45.3	43.1	42.4
Transport	43.4	42.0	41.8	41.4
Market services	42.4	41.7	41.2	40.9
Insurance	40.0	39.9	39.9	40.0
Commerce	42.7	42.0	41.4	41.5
Total	43.3	42.0	41.4	41.0

Source: OECD 1979.

In 1979 researchers at INSEE examined the consequences of a one-hour (25 per cent) reduction in the working week under four different sets of assumptions (Oudiz *et al.* 1979). One model assumed that working hours were reduced without lower output or wage compensation; a second that the introduction of reduced working hours was accompanied by wage compensation but no loss of production capacity. The first model predicted considerable job creation leading to a fall in unemployment of 62 000 in the first year and 108 000 by the third, although the cost was borne predominantly by wage earners working longer hours at low wages. The second model offered less hope of new employment, an adverse balance of trade, a 0.8 per cent drop in GNP and a 0.4 per cent increase in consumer prices.

The two other variants allowed for no loss of production and a 72 per cent compensation for lost wages but differed according to whether enterprises increased or reduced investment. In each case the degree of wage compensation was postulated to vary with income, ranging from 100 per cent at one-and-a-half times SMIC and below, through 50 per cent at wage levels up to three times SMIC, to zero compensation at higher levels. Under the assumption that firms did not reduce investment, business activity and employment increased at the end of the first year and unemployment was reduced by 35 000 compared with the first model variant. However, wages were predicted to rise faster than prices and more than offset the loss in monthly wages resulting from shorter working hours. The consequence was soaring inflation and a large trade deficit. The beneficial effects of shorter working hours on unemployment were much less evident under the assumption that firms did cut investment. The effects of the upswing due to increased wages were slight and short-lived and by the third year production was predicted to be lower than in the first variant. Inflation was accelerating as firms attempted to recoup profits and the balance of payments, which had deteriorated during the second year, was improving only because of a tightening of the economy brought about by inflation.

The main conclusion reached by the INSEE study was that the cost of reducing working hours could not be borne solely by management or labour but required a supporting policy which was linked to the jobs actually created. One example proposed was that social security costs might be reduced in those sectors where wages were low or working hours long.

The interdepartmental working party mentioned above (France 1981b) has also recommended that the promotion of employment through public works be extended (*Programme d'Emplois d'Utilité Collective*). The employment thus generated was viewed as a means of social reintegration, particularly for those who have exhausted their entitlement to benefit or who receive minimum assistance. Especially in the case of young people, training might be linked to the employment created so as to establish a gradual transition from total and prolonged inactivity to employment in a normal productive situation.

In 1979, an experimental programme was launched by the government in an effort to create 5000 jobs in community-related activities. The programme provides, under Decree Number 79–168 of 2 March 1979, for government grants to be made to community-based, non-commercial organisations for the purpose of creating new employment. A budget of 120 million FFr has been allocated to the programme which is partially financed, in the case of jobs created for persons under

26 years of age, by the European Social Fund. The projects will be supported by the State in decreasing proportion for up to two years after which the projects have to be self-financing.

Although it is hoped that the community-based job-creation projects will eventually become self-financing, they nevertheless represent a departure from the traditional emphasis of French employment policy on economic considerations. The experiment is at present on a very small scale and has been developed for the benefit of very marginal social groups including drop-outs, drug-addicts and prostitutes. It remains to be seen whether the experiment will be extended to assist those sections of the unemployed who are closer to the mainstream of French society. If it is extended in this way a concern for social profit will have triumphed over the longstanding concern for economic gain.

Poverty within the Labour Market

Unfortunately, the mere fact of employment does not always ensure that a person can avoid financial hardship and poverty. Wages in the declining industries and also in agriculture are often very low and the associated regional variations in income are substantial. In 1978, the index of average wages ranged from 139 FFr (national average = 100) for the Ile de France to 90 FFr for Limousin in the rural west, while the index in certain rural communes was as low as 74 (ILO 1980). Similarly, while circumstances of the self-employed — who, in France, constitute 17.6 per cent of the labour market (1980, ILO definition) — vary considerably, thousands of self-employed shopkeepers, craftsmen and farmers are thought to earn very little (Sinfield 1980). Many foreign workers, substantial numbers of whom entered France illegally, are also known to receive very low wages although no information is available on the actual extent of poverty among these groups or the variation within them (Sinfield 1980).

An examination of the occurrence of poverty in employment need not be limited to the consideration of income poverty. For example, occupations differ greatly in working conditions and in their safety record. Moreover, while the total number of work accidents and fatalities is falling, the severity of accidents is generally increasing. People who experience a serious industrial accident face a very significant risk of income poverty and very few are likely to avoid a considerable and prolonged drop in living standards. (Under *Assurance Obligatoire*, the main industrial injury scheme, the benefit payable is normally the product of reckonable earnings and the degree of incapacity. See UK (1980) for details of reckonable income.) Furthermore, as we have already seen, those who suffer lasting handicap also face a significant risk of long-term unemployment. It is impossible in the space available to consider French policy towards all types of poverty occurring within the labour market. Instead this section concentrates on income poverty and, in particular, on the performance of the national minimum wage.

The early introduction of a minimum wage in 1952 is at first sight surprising since French policy has not, until very recently, been much concerned with social minima (see Chapters 7 and 10). The *Salaire Minimum Interprofessionel Garanti (SMIG)* was initially set according to an estimate of typical monthly expenditure based on the minimum needs of a single worker. In effect it established an absolute poverty line — albeit a little above that established by Rowntree in his 1951 survey of York (Rowntree and Lavers 1951) — which, by an act of 1952, was to be protected against inflation. However, the introduction of SMIG must be understood in the context of a post-war economy under which all wage rates were determined by government legislation. SMIG was introduced in the Act of 11 February 1950 which also re-stored free wage negotiations and represented a residual control which was retained over minimum wage levels.

The interpretation of the minimum wage as a social minimum was finally dispelled when SMIG was replaced in 1970 by the *Salaire Minimum Interprofessionnel de Croissance (SMIC)*. In the years up to 1968, the purchasing power of SMIG was maintained as required by law but its value in relation to other wages fell considerably as workers benefited from the then buoyant French economy (see Figure 3.1). As a consequence of the industrial and political upheavals of 1968, the Confederation of Employers (*Conféderation Nationale du Patronat Français, CNPF*) and the main trade unions agreed to increase the real value of SMIG by 38 per cent, which more than offset the differentials that had emerged and was viewed as a deliberate attempt to reduce inequalities. In addition, the government undertook to modify the arrangements for uprating the minimum wage in order to keep pace with average wages and this led to the introduction of SMIC in 1970. Each year SMIC is uprated by the government on the basis of recommendations received from the *Conseil Supérieur des Conventions Collectives (CSCC)* which undertakes a review of the country's economic situation and performance. The membership of CSCC consists of the government ministers concerned, representatives of the employers' confederation and the main trade unions — in equal number — the Chairman of the social section of *Conseil d'Etat* and rep-resentatives of family organisations. SMIC has also to be uprated during the month following each increase of 2 per cent in the official retail price index, and the government may, at any time, raise the value of SMIC above the price index in order, for example, to keep it in line with a rapid rise in other wages.

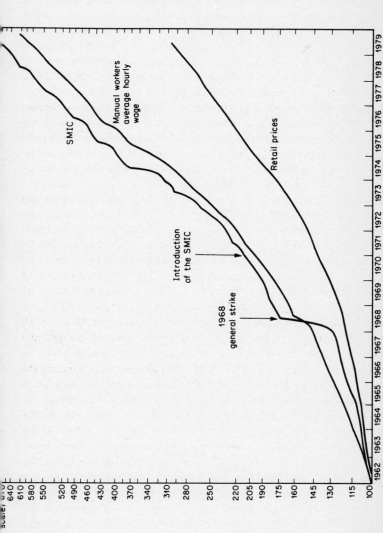

Figure 3.1 Comparative trends of SMIC, average manual wages and retail prices, France 1962–79

Notes: Index: January 1962=100. Before 1970, SMIC=SMIG

Source: France 1980

How successful has SMIC been in raising the income of low paid workers and in reducing social inequality? Figure 3.1 shows that since its introduction, SMIC has kept well ahead of prices and has also risen faster than average real wages. Between 1970 and 1979, the real value of SMIC increased by 64 per cent compared with a 49.5 per cent increase in average wages. By October 1979, the earnings of a full-time worker receiving SMIC (assuming 174 hours worked per month) were equivalent to 63.7 per cent of the average earnings of manual workers and 52 per cent of the average for all wage-earners. However, the relative increase in the level of the minimum wage has been uneven and most of the improvement was achieved before the slow-down in economic growth which has occurred since 1974 (OECD 1979). There is also an important distinction between net and gross SMIC, which is frequently overlooked. During 1979, rises in the contributions for old-age insurance, unemployment assurance and health cover were such as to increase the discrepancy between the net and gross figure from 10.3 to 12.8 per cent, thereby reducing the real net purchasing power of SMIC by 2.5 per cent.

It is impossible to establish the precise number of workers who earn SMIC because information on wage levels is not collected from firms with less than 10 employees. The omission of small firms is serious since they are less unionised and tend to pay lower wages. However, Table 3.5

Table 3.5   Workers receiving SMIC, 1979

		% receiving SMIC	
	Male	*Female*	*All*
Manual workers	4.2	11.5	5.9
Non-manual workers	1.0	2.7	1.7
All workers	3.0	6.2	4.0

Source: France 1980.

shows that, for firms employing at least 10 persons (excluding those in agriculture), around 4 per cent of workers receive the minimum wage. It also reveals that the proportion of workers earning SMIC varies greatly according to the worker's sex and type of work, with women being twice as likely to be paid at SMIC levels. Partly reflecting differences in the composition of the workforce and in the numbers of female workers, the incidence of minimum wage rates differs markedly between industries (see Table 3.6). Therefore, while minimum wage rates are received by 38.6, 12 and 10 per cent of the labour force in the cleaning, hotel and catering, and clothing industries respectively, the proportion is much lower in the construction industry (6.4 per cent) and the retail trade

*Table 3.6   Proportion of the workforce in selected industries
receiving SMIC, 1974—9*

	% of workforce receiving SMIC		
	July 1974	July 1978	July 1979
Sanitation (*Hygiène: nettoyage de locaux, blanchisserie*)	46.9	33.5	38.6
Catering and hotels (*Restauration et hébergement: salariés au pourboire*)	13.6	10.6	12.0
Clothing	20.2	9.7	10.0
Other manufacturing (*Autres industries manufacturières: articles de Paris*)	9.9	7.4	9.4
Leather	17.9	8.6	8.5
Footwear	14.8	8.3	7.8
Food wholesaling	10.7	6.8	7.7
Timber and furniture	12.1	7.3	7.0
Non-food retailing	8.6	4.3	6.1
Building and civil engineering	7.7	5.5	5.4
Plastics	9.3	4.9	5.3
Car repairs and sales	8.1	4.9	5.2
Food industry	9.2	4.9	5.2
All industries	5.8	5.5	4.0

Source: France 1979c.

(5.6 per cent) and lower still in the large-scale, heavily unionised car and steel making industries (0.3 and 0.2 per cent respectively). Table 3.6 shows that the proportion of workers receiving SMIC decreased significantly between 1974 and 1978 but rose again slightly in 1979.

It is more difficult to estimate the number earning less than SMIC but it is thought to exceed the number protected directly by SMIC and to comprise between 6 and 8 per cent of wage-earners. Certain groups — such as apprentices — are excluded by legislation from the SMIC provisions but in other cases, particularly in the construction and commerce sectors, employers are known to pay less than the stipulated rate. Employers who contravene the legislation and who are caught by the Ministry of Labour's Inspectorate (*Inspecteurs du Travail*) are liable to fines ranging from 600 FFr to 2000 FFr for each employee paid less than SMIC. Finally, the self-employed are necessarily excluded from minimum wage legislation. All in all, therefore, SMIC provides only a very partial 'safety net' even for those in work.

A number of more theoretical problems are inherent in a minimum wage although in practice they may be readily overcome. Linking SMIC to the index of prices runs the risk of accelerating general wage inflation through its impact on low wage rates. In an attempt to prevent this the

1970 legislation expressly forbade the linking of wage rates to SMIC in collective agreements. In practice, the level of SMIC has been implicated in wage inflation but only to a very limited extent. For example, a study by INSEE in 1978 estimated that a 2 per cent increase in SMIC raises total wages by 0.1 to 0.3 per cent (France 1978).

A second consideration is that minimum wage legislation may restrict the employment opportunities of marginal groups. The official French view is that this fear is without foundation although certain steps have been taken which serve to minimise the potential discriminatory effect of SMIC. Thus, the rate of SMIC is reduced in the case of young workers who are aged under 18 and have less than six months' relevant experience. (The reduction is 10 per cent for persons aged between 17 and 18 and 20 per cent for those under 17.) Also, while adult disabled workers are entitled to receive the full rate of SMIC, their employers can recover part of the expense from the State to the extent of 10 per cent of wages paid to workers suffering from a substantial disability and up to 20 per cent in more severe cases. The fact that reimbursements are not available for slightly disabled persons may help partially to explain the over-representation of this group among the long-term unemployed (see above).

Traditionally, SMIC has received support from both sides of industry for it is seen as a means of combating low pay while at the same time encouraging firms to improve their productivity. A possibility, if economic conditions do not rapidly improve, is that the minimum wage will come to be criticised as a factor in high wage costs which themselves shift the balance away from labour towards capital-intensive modes of production and at the same time limit the profitability necessary for investment to create new employment. For the moment, however, minimum wage policy continues to be viewed in most quarters as a success.

Perhaps the most important deficiency of a minimum wage in the fight against poverty is that it can be effective only against monetary poverty and, even in this respect, its benefit is personal and in no way influences the more significant socio-economic precursors of poverty. Furthermore, SMIC does not necessarily guarantee even an adequate income since it takes no account of wage earners' family commitments, which, in the case of children, are met with varying degrees of generosity through the family benefits system (see Chapter 7) but which are generally more limited for other categories of dependants. Likewise, because for certain groups the tax threshold is set below SMIC, the minimum wage may be eroded by taxation. (Single persons would generally be affected in this way and so might lone parents with a single child.) Similarly, a person earning the equivalent of SMIC is liable to national insurance contributions which, as in 1979, may be increased so as to reduce the net value of SMIC. Finally, because SMIC is a guaranteed *hourly* wage, it offers no protection against the effects of short-time working which in times of adverse economic conditions, such as the present, may dramatically reduce take-home pay. Nor does it do much to alleviate the financial uncertainty of those employed in *travail précaire*.

This is not to say that SMIC has proved ineffective in the fight against poverty at work. It has significantly improved the living standards of many low wage earners and will continue to play an important part in French policy, but while the minimum wage is a necessary element in attempts to reduce poverty within the labour market, it remains just one of many.

References

CSC 1980, *Unemployment in France*, London, Civil Service College, Mimeo.

EC 1978, *Comparative tables of the social security systems in the member states of the European Communities*, 10th edn, Brussels, Commission of the European Communities.

France 1978, *Economie et statistiques*, 100, May.

France 1979a, 'France: Avis et rapports du Conseil Economique et Social, La lutte contre la pauvreté', *Journal Officiel*, 9, 6 March, pp. 365–443.

France 1979b, *Unemployment benefits in France*, London, Le Conseiller pour les Affaires Sociales, Ambassade de France en Grande-Bretagne, Mimeo.

France 1979c, *Bulletin mensuel des statistiques du travail 65*, Paris, Ministère du Travail et de la Participation. (Also earlier volumes.)

France 1980, *The national minimum wage in France*, London, Le Conseiller pour les Affaires Sociales, Ambassade de France en Grande-Bretagne, Mimeo.

France 1981a, *Préparation du huitième plan*, Rapport de la Commission *Protection Sociale et Famille du VIII-eme Plan: annexes*, Paris, la Documentation Francaise.

France 1981b, *Contre la précarité et la pauvreté: 60 propositions*, Paris.

FRS 1980, *La pauvreté et la lutte contre la pauvreté*, Paris, Fondation pour la Recherche Sociale.

ILO 1980, 'Income distribution: France', *Social and Labour Bulletin*, January.

Maclouf, P. (Study Director) 1980, *La crise dans Saint Quentin*. Etude pour le Commissariat Général du Plan, Paris, Institut d'Etudes Politiques de Paris.

Merle, V. 1979, *Premiers résultats de l'enquête auprès des demandeurs d'emploi inscrits depuis plus de 12 mois à l'ANPE*, Paris, Agence Nationale pour l'emploi, Mimeo.

OECD 1977, *France*, OECD Economic Surveys, Paris.

OECD 1979, *France*, OECD Economic Surveys, Paris.

Oudiz, G., Raoul, H. and Sterdyniak, H. 1979, 'Réduire la durée du travail, quelles conséquences?, *Economie et Statistique*, 111, pp. 3–18.

Outin, J. L. 1979, *Familles et droits sociaux. Les modalités d'accès aux prestations familiales*, Etudes CAF, Paris.

Pitrou, A. 1978, *La vie précaire*, Paris, CNAF.

Rowntreee, B. S. and Lavers, G. R. 1951, *Poverty and the welfare state: a third social survey of York dealing only with Economic Questions*, London, Longmans.

Sinfield, A. 1980, 'Poverty and inequality in France' in V. George and R. Lawson (eds), *Poverty and Inequality in Common Market Countries*, London, Routledge and Kegan Paul.

UK 1980, *Social benefit tables for member states of the European Communities*, Position at 1 January 1980, International Relations Division, Department of Health and Social Security. Mimeo, London.

4 The Netherlands: Minimum Wage and Unemployment Policies

*A. A. M. van Amelsvoort** *

Introduction

Poverty is seldom referred to either in Dutch social security legislation or in accompanying official government statements. Nevertheless, major advances in the welfare state since the Second World War have done much to eradicate the poverty that was common during the inter-war years. Moreover, they have been accompanied by a distinct change in the conception of poverty (see Nauta 1980).

The factors generating post-war improvements in social security have been multifarious. First, there was, after the Second World War, an atmosphere of great mutual solidarity — a corporate feeling of responsibility for the society — and a significant degree of agreement between employers and workers as to the main social problems and the appropriate solutions. The latter factor was particularly important since employers and workers played key roles in the evolution, implementation and financing of social security. Secondly, the idea grew to be accepted that a worker should be guaranteed a sufficient income to support himself when sick, disabled or unemployed, and that this could best be achieved through provision of a minimum level of subsistence. Thirdly, benefit levels in The Netherlands have traditionally been related directly to wages — *Equivalentieveginsel* (the equivalence principle) — and the coincidence of reforms with a period of exceptional economic growth facilitated the establishment of high income replacement ratios. Fourthly, given the long-standing involvement of employers and labour in social security provision and the linking of benefit levels to wages, it was inevitable that social security would become an element in wages policy and wage negotiations. Uniquely, this has led to a coupling of social security benefits with the minimum wage, and a linking of both to movements in the wage index. Finally, a fundamental objective of the Dutch welfare state has been the reduction of inequality, the results of which are seen in, for example, the guaranteed minimum level of subsistence and the levelling effects of income policy.

Coincident with the improvements in social security — and linked symbiotically with the goal of reduced inequality — has been a shift in

*Adapted by Robert Walker from the original seminar paper.

the social meaning of poverty (Nauta 1980). Immediately after the Second World War, poverty was viewed more as a problem of deviance than of deprivation with the solution to be found in the improvement of individual behaviour. By the mid-1960s, however, an appreciation of the social context of poverty had become evident and the view that social structures could cause both poverty and deviance had attained ascendancy. The widespread acceptance of this view was itself instrumental in legitimising the high levels of benefit paid to social security claimants.

During the 1970s the levels of benefit continued to rise much faster than wages (see Table 4.1) while the number of recipients, particularly the disabled and unemployed, increased substantially (Table 4.2). As a result, expenditure on welfare benefits increased from 14 per cent of National Income in 1967 to 23 per cent in 1979. Moreover, increased welfare expenditure in the latter half of the decade coincided with a deteriorating economic situation and was accompanied by an increased debate as to the legitimate cost of welfare and the legitimate frontiers to solidarity.

Table 4.1   Differential increases in the value of the minimum wage and selected social security payments, The Netherlands, 1968--78

	Rise in real income[1] 1968—78 (%)
Minimum wage	40
General old age pension (AOW)	70
Modal wage[2]	25
Disability benefit (WAO) for a model employee	29

1 For a married man without children.
2 The modal wage is that earned by an employee with two children aged under 16. It is marginally below the level at which compulsory health insurance premium is payable.

This chapter is divided into two. The first explains the origin and workings of the minimum wage; the second details measures to alleviate the worst effects of unemployment. In both cases it will be noted that legislation tends to lag behind economic and social changes that may in themselves be the partial product of earlier legislation.

The Minimum Wage
The minimum wage has come to occupy a key position in the Dutch Welfare State, guaranteeing a minimum income for those in work and, through a mechanism known as 'coupling', providing a base level for social security benefits.

Table 4.2   Social security benefits, The Netherlands, 1969—77

Scheme	Benefits payable as at 31 December	
	1969 (000s)	1977 (000s)
General Old Age Pensions Act (AOW)	1035	1252
General Widows and Orphans Benefits Act (AWW)	154	172
General Disablement Insurance Act (WAO)	194	405
General Disablement Benefits Act (AAW)	–	114
Sickness Benefits Act (ZW)[1]	179	254
Unemployment Insurance Act (WW)[1]	26	52
Unemployment Benefits Act (WWV)[2]	26	88
Government Unemployment Assistance Scheme (RWW)	8	71
National Assistance Act (ABW)	183	168

1 Average per working day.
2 Average per year.

Source: Nauta 1980.

The origins of the minimum wage date back to 1946 and must be understood in the context of the long-established system of centralised wage negotiations. 'Coupling', however, was only introduced in the early 1970s and it was not until 1978, under the government headed by Den Uyl, that social assistance rates for a couple were equated with the minimum wage.

Wage bargaining and the minimum wage

From immediately after the war until 1959 wages in The Netherlands were fixed centrally in relation to changes in price levels and productivity. This process was facilitated by the presence of government influence throughout all stages of the wage determination process (OECD 1966). Underpinning the system was a minimum budget drawn up for unskilled workers, which included expenses for food, rent, gas, electricity, insurance contributions, etc. This budget was accepted as a basis for fixing minimum hourly wage rates throughout the economy although with slight variations between industrial sectors.

Tight labour market conditions during the late 1950s eventually led increasing numbers of employers to exceed legal maximum wage rates. Consequently, in 1959 a differential policy was introduced whereby wages in each industry could depart from nationally proposed guidelines in accordance with variations in productivity. The new system created the possibility that minimum wage rates in different industries might diverge and, to prevent this, a general minimum wage was introduced in

1966 and fixed at 120 guilders per week. However, unlike previous minima, the level of the new minimum wage was unrelated to any notion of need, but reflected instead the balance of power in negotiations between employers and trade unions (Fase 1980).

A wage explosion in 1963, followed by a wage pause in 1966, precipitated an end to the guided wage policy in 1968. Since then the determination of wages has, in principle, been in the hands of the two sides of industry, although in practice, government intervention has been frequent. Coinciding with the 1968 change, a statutory minimum wage scheme was introduced which included provisions for indexation (the same Act gave employees entitlement to a minimum holiday allowance). Initially, the minimum wage was indexed to price increases — the mechanism appropriate when a minimum is based on need — but from 1962 the minimum wage was linked to wages. It is increased twice each year in January and July in line with changes in the official index of negotiated basic wage rates for the preceding April to October and October to April periods respectively. In addition, the Minister of Social Affairs has power to introduce special 'structural' increases to the minimum wage if increases in actual earnings — particularly among the lower grades — rise faster than average rates. Such increases are limited to once every three years and must be made in consultation with the Social and Economic Council.

The scope of the minimum wage has also been extended since its introduction. In 1966, it became applicable to women and in 1974 a minimum youth wage was introduced. Currently, the minimum applies to all employees aged between 23 and 65 years working more than one-third of the normal working week (i.e. generally 40 hours). The wage is reduced by 7.5 per cent for each year that an employee is younger than 23. After 1974, the emphasis of incomes policy shifted towards redistribution among wage earners (OECD 1979). The minimum wage was increased more rapidly and the principle that fiscal policy should maintain purchasing power for those earning up to the 'modal' wage was added to the consensus, between the government and the two social partners, that wage agreements should include indexation. Also the use of job classification in fixing wage rates increased and is now employed by 25 per cent of large businesses and, less formally, by another 35 per cent.

It remains to be seen how far the deteriorating economic situation and the resultant statutory intervention in wage bargaining (which culminated in a temporary wage freeze in January 1980) will undermine progress towards greater wage equality. In 1979, the minimum wage was linked to net rather than gross changes in contractual wage rates and minimum income and fiscal policies since 1979 have generally sought only to protect the earning power of those on minimum incomes.

Low wages

How successful has the Dutch minimum wage been in protecting or improving the position of the low wage earner? Table 4.1 shows that during the period 1968 to 1978 the minimum wage rose much faster than 'modal' income and that by April 1979 the statutory minimum wage was estimated by the Dutch Central Bureau of Statistics to represent 75 per cent of the average gross earnings of all manual workers in manufacturing industry (O'Riodan 1981). On this basis, the level of the Dutch minimum wage, relative to average wages, considerably exceeds that in France or Belgium, is broadly the same as in Denmark, but falls somewhat short of the agreed minimum in Norway (O'Riodan 1981).

Minimum wages in The Netherlands are therefore high by international standards and have been increasing. However, from Table 4.3 it can be seen that most of the improvement has occurred since minimum wages were indexed to average wage rates and that during the previous

Table 4.3   *Change in real disposable income for different income groups, The Netherlands, 1964—77*

Income		% Annual change in real disposable income					
	Average 1964–8	Average 1969–73	1973	1974	1975	1976	1977
Minimum wage	3.5	2.7	4.1	5.0	4.5	2.0	2.0
Wage just above minimum	4.9	3.8	3.3	3.0	3.5	1.5[2]	3.0[2]
Modal wage[1]	4.7	3.3	1.5	2.5	3.0	0.5	2.5
2 × modal[1]	3.8	2.8	1.4	0.5[2]	1.0	−1.0	1.5
4 × modal[2]	3.6	1.8	0.9	−2.0	−1.5	−2.0[2]	1.5

1 See Table 4.1 for definition of modal wage. The wife is not considered to be contributing to household income.
2 Rounded up to nearest 0.5 or 1.0.

Source: Nauta 1980.

decade minimum wages fell relative to modal wages. Moreover, part of the rapid increase between 1973 and 1975 reflected the trend in collective agreements to incorporate bonuses, etc. into basic rates which had little effect on actual earnings but a considerable impact on the index used to adjust minimum rates. Thus at least part of the improvement in minimum wage rates has been unintentional. Since 1979, policies of wage restraint have had a complex effect on the minimum wage. In essence, while the policies have sought to favour the low paid by allowing for proportionately greater wage increases, the real value of the minimum wage has been eroded by price inflation.

Figures for 1976 show that overall about 10.5 per cent of employees earned minimum wages although half of these were persons aged under 23. In fact, 30.3 per cent of under-23-year-olds received the minimum wage income compared with only 2.1 per cent of adult male employees. The corresponding figure for female employees was 18.7 per cent, which reflects the continuing pattern of lower female earnings (Netherlands 1976). Moreover, women — particularly those working part-time — and young people are over-represented among the 1.7 per cent of employees (illegally) paid below the statutory minimum (Netherlands 1979b). Illegally low wages are also thought to be prevalent among foreign workers (Nauta 1980). Employers paying less than minimum wage rates are not subject to any penalties but employees can enforce payment through the courts. For obvious reasons, the minimum wage cannot be extended to the self-employed but, as Table 4.4 illustrates, incomes amongst certain groups of self-employed (e.g. small-scale tradesmen and farmers) are very low.

Table 4.4   Proportion of wage earner and self-employed households with income less than social assistance levels, The Netherlands, 1977

Household type	Households with income below national assistance level	
	Wage earners	Self-employed
No children	1.8	11.7
1 child	4.1	19.7
2 children	5.7	24.7
3 or more children	19.5	37.2
All households	4.7	18.8

Source: Adopted from Nauta 1980.

Since minimum social assistance scale rates for a couple are set equal to the net minimum wage, it follows that where a worker receiving the minimum wage has a family, the household income is likely to fall below assistance levels. In 1977, it was estimated that 4.7 per cent of households with earned income received less than social assistance and that the proportion for households with three or more children was four times greater (see Table 4.4).

In The Netherlands, minimum wage legislation has assisted in reducing wage disparities, established a level of minimum earnings that is high by international standards and contributed to eradicating absolute poverty among those at work. However, what is unique about the Dutch minimum wage is the role it plays in establishing the incomes of those outside the labour market.

Social security and the minimum wage
Figure 4.1 explains how social security payments are coupled with the

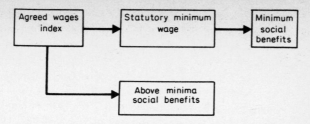

Figure 4.1   *The coupling of benefits with wages, the Netherlands*

Source: Nauta 1980

minimum wage. Every six months, the minimum wage is increased in line with the agreed wages index and at the same time social assistance scale rates are raised. (Since 1978, social assistance for a couple has equalled the minimum wage.) Likewise above-minimum benefits, e.g. unemployment benefit (*WW*) and sickness benefit (*Ziektewet*) which are related to former earnings, are also increased. This system thereby guarantees a common minimum income whether in or out of work, automatically maintains differentials between the different benefits and ensures that all benefit recipients share in the increased living standards of workers.

The other side of the same coin is that indexation adds significantly to the upward movement of social security expenditure. Benefits are related to wages but these in turn are linked to prices so that benefits must rise at least as fast as prices. Also, if earnings move ahead of prices, social security recipients share in the increase whether it results from genuine gains in productivity or simply from a twist in the inflationary spiral. Moreover, the situation is exacerbated by the precise form of linkage between social minima and wages. Benefits − net of tax and social security contributions − are set approximately equal to average net minimum wages. However, recipients of benefits normally pay less tax and social security than those on average wages. Thus, if the government attempts to keep wage costs down by contributing to the social insurance funds, the resulting increase in average net wages (as a result of the decrease in employees' contributions) leads not only to an increase in net social benefits but also to an increase in the gross level of social benefits. Consequently, the effect of a direct government contribution to the social insurance system can be an increase in the overall expenditure of social security (Sprake 1978).

The 'Carousel' effect described above has been one element in increased social security expenditure. (Other factors include demographic ones and the natural tendency for social expenditure to increase with national income.) General government expenditure increased from 52 per cent of national income in 1970 to 62 per cent in 1978 and to an estimated 67 per cent in 1981 with one-third of the 1979—81 increase being due to increased expenditure on social security (OECD 1981). The increasing scale of government transfers to social insurance funds is perhaps best appreciated when set against the income generated by Dutch natural gas (see Table 4.5). It would be wrong, however, to suggest that North Sea gas has deliberately been used to fund increased social security (one of the alleged features of the so-called 'Dutch disease'). Indeed, even over the period 1952—66, i.e. prior to the large-scale exploitation of natural gas, growth in *per capita* expenditure on social security exceeded that of most other countries (Kaim-Caudle 1973). Nevertheless, the revenue from natural gas has certainly made social security increases possible.

Table 4.5   Funding of social insurance, The Netherlands, 1973—80

Social insurance fund items	Items as a proportion of national income						
	1973 (%)	1974 (%)	1975 (%)	1976 (%)	1977 (%)	1978 (%)	1980 (%)
Expenditure	18.9	19.9	22.1	22.2	23.0	23.8	23.4
Contributions (employers and employees)	18.3	19.9	20.5	20.1	19.9	20.4	20.7
Government transfers[1]	1.0	1.0	1.9	2.7	2.5	3.2	3.1
Gas reserve	1.1	1.6	2.8	3.4	3.8	3.8	3.4

1 From 1978 onwards, 0.5 per cent of this is accounted for by wage-cost subsidies.

Source: IMF Staff Paper reproduced in Sprake 1978.

The increased social security expenditure has also acted to increase labour costs. Over the period 1965 to 1978, employers' social security contributions rose from 15 to 25 per cent of gross salaries (Sprake 1978). Moreover, this increase would have been even larger had the government not made substantial contributions to the social insurance system from general revenues.

Another supposed symptom of the 'Dutch disease' is that high benefit levels have reduced the will to work and that this is demonstrated by the coexistence of unemployment with labour shortages (OECD 1980). It must be said, however, that some of the shortages reflect real shortages of specific skills and, moreover, that the increased unwillingness of people to undertake unattractive jobs is a phenomena which is not restricted to the Netherlands.

To summarise, the minimum wage is an integral and long established element in the highly centralised system of wage bargaining in The Netherlands. More recently, it has become a cornerstone of the social security system and provided a mechanism for the integration of income levels between employed and non-employed. Inevitably the system is imperfect and the imperfections have become more apparent with the decline in economic growth, or at least the system's critics have become more vocal. Nevertheless, the use made of the minimum wage in protecting and enhancing low incomes has been substantial and there is still no sign that the role of minimum wages is to be significantly reduced.

Unemployment Benefits

The Dutch social security system consists essentially of a number of social insurance schemes run on strict insurance principles, supplemented by national schemes funded from general government revenue. Between 80 and 90 per cent of the costs of social insurance and health care are met by the contributions of employers and employees (Sprake 1978). The social insurance schemes are generally administered by quasi non-governmental agencies comprising representatives of both sides of industry. Responsibility for unemployment (*WW*), sickness (*ZW*) and disability insurance rests with the 26 Industrial Insurance Boards under the aegis of the Social Insurance Council. (Some of the Boards have elected to delegate administrative tasks to the *GAK*, Joint Administrative Office.) The Minister of Social Affairs has overall responsibility for the level of benefit and the scope of the scheme but the Ministry does not normally concern itself with day-to-day operations.

Against the backcloth of total spending on social security, expenditure on unemployment benefit is small, representing just 5.7 per cent of the total, with another 0.6 per cent spent on employment measures. Nevertheless, expenditure on unemployment benefits increased disproportionately during the 1970s.

Pattern of unemployment

Registered unemployment (including persons engaged in public works projects) has increased five-fold from 56 000 man—years in 1970 to 260 000 man—years in 1980. Most of this increase was concentrated between the years 1971/2 (a 66 per cent increase), 1974/5 (a 44 per cent increase) and 1979/80 (a 15 per cent increase). The decade also witnessed a shift in the nature and composition of unemployment. Significantly, adult male unemployment fell consistently from the OPEC-induced peak in 1975 until mid-1980 accompanied by an increase in unfilled vacancies. In contrast, registered unemployment among women increased sharply from 5.9 to 8.5 per cent between 1976 and 1979, although total female employment also increased significantly. The rate of unemployment among women is higher than among men but the average duration is much shorter. As in other countries, unemployment among young people is high but did not deteriorate in relative terms between 1976 and 1980.

During the 1976—9 period, the rate of economic growth exceeded improvements in productivity by amounts sufficient to keep pace with the increased labour supply but failed to reabsorb all the labour shaken out during the preceding recession. Over the same period the proportion without work for more than one year increased from 20 to 25 per cent. Moreover, the employment situation has deteriorated further since 1979 as the creation of new employment has fallen short of the 1 per cent annual increase in labour supply.

Development of unemployment schemes

Poverty resulting from unemployment has been a recurring problem down through the ages. Originally, solutions were sought in compulsory work and job creation with the churches and local authorities providing food and money as charity or poor relief. Then with the rise of the trade unions in The Netherlands in the second half of the nineteenth century, collective schemes were created to assist unemployed members, the so-called unemployment relief funds. By the beginning of the twentieth century the first municipal unemployment relief funds were being set up and in 1917 the Unemployment Decree — the first national insurance measure — was instigated and remained in force until the start of the Second World War. This provided a government subsidy to the voluntary Unemployed Associations' Relief Funds which were usually founded by trade unions and were financed by members' contributions. The subsidy amounted to 100 per cent of the members' contributions but the maximum benefit was limited to 70 per cent of the insured person's wage. At the end of the 1930s, there were approximately 600 000 employees insured in this way but the schemes gradually died out during the Second World War.

A national insurance scheme was proposed during the inter-war years but controversy about the role of the trade unions and the share of the cost to be borne by employers delayed legislation until the 1949 Unemployment Insurance Act (*WW*). This Act, implemented in 1952, provided a statutory scheme for compulsory employee insurance against the financial consequences of unemployment but was limited to workers earning less than about 120 per cent of the modal wage. Entitlement was restricted to 21 weeks and the level of benefit was differentiated with married householders receiving 80 per cent of their wage, unmarried householders 70 per cent and other people 65 per cent.

Major improvements to the scheme were introduced around 1965. The period of entitlement was increased to 130 days; the cover was extended to all employees regardless of their earnings; the benefit itself was standardised at 80 per cent of former wages and the maximum benefit was doubled. In addition, a new scheme was introduced, the Unemployment Benefits Act (*WWV*), which provided benefit equal to 75 per cent of former wages for two years for those no longer eligible under the *WW*. This scheme represented a major break with earlier practice in that benefits were funded solely from general taxation and not by contributions.

Somewhat earlier, in 1963, the National Assistance Act (*Algemene Bijstandswet*) was passed, which in principle gave all Dutchmen entitlement to benefit, covering basic living costs. (By providing persons with legally enforceable rights this Act finally dispensed with the idea of assistance as relief.) Within the framework of the Act, a separate scheme was created for unemployed persons falling outside the scope of the *WW* or *WWV*. The scheme, the Government Unemployment Assistance Regulations (*RWW*), is administered by local authorities and benefits, which are related to the minimum wage, are subject to means-test.

Current provisions

The three unemployment schemes, *WW*, *WWV* and *RWW*, coexist either providing benefit sequentially or under the second and third schemes when a person is ineligible for the first or second.

The *WW* was intended as the main form of protection against unemployment. Membership of the scheme provided by the appropriate Industrial Insurance Board is generally compulsory. Premiums are related to the two forms of benefit payable under the Act: redundancy and unemployment benefit.

Payments for the redundancy fund are set by the Industry Insurance Board and depend on the volume of unemployment in a specific branch of industry. They are paid by employers who deduct 50 per cent from employees. The premium for unemployment insurance is the same for all branches of industry and is determined by the General Unemployment Fund subject to ministerial approval. Contributions are in the ratio 2 : 1 : 1 for government, employers and employees respectively.

Unemployment benefit and redundancy benefit both amount to 80 per cent of former earnings subject to maximum and minimum payments. (The minimum payment seeks to guarantee income above the social minimum.) Both benefits are taxable and insurance contributions are payable to funds other than the *WW*. However, whereas unemployment benefit is payable for 130 days (based on a five-day-week), redundancy benefit is only payable for 40 days. Eligibility criteria are correspondingly stricter in the case of redundancy with entitlement being dependent on 130 days insured employment in the same industry within the preceding six months. Only 65 days' employment in any industry is necessary for receipt of unemployment benefit or six weeks immediately prior to claiming. Payment of benefit is also subject to registration for employment at the local employment office and may be stopped if the claimant fails to accept suitable employment or actively to seek it.

As noted above, the Unemployment Benefits Act (*WWV*) exists to provide benefit to those who are ineligible for benefit under the *WW*. However, the same criteria apply with respect to employment records and certain groups of workers are excluded, namely those aged 65 or over, married women who are not breadwinners or permanently separated from their spouse, and recipients of certain benefits. Benefit, which is payable for a maximum of two years, is marginally lower (i.e. 75 per cent of former wages) than under the *WW*, but the minimum is virtually the same. Although *WWV* is administered by local authorities as is unemployment assistance (*RWW*), it is regarded as a component of the insurance system.

An interesting characteristic of both the *WW* and the *WWV* is that a supplementary wage benefit may be payable if an unemployed person accepts employment at a rate of pay clearly below his normal earnings. This supplement may be paid for six months or two years for a person aged under 45 under the *WW* and the *WWV* respectively, and for up to one or three years respectively for someone aged 45 or over. Benefits are also payable to formerly part-time workers on a *pro rata* basis.

Table 4.6   *Net monthly payments in the event of unemployment,*
The Netherlands, 1 January 1980

	WW (£)	WWV (£)	RWW (£)
Minimum[1]	319	317	–
Modal	358	336	–
Maximum	610	573	–
Married[1]	–	–	317
Single above 21 years[2]	–	–	222
Lone-parent families[3]	–	–	285

1 Equals the net minimum wage.
2 Equals 70 per cent of the net minimum wage.
3 Equals 90 per cent of the net minimum wage.

Table 4.6 records the value of benefits payable under the three schemes as at 1 January 1980, and Table 4.7 relates the average benefit received to average income and average wages. Benefit levels are high by international standards and would be even higher were it not for the

Table 4.7   *Relative value of selected social security benefits,*
The Netherlands, 1977

Source of income	Value in relation to:	
	(a) Average income	(b) Average wages
Wages	110	100
Self-employment	109	99
Unemployed benefit (WW)	78	71
Unemployed benefit (WWV)	72	66
Disability insurance (WAO)	89	81
National assistance (ABW)	71	65

Source: Nauta 1980.

fact that claimants tend to have low job status, limited education and formerly low wages. Nevertheless, it remains true that most workers would experience a significant drop in income on becoming unemployed.

Recent developments

The developing problem of unemployment described at the start of this section has begun to undermine the rationale of the benefit system. Table 4.8 shows that a minority of the unemployed are now supported by the first-line insurance benefit (WW) which in 1979 accounted for

Table 4.8   *Recipients of unemployed benefits by scheme,*
The Netherlands, 1979

	Number of recipients[1]
Unemployment Insurance Act (WW)	45 000
Unemployment Benefit Act (WWV)	85 000
Government Unemployment Assistance Regulations (RWW)	70 000
Other	10 000

1 Average per year.

only one-third of expenditure on unemployment benefits. Neither unemployed young people nor the long-term unemployed — both groups which have grown disproportionately with the shift from cyclical to structural unemployment — can be satisfactorily protected by contribution-based benefits. Moreover, the balance of funding has been shifted from employers and employees — who contribute only to the WW — towards government, thus eroding the principle of risk insurance.

Another significant development which has attracted much attention recently is that recorded unemployment is providing an increasingly un-reliable guide to the true level of unemployment. For example, many of those receiving full disability pension (the number of recipients increased at an annual rate of 10 per cent throughout most of the 1970s, OECD 1980) should properly be counted as unemployed since they are only partially disabled. Also, certain groups who have lost their entitlement to unemployment benefit — primarily married women — may neverthe-less wish to work. Moreover, while the proportion of women going out to work has traditionally been low in The Netherlands, this pattern is likely to change substantially.

A third development has been the growing concern about non-material aspects of benefits. One component of this concern, already mentioned, relates to the possible disincentive effects engendered by high benefit levels. Formerly, the administrative response to such problems has been to impose penalties against those who fail to accept suitable work or training. Now the idea which is gradually gaining ground is that unemploy-ment schemes should contain a range of instruments designed to prevent unemployment or to shorten the periods of unemployment, for example, by making greater use of retraining and refresher courses. Another aspect of the same concern relates to the extent to which the unemployed may engage in unpaid community-based activities without losing their entitlement to benefit. New rules have been drawn up to cover this contingency and are currently being evaluated.

Unemployment and social policy

Policy towards unemployment must be seen alongside developments in other areas of policy and most importantly the growth in the scale of social security. Over the period 1969 to 1978 the number of claims made on the social security system increased at an annual rate of 4.3 per cent. Part of this rise was a consequence of demographic factors but to a large extent it was due to the down-turn in the economy. Moreover, oppor-tunities for reducing the number of claims in the future will depend largely on the number of jobs available.

One increasingly important sub-area of policy — bringing together both social and economic objectives — is concerned to curb the rise in social security claims which, in the case of unemployment, means striving to limit the degree of unnecessary unemployment. To achieve this goal there has been a number of policy initiatives since 1978. These have sought:

(a) improved performance of the labour exchange system partly by means of the introduction of a new type of labour exchange (see OECD 1980);

(b) increased co-ordination between national and local agencies in the implementation of existing programmes;

(c) better understanding of special problems in the labour market and ways of overcoming them;

(d) enhanced occupational mobility achieved through better information and increased and improved training (the largest single training programme is concentrated on school leavers);

(e) promotion of job placement for young people, the long-term unemployed, handicapped persons and, on a temporary basis, immigrants, to be achieved primarily by wage subsidies to employers and contributions to workers' removal expenses (OECD 1980);

(f) to test new ideas including experimental public works projects, a temporary employment programme for young people and sheltered workshops;

(g) redistribution of existing employment through extension of the early retirement schemes agreed by the social partners and incorporated into the yearly wage contracts. (These have generally been financed through increased social security contributions at the sectoral level which have normally been met out of increased earnings, OECD 1980).

The rapid growth in social security in The Netherlands, both in the numbers of schemes and claimants, has not only increased costs but has also resulted in a system of enormous complexity. To overcome these problems, recent studies have recommended that the system should be made more client-oriented and, through decentralisation, more accessible and less unwieldy.

Another important development has been a broadening in the aims of social security policy. There has been a clear move away from employers' risk insurances to national insurance that provides universal coverage and uniform non-contributory benefits. Correspondingly, unemployment must increasingly be seen as a social risk with solidarity, rather than insurance pure and simple, providing the underlying rationale for the benefit system. Moreover, the notion of solidarity must be two-dimensional, involving solidarity on the part of the community with the individual, but also solidarity on the part of the individual with the community. The latter dimension means that individuals must contribute to the insurance schemes in accordance with their ability and make as few claims as possible. The former can be seen in a definite shift in the objectives of the Dutch social security policy. To the original objective of providing a guaranteed income have been added new ones concerned with maintaining the social position of the claimants and providing them opportunities for personal development.

A new unemployment benefit scheme?

The premises underlying a new system of unemployment benefit currently being developed by a team of civil servants, reflect the developments described above:

(a) the new scheme should increase homogeneity of policy, administration and implementation and provide optimum correlation between the primary social objectives and those of employment and labour market policy;

(b) it should constitute a step towards an integrated system of insurance for loss of wages and perhaps for loss of income;

(c) benefit should be available to the fully and partially unemployed, including those whose unemployment is due to disablement;

(d) entitlement to benefit should be more dependent than formerly on length of service;

(e) the scheme should provide equality of treatment for men and women in accordance with EC directives;

(f) local authorities ought eventually to be responsible for administration;

(g) the cost of the system should remain the same.

In detail, the scheme is likely to consist of a flat-rate component with a supplementary benefit. The flat-rate element will be fixed at a socially acceptable minimum level in accordance with the solidarity principle. This guaranteed minimum will probably equal 70 per cent of the minimum wage with the benefit dependent on family composition and means.

The supplementary benefit, on the other hand, will reflect loss of wages and will probably be fixed at about 80 per cent of a notional figure dependent on former wages, length of service and possibly age. This will fall to 70 per cent after a period of time. Payment of the supplementary benefit will be limited to, perhaps, 130 days and a limit may also have to be placed on the flat-rate component.

Conditions for receipt of the flat-rate and supplementary benefits will be analogous to those existing for the *WW* and *RWW* respectively, and penalties for abuse will be maintained. School-leavers and formerly self-employed workers will be entitled to the flat-rate benefits and eligibility may be conferred on other groups. Finally, the scheme will incorporate provisions geared to re-entry into working life that are complementary to those available under employment policy.

Conclusion

Every social security system should be under continual review to ensure that it responds effectively to social and economic change. Otherwise the initial underlying premises may cease to apply and the system begins to exacerbate the very problems it was designed to solve. The Dutch system of unemployment benefits evolved to protect a minimal number of people against short periods of cyclical unemployment and it was then reasonable that the cost of insurance should be borne by those at risk. Today's structural unemployment has undermined the financial basis of the system at a time when a new form of social contract was already operative in other branches of social security. Consequently, it is time to consider a new system of benefits more attuned to present circumstances.

In the same way the minimum wage has evolved to meet changing circumstances. Formerly, it represented simply the converse of statutory maximum wages determined by government. Today, it lies at the centre of economic and social policy. How far minimum wages and indexation contribute to the problems of the Dutch economy is an issue of current political debate and we must wait and see whether a fundamental realignment of wages and social security payments will prove necessary to reverse our economic fortunes. To date, incomes policies have curbed the automatic indexation of wages but have sought to maintain the relative, though not the real, value of the minimum wage and social security benefits.

References

Fase, W. J. P. 1980, *Vijfendertig jaar loonbeleid in Nederland, terugblik en perspectief*, Alphen aan de Rijn.

Kaim-Caudle, P. R. 1973, *Comparative Social Policy and Social Security*, London, Martin Robertson.

Nauta, A. P. N. 1980, *Poverty in the Netherlands — A Report to the Commission of the European Communities*, Social en Cultureel Planbureau, Ritswijk.

Netherlands 1976, 'Minimumloontrekkers, het aantal', *Sociale Maandstatistiek*, pp. 508—16.

Netherlands 1979a, *Beloningsmethoden in Nederland*, Loontechnische Dienst, Hague.

Netherlands 1979b, *Naleving, de, van de Wet Minimumloon en de minimumvakantiebijslag*, Loontechnische Dierst, Hague.

OECD 1966, 1979, 1980, 1981, *Netherlands*, OECD Economic Surveys, Paris.

O'Riodan, M. 1981, 'Minimum wages in Europe', *Low Pay Review*, 5.

Scholten, G. 1979, *Functiewaardering met mate*, Alphen aan de Rijn.

Sprake, A. D. 1978, *Social Insurance in The Netherlands*, Mimeo.

5 West Germany: Poverty, Unemployment and Social Insurance
*Karl Furmaniak**

I begin with the assertion that there are virtually no working poor in Western Germany. Poverty — where it exists — affects mainly those outside the working population and is concentrated among the elderly, incomplete families and those who have been handicapped from early youth.

In the first part of this chapter I shall seek to establish the validity of my opening assertion — subject to certain qualifications — and then proceed to examine why this should be so. The second part is concerned primarily with the rise of unemployment and focuses on the way in which the West German system of social insurance has been used to restrict the growth in unemployment and to limit the impact of poverty among the unemployed. Finally, I shall consider some of the inevitable consequences of a social security system that is founded on social insurance principles and which means that not insignificant numbers of people remain at risk of poverty even within a country as prosperous as the Federal Republic of Germany.

Poverty and Employment
Any definition of poverty or of a poverty threshold must necessarily be somewhat arbitrary and this is especially so since both concepts are the subject of intense discussion in the Federal Republic (Henkel 1978). Taking the level of means-tested social assistance payments (*Sozialhilferegelsatz*) as a rough measure of the poverty threshold has both advantages and disadvantages. First, *Sozialhilfe* is perhaps the most commonly used definition in West German studies of poverty (see Chapter 8). Secondly, in so far as an official poverty line exists at all in West Germany, it is usually taken to be equal to, or slightly less than, *Sozialhilfe* levels. (The Federal Social Aid Act, *Bundessozialhilfegesetz* — BSHG, seeks to secure for every citizen 'the possibility to lead a life in conformity with human dignity'.)

---

*In association with Robert Walker.

On the other hand, several negative implications follow from the adoption of *Sozialhilfe* levels as a poverty line. Attention is focused on income poverty to the exclusion of other forms of poverty — social, psychological, cultural, etc. — which prevents a full understanding of the precedents and antecedents of poverty (Brenner 1978). Furthermore, it has been argued that:

> compared with other European countries, Germany's record appears more favourable when poverty is defined purely in terms of money income than when one uses a definition which takes into account access to schools, medical care or housing or, more generally, attitudes towards the poor and their chances of participating in cultural activities and maintaining social content. (Lawson 1980: 195).

Secondly, the use of *Sozialhilfe* levels predicates a relative, normative definition of poverty. Thirdly, since *Sozialhilfe* is defined for households, the household becomes the unit of analysis in the assessment of poverty. This may be appropriate in many circumstances especially in the measurement of income poverty. Nevertheless, it must lead to an underestimation of the loss of independence — particularly among women, young people and the elderly — resulting from low income.

In 1980, the basic maintenance element (*Regelsatz* of *Sozialhilfe* amounted to 309 DM per month to which must be added supplements for housing costs, heating, and extra needs (*Mehrbedarf*). The average total payment for a married couple with two children is equivalent to about 40 per cent of average gross earnings of skilled men in manufacturing industries.

With the further qualification that 'working' is taken to mean full-time employment (of about 40 hours per week) for wages or a salary and on a normal contract basis, it is now possible to consider my initial assertion that there are virtually no working poor in Germany. Table 5.1 shows the monthly net household income for various categories of earner derived from a national sample survey of incomes. In 1978, only 1 per cent of all gainfully employed persons working full time lived in households with a monthly net income of less than 1000 DM and even among unskilled workers, the corresponding figure rose only to 2 per cent. 1000 DM was well above the 1978 *Sozialhilfe* level for a two-person household and marginally exceeded that for households consisting of two adults and a dependent child (assuming receipt of housing allowance). Therefore, in 1978 less than 1 per cent of households with at least one member in full-time employment fell beneath the poverty threshold. (Table 5.1 also reveals that marginally more self-employed persons earned less than *Sozialhilfe* levels although accurate assessment of income is particularly difficult for this group.)

Percentages/DM

Table 5.1 Net monthly household income, West Germany, 1978

| Net monthly household income (DM) | All gainfully employed (%) | Gainfully employed working full time aged 18 to 65 years | | | | | Pensioners (%) | Self-Employed (%) |
| | | Manual workers | | | All employees (%) | Tenured public officials (%) | | |
		a. all (%)	b. unskilled/ semi-skilled (%)	c. skilled (%)				
0 – 999	1	1	2	1	1	0	22	3
1.000 – 1.499	9	15	17	13	6	2	27	5
1.500 – 1.999	20	27	26	28	15	16	22	13
2.000 – 2.499	23	22	22	23	24	20	13	18
2.500 – 2.999	17	16	16	16	18	18	7	14
3.000 – 3.499	14	9	7	10	16	19	4	13
3.500 – 3.999	6	3	2	4	8	10	2	10
4.000 or above	10	5	6	5	12	14	2	25
Average net household income (DM)	2560	2290	2230	2340	2730	2880	–	2990
Personal net income as % of net household income	68	63	60	65	69	73	71	76

1 Net of taxes and social security contributions.

Source: Becker and Ruhland 1979.

Similar results were obtained in a model comparison of disposable income and social assistance rates conducted for 1977 (Brenner 1978). This study defined disposable income as income remaining after deduction of taxes and social insurance contributions and after receipt of children's allowances (*Kindergeld*), housing allowances (*Wohngeld*) and training assistance (*Bundesausbildungsförderungsgesetz*). Disposable income was found to exceed *Sozialhilfe* levels for all groups except low income, unskilled workers with four or more children (see Table 5.2).

Table 5.2   Social assistance requirements and the disposable income of unskilled industrial workers, 1977

Unskilled worker[1]	2 children (DM)	4 children (DM)
Average gross earnings per month[2]	1 860.00	1 860.00
Legal deductions[3]	522.06	514.36
Net wage	1 337.94	1 345.64
Children's allowance	120.00	360.00
Housing allowance	43.00	113.00
Disposable income	1 500.94	1 818.64
Social assistance requirements[4]	1 392.00	1 875.00
Difference between disposable income and social assistance	+108.94	−56.36

1 Performance group 3 (i.e. 13.3 per cent of industrial workers). Assumes sole male earner.
2 Wages for normal workers in July 1976 with an increase in tariff wages of 6.5 per cent assumed for July 1977.
3 Wage tax, church tax (rate: 9 per cent of wage tax less children's allowance), social deductions 16.6 per cent.
4 Standard needs for subsistence plus an overall amount for non-recurrent subsidies (15 per cent of the standard rates).

Source: Brenner 1978.

Several factors account for the findings in Table 5.1. First, the household income of low wage earners is frequently supplemented by the earnings of working wives. Indeed, it appears that the lower the income of the head of household, the higher is the percentage of working wives and the greater the proportion who work full time (Hofbauer 1979). Clearly although income poverty may be avoided by this means, significant social costs may be entailed reflecting, for example, expensive and perhaps inadequate child care.

Secondly, the income figures presented in Table 5.1 include receipt of *Wohngeld*, the means-tested housing benefit payable to tenants and owner occupiers. *Wohngeld* payments are dependent on family (i.e. household) size, family income and housing costs, the last of which is in turn dependent on location. Assuming average rent and standard work expenses, as accepted by the tax authorities (work expenses are deducted from the assessment of income), a couple with two children on two-thirds average earnings would stand to gain *Wohngeld* equivalent to 7 per cent of their gross earnings. Depending on their housing expenses, a family of similar size might still be eligible for *Wohngeld* with an income 14 per cent above average earnings (Bradshaw and Piachaud 1980). In 1976, some 7 per cent of all households received *Wohngeld* (FRG 1979) although many more were thought to be eligible; according to some estimates take-up is as low as 50 per cent (Lawson 1980b).

In discussing Table 5.1, little account so far has been taken of the impact of family size. The West German wage system ignores the question of family poverty (see Chapter 9) since, except in the public service, wage differentials do not take account of marital status or family size. The last remnants of this formerly quite common provision were eliminated in the 1950s on the initiative of employers in keeping with their professed adherence to the principles of a market economy. The unions concurred partly in the belief that family-based differentials could damage the employment opportunities of persons with families, but also because they saw it as the duty of the whole society to make adequate provision for the family rather than the function of the wage bargaining process.

Whether West German society has made adequate provision for the family is an open question (see chapter 9 and Bradshaw and Piachaud 1980) for, as table 5.2 shows, unskilled workers with four or more children are likely to be eligible for *Sozialhilfe* even after payment of *Kindergeld*. However, in practice only a small minority of the families who claim *Sozialhilfe* include a full-time worker (Brenner 1978).

Wage bargaining and the trade unions

It is necessary to consider the process of wage bargaining and the role of the trade unions in order fully to appreciate why there are so few working poor in West Germany.

The view of the Federal government, which is shared by all parties in the *Bundestag*, by the unions and by the employers, is that the settlement of wages and salaries should be the sole responsibility of unions and employers. This policy is strictly adhered to with the result that there are no wage-price guidelines and no incomes policy or minimum wage. Between 1967 and 1977 tripartite talks were held under the 'law on economic stability and growth', the so-called '*Konzertierte Aktion*', but these had no binding character and ended with the tensions arising from a lawsuit brought by employers against the 'codetermination law' (*Mitbestimmungsgesetz*). Nevertheless, a great number of informal contacts remain between government, unions and employers and operate at various levels.

The unions themselves have always been aware that the consequences of their collective bargaining could necessarily affect the economy as a whole. (Interestingly this stance by the trade unions was anticipated by both Bismarck, shortly after the unions were legalised, and by the socialist theoretician Bernstein in 1899 (Rothfels 1953; Bernstein 1973).) But while the unions have, with good reason, always refused to be held responsible for the fate of the economy they have, in their negotiations, taken account of the fear of inflation which is a pervasive feature of German public opinion. This distinctly moderate stance has elicited consistent praise from both the present government and, in somewhat more muted terms, from employers' representatives (Handelsblatt 1980). It may also have facilitated the continuingly high levels of entrepreneurial income that characterise the German economy (see Krejci 1976).

The system of autonomous settlements which takes account of the overall economic picture can only be understood in its historic context. The majority of the German population tends to subscribe to the ideal of '*Sozialer Friede*' (literally, social peace) that is incompatible with talk about, or even less the practice of, class struggle. Nevertheless, the majority of people are also aware that strikes are a necessary part of the bargaining process (Becker and Ruhland 1979). Equally, it is generally accepted that the autonomy of collective bargaining and the social environment in which it took place were major factors in attaining full employment during the 1950s and preserving it, with an interlude in 1967, until 1974, while simultaneously maintaining low inflation, high growth rates, and a balance of payments surplus. The high growth of productivity over this period enabled most workers to obtain substantial improvement in their standard of living and facilitated the high tax yields necessary to fund West Germany's expanding social programmes (Lawson 1980a).

Within this social and economic climate, membership of trade unions has increased steadily so that by 1979 42.8 per cent of all gainfully employed persons in the FRG were unionised (FRG 1979: 294). About five out of six of those unionised belong to the German trade union federation *Deutscher Gewerkschaftsbund* (*DGB*) which is organised on an industry basis. The fact of a single powerful union per industry has led trade unions to seek a careful balance between different groups in the labour force and has restrained the ambitions of the strategically well placed (Janzen 1979). What is more, the fairly high degree of voluntary unionisation (there are no closed shops in West Germany) has resulted in the adoption of union wage rates throughout much of the West German economy, including those sectors that are weakly unionised. Indeed, the Minister of Labour and Social Affairs has power to extend the application of collective agreements to all businesses within a particular industry even where employers are not party to the agreeement in question. Moreover, since most social insurance benefits are linked to former earnings (see below), the trade union movement plays a significant role in establishing the social wage.

Despite continuing employer resistance, the West German trade unions have consistently fought for disproportionate wage increases for the lowest earners. This is of course in keeping with the strong socialist strain in their tradition. There is insufficient data from which to draw positive conclusions but it does appear that the trade unions have met with some success in recent years as is indicated by the modest reduction in the dispersal of earnings shown in Table 5.3. This is further supported by comparison with France (Lutz 1976). An exploratory study of the French and West German metal-working industries has shown that the earnings ratio of skilled to unskilled workers is considerably higher in France (1.25) than in West Germany (1.15).

Table 5.3   *Relative incomes of different occupational categories, 1968—78*

Index numbers

	Net personal income		Net household income	
	1968	1978	1968	1978
Workers	86	83	88	90
Employers	110	107	117	107
Tenured public officials	130	121	111	113
Self-employed	142	131	121	117
Index: average net income of all gainfully employed	100	100	100	100

More general international comparisons point also to the distinctive nature of inequality in West Germany in which the high proportion of income received by the rich is compensated for by comparatively low proportions received by those in the middle to low middle ranges of income distribution. The result is that low-income households are relatively better off in West Germany than in most other Western countries (Lawson 1980a; see also FRG (1981) which gives a much more optimistic picture).

Unemployment, Poverty and Social Insurance

It is generally believed that the system of autonomous collective bargaining was an important factor in maintaining full employment up to 1973. Since then, however, the system has functioned much less effectively as drastically increased oil prices and a floating Deutschmark have come to dominate the economic environment. Therefore, although inflation and unemployment have remained lower than in other countries, unemployment reached a million in 1975 and was still in excess of 850 000 in 1980 (Table 5.4). Moreover, while unemployment has fallen gradually since 1975, the employment opportunities of certain groups

Table 5.4   Structural characteristics of unemployment, West Germany, 1973–9[1]

	Units	1973	1974	1975	1976	1977	1978	1979
Total unemployment	000s	219	557	1105	898	911	865	737
Rate of unemployment	%	1.0	2.4	4.4	3.9	4.0	3.8	3.2
Males	%	0.7	2.0	3.7	3.0	3.0	2.7	2.2
Females	%	1.4	3.2	5.5	5.5	5.7	5.5	4.8
Foreigners								
Absolute	000s	16	67	133	79	80	90	77
% of total	%	7.3	12.0	13.2	8.8	8.8	10.4	10.5
Rate of unemployment	%	0.6	2.8	5.8	3.8	4.1	4.6	3.9
Age of unemployed								
Under 20	%	9.6	12.5	11.5	11.4	11.6	10.6	9.3
20–49	of total	61.0	68.3	71.3	69.2	69.2	68.4	66.0
50 and over		29.4	19.1	17.2	19.4	19.4	21.0	24.7
Average duration of unemployment								
White collar, total	000s	86	138	340	383	381	343	299
Under 3 months	%	61.7	58.9	45.4	42.1	40.9	40.9	42.5
Over one year	of total	4.9	4.0	7.8	14.3	16.5	17.8	16.5
Blue collar, total	000s	133	373	666	515	530	521	438
Under 3 months	%	54.3	56.5	40.2	40.9	42.0	40.7	41.4
Over one year	of total	10.9	5.7	10.6	20.6	20.0	22.0	22.1
Memorandum items:								
Short-time workers	000s	36	265	639	94	158	109	37
Unemployed/vacancies	Ratio	0.4	1.9	4.3	3.9	3.9	3.4	2.3
Participation rates[2]	%	56.4	55.8	55.4	54.9	54.5	54.4	54.3
Males	%	76.2	74.8	74.2	73.2	72.4	72.0	71.8
Females	%	39.0	39.0	39.0	38.9	38.8	38.9	38.9

1 As of September each year, not seasonally adjusted.
2 Population aged more than 14 years — average for year.

Source: OECD (1980).

have markedly worsened. This is true of older workers — especially those aged over 55 — and also of persons with health problems. The unemployment rate amongst foreign workers (*Gastarbeiter*), many of whom returned home as employment difficulties increased, is still above the national average, although it has improved recently. Likewise, although unemployment among women has declined in sympathy with the general trend, the improvment has been significantly less marked than for men. Moreover, women are disproportionately represented within the *Stille Reserve*, that section of the potential labour force which is not shown in official unemployment statistics. The circumstances of one group — the under 20s — have improved appreciably as a result of an increased demand for apprentices (see below) although unemployment in the age group 20–25 remains much above average. Finally, as can also be seen from Table 5.4, the average duration of employment appears to be increasing.

Despite the fact that unemployment has fallen only slowly since the 1975 recession, there is considerable evidence that most of the unemployment — perhaps, on some estimates, as much as 90 per cent — is cyclical rather than structural in nature (OECD 1979; Cramer 1976). Therefore, the government's response, particularly marked during the period 1977 to 1979 when fiscal and monetary policies were both expansionary, has been to persist with a policy of full employment and to maintain a moderate Keynesian line. The results have been moderately successful. For example, the series of fiscal measures introduced in 1977, which reduced income and wealth taxes and increased the medium-term public investment programme (see OECD 1978), is estimated to have generated 160 000 additional jobs in 1978–9, or perhaps as many as 300 000 if the effect of additional public sector employment is included (OECD 1980). On the other hand, Federal deficit spending has been made partly ineffectual by municipal and *Länder* budget contraction. Furthermore, there have been increasing Friedmanite tendencies in the autonomous West German Federal Note Bank (*Deutsche Bundesbank*) and the policies of the Federal government itself have been strongly moderated by the fear of inflation.

In themselves demand-management policies proved ineffective in controlling the high tide of unemployment and consequently a number of special programmes of relief work, retraining and job placement have been introduced. In most cases, these have been administered under the existing unemployment insurance scheme.

Social insurance

The West German system of social security owes much to its origins in the 1880s and the major compulsory social insurance schemes can be traced to the Imperial Message to the Diet given on 17 November 1881. (The welfare activities of the municipalities constitute an important exception and their medieval roots are still evident in the current social assistance legislation.) One explicit goal of the Imperial Message (Germany 1881) was an attempt to counteract socialist agitation among workers by offering an element of social pacification in addition to the usual methods of police repression. The Prussian ruling class felt quite competent to deal with the traditional — mainly rural — poverty which, though quite severe in certain regions, was susceptible to the traditional methods of social control that included, in extreme cases, military action. The industrial workers, however, presented a more intractable problem since they were generally beyond the reach of oppressive methods of social control. Furthermore, they were made more receptive to socialist ideas by their precarious circumstances which were further exacerbated by the absence of extended families and the support and security which they can offer. Indeed Bismarck himself stressed that uncertainty and old age were the major sources of workers' grievances (Rothfels 1953).

In order to pacify the workers and to marry their interests to those of the State, Bismarck proposed *small* old-age and invalidity pensions, work accident insurance and sickness insurance for blue-collar industrial workers. Bismarck noted that the numerous small pensions distributed by the French government created a large group with vested interest in the *status quo* and for this reason he argued that contributions should be borne solely by employers and by the State (Born 1960). However, Bismarck's officials, to whom he necessarily had to entrust the details of legislation, adhered to a Manchester liberal creed and believed that if social security were to be introduced at all, it should be constructed on social insurance principles. Their view held sway and until this day the West German system of social security is largely financed by insurance contributions. Currently, the pension, sickness, accident and unemployment funds are 61 per cent financed by contributions; the contributions of the insured account for 22 per cent, those of employers for 23.6 per cent and the residual 15.5 per cent comprises 'fictitious' contributions attributable to employers who, for example, in the public sector pay benefits from their general budget rather than contributing to insurance funds (FRG 1978).

The strong insurance orientation of West German social security has a number of important consequences. Perhaps the two most significant are first, that benefits are linked to wages lost or to damage suffered and, secondly, that coverage is restricted to the gainfully employed and, to a limited extent, to their dependants. It follows from the linking of benefits to wages lost that the benefits payable are not uniform but reflect instead financial differentials established in the labour market. To a degree, the level of benefit is viewed as a reward for former work that reflects the value of that work (Jantz 1961). This, in turn, has hindered development of the notion of a 'poverty line' below which incomes should not be permitted to fall (see above) and diverted attention away from the possibility of employing the social security system as a mechanism for the vertical redistribution of income.

The circumstances of groups denied insurance cover because of their failure to participate in the labour market have often been precarious. Increasingly, however, legislation has been amended to include those groups but often only by allowing for the establishment of fictitious work histories. This serves to maintain a semblance of the insurance principle but with the result that the schemes have become inordinately complex.

Other consequences of the insurance orientation of West German social security are worth noting. The actuarial desire to minimise outgoings and maximise contributions, in order to maintain financial solvency, has caused the insurance funds to stress the desirability of a rapid return to the labour market and thereby also the importance of rehabilitation. The emphasis on rehabilitation, which is shared by most of the West German insurance funds, is readily compatible with the importance of employment in establishing social status. Less beneficial, however, has been the development of separate insurance schemes to cover different risks, which has resulted in the segmentation of welfare and created significant problems of co-ordination when attempting to meet the needs of the multiply deprived. Furthermore, insurance schemes may be unable to protect small numbers of people with desperately disorganised lifestyles.

The unemployment insurance scheme

The first system of contributory unemployment insurance was not introduced in West Germany until 1927, over 40 years after the other branches of social insurance had been instituted. However, the main tenets of the original law have been followed in all subsequent legislation although the emphasis has gradually changed (Kaim-Caudle 1973). Significantly, the current law (*Arbeitsförderungsgesetz (AFG)* of June 1969) has as its primary aim the prevention of unemployment by means of a positive employment policy, with financial support for the unemployed being a secondary objective. Nevertheless, it is appropriate first to consider the measures for income support and then to examine other aspects of the 1969 law.

Two unemployment benefits are payable under the unemployment insurance scheme, an insurance benefit (*Arbeitslosengeld*) and an assistance-type payment (*Arbeitslosenhilfe*). Both benefits are administered by the *Bundesanstalt für Arbeit* (Federal Labour Agency) and payable by local unemployment offices (*Arbeitsamt*).

All employees who work for 20 hours or more per week are compulsorily insured against unemployment and currently contribute 1.5 per cent of their gross pay to the insurance scheme with employers making a similar contribution on their behalf. As unemployment is not an insurable risk in the actuarial sense any deficit is funded by the Federal government. As a result of record levels of unemployment the insurance scheme went deeply into the red in 1975 and had to be supported by massive subventions from Federal funds. At the same time high unemployment reduced the income of the old-age pension and health insurance funds, exacerbating already serious mismatches between financial inflows and outflows. The unemployment fund deficit was readily met by increasing contributions by 1 per cent (since reduced again) and by 1977 the *Bundesanstalt für Arbeit* was once again in surplus. For a range of political reasons the same simple expedient of increasing contributions was impossible with respect to the old-age pension and health insurance funds and the dilemma was resolved partially by means of a transfer of funds from the unemployment scheme. This was achieved by making the *Bundesanstalt für Arbeit* responsible for the payment of pension contributions in respect of the unemployed receiving either *Arbeitslosengeld* or *Arbeitslosenhilfe*. From the unemployed claimants' point of view, therefore, since 1977 they have been technically insured free of charge under the compulsory old-age pension and invalidity scheme, whereas there was only a restricted and partial coverage before. Moreover, spells of unemployment affect the value of their future pension rights less since they are calculated on the basis of a 'fictional' income during the period of unemployment equal to their previous 'usual' net pay.

Arbeitslosengeld amounts to 68 per cent of the 'usual' pay, net of tax and social security contributions, received during the last four weeks of insured employment. No additions are payable to take account of marital status or family size but the benefit is tax-free. It is payable for a period varying from 78 days to a maximum of one year according to the length of insured employment. Once entitlement to benefit is exhausted (or there is no initial entitlement because the person has less than six months' contributions) an unemployed person becomes eligible for *Arbeitslosenhilfe*. Under this scheme an unemployed person receives 58 per cent of his former net 'usual' pay, tax-free. Both benefits are subject to an effective maximum (2072.20 DM per month in 1980) as a consequence of a contribution ceiling which is fixed at roughly twice the average gross earnings figure for employees. However, unlike *Arbeitslosengeld*, receipt of *Arbeitslosenhilfe* is subject to a means-test which is rather unusual for an insurance benefit. Moreover, the effect of the means-test, which applies to the household, is quite severe and limits dramatically the numbers of women and young people who are eligible. In 1975, for example, 157 000 of the 250 000 enemployed who theoretically might have been entitled to *Arbeitslosenhilfe* because they had been out of work for more than a year failed to qualify. In fact, on occasions the level of *Arbeitslosenhilfe* may be such that it has to be supplemented under the general public assistance scheme (*Sozialhilfe*).

In contrast with insurance benefits, the public assistance scheme is generally more meagre than its counterpart in Britain (Lawson 1980a, 1980b). The scheme is administered by local authorities and by the *Länder* who are also responsible for its finance. The individual *Länder* are also responsible for setting the basic rates although there has recently been a tendency towards a national and relatively uniform policy. This has been encouraged by the use of a common basket of goods (*Warenkorb*) to define the basic 'needs' of claimants and their dependants. Although *Sozialhilfe* is payable to people in employment – 'demonstrable need' is the fundamental criterion of eligibility – the *Länder* usually aim to set scale rates below local wage rates for the lower paid. This necessarily proves difficult with respect to large families, but even so very few workers simultaneously receive *Sozialhilfe*.

Recipients of *Sozialhilfe* increased in number throughout the 1970s partly as a result of additional unemployment and partly because benefit levels rose faster than wages. In 1970 there were 749 000 beneficiaries (including dependants) but by 1977 this figure had risen to 1 362 000. Nevertheless, there is still a significant problem of low take-up which, among other things, is exacerbated by the fear that the authorities might approach parents and children who, under the social assistance law, are liable to pay maintenance (Brenner 1978).

The amount of poverty generated by unemployment is hard to establish. Without doubt unemployment causes severe loss of income so that in 1978, unemployment reduced the average net household income of the unemployed by 600 DM (FRG 1978). Also, reduced employment opportunities mean that women and young people are less able to supplement the income of the poorly paid bread-winner. On the other hand, because a high proportion of the unemployed (85 per cent) live in households with at least one fully employed person, the household income, though significantly reduced, is likely to remain above *Sozialhilfe* levels. Moreover, during recent years the period of unemployment has averaged around 13 weeks so that very few of the unemployed have exhausted their entitlement to insurance benefits. In 1978, the average monthly personal income of unskilled workers was 1450 DM per month. Fifty eight per cent (841 DM) of this, or the amount that the average unskilled worker would have received in *Arbeitslosenhilfe*, was well above the *Sozialhilfe* level for a childless couple. When housing and children allowances (*Wohngeld* and *Kindergeld*) are taken into account it is obvious that a large majority of the unemployed remain above social assistance levels.

Certain groups are necessarily at greater risk of poverty caused by unemployment. Some, for example, women, young people and the irregularly employed who are not living in households with other workers, are at risk as an almost inevitable consequence of relating benefit to the record of contribution (see also below); others because benefits are related to previous earnings and thereby reflect differentials established in the labour market. Families of the unskilled are likely to be at particular risk since an unemployed man with a non-working wife and more than two children, who had previously earned the average wage for an unskilled worker would generally be entitled to *Sozialhilfe*. Moverover, there is evidence to suggest that for reasons of shame the unemployed are in practice more reluctant to claim benefit than are other groups. Nevertheless, the weight of evidence is that unemployment has not created a quantitatively major problem of income poverty. (In part this is due to the built-in dynamism of unemployment benefits which is achieved by linking them to former wages.) Unemployment may have increased the numbers receiving *Sozialhilfe* but the proportion of the unemployed who are eligible for social assistance remains very low. Only 3 per cent of a representative sample of unemployed surveyed in 1978 stated that they received *Sozialhilfe* payments (FRG 1980). The less than satisfactory social assistance statistics for the same year show that 10 per cent of *Sozialhilfe* recipients simultaneously receive *Arbeitslosengeld* or *Arbeitslosenhilfe*. The latter figure is the sum for the whole year and must be divided by the unknown average duration of receipt to yield the actual number of people affected. Nevertheless, it can be adduced that the number of registered unemployed who are legally entitled to *Sozialhilfe* payments (i.e. including those who fail to claim it) is less than 50 000 or 5 per cent of the unemployed.

Training provisions under the unemployment insurance scheme

The scope of insurance in West Germany is not limited to the provision of unemployment benefits. The AFG recognises the need to promote growth and avoid unemployment and therefore places great emphasis on vocational education as a means of adapting the skills of workers to changes in production and technology. The *Bundesanstalt für Arbeit*, which as the Federal Institute for Placement and Unemployment Insurance before 1969 had little involvement in training, now funds four principal forms of vocational education: vocational training which aims to provide skills necessary to practice a trade or profession; vocational further education which seeks to supplement and expand existing skills; vocational retraining which aims to equip workers to change occupations; and vocational rehabilitation (see below) which helps the handicapped to remain or to become self-supporting.

The *Bundesanstalt für Arbeit* is also empowered to encourage training through the provision of grants. Under the AFG all insured persons, whether employed or unemployed, and certain groups without insurance cover, such as housewives and previously self-employed persons, may apply for government assistance to cover the expense of training. If the *Bundesanstalt für Arbeit* considers the training to be an appropriate means of avoiding unemployment it will bear the cost of tuition, books, travel expenses, and, if necessitated by the location of training, accommodation. In 1980, the number of people benefiting from training and retraining financed by the *Bundesanstalt für Arbeit* was 153 000.

During training the person is also entitled to a maintenance allowance (*Unterhaltsgeld*) equivalent to 80 per cent of the usual net pay. The *Unterhaltsgeld* is set deliberately at a higher level than either of the two unemployment insurance benefits in order to provide an immediate incentive to retrain. Unfortunately, the take-up of training schemes is not entirely satisfactory since skilled workers have tended to take most advantage of retraining whereas the risk of unemployment is highest among those with the lowest occupational skills. In this respect, therefore, the system tends to provide least for those in greatest need. The problem is partly the result of an inherent middle-class bias among educators and educational institutions which means that they have not adapted satisfactorily to the needs of unskilled workers. To overcome this problem an experimental programme of retraining on the shop floor was launched and ran between 1979 and 1981. Nine hundred million DM were budgeted for the programme which benefited 45 680 people.

Apprenticeships

The aim of facilitating economic growth and employment by means of a highly skilled labour force is reflected in the very large system of three-year apprenticeships and in the concomitant belief that all school leavers should have an opportunity to acquire vocational qualifications. (In 1976, apprenticeships covered about 500 occupations, although the number of separate schemes has since been reduced through rationalisation.) Indeed, although compulsory full-time education in West Germany finishes at age 15 (or 16 in certain *Länder*) compulsory part-time education continues for a further three years. Two-thirds of young people attend part-time vocational school while the remainder continue in full-time education. Ninety-two per cent of those in part-time vocational schools are simultaneously serving an apprenticeship. The cost of the on-the-job component of the apprenticeship is met by the employer (and, to the extent that apprentice pay is relatively low, by the apprentice), while the training schools — which apprentices usually attend for 8 to 12 hours per week — are government financed.

In 1976, to cope with the demographic bulge of school leavers (rising from 700 000 per year in the early 1970s to 950 000 in 1982), the government introduced a provisional law (*Berufsbildungsgesetz*) to ensure a sufficient number of apprenticeships. The main provision permitted a special levy to be raised from larger firms whenever the number of apprenticeships offered in a given year failed to exceed demand by at least 12 per cent. The levy would be used to provide financial incentives for firms, particularly small-to-medium sized ones, to increase their number of apprenticeships. The impact of the scheme has already been noted above with respect to the drop in the number of young people out of work. (The scheme came to an abrupt end in 1981 when the Federal Constitutional Court declared the provision unconstitutional on technical grounds.)

Other measures to reduce unemployment

The policy principles laid down in the AFG have resulted in a shift in emphasis away from attempts to treat the symptoms of unemployment towards the creation and development of preventive measures (Hanby and Jackson 1979). The shift is evident in the increasing involvement of the *Bundesanstalt für Arbeit* in vocational training (see above), in the creation of a comprehensive policy on occupational choice and in the restructuring of careers advice into an integrated programme of assistance lasting throughout working life. Rather less consistent with the new emphasis have been various attempts since 1974 to assist certain groups of unemployed who appear to be particularly disadvantaged in their search for employment.

One such scheme which has attracted much attention is the job-creation programme (*Arbeitbeschaffungsmassnahmen, ABM*). Under the ABM, the *Bundesanstalt für Arbeit* may grant subsidies and loans to public corporations, private undertakings or institutions which provide additional jobs 'in the public interest'. The scheme is financed from the unemployment insurance fund and the amounts available are distributed, taking into account regional differences in the severity of unemployment. The subsidies available to the employers range from 60 to 120 per cent of the remuneration that employees have received.

The ABM has come in for criticism from both sides of industry. The *Bundesvereinigung Deutscher Arbeitgeberverbände* (*BDA*), the main employers' organisation, has argued that the need for such a measure could be much reduced by making the educational system more responsive to the needs of industry, while the DGB, the principal trade union organisation, has tended to view the ABM as a simple subsidy to employers which potentially lessens the volume of permanent employment. The responses of certain of the *Länder* governments have also been less than enthusiastic, in part because of the uncertain nature of the employment created.

In truth, the ABM was initiated as a temporary measure and is more of a palliative than an effective remedial programme. Nevertheless, the programme provided 41 250 jobs (monthy average) in 1980 and generated employment for around another 41 000 as a result of multiplier effects. Although the jobs were typically of short duration (i.e. six months) the persons employed will have benefited from the work experience (despite receiving little training) and avoided, to some extent, the stigma of unemployment. In the long term the displacement effects of the programme might be quite substantial but there is little evidence that the ABM has had a significant effect on the level of permanent employment in the short term (see Hanby and Jackson 1979 for a fuller evaluation of the ABM).

Another measure introduced on a temporary basis but which has become more or less permanent is the subsidy for employers who increase their workforce by employing long-term unemployed (*Eingliederungsbeihilfen*). When the scheme was introduced in 1969, employers who recruited persons who had been unemployed for more than three months were able to claim a lump sum payment for each new employee equivalent to 60 per cent of the union wage over a six-month period. However, subsidies have subsequently been increased to 80 per cent of the union wage for up to two years. Under the same scheme persons who had been unemployed for at least six months and who accepted a job in an unfavourable location were paid a mobility allowance but this measure has lapsed. The unemployed may, however, claim a removal allowance (*Umzugskostenbeihilfe*) and a resettlement grant (*Trennungsbeihilfe*) and certain travel expenses when applying for a new job. In 1979, 113 716 persons benefited from the wage-cost subsidy and 450 845 received the allowances associated with taking up a new job.

An older quota system was reaffirmed under the Severely Disabled Persons Act of 23 April 1974 (*Schwerbehindertengesetz*) which obliges all employers with more than 15 employees to ensure that 6 per cent of their labour force comprises persons officially recognised as being severely handicapped (*Schwerbehinderte*). If they fail to do so, employers are assessed 100 DM per month for every job falling below the required quota. These compensatory payments are used to subsidise the adaptation of workplaces to the requirements of the severely handicapped.

Finally, two schemes exist which are designed to prevent workers being laid off due to inclement weather or to a down-turn in the economy. In addition to protecting individual workers, both schemes seek to ensure that employers do not lose experienced labour and, in the case of the former scheme, that losses to the national economy resulting from seasonal inactivity are avoided. Affected individuals may claim 'short time allowance' (*Kurzarbeitgeld*), which is paid by the employer and reimbursed by the *Bundesanstalt für Arbeit* provided that a third or more of employees in an establishment are idle for at least 10 per cent of time during a four-week period. (In later weeks an employer will be reimbursed if only 10 per cent of employees are on short time.) The level of allowance, which is tax-free, is set at 68 per cent of the loss in 'usual' net pay and is payable for six months although this period may be extended to 24 months in special regions by an ordinance of the Federal Minister of Labour. In 1979, payments equivalent to 88 000 man-years were made and it is estimated that 40 000 jobs were thereby saved (Bach *et al*. 1979). Persons laid off in the construction industry as a result of poor weather conditions are entitled to claim 'bad weather allowance' (*Schlechtwettergeld*) which is also tax-exempt and fixed at 68 per cent of usual net pay. Nine hundred and eighty-nine thousand construction workers received an average of 23 work days' allowance during the 1979–80 winter.

Although the range of instruments designed to avoid unemployment, and with it the possibility of poverty, is quite impressive, some caution is necessary. It has been estimated that if West Germany had used these instruments to the same extent as Sweden, unemployment might have been reduced by 3.3 per cent instead of by little more than 2 per cent. On the other hand, the marginal impact of expenditure in West Germany seems to be markedly higher than in Sweden (Johanesson and Schmid 1979).

Sickness, accident and invalidity provisions

A discussion of the extent of poverty among the labour force is incomplete without reference to persons affected by sickness, accident and invalidity. More than half of all males in West Germany have to retire because of failing health several years before reaching the statutory retirement age of 63 and many of these must be considered as involuntarily out of work. Likewise, in 1978, 8.4 per cent of the West German labour force suffered a spell out of work due to industrial accidents (FRG 1979).

It is impossible here to detail the measures which protect workers from the full consequences of sickness, accidents and invalidity. In brief, employers are obliged to pay full wages during the first six weeks of sickness. Thereafter, the employee receives 80 per cent of his gross wage, which is usually equivalent to the full net wage, in sickness insurance benefit (*Krankengeld*). There are similar provisions in the case of industrial accidents. If permanent invalidity results, a pension (*Unfallrente*) equivalent to 66.7 per cent of the gross wage received during the year immediately prior to the accident is awarded and in the case of partial invalidity the pension is awarded *pro rata*. In the case of invalidity due to other causes an invalidity pension (*Erwerbsunfähigkeitsrente*) of 70 per cent of the former net wage is normally paid. However, because invalidity pension is based on lifetime earnings benefit levels are extremely variable.

Rehabilitation

A further feature of the West German social security insurance system is the importance attached to rehabilitation. This has already been seen in the emphasis placed on retraining. In the case of sickness and invalidity it is probably true to say that rehabilitation takes precedence over pensions.

In principle, rehabilitation is provided for everyone who needs it. All branches of the social insurance scheme provide rehabilitation and under social assistance legislation rehabilitation is available to those not covered by any of the insurance schemes. The stress on rehabilitation — 822 344 people benefited under the insurance schemes (excluding health) in 1978 and 85 per cent were able to resume or start work — is encouraged by the insurance approach inherent in the West German system. It is in the interest of the individual insurance agency to avoid paying pensions if at all possible and this, in turn, has a socially desirable consequence. In West Germany 'paid employment' is accepted to be, for men at least, the mandatory role from the time of leaving school until the age of retirement. It follows, therefore, that to be unable to work is to be reduced to playing a more or less marginal role in society and that successful re habilitation to work means the re-integration of a person into the mainstream of West German society.

Limitations of Social Insurance

The exclusion of certain groups from the most important provisions of West German social security is an almost inevitable consequence of the insurance orientation of the system and of its origin as an instrument for the protection of *industrial* workers. Nevertheless, during the 100 years of its existence coverage has been extended gradually to embrace practically all gainfully employed persons working regularly and earning more than a negligible income. Most recently, voluntary or mandatory coverage has also been given to certain groups of self-employed workers.

The self-employed

In theory, all 2.4 million self-employed are excluded from the West German social insurance system although in reality large numbers of the self-employed are able to obtain cover under the insurance system on a voluntary basis and many are included compulsorily. For example, most farmers are covered by the compulsory sickness insurance scheme although they do not receive compensation for lost wages. Similarly, licensed master craftsmen are obliged to join the old-age and invalidity pension schemes.

The dependants of the self-employed who work for wages in family businesses are, in general terms, treated like all other gainfully employed persons. However, because there is a large arbitrary element in the fixing of their wages — reported wages, for example, may be below the insurance minimum — *de facto* coverage by social security is ineffective. Consequently, dependants of the unsuccessful self-employed are at a considerable risk of poverty. In practice, few people are involved because the self-employed are relatively successful and the number of dependants working in family businesses is steadily decreasing. Nevertheless, a disproportionate percentage of the poor of working age are comprised of former self-employed persons or their dependants who did not voluntarily enter the social security system or are still in business.

There is little prospect of changing this state of affairs since one of the coalition parties and the opposition are both opposed to taking away the 'freedom' of the self-employed to become poor through the failure of their business.

Persons outside the labour force

The most important group of people for whom the West German social security system makes insufficient provision are those who have not or cannot become members of the compulsory social insurance schemes. This group has two main components: persons finishing formal education without having previously been employed and persons unable to work in gainful employment.

The first group consists mainly of unemployed young people and tends to attract a great deal of media attention. It is argued, for example, that employers discriminate against younger workers (Melvyn 1977); that the young are over-educated and have excessive aspirations (OECD 1977); and that the least qualified are at an increasing disadvantage due to a 'trading-down' of occupational expectations in the job market (Hanby and Jackson 1979). Consequently, disillusionment sets in and cynicism develops about the value of training and the chances of employment, which hinders future integration into the workforce and into society generally (Schober-Gottwald 1977). While these points may or may not be true the problem of poverty is a relatively small one and in May 1980 only 2.9 per cent of young people aged under 20 had been registered as unemployed for more than one year. The main reason for this is that the West German occupational training structure still channels the large majority of young people through a three-year apprenticeship, albeit at a fairly low wage. The apprentice wage, which incidentally is open to negotiation by the trade unions, is nevertheless above the poverty line in circumstances where the apprentice is living with his parents and a Federal education subsidy (*Bafög*) is available in exceptional cases.

The second group comprises primarily people who are already handicapped before reaching working age. After the death of their parents there is, in principle, no provision except for *Sozialhilfe*. To meet the needs of this group, coverage of social insurance has been extended by establishing a fiction of work or by assuming fictitious wages. The legislation (*Gesetz über die Sozialversicherung Behinderter*) stipulates that handicapped persons working in offices or organised workshops for the handicapped are covered by the social security scheme, even if their wages are below the minimum necessary for compulsory insurance, or indeed, if they receive no wages at all. Handicapped people working under this law are insured as if they are earning 75 per cent of the national average wage.

This exceptional scheme illustrates another feature of German social security. Where ordinary provisions or coverage under the compulsory insurance scheme are insufficient this is usually remedied not by abandoning the insurance principle altogether, but rather by altering the rules of insurance in what may appear to be an arbitrary way. However, in this case the approach is seen as having the same socially desirable consequences as the emphasis on rehabilitation: it establishes the handicapped as 'ordinary' members of the workforce and thereby increases their self-esteem and social integration.

Women

Women suffer doubly under insurance-based schemes. First, the level of benefit is set as a proportion of earnings, which reflects past and present wage discrimination against women. Secondly, women generally interrupt or discontinue employment in order to raise children. This is most serious in its consequences when benefit entitlement is dependent on lifetime earnings as is the case with old-age and invalidity pensions. Moreover, if the family breaks up through divorce or desertion and the husband defaults on alimony, the uninsured woman with small children is solely dependent on *Sozialhilfe*

Conclusion

A major element in reducing poverty must be a full employment policy. However, as West German experience demonstrates, such a policy can only be effective when the trade union movement is strong enough both to act responsibly and at the same time to achieve an acceptably high industrial and social wage for its members.

It is in this context that the West German social security system has largely eliminated poverty among those in the labour force. However, much less attention has been given to the development of social security provisions for those outside the labour force and, consequently, poverty tends to be concentrated among the handicapped, the old and among broken families.

The West German emphasis on insurance-based social security has two positive advantages. First, it encourages rehabilitation and thereby places the goal of social integration above well-provided exclusion from working life. Secondly, people may be more ready to pay insurance contributions rather than taxes since the former provide benefits which are explicitly related to contributions. As nations reach what seems to be the politically acceptable upper limit of personal taxation this may become an increasingly important factor in attempts to protect the relative position of the least advantaged.

Nevertheless, the advantages of an insurance-based approach have to be weighed against three negative consequences. Insurance-based systems seem unable to cope with a hardcore remnant of poverty extending to about 1 per cent of the population. This 'hardcore' comprises persons who are severely handicapped or who, for long periods of their working life, are socially or mentally extremely maladjusted. This group would be better served by flat-rate payments.

Insurance systems also tend to fragment provision and to raise the threshold that has to be mastered in order to benefit from social security. This necessarily follows from the need for claimants to prove entitlement to benefit, which frequently calls for communication skills that are lacked by a significant proportion of the population. Moreover, individual insurance schemes cover only certain contingencies and fail to take account of needs which fall outside their fields of reference. At best the client with multiple needs will be advised to apply additionally elsewhere. In theory, these difficulties are surmountable, but attempts to mount 'integrated' counselling and referral services under the *Sozialgesetzbuch* have not been encouraging. Insurance systems, therefore, seem particularly unfitted to meet the needs of the multiply deprived who require complicated packages of monetary provision, goods and services.

Finally, insurance-based systems exhibit a 'blind spot' with respect to the importance of providing goods and services such as counselling services, home helps, specialised housing, etc., which are not adequately catered for by the market economy. This arises from the inevitable actuarial orientation of funds which leads them to cover only clearly definable risks and to offer only certain circumscribed forms of provision. Funds have proved very loath to enter into obligations to meet needs, the definition of which is dependent upon a significant element of judgement on the part of social workers, counsellors, etc. Similarly, insurance funds have tended to avoid circumstances where claimants may require a range of services involving claims on different funds or agencies and leading, potentially at least, to demarcation disputes over who is financially responsible.

References

Bach, *et al*. 1979, 'Der Arbeitsmarkt in der Bundesrepublik Deutschland im Jahre 1980', *Mitteilungen aus der Arbeitsmarkt und Berusforschung*, 4, p. 512.

Becker, H. and Ruhland, W. 1979, *Bürger und Sozialstaat*, Bonn, Der Bundesminister für Arbeit und Sozialordnung.

Bernstein, E. 1973, *Die Voraussetzungen des Sozialismus und die Aufgaben der Sozialdemokratie*, 5th edn, Bonn, Dietz.

Born, K. E. 1960, 'Die Motive der Bismarckschen Sozialgesetzgebung', *Die Arbeiterversorgung*, 62.

Bradshaw, J. and Piachaud, D. 1980, *Child Support in the European Community*, Mimeo, University of York/London School of Economics.

Brenner, K. 1978, 'Economic (Income) Poverty in the Federal Republic of Germany', *Eurosocial Reports, (Centre for Social Welfare Training and Research, Vienna)*, 14, pp. 49–62.

Cramer, E. 1976, 'Zum Problem der Strukturellen Arbeitslosigkeit', *Mitteilungen aus der Arbeitsmarkt und Berufsforschung*, 2, pp. 221–4.

FRG 1978, *Sozialbericht '78*, Bonn, Der Bundesminister für Arbeit und Sozialordnung.

FRG 1979, *Gesellschaftliche Daten 1979*, Bonn, Presse und Informationsamt der Bundesregierung.

FRG 1980, 'Statistiches Bundesamt', *Sozialhilfe*, vol. 13, no. 2, Stuttgart Kohlhammer.

FRG 1981, *Das Transfersystem in der Bundesrepublik Deutschland*, Bonn, Mimeo.

Geissler, H. 1976, *Die Neue Soziale Frage*, Freiburg, Herder.

Germany 1881, *Stenographische Berichte über die Verhandlungen des Reichstags*, vol. 66, V, Legislaturperiode.

Hanby, U. J. and Jackson, M. P. 1979, 'An Evaluation of Job Creation in Germany', *International Journal of Social Economics*, vol. 6, no. 2.

Handelsblatt 1980, 16 October, p. 3.

Henkel, H. 1978, 'Poverty in the Federal Republic of Germany: the Political Discussion', *Eurosocial Reports (Centre for Social Welfare Training and Research, Vienna)*, 14, pp. 63–70.

Hofbauer, H. 1979, 'Zum Erwerbsverhalten Verheirateter Frauen', *Mitteilungen aus der Arbeitsmarkt und Berufsforschung*, 12, p. 223.

Jantz, K. 1961, 'Pension Reform in the Federal Republic of Germany', *International Labour Review*, 83.

Janzen, K. H. 1979, In *Protokoll einer Schichtarbeiterkonferenz*, Saarbrucken, 29 April.

Johanesson, J. and Schmid, G. 1979, *Die Entwicklung der Arbeitsmarktpolitik in Schweden und der Bundesrepublik Deutschland*, Berlin, Institut für Management und Verwaltung, Mimeo.

Kaim-Caudle, P. R. 1973, *Comparative Social Policy and Social Security*, London, Martin Robertson.

Krejci, J. 1976, *Social Structure in Divided Germany*, London, Croom Helm.

Lawson, R. 1980a, 'Poverty and Inequality in West Germany' in V. George and R. Lawson (eds), *Poverty and Inequality in Common Market Countries*, London, Routledge and Kegan Paul, pp. 195–232.

Lawson, R. 1980b, *Social Assistance in the Federal Republic of Germany*, Report prepared for the European Commission, Mimeo.

Lutz, B. 1976, 'Bildungssystem und Beschäftigungsstruktur in Deutschland und Frankreich' in Hans-Gerhard Mendices *et al.*, *Betrieb-Arbeitsmarkt-Qualifikation I*, Frankfurt, Aspekte, p. 110.

Melvyn, P. 1977, *Youth Employment, Roots and Remedies*, World Employment Programme Research Working Paper, Geneva, ILO.

OECD 1977, *The OECD Observer*, Paris, pp. 31–6.

OECD 1978, *Germany*, OECD Economic Surveys, Paris.

OECD 1979, *Germany*, OECD Economic Surveys, Paris.

OECD 1980, *Germany*, OECD Economic Surveys, Paris.

Rothfels, H. (ed.), 1953, *Bismarck und der Staat*, 2nd edn, Stuttgart, Kohlhammer.

Schober-Gottwald, K. 1977, 'Jugendarbeitslosigkeit: eine Zwischenbilanz', *Berufsbildung in Wissenschaft und Praxis*, 1.

6 Denmark: Policies to Combat Unemployment and Low Incomes
*Robert Walker**

Introduction

Denmark is an exceedingly prosperous country. In 1978 its *per capita* income was exceeded only by that of Switzerland while private *per capita* consumption of $US 6000 placed it fourth in the OECD league following Switzerland, Belgium and the USA (OECD 1980). At the same time government expenditure and taxation is high. Current government revenue in 1978 amounted to 49 per cent of GNP (compared with 39 per cent in the UK) of which 19 per cent was raised from direct taxation and 37 per cent from indirect. Furthermore, social welfare expenditure is financed from general taxation to a far higher extent than in most other countries (EC 1979).

However, the 1970s were rather lean compared with the fat years of the 1960s. The Danish economy suffered a severe recession after the increase in oil prices in 1973/4 and had not fully recovered at the time of the second increase in 1979. Declining economic growth brought with it a questioning of the nature of Danish society and of the role of social welfare. Even during the boom years, doubt had arisen as to whether economic growth and full employment could in themselves reduce social inequalities. In 1969, Bent Hansen published *Prosperity without Welfare* which demonstrated that little redistribution of personal income had occurred and that even the redistributive consequences of public fiscal and expenditure policies had been negligible (Hansen 1969). Two years later a special committee of the Union of Unskilled and Semi-skilled Workers (SID) reported that large wage differences still existed in Denmark and that low pay was only one facet of a more extensive problem of inequality (cited in Boeck *et al.* 1977). By 1973 the ruling Social Democratic party had responded with a report *The Demand for Equality* (Socialdemokratiet 1973) and in 1976 the Social Democratic government set up a Low Income Commission which was expected to complete its final report in 1981.

*I should like to thank Kaj Westergaard and Kühn Pedersen for their help in the preparation of this chapter. Remaining errors are regrettably mine.

Reforms, instigated in the late 1960s and early 1970s, in the administration of social welfare were a consequence of the same process of appraisal. Research conducted by the Danish National Institute of Social Research had not only shown that the needs of individual families frequently required the intervention of many separate agencies, but also that many of their problems were preventable by a unified approach (see Petersen 1976). As a result, a number of measures were introduced to unify social insurance and social services in Denmark and to shift the emphasis towards participation:

> the emphasis is on preventing social casualties and offering people a chance of rehabilitation through a wide variety of social services. It is hoped that a new-found sense of security and well-being will prompt the individual to become a productive member of society. (Duvå 1976: 15).

In 1973, existing social insurance funds were replaced by a public health service, funded primarily by local and regional taxation, which provided free medical care on a means-tested basis. (The availability of free medical care was extended to all in 1976.) A unified system of daily allowances for sickness, maternity and work accidents was also established in 1973. This offered benefits of 90 per cent of previous earnings to the entire active working population. In 1976, the process of reform was concluded with a new social assistance act (*Bistandsloven*).

Despite the concern which precipitated the reforms of the early 1970s, the average Dane did not seem to have been much disturbed by an awareness of deprivation among the disadvantaged. So Knud Bidstrup (1976: 14) could conclude, in 1974, that: 'The country (Denmark) has pretty well succeeded in living up to the ideal expressed in an old song, "that few should have too much and fewer still too little".' Moreover, the apparent affluence of Danish society combined with a confidence as to the overall effectiveness of social welfare has meant that the concept of poverty is generally viewed as anachronistic within the Danish context and that the possible existence of poverty, either absolute or relative, is scarcely ever acknowledged (Boeck 1977). Consequently, when a national sample of Danes was asked, 'Are there at the present time in your town, part of town or village, people whose general standard of living you consider to be very bad compared with that of other people, that is people really in poverty?' only 16 per cent replied in the affirmative compared with 47 per cent in the EC as a whole. Likewise, the Danish sample were by far the most contented with the action taken by the authorities to combat poverty (EC 1977; see also Chapter 2 above).

While the economic downturn caused some people to consider the permanence of social inequalities, it provoked others to question the cost of state provision and to challenge the 'aura' which had previously held social welfare above the level of ordinary partisanship (Duvå 1976). The 1973 election saw the emergence of the Progressive Party as a major political force campaigning on a manifesto of tax cuts and reductions in the public sector. This, together with the break away of right-wing Social Democrats, severely weakened the position of the ruling Social Democrats. The Social Democratic Party has since re-established its authority but in doing so has been forced to fight three general elections in the space of five years. Moreover, in its attempt to reverse the rapidly deteriorating balance of payments the government has adopted policies to restrict demand and restrain wage costs and as a consequence has lost the support of its former ally, the Trades Union congress (*Landsorganisationen i Danmark, LO*). The break came in 1977 as a result of the provisions of an incomes policy, spelt out in the so-called 'August Agreement' (see below), and the failure of the government to introduce plans for economic democracy. Since then the LO has continued to assert that, in ignoring demands for taxation and social policy reform, the Social Democratic party has abandoned its social democratic principles.

This chapter concentrates on some of the measures introduced in Denmark to limit financial inequalities resulting from participation in the labour force or exclusion from it. The next section examines the dispersal of income and the prevalence of low wages. Then, the labour market measures which have been introduced to check steadily rising unemployment are reviewed and, in the final section, the unemployment insurance and social assistance schemes are described and evaluated with respect to their ability to maintain the living standards of the unemployed and to counteract the increased inequality frequently associated with high levels of unemployment. Wherever possible, an attempt is made to assess the effectiveness of the Danish measures in reducing inequality but this is seldom easy. Many of the policies were not introduced in order to reduce financial inequalities and have not been monitored with respect to such an objective. In these circumstances, therefore, egalitarian criteria of effectiveness are inappropriate. Moreover, adequate data is frequently unavailable.

Dispersion of Wages

It is necessary first to understand the process of private sector wage bargaining in Denmark, which provides for the signing of a legally binding collective agreement between individual employers and national trade unions. Currently, agreements generally last for two years and include an element of indexing. During the currency of an agreement, industrial stoppages are illegal.

The first step in the process is for a national agreement to be sought between the *Dansk Arbejdsgiverforening (DA)*, the Danish Employers' Confederation to which most large employers are affiliated, and the LO, the Danish Federation of Trades Unions which negotiates on behalf of about 40 national independent unions which are themselves affiliations of local unions. This national agreement usually covers such matters as minimum wages, hours of work, cost of living compensation and certain social benefits. Once a national agreement has been reached, the national unions try to conclude collective agreements with employers that take account of factors specific to the industries concerned. A statutory conciliation board is available to mediate should parties at either level of negotiation fail to reach agreement.

The last national agreement reached freely without government interference was in 1973[1]. Since then the agreement has been prolonged on three occasions as part of the government's incomes and prices policy. In March 1975 a 1 per cent increase in wages was permitted together with increases above 1 per cent for the lowest paid and some compensation for changing the base year of the wage-regulating price index. The 'August Agreement' for 1976 provided for a 2 per cent increase per annum in real income and 4 per cent indexation for the two years from 1977. September 1978 saw the introduction of a six months' wage and price freeze and the two-year agreement proposed by the government in March 1978 stopped payment of two cost of living bonuses due in September providing for an increase in holidays in lieu. A further wage and price freeze was introduced in November 1979 and at the same time oil costs were excluded from the key index of consumption prices used in wage indexation. The cost of living bonus due in 1980 was also forgone.

Although the established process of negotiating collective agreements slowly fell into disuse in the 1970s the nature of the agreements has changed little. Two points are worth noting. First, the LO argue that centralised bargaining has led to what is termed the 'solidarity in wages policy'. Essentially, this asserts that the strength of the trade union movement has been directed towards obtaining larger wage increases for the low paid thereby reducing differentials (Carlsen 1977). The rewards for this policy can be seen in the marked reduction in differentials achieved in the early 1970s (see below) and in the provisions included in each round of incomes policy. Exceptional increases for the lowest paid equal to 2 per cent in the total wage bill were allowed under the March 1975 agreement and up to a limit of 225 million Kroner under the 1976 settlement. The 1976 'August Agreement' introduced a minimum

1   1981 saw a return to a voluntary wage settlement.

wage into collective agreements which was implemented in April 1977 and the level of this was subsequently raised in March 1979 and 1980 although insufficiently to maintain its relationship with average earnings (Table 6.1).

Table 6.1   *Wage and benefit levels in Denmark, 1976—80.*

	% of average wage (for 40-hour week)				
	1976	1977	1978	1979	1980
Average wage (gross)					
(a) Hourly rate (Kr)	(34.43)	(37.81)	(41.50)	(45.74)	(49.62)[3]
(b) Base for 40-hour week = 100 %	100	100	100	100	100
Minimum wage	—	76.7	73.0	71.3	72.0
Maximum daily cash benefit[1]	80.2	81.3	81.3	78.3	78.9
Social assistance: rate of continuing assistance[2] for:					
(a) Single person	26.9	26.4	27.2	27.2	27.5
(b) Couple	44.1	46.0	48.6	50.9	51.7
(c) Children's allowance	5.0	4.9	5.0	4.8	4.8

1 *Dagpenge-maksimum* — calculated from daily rate assuming a six-day week.

2 *Varig hjælp* — calculated from annual rate assuming a 52-week (year), plus a pension contribution.

3 Second quarter of 1980.

Source: *Arbejdsdirektoratet*: personal communication.

Secondly, collective agreements include provision for a twice-annual cost of living increase which favours the low paid. Wage indexation is based on movements in the consumer price index, net of indirect taxes, subsidies and (since 1980) energy costs. A 'portion' or flat-rate increase of 0.90 Kr per hour (from December 1979) is released when the price index moves upwards by three index points. Salary earners and civil servants, who had previously received a percentage compensation equivalent to the increase in the price index, were brought into the scheme in 1975 and the OECD estimated that by 1979 indexation provided workers with protection equivalent to 55 per cent of any increase in the price index (OECD 1979).

To what extent have these egalitarian wage policies succeeded in reducing differentials? Pedersen (1976) has shown that there has been a long-term secular trend towards reduced differentials but, as Tables 6.2 and 6.3 show, the rate of progress has varied markedly. The general wage agreement and indexation have normally produced relatively larger contractual increases for unskilled workers — and particularly for women — than for skilled ones. However, during the 1960s and early 1970s when the economy was close to full employment, high wage-drift for skilled

Table 6.2 Wage increases by components and occupational groups

Date	Skilled workers				Unskilled workers				Women			
	Total wage increase	Components of increase (=100%)			Total wage increase	Components of increase (=100%)			Total wage increase	Components of increase (=100%)		
		Wage agreement	Indexation	Wage-drift		Wage agreement	Indexation	Wage-drift		Wage agreement	Indexation	Wage-drift
1966–70	9.5	25	28	47	10.5	33	34	33	10.8	36	45	19
1970	10.8	10	26	64	9.6	13	36	51	8.9	14	55	31
1971	13.0	33	29	37	16.2	42	29	29	17.8	56	32	12
1972	10.4	13	32	55	10.3	25	39	36	12.2	42	40	18
1973	13.2	7	23	70	13.1	14	28	58	16.6	52	26	22
1974	20.9	9	43	48	22.4	16	48	36	24.9	18	50	32
1975	20.4	24	44	32	20.9	31	51	18	22.8	32	52	16
1976	11.8	5	55	40	12.0	10	63	27	13.5	12	62	26
1977	8.8	18	38	44	11.4	22	34	44	12.6	25	33	42
1978	10.8	18	29	53	9.1	31	39	30	9.0	38	42	20
1979	10.3	9	27	64	10.2	13	31	56	10.4	15	34	51

Source: *Arbejdsdirektoratet* from figures supplied by DA.

Table 6.3   Wage structure[1] selected years (skilled worker,
Copenhagen = 100)

	1965	1970	1973	1976	1979
Copenhagen area					
Skilled workers	100	100	100	100	100
Unskilled workers	83	84	86	86	86
Female workers	62	65	70	75	77
Other areas					
Skilled workers	86	85	87	87	88
Unskilled workers	71	72	76	77	77
Female workers	56	58	65	70	71
Coefficient of variation	0.46	0.42	0.34	0.27	

1 Standard calculation, assuming the same distribution of workers as in 1962/3.

Source: OECD 1980.

manual workers largely offset the influence of 'egalitarian' settlements and indexation. After 1973, there was a marked increase in the contribution of indexation and a trend towards more egalitarian statutory agreements. Furthermore, the weak cyclical position, together with the acceleration of consumer prices, reduced the importance of wage-drift which has traditionally favoured skilled wage-earners in higher income brackets (OECD 1978). The period up to 1977 also witnessed a relative improvement in the level of wages compared with salaries (and a lessening of salary differentials) due to a marked reduction in expansion of the public sector and, after 1975, to the extension of flat-rate indexation to salaries. Significantly, the 1977 collective agreement might have been reached voluntarily had the employers not objected at the last moment to provisions which, they claimed, gave too much to the lower paid and consequently posed a threat of new claims for the restoration of differentials (Dean 1980).

Since 1978, the trend towards reduced dispersal of income has been halted and, to some extent, reversed. Incomes policies have held down contractual increases but cancelled a number of index 'portions' to the relative detriment of the low paid. More important, however, wage-drift which has been running at 5 per cent — suggesting a tendency for wage bargaining to become decentralised — has favoured skilled workers in comparison with unskilled and women workers. This reversal of the long-term trend is inevitably a consequence of many factors and the data itself is open to question (compare OECD 1979 and 1980). Nevertheless, the OECD (1979: 14) conclude that:

At the micro level it cannot be excluded that this development is related to efforts made in recent years to reduce wage dispersal — despite differences in productivity — and that the egalitarian profiles of the 1975 and 1977 wage settlements have led to attempts to restore the previous wage structure through wage drift.

Tables 6.2 and 6.3 take no account of the impact of taxation which has increased steadily in recent years with the result that, according to the OECD (1980), the real disposable income of individual wage-earners has remained stagnant. Furthermore, recent increases in the tax burden have been largely effected through higher indirect taxes which may be assumed to have adversely affected disposable incomes of the lower paid. (This has been proposed as a reason for increased rates of economic activity among married women, OECD 1980.) Moreover, even before the latest increases, Adam Trier concluded from an extensive literature review that taxation 'had not been able to contribute much to the levelling of income' (Trier 1977: 11). Wage dispersal in Denmark does appear to be less than elsewhere in Europe (e.g. see Table II.5 above).

The differentials that remain are nevertheless significant for they are replicated in the payment of earnings-related insurance and assistance payments (see below). In 1979, provisional estimates of wage rates for unskilled male workers averaged less than 75 per cent of skilled wages in Copenhagen in 10 of the 22 industrial sectors defined by the DA; and the situation was considerably worse for unskilled female workers for whom the corresponding number of sectors was 19. Furthermore, the minimum wage — though relatively high — still only equates to 59 per cent of average skilled wages in Copenhagen, although the number of workers who actually receive the minimum is unfortunately unknown.

It may be that the time of minimum wage differentials has already passed. It is increasingly being argued (e.g. OECD 1980) that the minimum wage is set too high and it has now been officially implicated in the slackening of demand in certain sectors of the labour market (Denmark 1980a). Moreover, there are substantial pressures to halt and even reverse the trend towards greater equality in the wage structure. Most significant among them, the Economic Council, has argued in a report published in December 1980, that the demand for a 'fair structure of wages' is not necessarily compatible with the working of the Danish economy (Denmark 1980a: 77).

Unemployment

With the exception of 1979, unemployment has risen every year since 1973 when the first round of OPEC price increases resulted in a six-fold rise in unemployment within the space of 12 months. Indeed, Table 6.4,

Table 6.4   Development of employment and unemployment in Denmark, 1973—9

Thousands

	1973	1975	1977	1978	1979[1]
Employment	2426	2365	2448	2508	2529
Unemployment	20	121	131	137	98
Early retirement scheme	—	—	—	—	45
Total labour force	2446	2486	2579	2645	2672

1 Source: OECD 1980.

Source: Denmark 1980b.

which is based on autumn labour market surveys, may well understate the true growth of unemployment and the OECD, on the basis of a regular weekly count, report a figure of 190 000 — 7.1 per cent of the workforce — for late 1978 (OECD 1980).

On the supply side, Table 6.4 shows that labour growth is accelerating and that by 1977/8 the net annual increase was double that in 1972/3. About a third of this growth can be attributed to increases in the size of the age groups with highest activity rates (i.e. those aged 25—69). A more important component, however, has been the marked increase in female activity rates — rising from 64 per cent for women aged 25—59 in 1972 to 75 per cent in 1978 — which in turn reflects a radical change in the pattern of women's withdrawal from the labour market. This phenomenon is expected to wane in the 1980s but even so the number of women in the labour force is expected to grow by 144 000 (12.5 per cent) between 1979 and 1987 and to account for 65.2 per cent of the increase in labour supply.

The slack demand for labour has been largely conditioned by a sluggish economy and especially, since 1976, by a tight economic policy pursued in reaction to a deteriorating balance of payments. Between 1973 and 1979 overall employment grew by 4.2 per cent but did not match the increase in potential labour. Furthermore, global figures conceal a steady decline in primary sector employment and a severe slump in the secondary sector in 1975, which was not followed by a recovery to 1973 levels until 1978. Only the tertiary sector has shown a consistent gain in employment attributable largely to expansion in public employment. Indeed, employment in the public sector increased by 23.4 per cent between 1973 and 1978, while employment throughout the rest of the economy actually declined (Denmark 1980b). Since government policies are likely to continue unchanged for some time ahead (OECD 1980), new labour opportunities will probably continue to lag behind labour supply.

A new method of compiling unemployment statistics was introduced by the Danish Ministry of Labour in 1979 which permits some insight into the nature of the unemployment experienced. Over the period 1 January to 17 June, during which employment grew steadily, 456 000 persons experienced unemployment. For a sizeable number the experience of unemployment consisted solely of short-time working (32.9 per cent of the 158 000 out of work on 17 June) and for others unemployment was short-lived. Of those affected by unemployment during the six-month period, 71 000 (15.6 per cent) were unemployed for less than 5 per cent of the time. However, one third of those who were unemployed on 1 January were also unemployed on 17 June and 47 000 (10.3 per cent) were unemployed for at least 95 per cent of the total period.

Turnover from week to week was considerable, averaging 25–30 000, though with large variations. Turnover also varied markedly according to occupation and was highest amongst the semi-skilled, particularly those in the building and construction industry, and lowest amongst commercial and clerical employees and other groups of white-collar workers.

Table 6.5 shows that the risk of unemployment is highest amongst the young. This situation is by no means new and the position of the young has not deteriorated greatly in recent years. What has changed, however, is the extent to which the problem has become one of female unemployment. In this respect the problems of the young mirror those of women generally in Denmark for although female employment has increased markedly since 1975, so too has the extent of unemployment. In October 1979, women accounted for 59.9 per cent of the unemployed and were twice as likely as men to be without work. Furthermore, there is some evidence that women are disproportionately represented amongst the long-term unemployed (Denmark 1980b).

So far we have ignored the impact of government policy on the employment situation. Since 1975, successive governments have adopted macroeconomic policies designed to place domestic demand under an increasingly tight rein and which have thereby constrained labour market expansion. We have already discussed the restrictions which have been placed on the automatic indexing of wages and the series of wage and price freezes that began in September 1978. Taxation has also been increased. VAT was first raised from 18 to 20 per cent — a move which the LO claimed added 10 000 to the numbers unemployed. It was then increased further, in June 1980, to 22 per cent as part of the package of measures enacted by Parliament which the OECD estimated would reduce domestic demand by 2 per cent (OECD 1980).

While curtailing domestic demand the Danish government have, under

Table 6.5   Unemployment in Denmark by age and sex, October 1979

		Number of unemployed (000s)	Proportion of insured persons (%)
Males aged	−24	12.6	7.5
	25−59	38.1	5.2
	60+	4.9	5.7
Total		55.6	5.6
Females aged	−24	27.5	16.7
	25−59	53.0	10.2
	60−	2.7	9.2
Total		83.2	11.5
Total		138.8	8.0

Source: Denmark 1980b.

intense pressure from the LO, simultaneously adopted a number of innovative measures designed to stimulate employment growth. Two employment bills were introduced in 1976 and 1977 respectively. The second (B11) — associated with what has come to be called the Second or August Compromise — involved public expenditure of the order of 10 billion Kr between 1977 and 1980. A quarter of the funds were to be directed towards increasing employment in agriculture, forestry, fishing, manufacturing industry and tourism; one-fifth each towards energy conservation and labour market policies (including direct job creation); and the remainder towards a variety of measures ranging from public construction projects to the relaxation of employers' sickness benefit obligations. Certain of the measures introduced under B11 and intended to expire in 1980 have since been extended.

The labour market measures are of special interest in that they illustrate how economic objectives — the creation of a skilled, confident and flexible labour force — may be married with social goals concerned to protect the individual from the worst effects of unemployment. Furthermore, these measures need to be seen against an unemployment insurance system which attempts to maintain a person's living standards for as long as is necessary.

Jobtilbudsordningen (job offer scheme)
The *Jobtilbudsordningen*, introduced in June 1978 as a temporary amendment to the Employment Service and Unemployment Act, obliges county Labour Market Boards (*Arbejdsmarkedsnævn, AMN*) and local

government to offer every insured long-term unemployed person a 'reasonable' job lasting for at least nine months. The aim is to return the long-term unemployed to a normal work situation so as to counteract the disabling effects of unemployment while at the same time providing on-the-job training. In macroeconomic terms the scheme is seen as contributing to the total level of employment.

For the purpose of *Jobtilbudsordninges*, the definition of long-term unemployment is restricted to persons who are in danger of losing their entitlement to unemployment benefit (*Arbejdsløshedsdagpenge*) under the '26 week rule'. This rule stipulates that *Arbejdsløshedsdagpenge* is payable only to those insured persons who have worked for 26 weeks within the last three, or exceptionally, four years (see below). Consequently, the relatively small number of people likely to benefit under this scheme (about 10 000 per year) are among the most disadvantaged with regard to employment opportunities.

Placing persons in suitable employment has not proved easy. It had been hoped that large numbers of people would be found jobs in the private sector and to this end the government is prepared to grant employers a subsidy 'towards the cost of retraining' of 22 Kr per hour for the first 13 weeks, declining to 11 Kr per hour for the last 13. This subsidy is only available if the job offer increases the level of employment in the undertaking concerned. In practice, so few job offers were forthcoming from the private sector that local authorities have been forced to provide posts themselves or to find openings in other public or publicly supported organisations (Table 6.6).

Table 6.6   *The job offer scheme for long-term unemployed: offers, October 1978 – June 1979*

	Males	Females	Total
Private sector	723	927	1650
Municipalities	1656	2975	4631
Other public employment	293	454	747
Total number of job placements	2672	4356	7028
Refusals	1216	2199	3415
Total number of persons	3888	6555	10443

Source: Denmark 1980b.

Youth unemployment measures

The employment plan B11 also placed a responsibility on local authorities to set up initiatives to counteract unemployment among under 25-year-olds. The Youth Unemployment Programme (*Foranstaltninger vedr. afhjælpning af ungdomsarbejdsløsheden*), authorised under Act No 488 which came into force on 14 September 1977, was designed to supplement general employment and education policies and was very much modelled on UK initiatives. However, as with other recent Danish social legislation, the Act provided the maximum scope for local initiatives and sought to encourage local authorities to set priorities and initiate projects sympathetic to their local labour markets.

Under the scheme local authorities were able to launch special employment projects for young people; to give subsidies to private organisations so as to reduce the wages and training costs of employing additional young people; to initiate or subsidise training courses and information and guidance provisions for young people; and to establish special apprecticeships and training posts within the local authorities themselves. An amount of 500 million Kr was to be allocated for each of the years 1978, 1979 and 1980 with about 6 per cent of the costs falling on local authorities. (The local government contribution represents about 40 Kr and 20 Kr per head of the population for local and county authorities respectively.)

A pilot project is also under way in two counties to determine the vaue of a 'guarantee' of further education, training or employment for all unemployed persons aged under 25 years. The emphasis is on education with individual assessment and vocation guidance envisaged and, in appropriate cases, preparatory courses to equip candidates for entry to their desired training. Employment of at least nine months' duration will be offered to those who refuse further training. It is anticipated that a full national scheme will be implemented in 1982.

Relief projects

The Danish government has traditionally financed public relief schemes but in recent years the number of state-subsidised employment projects (*Beskæftigelsesarbejder efter a-lovens* § 97a) has grown substantially and the proportion of places taken by young persons (aged under 25) has been increased to almost two-thirds (1979). Projects are normally initiated by county and local authorities although some schemes have been sponsored by private individuals, non-profit concerns and central government. In order to qualify for the subsidy (based on a fixed rate per hour of employment generated), projects have to receive approval from the AMN.

Efterløn (early retirement wage)

The *Lov om arbejdsformidling og arbejdsløshedsforsikring m.v.* was the first legislation to follow recommendations made by the committee on work sharing (*Udvalget af 1977 om Fordeling af Arbejdet, UFA*) established under the August Compromise II in 1977. Under this scheme, members of recognised unemployment insurance funds between the ages of 60 and 66 are permitted to retire and to receive a 'wage' equivalent to *Arbejdsløshedsdagpenge* (subject, from June 1980, to a maximum of 81 693 Kr per annum) for as long as he/she would have been entitled to benefit (i.e. 2½ years maximum). After this period the retirement wage decreases to 80 per cent of the benefit for a two-year period and thereafter to 60 per cent until the person reaches the retirement age of 67. Certain restrictions are imposed; for example, to be eligible persons must have been members of recognised insurance funds for 5 of the 10 years prior to retirement.

The objective of the scheme is to release jobs for younger people by permitting early retirement and by easing the financial transition from employment to retirement. *Arbejdsløshedsdagpenge* generally amounts to 90 per cent of previous earnings (up to a maximum) which means that for most people the scheme provides a gradual tapering of income. It is particularly attractive to older workers who may retain 90 per cent of earnings until they become eligible for an old-age pension and for low paid workers who are unlikely to be hit by the benefit ceiling.

The *Efterløn* scheme, which is administered by the unemployment insurance funds rather than the government, does not place any obligation on employers to fill posts vacated. Moreover, the scheme is open to the unemployed — providing they are eligible for *Arbejdsløshedsdagpenge* — and also to the self-employed. It is clear, therefore, that the job-replacement ratio (i.e. the ratio of posts filled to posts vacated) resulting from this legislation is unlikely to approach anything near unity (see below).

The *Efterløn* scheme has also been justified (Denmark 1980b) in terms of its direct social benefit, namely releasing the tired and frail from the burden of demanding labour. In this respect, the legislation may be seen as a small step towards bringing the high Danish statutory retirement age (67) more into line with that of other European countries.

Other redistributive measures

A number of other schemes designed to distribute existing employment have recently been introduced or are currently under discussion. The renewal of collective agreements on 1 March 1979 increased holiday entitlement from four to five weeks. The increase was introduced in order to compensate for the loss of two indexed increments as part of the wage-freeze and was staged over two years. In January 1980, the Committee on Work Sharing (UFA) produced a report which included a draft Bill designed to reduce overtime (UFA 1979). Under the provisions of the Bill the amount of annual overtime would be set at 200 hours per year for each employee with all overtime compensated for by time off in lieu (on an hour-for-hour basis). Overtime bonus would still be payable either in the form of cash or as an additional payment in lieu. The recommendation would not affect existing collective agreements which include restrictions on overtime and provisions for compulsory rests.

Finally, following the joint report of the Council on Equality (*Ligestillingsrädet*) and the Commission on Children (*Børnekommissionen*) published in 1978, legislation is expected to provide the right of absence and protection against dismissal in connection with pregnancy and confinement (*Børnekommissionen*, 1978).

Training

In the interests of developing a skilled and flexible labour force the Danish government has long provided vocational training schemes. In recent years, the number on vocational training schemes provided by the Danish government has been greatly increased and new courses have been introduced tailored specifically to the needs of the unemployed. Under the 'Rearrangement' of the Ausust 1977 Employment Act in 1979 additional funds have been allocated to existing vocational training and new funds provided for training in the fields of commerce and trade. Even so the increase in the number of training places provided has not kept pace with increased unemployment.

A significant motivation in the development of courses has been the considerable concern expressed in Denmark over the so-called 'paradox problem', i.e. the coexistence of large numbers of unemployed and employment vacancies. The discussion has drawn attention to special employment surveys which have shown a pronounced tendency for job offers presented to employment offices to be turned down or to result in employment of unexpectedly short duration (OECD 1980). Research findings, notably those published recently by *Landsarbejdsnævnet* (LAN, National Labour Board), have demonstrated that there is often a mismatch between job requirements — primarily for skilled labour, especially in the private sector — and the qualifications of job seekers who are predominantly unskilled men, women and young people with relatively little experience (*Landsarbejdsnævnet*, 1980).

Vocational training in Denmark falls into two categories: general and specific. The former, which is the responsibility of local Labour Market Boards (AMN), is intended mainly for employed workers who wish to enhance their skills although the number of unemployed candidates has increased rapidly in recent years. Specific training is planned centrally by the *Direktoratet for Arbejdsmarkedsuddannelser* (Directorate for Adult Vocational Training) and is of much more recent origin. Two separate work experience courses are provided, one (*Erhvervsintroducerende Kurser for Unge, EIFU*) for unemployed persons between 15 and 25 years of age and one for the long-term unemployed (*Erhvervsintroducerende Kurser for Langtidsledige, EIFL*).

Evaluation of labour market policies

To what extent do the measures described above reduce the levels of unemployment or, more especially, how far have they facilitated the employment of those most at risk in the labour market, namely women and young people?

The introduction of the early retirement scheme (*Efterløn*) in January 1979 seems to have resulted in a marked but one-off reduction in unemployment. Almost 50 000 took early retirement in the first year of the scheme, which was three times the number anticipated and half of all those eligible. Sixty per cent of applicants retired from employment while the remainder were drawn from the lists of unemployed. Approximately 75 per cent of the 30 000 jobs released by the scheme were subsequently filled but it is impossible to say how many unemployed benefited directly or indirectly from these vacancies. To the extent that most of the jobs were for unskilled or semi-skilled workers, many of the unemployed could have been potential beneficiaries. On the other hand, only 22 per cent of the posts were previously occupied by women although women constituted 59.9 per cent of the unemployed in October 1979. Because of the popularity of the scheme in the first year its potential for releasing jobs was rapidly exhausted. Not surprisingly, relatively few jobs were released in 1980 and the numbers becoming available in future years can be expected to rise only very gradually.

The job offer scheme (*Jobtilbudsordningen*), which is demand led, has had to offer 2500 posts each quarter. Assuming all posts last the statutory nine months (some last longer), the scheme will be contributing some 7500 jobs at any one time. However, more important criteria of success are first, the number of posts which remain in existence after nine months and which therefore constitute a gain in employment and, secondly, the number of people who remain in the post or readily obtain alternative employment as a consequence of work experience acquired under the scheme. Unfortunately, no information is available although, intriguingly, of those offered jobs under the scheme in 1979 about 40 per cent declined to take them. This has been interpreted in some quarters as evidence that official unemployment figures are inflated due to the inclusion of significant numbers of people who are not genuinely seeking work (OECD 1980).

Table 6.7 summarises the impact of measures to combat youth

Table 6.7   Special employment and training offers to young unemployed persons under the age of 25 (1 January — 31 December 1978)

		Males	Females	Total
I	Relief projects	7 240	6 960	14 200
II	Support to employment in private undertakings	1 800	700	2 500
III	EIFU courses	1 500	4 500	6 000
IV	Apprenticeships and training places in private undertakings	3 300	2 100	5 400
V	Apprenticeships and training places in public undertakings	430	1 200	1 630
VI	Contributions to fees paid by students of folk high schools, etc.	240	390	630
VII	Other municipal activities in connection with training, etc.	300	600	900
I—VII	Total	14 810	16 450	31 260
VIII	Courses initiated by the county authorities — estimated figure			2 500
IX	Payment of unemployment benefits during courses at folk high schools etc.			1 300
X	Courses at commercial or technical schools (financed by the State)			300
XI	Courses for long-term unemployed			1 200
I—XI	Total number of persons benefiting from extraordinary measures for young persons			36 860

Source: Denmark 1980b.

unemployment in 1978 when unemployment among those aged under 25 was 13 per cent. (The table conceals an indeterminate degree of double counting due to people benefiting under more than one scheme.) The measures have succeeded in limiting youth unemployment in the short term and, adopting a longer term perspective, must constitute an investment in the labour force which should pay dividends later. However, the biggest single initiative is relief work which is generally limited to 26 weeks and provides precious little work training. Furthermore, it may be that despite government insistence that projects undertaken through relief work would not have been carried out otherwise, relief work represents merely a redistribution of employment towards the young and, perhaps, a redistribution forward in time which thereby reduces future employment opportunities. It has even been argued, by no less a body than the OECD (1980), that relief work actually encourages unemployment by qualifying young people for higher unemployment benefits and thereby lessening work incentives once relief work has ceased.

Some doubts have also been expressed about the effectiveness of special training schemes. Surveys (cited in Denmark 1980b) have shown that while almost 60 per cent of participants take up employment on completion of an EIFU course, over half of these obtain short-term posts in public employment projects. The 40 per cent who do not take up employment are equally divided between those who seek further training and those who return to unemployment. EIFU courses may therefore serve merely to postpone unemployment for between 20 and 70 per cent of participants.

Available evidence makes it difficult to determine whether people graduating from adult training schemes face similar problems in obtaining stable employment. However, it is known that only 62 per cent of trainees on courses for the semi-skilled have guaranteed employment on completion of the course so that the remainder must presumably spend at least some time unemployed. Indeed, a comparison for 1979 of the proportion of semi-skilled trainees who were employed directly prior to training with the proportion who had employment awaiting them on completion of their training reveals no change at all in their employment prospects (Pedersen 1981).

Benefits for the Sick and Unemployed

The distinctive character of Danish social policy is most apparent with respect to the benefits provided for people temporarily excluded from the labour market. Specifically, the long standing policy objective to try and maintain a person's standard of living during temporary loss of income determines the structure of both insurance and assistance benefits. Consequently insurance benefits for sickness (*Sygedagpenge*) and unemployment (*Arbejdsløshedsdagpenge*) are paid at 90 per cent of the previous gross wage which means that benefit levels are generally much higher than in most other European countries (but see below). Benefits are also payable for longer periods: *Sygedagpenge* is payable indefinitely, for five weeks by the employer in the case of employees and thereafter by the State; and *Arbejdsløshedsdagpenge* for three and a half years. As a consequence of the high level of benefits, supplementation by social assistance is seen as necessary only to meet exceptional needs and, unlike most other countries, assistance is not usually payable to persons who are eligible for social security benefits (Lawson 1980, see also below).

The level and duration of *Arbejdsløshedsdagpenge* has not been without its critics, most notably among the Conservative and Progressive parties. It has been argued that benefits are too high when account is taken of the expenses associated with full-time employment (transport, child care, etc.), high marginal tax rates and the indirect benefits associated with redundancies and that this, in part, explains the coexistence of high numbers of unemployed and vacancies (OECD 1980).

However, the Danish approach to social provision for those temporarily excluded from the labour force can be defended on a number of grounds. Recourse to natural justice demands that no person should be (further) punished for not working when the fault is not their own. Such an argument has added force when unemployment is used as an aspect of demand management as has been the case in Denmark for much of the 1970s. A second argument voiced strongly in Denmark is that decisions pressurised by unaccustomed shortage of income are unlikely to be wise or beneficial, either for the individual or for the community (Westergaard 1980). Moreover, the security of adequate financial support in the event of unemployment may make the labour force more willing to facilitate technical change and thereby to foster increased productivity. Taking a more pragmatic approach, Danish research has shown that most cases of social hardship are very short-lived (Mortensen 1977), with the implication that in normal circumstances the costs of generous provision may not be excessive. A final consideration relates to the long-term repercussions (debt, marital instability, etc.) which may result from financial hardship and which can place even greater demands on the public purse.

The immediately preceding argument was instrumental in the major reforms of social legislation during the early 1970s and held sway in Denmark throughout the rest of the decade in spite of a slack economy and markedly increased levels of taxation. The rate of *Arbejdsløshedsdagpenge* (i.e. the daily cash benefit − *Dagpenge-maksimum*) was increased from 80 to 90 per cent of previous gross income (*d.v.s. samlede indtjening frankrukket overarbejdsbetaling*) in 1970; and the maximum amount payable has risen from about two-fifths of average earnings in 1969 to 90 per cent in 1980 − a ratio which is fixed by statute and adjusted twice a year in line with inflation. (In practice, the second ratio is somewhat less than 90 per cent because the administrative definition of average wages relates to the preceding year, see Table 6.1.)

Likewise, an Act of 1972 replaced the flat-rate sickness benefit with one related to previous earnings. (*Sygedagpenge* and *Arbejdsløshedsdagpenge* are both taxable.) The grave unemployment situation in 1977 resulted in a temporary relaxation of the so-called '26 weeks rule': entitlement to *Arbejdsløshedsdagpenge* became conditional upon 26 weeks' work within the last four years prior to unemployment rather than within the last three years. At the same time a 'moratorium' was introduced so that in 1978 no person lost entitlement to *Arbejdsløshedsdagpenge* due to their length of unemployment.

The sickness and unemployment schemes differ both in the method of funding and (see below) administration. The system of cash sickness benefits (*Sygedagpenge*), which complements a comprehensive and largely 'free' health-care service, is financed by a 10 per cent tax on income and covers the entire economically active population (with voluntary insurance for the self-employed). Employers do not make regular contributions to the sickness scheme but are obliged to pay benefit during the first five weeks of illness and are only refunded for weeks 4 and 5. (Small employers may insure against the expense incurred.)

Unemployment insurance (*Arbejdsløshedsdagpenge*), which is technically voluntary (but see below), is funded from fixed contributions made by employers (522 Kr for the second and additional employees, 1980) and employees (783 Kr) and by an increasing state subsidy (UK 1980). In 1968, the state paid 82 per cent of the cost of *Arbejdsløshedsdagpenge* (itself the highest proportion of any year in the 1960s) against 11 per cent by insured employees and 7 per cent by employers (Kaim-Caudle 1973). In 1980, the corresponding figures were 88, 8 and 4 per cent (Denmark 1980d).

Recent amendments to the Employment Service and Unemployment Insurance Act (*Lov om Arbejdsformidling og Arbejdsløshedsforsikring m.v.*) have tightened up the administration of benefits to prevent alleged abuse, especially in respect of the rules governing part-time employment. Legislation permits part-time workers to insure against unemployment and to draw *Arbejdsløshedsdagpenge* commensurate with their previous earnings. It also enables full-time insured workers to work part-time and to claim benefits for the hours they are not working. Amendments in 1979 restricted the time for which part-time insured workers can receive benefit (12 weeks in any year) and made it a condition that full-time insured workers should only receive benefit if they were prepared to accept full-time work when on offer. Equally, no person was to be allowed to benefit financially through part- or full-time unemployment nor, whilst receiving *Arbejdsløshedsdagpenge*, to undertake work that would normally have been offered as 'proper paid work'. The amendments also closed a loophole under which employers had been reducing labour costs by laying off employees over bank holidays only to re-employ them immediately afterwards.

Although regulated and largely financed by central government, *Arbejdsløshedsdagpenge* is administered by the unemployment insurance funds. The 57 (1980) recognised funds are effectively private associations comprising wage earners or self-employed persons and have traditonally been closely connected with individual trade unions. Indeed, although membership of the funds is technically voluntary, trade union rules frequently oblige members to join. (Non-union members are not prohibited from joining a fund but union membership is effectively a condition of employment in many occupations.) The role of the funds differentiates unemployment benefit from other branches of Danish social policy, including *Sygedagpenge* provisions, where the state is the predominant agent of social welfare. Also by making eligibility for benefit dependent on membership of the fund, and, through application of the '26 weeks rule', on a person's contribution record, unemployment insurance departs from the principle of entitlement by way of Danish residency which is enshrined in most other social legislation. (Mortensen 1977.)

In 1979, 30.6 per cent of workers (25.7 and 36.8 per cent of men and women respectively) were not covered by unemployment insurance, with the slightly higher proportion of women reflecting the fact that almost two-thirds of part-time employees are uninsured. A significant number of those without insurance cover will be civil servants who have *de facto* tenure of employment but unfortunately no information is available which facilitates a comparison of the extent of insurance cover between industrial sectors and skill levels. However, a simple comparison between the proportion of insured in work (69.4 per cent) and in unemployment (88.3 per cent) suggests that those without insurance tend on average to face a lower risk of unemployment (Denmark 1980c). Nevertheless, between 1973 and 1977 operation of the '26 weeks rule', together with the voluntary nature of insurance, resulted in a 16-fold increase in the number of uninsured unemployed (see below).

Inevitably, the earnings-related nature of Danish unemployment and sickness benefits mean that the remaining inequalities of the labour market are, to some extent, projected or 'mapped' onto those who are out of work. The extent of 'mapping' is limited however by the ceiling imposed by the *Dagpenge-maksimum* which, in practice, is less than 80 per cent of average male earnings (see Table 6.1). Around two-thirds of unemployed men and one-third of women were affected by this ceiling and consequently receive less than 90 per cent of previous earnings. It is not clear to what extent the upper limit of *Dagpenge-maksimum* is determined by pragmatic considerations of cost or perceived disincentive effects rather than with respect to egalitarian objectives. However, the effect is to reduce considerably the dispersal of benefit payments at the inevitable expense of another policy objective, namely the maintenance of living standards resulting from temporary loss of earnings.

When entitlement to *Arbejdsløshedsdagpenge* is exhausted or, as with school leavers, no insurance contributions have been made, a person will usually be eligible for (means-tested) social assistance. Unlike most other countries, the transition from insurance to assistance benefits does not necessarily entail a drop in living standards. Two forms of assistance are payable under the 1974 Social Assistance Act (*Vijstandsloven*): temporary assistance (*Midlertigid hjælp*) and continuing assistance (*Varig hjælp*). *Varig hjælp* consists of standardised benefits for people without prospects of returning to the labour force. The payments are essentially equal to national minimum pension levels and consequently are low in relation to average wages (see Table 6.1). However, most unemployed would be entitled to *Midlertigid hjælp*, which is intended to maintain a family's living standard and is payable up to a maximum which would not normally exceed 90 per cent of a claimant's previous income. *Midlertigid hjælp* has two regular components:

(a) A maintenance allowance, paid at standard rates, to cover essential needs such as food and clothing;
(b) An allowance for fixed expenses to include items such as rent, insurance, utilities and hire-purchase.

In addition, claimants may be entitled to an allowance under the housing allowance scheme (*Boligsikring*) although this would be taken into account in assessing benefit.

Lawson (1980), in his review of Danish social assistance, identified three distinctive features:

(a) the emphasis on maintaining living standards which has already been stressed;
(b) the development of social security such that social assistance provides only supplementation to meet exceptional needs;
(c) an emphasis on the integration of financial aid (social assistance is administered and 50 per cent financed by the 257 local authorities) with employment services, practical social work and counselling.

However, these objectives have proved difficult to meet as public expenditure has been reduced and the numbers receiving assistance, particularly the unemployed, have grown. In 1969/70, under the old system of social assistance, 95 739 people claimed benefit, that is approximately

4.3 per cent of the population aged 18 to 66. By 1974/5 these figures had risen to 100 079 to 200 091 and 7.5 per cent (UK 1978) and in 1977, under the new scheme, 190 384 and 500 259 were in receipt of temporary and continuing assistance respectively. As recently as 1973, only 1358 persons were unemployed and not entitled to unemployment benefit, but by 1977, the roughly comparable figure of unemployed persons claiming temporary assistance had soared to 22 219 (Denmark 1980b). It will be interesting to see whether this extreme situation leads to attempts to simplify and standardise social assistance as has already happened in the UK.

Concluding Remarks

Denmark has succeeded in eradicating poverty, both absolute and relative, from the political and social consciousness. Most Danes believe that poverty no longer exists and are content that it is adequately prevented by the state system of social protection. This is not to say that the existence of inequality is denied (see Duvå 1976), but rather that egalitarian policies, particularly in respect of the labour market, are believed to have been markedly successful. This is certainly the view of the Social Democratic government and, with minor reservations, of the trade union movement.

As a result of the lack of interest in poverty and inequality, little material is available which permits an assessment of the success of Danish policies when compared with those of other European countries. Certainly, the centralised nature of wage bargaining facilitates an egalitarian approach and government attempts to redistribute labour through, for example, the early retirement wage, have been taken further than elsewhere in Europe. Likewise, the social security system is unique in that it is founded on the belief that socially constructive decisions are fostered by the longer term maintenance of living standards. However, these policies have been shown not always to fulfil their stated objectives. Moreover, government's failure to stem the increase in unemployment is resulting in problems of a new order of magnitude while at the same time the slackening rate of economic growth is beginning to reveal the high costs of social provision.

Set against a ground swell of opinion that tax rates are too high, respected authorities are now arguing that the trend towards equality has gone too far for the good of the Danish economy. Already government measures such as increased VAT, modifications to the price index and the forgoing of indexed pay increases have differentially affected the less advantaged. Ironically, if these trends continue, Denmark may yet be forced to rediscover poverty.

Denmark: Policies to Combat Unemployment and Low Incomes 183

References

Bidstrup, K. 1976, 'Living standards' in M. K. Bjørnsen and E. Hansen (eds), *Facts about Denmark*, Copenhagen, Politikens Forlag.

Boeck, P. *et al.* 1977, *Poverty in Denmark*, Copenhagen, Danish Low Income Commission, Mimeo.

Børnekommissionen, 1978, *Barselsorlov* (joint report by the Børnekommissionen and Ligestillingsrådet).

Carlsen, P. 1977, *The Danish trade union movement*, Copenhagen, Landsorganisationen i Danmark.

Dean, A. J. H. 1980, *Pay bargaining arrangements in Denmark, Finland, France and the United States*, London, National Institute of Economic and Social Research, Mimeo.

Denmark 1980a, *Dansk økonomi, December 1980*, Copenhagen, Det økonomiske Råd.

Denmark 1980b, *Labour market and labour market policies: report on the development in Denmark in 1979*, Copenhagen, Ministry of Labour, (Arbejdsdirektoratet) Economic-statistic Adviser.

Denmark 1980c, *Statistisk arbog*, Copenhagen, Denmark.

Denmark 1980d, *Description of the Danish unemployment system*, Copenhagen, Ministry of Labour (Arbjsdsdirektoratet) 2.kt.j.nr.80,- 7/79.

Duvå, V. 1976, 'Social welfare' in M. K. Bjørnsen and E. Hansen (eds), *Facts about Denmark*, Copenhagen, Politikens Forlag.

EC 1977, *The perception of poverty in Europe*, Brussels, Commission of the European Communities.

EC 1979, *The European social budget 1980—1975—1970*, Brussels, Commission of the European Communities.

Hansen, B. 1969, *Velstand unden velfoerd*, Copenhagen, Fremad.

Kaim-Caudle, P. R. 1973, *Comparative Social Policy and Social Security*, London, Martin Robertson.

Landsarbejdsnævnet (LAN) 1980, *Rapport om landsarbejdsnævnets undersøgelse af den samtidige forekomst af legigbed og ubesatte pladser (Paradox II)*, Copenhagen, LAN, June.

Lawson, R. 1980, *Social assistance in Denmark*. Report prepared for the European Commission, mimeo.

Mortensen, E. A. 1977, *Social security, Danish style*, Copenhagen, Ministry of Foreign Affairs, Fact Sheet.

OECD 1978, *Denmark*, OECD Economic Surveys, Paris.

OECD 1979, *Denmark*, OECD Economic Surveys, Paris.

OECD 1980, *Denmark*, OECD Economic Surveys, Paris.

Pedersen, K. 1981, *Minute concerning the number of participants in and expenses for labour market education*, Copenhagen, Ministry of Labour (Arbejdsdirektoratet).

Pedersen, P. J. 1976, 'Long-run trends in the occupational and geographical wage structure in Denmark*, Nationalokronomisk Tidsskrift.

Petersen, J. M. 1976, *Aspects of the development in social protection in Denmark in the period 1965 to 1975*, Brussels EEC Working Group on concentration of Social Protection, Working Paper DK, January.

Socialdemokratiet, 1973, *Kravet om lighed*, Copenhagen, Forlaget Fremad.

Trier, A. 1977, *Financing of social security in Denmark*, Mimeo.

UFA 1979, *Betænkning om begræning af overarbejde og om afspadsering*, (Udvalget af 1977 om Fordeling af Afspadsering), Copenhagen, Schultz Bogtryk.

UK 1978, *Public assistance in Denmark*, Social Assistance Review, Working Paper 32, London, Department of Health and Social Security.

UK 1980, *Social benefit tables for member states of the European Communities: position at 1 January 1980*, London, Department of Health and Social Security.

Westergaard, K. 1980, *Talk given at the 'Responses to Poverty' seminar*, Civil Service College, Sunningdale, 20 May.

Part III   Family Policies and Poverty
*Editorial Overview**

The term 'family policy' can refer to a wide range of social policies concerned with relationships between the sexes and the generations (see Land 1978). However, it is used here in the narrower sense of collective provision towards sharing the costs of children. Thus the chapters on France, West Germany and The Netherlands in this part examine measures such as family allowances or child benefits, tax allowances and payments made for children in social insurance and assistance schemes. Some attempt is also made to take account of other social services in which the costs of children are affected.

The Development of Family Policies

Family allowances and other measures supplementing family income are an important means of reducing inequality between rich and poor and certainly have a crucial role to play in any state action against poverty. Historically, however, other considerations have often been more influential. During the first half of this century, statutory family benefits were introduced in a number of European countries — as different as Sweden, France and Nazi Germany — for overtly pro-natalist reasons. There were also distinctly nationalistic overtones and, in some instances, eugenicist influences with their bias against 'the poorer stock'. In Nazi Germany, the elaborate Aryan family policies stressed 'the moral and patriotic duty of bearing children for Hitler's Reich — within wedlock if possible, without if it necessary' (Shirer 1960).

In addition, the early family allowances enjoyed considerable support amongst liberal and conservative opinion as a means of aiding labour mobility, promoting work incentives and discipline and keeping wages down. For the same reasons, labour movements, including most of the British trade unions and some of the early women's organisations, were often fervent opponents of this kind of family support. The arguments

*Roger Lawson took lead responsibility for this overview.

and counter-arguments were fuelled by reports of the French experience. It was claimed, for example, by a director of the French Family Allowance Fund, that

> the payment of [family] allowances had prevented trade unions from making use of family men for helping in their 'revolutionary' aims, [and] the majority of family men among workers had remained outside the 'class struggle'. (quoted in Field 1982)

Since the end of the Second World War, by contrast, the sources of support for family policies in most countries have been concerned more explicitly with the welfare of children and their families. However, this still embraces a variety of ideological concepts and practical targets, as is well illustrated in the three countries examined here. In West Germany, the reaction against Nazi policies led initially to a reassertion of traditional family obligations and assumptions about the family's superiority over other social institutions (Dahrendorf 1965). It was widely held that the primary aim of a 'family policy' should be to preserve the autonomy and cohesion of the family, and that the most effective measures were constitutional guarantees and legal safeguards designed to protect marriage, family ties and parental prerogative. Many social welfare measures, including family allowances, were viewed with suspicion because of their intrusion into family responsibilities. Moreover, as an official report observed, family policy 'had to dissociate itself from the reproach that it was, even if not explicitly, an instrument of population policy, and that children's allowances were bonuses which...favoured those who without restraint brought children into the world.' (*Sozialenquete* 1965).

Since the early years of the Federal Republic such attitudes have gradually given way to newer concepts of child support. Significantly, the changes were at first prompted by a concern with maintaining economic growth. The 1960s saw a lively debate on the family's influence in promoting economic advance and on the role of 'social investment', though its impact was felt more in education than in social security and the social services. As the West German chapter stresses, more important changes occurred during the past decade or so under the aegis of the Social Democratic-Liberal coalition. At least, the aspirations of policy makers have now moved closer to those found in Scandinavia, with their emphasis on recognising and accepting 'irregular' forms of family life, improving the status of mothers and children and helping the disadvantaged. As will be evident, in practice not all has changed so much, especially for the lone parent or immigrant worker's family.

A similar shift in priorities towards poorer families and those with special needs, such as one-parent families, has been apparent during the past decade in France. Compared with most other European countries, however, France has long had 'a more conscious, clearly defined concept of a family policy, which finds expression firstly, in statutory and volun- tary institutions whose primary or even sole purpose is to promote the welfare of the family, and secondly, in a whole range of statutory bene- fits to which the parents of the nuclear family are entitled as of right' (Rodgers 1975). Since 1945, but especially during the 1950s and 1960s, these measures have been an extremely important source of income for many French families, entailing high social expenditures. In the early 1960s, for example, family allowance expenditures alone exceeded those on state pensions, whereas in the UK the costs of family allowances were less than one-seventh of the costs of pensions (ILO 1972). Unlike the Scandinavian countries, where family expenditures have also been high. '*la politique familiale*' has traditionally been distinguished by its empha- sis on a horizontal rather than vertical redistribution of family costs. Moreover, until recently, the policies were designed mainly to com- pensate 'normal' families for the costs of child-rearing, partly because of the continuing concern with the birth rate but more generally to strengthen the family as an economic unit and social institution. Another feature of French policies — with important consequences for women, especially lone parents — has been the notion that family allowances are a '*sursalaire*' or supplementary wage, financed by employers, and hence the emphasis on employment in an occupation covered by social insur- ance as the basis of most rights to benefits.

The French chapter reveals how, since the early 1970s, policies have begun to adapt both to changing attitudes to women's and children's rights and also to the discovery that even the relatively generous family benefits have by no means eliminated family poverty. From our pers- pective, the most interesting aspects of this change have been the intro- duction of new 'social minimum' benefits, including a special allowance for lone parents, and the move towards a more selective approach to family allowances. Compared with selectivity in the UK, the French version appears to have certain advantages, not least because of the con- tinuing importance of more wide-ranging universal benefits. Nevertheless, recent reports suggest that the French are increasingly concerned with the complications of official procedures associated with means-testing (compare Sinfield 1980) and with the problems of defining acceptable minimum standards.

Important developments have also been taking place recently in The Netherlands. Indeed, of the three countries in this section, the Dutch have undertaken the most systematic review of family policies. The Dutch chapter reports this in some detail, and it will be seen that it has embraced fundamental questions about the basic costs of children and the lifecycle of family needs. The deteriorating economic situation has also helped focus attention on the risks of family life, especially for the growing numbers of lone parents. Prior to this, Dutch family policies have had a relatively uneventful history, more or less free from demographic controversies. Family allowances have formed an integral part of the social security system since the 1940s, but have had little to do with the attack on poverty. Other policies, including the statutory minimum wage, have sought to achieve that objective. Family allowances and tax policies have been more concerned, and quite explicitly so, with redistributing income to those with family responsibilities within each income group. It is the consequences of this policy which are now being seriously questioned. Various studies have shown a general lack of correspondence between incomes and the extent of family responsibilities, but with the problem much more acute for poorer and larger families than was previously appreciated. Similarly, there has been growing concern with the extent of poverty amongst lone parents. The Dutch report on poverty prepared for the European Commission shows lone-parent families to be most at risk: more than a third of lone parents have incomes below the national assistance norm (EC 1981).

The EC's final report on poverty reveals how problems like these are evident throughout Europe. No government can yet claim to have developed clear and well thought out policies to combat poverty due to family responsibilities or low earnings. More generally, most governments have been slow to recognise the extent to which certain economic and social forces have tended to develop adversely to the interests of the family. As Margaret Wynn observed, at a time when it was unfashionable to talk about such trends, post-war welfare state developments have often been biased against families. While the prolongation of education has placed a greater burden on families, other costs of bringing up children have risen rapidly in Western countries. At the same time,

> the great majority of recipients of pensions, sickpay, medical services, unemployment pay are non-parents . . . . The extension of these services has therefore reduced substantially the resources available to parents for bringing up the next generation at a time when the rearing of children is becoming an ever more exacting and expensive task. (Wynn 1970)

In most countries, there is now ample evidence to support this, and indeed to show how the working mother, whose job is now increasingly vulnerable, has done far more than post-war governments to raise the standard of living of her family. Unless account is taken of these broader trends, it is difficult to see how family poverty can be adequately tackled.

Comparisons of Child Support and Family Poverty

A comparison of the current value of child support in the European Community is provided by Bradshaw and Piachaud (1980). Their approach was to calculate what, under normal circumstances, a number of model families of different size and different income levels should be receiving by way of family allowances, taxation and the principal social services. Although the study (which was restricted to two-parent families with a working head) revealed a wide diversity in the pattern and value of benefits in 1980, it also showed that the levels of child support in France, Belgium and Luxembourg were consistently ahead of other countries while those in Italy and Ireland lagged behind.

Table III.1   The value of child support in selected countries, 1980

| | Earnings[1] | Additional income[2] as a % of net income[3] of a couple with no children | | |
		1 child	*2 children*	*4 children*
France	a	15.2	34.1	101.9
	b	6.4	20.7	68.1
	c	2.0	9.5	45.0
The Netherlands	a	6.8	17.8	41.5
	b	5.0	13.1	30.5
	c	1.4	5.2	16.3
West Germany	a	7.5	18.4	53.9
	b	3.0	8.8	33.7
	c	2.2	6.2	22.0
UK	a	9.6	24.1	54.6
	b	6.1	12.1	25.1
	c	4.0	8.1	16.1

1 (a) Two-thirds average earnings; (b) Average earnings; (c) One-and-a-half times average earnings. Estimated earnings for January 1980.
2 After family allowances, social security tax, education and health gains and losses, and housing allowances.
3 Net income of couple equals gross income less income tax and social security contributions.

Source: Adapted from Bradshaw and Piachaud 1980.

Table III.1 summarises the Bradshaw and Piachaud findings with respect to the countries featured in this volume, and Table III.2 relates the level of child support to the child element included in the international poverty standard. It can be seen that the government's contribution towards the 'costs' of children increases with family size in France and

Table III.2   *Child support in relation to the international poverty standard, selected countries, 1980*[1]

| | Earnings | Additional income as a % of the child element in the international poverty standard[2] | | |
		1 child	2 children	4 children
France	a	52.6	60.3	79.1
	b	32.2	53.2	76.8
	c	14.7	35.7	74.2
The Netherlands	a	33.9	45.4	46.4
	b	33.9	45.5	46.5
	c	13.7	26.0	35.8
West Germany	a	33.7	42.3	54.4
	b	19.1	28.7	48.2
	c	20.1	29.0	45.1
UK	a	43.9	56.4	56.0
	b	38.6	39.3	35.8
	c	36.2	37.4	32.6

1 For definitions see Table II.1
2 As defined by Beckerman 1979; see Annex 2A above.

Source: Adapted from Bradshaw and Piachaud 1980.

West Germany but that in The Netherlands and the UK it remains more or less constant, in proportional terms, for families with more than one child. In France, child support falls markedly with income — due in large part to the withdrawal of means-tested housing benefits — whereas in West Germany and in the UK there is little difference between families on average and one-and-a-half times average income or, in The Netherlands, between families with two thirds average and average incomes. Overall, West Germany is the least generous country with respect to four of the nine categories in Table III.2, specifically those relating to small families, while France is the most generous with respect to six. In the French case, support is directed particularly toward low income and large families and, in some cases, amounts to over 75 per cent of the child element in the international poverty standard. The UK is relatively generous to one-child families but large families, especially those with average or above average incomes, are much less favoured.

Table III.3 shows the composition of child support for families on two-thirds average incomes. Virtually all the assistance in The Netherlands is provided through the child allowance system but in West Germany, and especially in France, housing allowances are very important for

*Table III.3   The composition of child support for couples at
two-thirds average earnings, selected countries, 1980*

	Additons[1]	% contribution to total child support		
		1 child	*2 children*	*4 children*
France	a	9.9	44.9	71.9
	b	−1.3	2.6	1.8
	c	91.4	52.5	26.3
	d	52.6	60.3	79.1
The Netherlands	a	100.0	100.0	101.9
	b	0	0	−1.9
	c	0	0	0
	d	33.9	45.4	46.4
West Germany	a	58.6	70.1	82.4
	b	0	0	0
	c	41.3	29.9	17.6
	d	33.7	42.3	54.4
UK	a	83.3	66.0	72.9
	b	0	18.7	16.3
	c	16.6	15.3	10.8
	d	43.9	56.4	56.0

1 (a) Family allowances, social security and income tax.
  (b) Education and health gains and losses.
  (c) Housing allowances.
  (d) Additional income as a percentage of the child element of the international
     poverty standard = 100 per cent.

Source: Adapted from Bradshaw and Piachaud, 1980.

smaller families. In the UK free education, subsidised school meals and
transport make a significant contribution to the support of families with
two and four children, although since 1980 these areas have been among
the most severely affected by legislative constraints and expenditure cuts.

Bradshaw and Piachaud's study of how the family support system
works in theory needs to be set against national studies of poverty undertaken for the European Commission which report on the actual outcome
of policies (see Table 2.26 above, EC 1981). These reveal the persistence
of a traditional problem — the combination of low earnings and large
families — and the emergence of a new one, lone parenthood. Despite
modern child benefits, families with three or more children still rank
amongst the most exposed to poverty with, in France and West Germany,
over half falling beneath the 60 per cent disposable income poverty line.

(Relative to other groups, the enhanced risk of poverty faced by large families is actually lower in France than in other countries — probably because of the structure of child support described — but this is outweighed by the generally high incidence of poverty in France.)

However, the highest incidence of poverty in most countries appears now to be found amongst lone-parent families, particularly where there is more than one child. This in turn reflects the disadvantages of women in all parts of the labour market as well as in many aspects of social security (see EC 1981).

References

Beckerman, W. 1979, *Poverty and the impact of income maintenance programmes*, Geneva, ILO.

Bradshaw, J. and Piachaud, D. 1980, *Child support in the European Community*, London, Bedford Square Press.

Dahrendorf, R. 1965, *Society and democracy in Germany*, London, Weidenfeld & Nicolson.

EC 1981, *Final report from the commission to the council on the first programme of pilot schemes and studies to combat poverty*, Brussels, European Commission.

Field, F. 1982, *Poverty and politics*, London, Heinemann.

ILO 1972, *The cost of social security*, Geneva.

Land, H. 1978, 'Who cares for the family?' *Journal of Social Policy* vol. 7.3.

Rodgers, B. 1975, 'Family policy in France', *Journal of Social Policy*, vol. 4, no. 2.

Shirer, W. 1960, *The rise and fall of the Third Reich*, London, Pan.

Sinfield, R. 1980, 'Poverty and inequality in France' in V. George and R. Lawson (eds), *Poverty and inequality in Common Market countries*, London, Routledge and Kegan Paul.

Sozialenquete 1966, *Bericht der sozialenquete kommission*, Social Sicherung in der BRD, Bonn.

Wynn, M. 1970, *Family policy*, London, Michael Joseph.

7 France: Poverty and the Family
Claude Ameline and *Robert Walker*

We should like to touch upon some aspects of family poverty in France, outline some of the main programmes and provisions which attempt to combat it, and briefly discuss how successful existing policies seem to be in helping low income families. However, it is worth noting that until relatively recently poverty has not been a major issue in France.

Some evidence of this is apparent in the legislation. Here, the difference with Britain is a significant and long-standing one. While Britain has known some form of poverty relief scheme since the seventeenth century, with the Poor Law Act gradually evolving during the first half of this century into national assistance and then into supplementary benefits, French legislation has never sought to protect everybody in need without regard to the cause. Before social security began to develop in France in the 1920s, statutory assistance was available only to a few categories of people: the sick, the elderly, poor or abandoned children and unmarried mothers. Furthermore, that assistance was nearly always restricted to hospital care or accommodation. Only the victims of industrial injuries and sometimes families in grave need could receive financial help. When statutory social insurance and family allowances were first introduced in the 1930s, their purpose was not to combat poverty but to establish a form of mutual support, *solidarité*, first between wage-earners, then between wage-earners' families and eventually among all categories of worker and family. The aim of social security was thus to redistribute income horizontally within a number of occupational or demographic groups rather than vertically between income groups.

Today, the position is somewhat different. Social insurance and social assistance have both grown considerably since the war with improving provisions for ever more categories of people and situations, and with some financial transfers from the relatively more affluent social insurance schemes to the others. Apart from legislation covering various temporary circumstances like illness, unemployment, training periods, etc., certain provisions now give a permanent right to a guaranteed minimum income to specific sections of the population:

(a) wage-earners, through the *Salaire Minimum Interprofessionnel de Croissance* (national growth wage) which, for full-time workers, amounts to 52 per cent of all employees' average earnings (see below and Chapter 3);

(b) the elderly, through the *Minimum Vieillesse* (old-age minimum pension) which represents 31.2 per cent of the net average earnings for a single person and 62.4 per cent for a couple (see Chapter 10);

(c) the disabled, who are entitled to the same minimum as the elderly.

In addition, certain families now have — or will shortly be entitled to — a minimum guaranteed income as discussed below. It remains true, however, that French legislation does not provide a general safety net that would guarantee a certain amount of resources to anyone falling outside the scope of all specialised schemes.

The limited public debate about poverty is further confirmation that it ranks rather low among political issues. The poor themselves do not have a strong voice. Few of them belong to trade unions. They generally do not form clearly defined social or geographical groups. In fact, many are isolated for one reason or another, being unemployed, retired, widowed, etc. Some are self-employed. Others are foreigners (the foreign population in France is about 3.7 million, including 1.64 million workers); as such, they are not entitled to vote in national or local elections. While there are vocal lobbies campaigning for many groups, including women and families generally, a poverty lobby does not exist apart from an organisation, called *Aide à toute Détresse — Quart Monde*, which concerns itself primarily with the most disadvantaged families where economic, social and educational problems appear to be passed from one generation to the other.

The political parties, among them the socialists and communists, who would see themselves as most receptive to the needs of the under-priviledged, have traditionally preferred to advocate fundamental reforms with a view to eradicating what they consider as the roots and permanent causes of poverty, rather than try to alleviate poverty within the framework of present society. The political debate, therefore, has always tended to concentrate on broad issues such as the constitution or the structure of the economy rather than on social assistance.

Trade unions have sometimes taken a similar approach. More importantly, while they traditionally organise and defend all categories of workers — including the low paid — they have perhaps given less attention to some of the poorest groups in the community, for instance those who have fallen, or have always been, outside the employment market. Perhaps, a reason for their attitude — and for attitudes towards poverty generally — is that France did not experience unemployment on the same scale and for the same length of time as did some other countries during the 1930s.

All these reasons have contributed to minimise or obscure the debate on poverty. One may add that the steady and fairly rapid growth of the French economy since the war (about 4.7 per cent per year on average) led many people to believe that any residual poverty would gradually and spontaneously disappear. That belief was probably reinforced by the existence of the national minimum wage and the continuous development of social insurance, family benefits and education at all levels.

From the mid-1960s onwards, such conceptions began to be challenged by a number of studies sparked off by research undertaken in the USA and elsewhere (de la Gorce 1965; Klanfer 1965; Parodi 1969). It then became increasingly apparent that poverty still existed on a substantial scale. This growing awareness helped to bring about important advances in benefits and other legislation, first in favour of the low paid, then of the elderly and the disabled.

This trend has continued over the last few years. Further research and programmes have been launched under the auspices of the EC (see Lion 1980). New measures have been or are being introduced to help families, especially those with three or more children. The present worldwide economic depression makes it more difficult to improve social benefits continuously; but it also makes it more necessary for it threatens to give a new dimension to existing poverty.

Evaluating the Extent of Poverty

Despite the growing interest taken in poverty, relatively little is known on a national basis. (Sinfield 1980). Certain aspects of the French economy and society contribute to make any assessment difficult. For instance, there are large numbers of self-employed in agriculture, trade and other services about whom there is very little information. However, the indications are that many of these, particularly those in agriculture, may have very low incomes (Scardigli 1970).

Perhaps the most common reference point used in France is the *Salaire Minimum Interprofessionnel de Croissance* (*SMIC*) or minimum wage. SMIC is a gross hourly rate and, when used as an index of poverty, adjustments have to be made to take account of the numbers of hours actually worked, and of tax and social security contributions. Another problem is that SMIC is not related to family size. Also, the fact that SMIC has tended to move ahead of the rise in prices and, to a lesser extent, in average wages may result in an exaggerated increase in measured poverty outside the employees group.

The difficulty of using SMIC and the absence of a single, official reference point such as the supplementary benefits level in the UK has meant that researchers in France have failed to agree on a definition of poverty, or even on an established group of alternative definitions. They disagree even more about the size of the problem, its causes and possible remedies. Divergencies between different schools of thought and analyses are so marked that it is unusual for one body to refer to work carried out by another (Sinfield 1980).

The picture is further complicated by the fact that many authors include in their figures various overlapping groups of people who experience serious difficulties and face some sort of 'social exclusion', such as ill-treated or maladjusted children, drug addicts, the mentally ill, the homeless, etc. Estimates of the total number of persons in poverty or socially maladjusted thus range between 15 and 28 per cent of the whole population (Lenoir 1974 and Launay 1970 respectively).

Perhaps more interesting is an investigation conducted in 1977 in the medium-sized city of Rheims, 100 miles east of Paris (Debonneuil 1978). This study found that in 1975 2000 families out of 27 000 known to the local family benefits office (i.e. 7.4 per cent) had earned income equivalent to less than SMIC for a full-time worker. (Indeed the true figure might be higher due to differential reporting of low income families to the office.)

Of the heads of these low income families, 68 per cent were wage earners working more or less irregularly, 3 per cent were self-employed (tinkers, basket makers, etc.), 8 per cent were unemployed job seekers and 21 per cent were neither working nor seeking work, generally being ill or disabled; 84 per cent of the wage earners were manual workers.

A high proportion of the heads of families (24 per cent) turned out to be single women, while an equal number were either foreign workers or married to a foreigner. In only 6 per cent of families did both the man and the woman work, as compared with 50 per cent for Rheims as a whole. None of the 2000 families were owner-occupiers (the national proportion of owner-occupiers is 47 per cent) and 67 per cent lived in social housing. Many more were probably entitled to accommodation in social housing but, aware of the very high building and maintenance costs they incur, deficit-conscious local authorities often turn down applications from people with low and irregular incomes. For these people, therefore, the problems of insufficient resources are compounded by inadequate housing. Indeed, 33 per cent of the families surveyed lived in privately rented flats or houses which were generally too small, poorly maintained and lacking some basic amenities.

The housing problems were made especially disturbing by the larger size of the families concerned. Each family averaged 2.5 children as against 1.8 for other families in Rheims and 20 per cent had four or more (compared with an average of 8 per cent). Five per cent of children were away from home in the care of the local authority, either voluntarily or following a care order. The proportion, here, was three times the local average. Fourteen per cent were considered to be mentally subnormal or had repeated two or three years at school.

The most common and permanent problem for all 2000 families, however, was lack of money. Their earned income per day and per consumption unit barely reached a quarter of the average for manual workers' families. Sixteen per cent of them did not earn any income at all during 1975. As, in France, all sickness invalidity and unemployment benefits are contributory and almost completely earnings-related, the heads of families who became ill or unemployed could receive little or no help from social insurance. They had, therefore, to rely largely on family benefits, supplemented — but in a small part — by social assistance.

Family Benefits

The desire to assist poor families has only been one influence on the development of the French system of family benefits (see Ellingson 1979; Questiaux and Fournier 1978). Family allowances originated in the nineteenth century as wage supplements provided by private employers to their workers and in order to compensate parents for the costs of child-rearing as well as to maintain them at a standard of living comparable with that of other workers. This early emphasis on horizontal redistribution is still evident in the preponderance of universal schemes and the rather late development of selective benefits which are typically justified on grounds of economy, rather than a desire to achieve vertical redistribution. It also explains why until January 1978 most family benefits were payable only to heads of families who had worked in the preceding months. Similarly, the method of financing family benefits, based on contributions from employers can also be traced to the extension of employer-based schemes. However, this principle of financing is increasingly being called into question with the down-turn in the economy. The CNPF, the French Employers' Association, advocates a gradual shift towards the general revenue financing of family benefits in order to release company funds for industrial investment (Ellingson 1979).

The pro-natalist policies of successive governments have been even more influential in the development of the French system of family support. Statutory family allowances, introduced in 1932, were intended partially to encourage a recovery in the birth rate, which had been declining steadily for 150 years and was no longer sufficient to maintain an already relatively sparse population at its existing level. Equally, the reforms of the 1970s (see below) have been stimulated by a fear amongst French policy-makers that a decline in the population would lead to grave social and economic consequences. These policies have been paralleled by a desire 'to strengthen the family as an economic unit and social institution . . . as *la cellule de base de la societé*, the primary source of a nation's stability and integrity' (Lawson 1980a).

Although less important, the goal of social equity has nevertheless been evident in the development of family support in France. The first means-tested allowance was introduced in 1948 as a cash payment to assist with housing expenses. From 1972 onwards, several new benefits took household resources into account and played some part in bringing about a greater redistribution to lower income groups. Since 1978, under the so-called *Programme de Blois*, there have been further changes including the abolition of the work requirement and an extension of coverage to the entire population (Ellingson 1979). However, some of the distributional benefits of the selective schemes are offset by the family deduction under the French progressive income tax system, which favours higher income families over other groups (see below).

As part of the moves to concentrate family benefits on the most needy groups, specific allowances were introduced in the early 1970s for orphans, handicapped children and single parents among others. However, this policy of 'diversification', together with increased means-testing, resulted in a very complex system that has recently been the object of reform. These reforms have also begun to take account of the changing employment status of women (see below).

Currently, there are more than a dozen different family benefits which (in 1978) cost 45 148 million FFr or 2.54 per cent of GDP (including fiscal provisions, the proportion of GDP for 1976 was 3.2 per cent, as against 1.9 per cent for the UK). The benefits listed in Table 7.1 are all administered by the same agency and budgeted from the same fund (*Caisse Nationale des Allocations Familiales, CNAF*). The schemes are financed entirely by contributions from employers (9 per cent of employees' earnings up to a maximum of 4470 FFr per month in 1980) and the self-employed; and over the years the CNAF has built up substantial revenues which have been used to fund the deficits in other social security programmes. These surpluses are partly a consequence of inflation, which has eroded the value of certain benefits in relation to the cost of living, while, at the same time, contributions have closely followed the upward drift of wages (Fabius 1978).

Benefits are paid to most families through the offices of the 115 local funds (*Caisses d'Allocations Familiales*). The *Caisses*, which vary markedly

Table 7.1   *Family benefits in France, 1978*

	Number of recipients (000s)	Proportion of all expenditure on Family Benefits[1] (%)
Universal benefits		
Allocation Familiales (family allowances)	4318	48.5
Allocation d'Orphelin (guardian's allowance)	1310	2.4
Allocation Prénatale (pre-natal grant)	719	2.2
Allocation Postnatale (post-natal grant)	680	2.8
Allocation d'Éducation Spéciale (special education allowance for handicapped children)	—	0.8
Means-tested benefits		
Complément Familial (family supplement)	2724	19.3
Allocation Logement (housing allowance)	2724	11.6
Allocation de Rentrée Scolaire (school clothing and equipment allowance)	2302	1.6
Allocation de Parent Isolé (lone-parent allowance)	40	1.0
Prêts aux Jeunes Mérages (loan to young couples)	—	n.a.

1 This column does not sum to 100 because the disabled adult allowance is excluded.

Source: French Embassy, London.

in size from 4000 to 800 000 family beneficiaries, are technically independent organisations managed by governing bodies composed of representatives of employers, trade unions and family associations. (Family associations are groups organised on behalf of parents and other persons with dependent children; they receive some financial support from government.)

The CNAF supervises the local *Caisses* and allocates resources. The level of all family benefits is set as a proportion of a national base amount which is uprated once or twice a year, at least in line with prices and generally by a somewhat higher percentage so as partially to reflect the growth in average earnings (but see Fabius 1978 and below). All French family benefits are tax-free.

Allocation Familiales

Allocation Familiales was the first family benefit to be introduced and is still the most important, accounting, in 1978, for 47.3 per cent of the total cost of family benefits when 4.3 million families were in receipt. It became statutory for most wage earners in 1932 and in its present form dates back to an Act of Parliament of 22 August 1946.

Allocation Familiales is a universal benefit available to persons with at least two dependent children resident in France, whether or not they are the parents of the children. It is payable for:

(a) all children under 16 (or 17) including those who have left school, but have not started work;
(b) apprentices until the age of 20;
(c) children in further or higher education until the age of 20.

The age limit of 20 also applies to young persons who are disabled or suffering from a chronic illness that prevents them from earning a living, and to girls who remain at home to look after at least two younger siblings and to keep house.

The provision for *Allocation Familiales* to be paid for the first child was abolished in 1939. This decision was governed by considerations of cost, married to a belief among policy-makers that, since most families are likely to have one child even in the absence of financial inducement, financial incentives might be more cost effective when available for the second and subsequent child. However, the Sullerot Report, while continuing to adopt a pro-natalist policy, has recently recommended that the payment of *Allocation Familiales* should begin with the first child and that levels of benefit should be increased to meet the actual cost of child-rearing (France 1978). Needless to say this proposal did not find favour with the government under President Giscard d'Estaing.

Allocations Familiales vary according to the age and number of children (Table 7.2). The French recognise that older children have greater requirements and an age allowance may be payable to children aged over 10. For reasons of economy, however, this additional allowance is not paid for the eldest child in families with fewer than three children. Moreover, the level of additional benefit is somewhat arbitrary and has been the subject of some criticism by the *Union Nationale des Associations Familiales* and by certain trade unions (Questiaux and Fournier 1978). Indeed, there is little or no consensus of opinion in France as to the cost of a child and estimates frequently have more validity as bargaining points than as empirical assessments.

The pro-natalist intentions of French family policy are evident in the high level of benefits payable to the third and fourth child. In fact, as

Table 7.2   *Allocations familiales: levels of benefit, July 1980*

	Monthly rate (FFr)	Rate as a proportion of	
		(a) SMIC (%)	(b) Average wages (%)
Total for 2 children aged under 10	251	10.3	5.3
Total for 3 children aged under 10	710	29.3	15.1
Total for 4 children aged under 10	1148	47.3	24.4
Increment for each additional child under 10	388	16.0	8.3
Increment for each child aged between 10 and 15	98	4.0	2.1
Increment for each child aged over 15[1]	175	7.2	3.7

1 With the exception of the eldest child in families with less than three children.

Source: French Embassy, London; own calculations.

recently as the *Programme de Blois* measures, benefit for the third child was increased from 38 to 41 per cent of the base amount while that for the second child remained at 23 per cent. Clearly, the *Allocations Familiales* are seen as an important demographic tool by French policy-makers even though it is yet to be conclusively demonstrated that family allowances successfully stimulate the birth rate (Ellingson 1979).

The value of *Allocations Familiales* in relation to wages has been eroded since 1946 when the rate for the first child was set at 20 per cent of the average wage and for the third and subsequent children at 30 per cent (compare Table 7.2). Over the period 1970–7, family allowances increased by only 90 per cent compared with a rise of 146 per cent in SMIC. Nevertheless, *Allocations Familiales* can make a very significant contribution to the living standards of large families: Bradshaw and Piachaud (1980) have estimated that the income of a four-child family on two-thirds average earnings is increased by more than 40 per cent.

Allocation Prénatale and Allocation Postnatale (pre- and postnatal grants)

These two universal benefits reflect primarily demographic and health objectives but also represent a considerable financial bonus, particularly for low income families.

The *Allocation Prénatales* was introduced by an order of 5 February 1962 and is conditional upon the notification of pregnancy to a local insurance office before the third month and attendance at five compulsory medical examinations. The total grant (2165 FFr at 1 July 1980) is payable in three instalments on receipt of completed forms relating to the first three medicals. Official estimates suggest that only 2 per cent of mothers fail to meet the conditions (but see below).

The *Allocation Postnatale*, which was introduced in 1975 and modified by an Act of Parliament in 1980, consists of a lump sum of 2842 FFr for each of the first two children and one of 7158 FFr for the third and subsequent child. Therefore, in the case of the third child, for example, the benefits of both grants add up to 10 000 FFr or the equivalent of four months' income at SMIC levels. *Allocation Postnatale* is conditional on three preventive medical examinations held at one week, nine months and two years.

Complément Familial (family supplement)

Complément Familial is an income selective benefit which was introduced by an Act of 12 July 1977. The new benefit was designed to simplify the existing system, by replacing several benefits, including *l'Allocation de Salaire Unique*, *l'Allocation de la Mère au Foyer* and *l'Allocation pour Frais de Garde*, and to create a scheme that was neutral with regard to a woman's decision to enter the labour market. This second objective represented a considerable change since under the previous system it was possible for a family to lose benefit if the wife of an employed man chose to work. It also recognised a *de facto* change in the role of women in French society: women now make up 40 per cent of the French labour force and the proportion of families with children and a working mother might be in the region of 43 per cent.

Complément Familial also filled a gap in the previous system by making a benefit available to the first child. Payment of *Complément Familial* is subject to two conditions:

(a) the family must have at least one dependent child under three years of age, or at least three dependent children;
(b) the income of the family (assessed over the previous tax year) must not exceed a ceiling which varies with the number of dependent children.

The amount payable (455 FFr per month in July 1980) does not vary with family size.

The income ceiling was set in the expectation that about two-thirds of families with at least one young child or three children would be eligible for benefit. In this way it was hoped to help middle-income families who were thought to be relatively disadvantaged under the family allowance system. In the event, 2.724 million families (87 per cent) were receiving benefit in 1978, which suggests that the scheme is only excluding those with very high incomes.

Allocation de Parent Isolé (lone-parent allowance)

Although the *Allocation de Parent Isolé* introduced by an Act of 9 July 1976 accounts for only 1 per cent of the total cost of family benefits 1978, its special interest is that it incorporates the concept of a guaranteed minimum income for lone parents.

The *Allocation de Parent Isolé* is equivalent to the difference between a recipient's total income (including other family benefits) and the 'guaranteed' income which, as of July 1980, is 2186 FFr per month (equivalent to SMIC after tax and contributions) for lone parents with one child, with an increment of 547 FFr for each additional child.

Allocation de Parent Isolé may be paid to any lone parent who resides in France and is singly responsible for the upbringing of one or more children, regardless of whether they are a parent or relative of the child. *Allocation de Parent Isolé* may also be paid to pregnant women who do not yet have a dependent child provided they undergo a prescribed prenatal examination, in which case the guaranteed income is 1640 FFr per month.

A minimum income is only guaranteed in the short term, because *Allocation de Parent Isolé* is payable for one year or until the young child reaches the age of three. Had the benefit been paid in the longer term, the 100 per cent marginal withdrawal of benefit might have produced serious disincentives to work although this does not seem to be a major consideration of French policy-makers. In 1978, 40 000 families — 8 per cent of all lone parents with at least one dependent child — received *Allocation de Parent Isolé*.

Allocation Logement (housing allowance) and Allocation de Rentrée Scolaire (school clothing and equipment benefit)

Other means-tested benefits administered through the *Caisses d'Allocations Familiales* are tied to specific forms of household expenditure: most important are the *Allocation Logement* and the *Allocation de Rentrée Scolaire*.

The former benefit was introduced by an Act of 16 July 1971 with the twin objectives of helping families with their housing costs while at the same time ensuring basic housing standards. It is available primarily to families or persons with at least one dependent child and to childless couples for five years after marriage if, at the time of the marriage, neither partner was over 40 years of age.

The level of benefit is equal to the rent (or mortgage repayment in the case of owner-occupiers) actually paid — within a ceiling — less an amount which is dependent on the property meeting certain health and environment standards which sometimes precipitates a Catch-22 situation:

Allocation Logement is payable only with respect to dwellings of a certain standard, but families may be unable to afford accommodation of appropriate standard without first receiving the benefit. This problem is further discussed below.

(Low-income families are also helped by the provision of subsidised housing (*Habitations à Loyer Modéré*). Accommodation is provided at a rent dependent on income and family size and tenure is subject to an upper income limit.)

Allocation de Rentrée Scolaire is designed to assist parents with various expenses they incur for their school-age children at the beginning of the school year. A fixed payment (400 FFr in 1978) is made up to income ceiling of about 75 per cent of that applying to *Complément Familial*; 2.3 million families received this benefit in 1978.

Quotient Familial (family tax allowance)

A substantial part of the French aid to the family is achieved through the fiscal system and it has been estimated that, in 1966, removal of the *Quotient Familial* provisions would have doubled the number of families with four children living in poverty (Questiaux and Fournier 1978). However, if one considers indirect as well as direct taxation the disadvantages of the tax system for low income families probably outweigh the benefits.

The *Quotient Familial* works as follows. The joint income of the family (husband, wife and unmarried children aged under 18) is divided by a coefficient (*Quotient Familial*) which increases with family size, and a progressive tax schedule applied to the result to give a tax base. This is then multiplied by the same coefficient to yield the family's tax liabilities.

The family deduction under the progressive tax system clearly favours high income families and is of no benefit whatsoever to families below the tax threshold. (In 1980, all couples with a joint income equivalent to, or less than, SMIC would have been below the tax threshold irrespective of the number of children.) In addition, the French tax system depends heavily on sales taxes which, of course, are unaffected by the *Quotient Familial*.

The *Quotient Familial* also limits the funds available for further transfers to low-income families. Such transfers currently have to compete for priority against strong demands from the health service and for increased pensions. Additional funds could be generated by replacing the *Quotient Familial* with a fixed deduction related to the number of children as has been proposed by the Socialists when in opposition. However, such a reform would be likely to meet with strong resistance from high-income groups. It would also be opposed by family associations, who have always favoured horizontal rather than vertical income redistribution.

Aide Social (social assistance)

France has no statutory and comprehensive scheme which ensures that every person or family in need can receive a minimum income regardless of the cause of need. Nevertheless, specialised benefits are provided for certain groups subject, in most cases, to the *obligation alimentaire* which imposes a liability to maintain on spouses, all ascendants and descendants and parents-in-law. The benefits are administered by *départements* and/or *communes* and financed jointly with central government. The following are available to families:

(a) *Aide Médicale (medical aid)*: this scheme allows for the payment of medical and related costs incurred by people without insurance coverage. 1.56 million persons resorted to medical aid in 1977 and of the total expenditure of 4532 FFr million, 66 per cent was paid by central government and 34 per cent by local authorities.

(b) *Aide Sociale a l'Enfance (aid to children)*: under this scheme, *départements* can grant a monthly allowance to families without adequate income in order to help them maintain and educate their children. This allowance is usually reserved for children under 18 and is most often granted to prevent children being abandoned or taken into care. In certain exceptional cases the allowance may equal the maintenance payment made to foster families employed by the *département*, although it is normally much less. At the end of 1978, allowances were being paid for 192 000 children and averaged 237 FFr per month for each child. The cost is shared between central government (83 per cent) and *départements* (17 per cent).

(c) *Aide Sociale Facultative (discretionary aid)*: communes can also make discretionary payments or give help in kind (food or fuel vouchers, etc.) to any person in need. The extent to which they do so varies markedly from one commune to another but, in most cases, discretionary aid is likely to be very limited in its amount and duration.

Recent developments in French family support, especially the introduction of new and generous non-contributory benefits such as *Complément Familial* and *Allocation de Parent Isolé*, have led to the contraction of *Aide Sociale*. Nevertheless, many thousands of families still rely from time to time on these social assistance benefits which are significantly lower, relative to average wages, than in the other countries considered in this book and are administered more stringently (Lawson 1980a).

The Relevance of Exisiting Policies for Low Income Families

How relevant, then, is the French system of family benefits to the needs of low income families?

Some light has been shed on that question by the Rheims research discussed above (Debonneuil 1978) and by a subsequent study which further investigated the situation of a sample of 43 families among the 2000 already surveyed (ATD 1980). Both studies showed the importance of family benefits for the families concerned: on average, the full range of family benefits represented 46.2 per cent of their budgets, the proportion varying from 35 to 70 per cent. In terms of total income per consumption unit, large families were no worse off than others. Indeed, it would have been advisable for certain families to have several more children in order to increase their income — a strategy which has even more to recommend it following the most recent developments in benefits legislation (see above).

Most families (68 per cent) received *Allocation Logement*, but while the percentage was very high among council tenants (84 per cent, with the allowance covering 67 per cent of their rents), it was much lower among the other families (38 per cent). The latter, whose earned income was particularly low and who had therefore been refused a council house, found themselves doubly penalised because their accommodation did not meet the standards required to qualify for the housing allowance.

Other regular benefits paid to most or many of the 2000 families included *Allocation Familiale* paid to 64 per cent of them, and the *Allocation d'Orphelin* paid to one family out of five. Two important benefits now available — *Complément Familial* and *Allocation de Parent Isolé* — did not appear in the two surveys as they were introduced some time later.

Before 1 January 1978, benefits were paid only to heads of families who could show evidence of having worked for a certain period during the preceding months, or produce a satisfactory explanation of why they had not worked. For one reason or another, 8 per cent of all families had not met that condition in December 1975 and consequently did not receive any benefits during that month. Some of these families later had their situation reviewed and eventually received benefits but, in the meantime, their already tight budget had been seriously disrupted. The removal of the working condition as from 1 January 1978 thus meant a substantial improvement for the people who most depend upon benefits.

However, the Rheims' surveys revealed other problems which still exist. First, families sometimes had not heard about particular benefits, or were not aware that they could receive them. Others failed to comply with the relevant formalities, for instance declaring a pregnancy and undergoing the required medical examinations at certain prescribed times. The 43 families surveyed showed that, out of 13 births that took place in 1975, five families failed to secure the whole of their pre-natal and post-natal allowance.

Secondly, the housing and family support objectives of the *Allocation Logement* frequently seemed to be in conflict. (A problem exacerbated by the rules governing the allocation of social housing). The insistence on good quality housing as a prior condition of entitlement effectively condemned the poorest families to the worst housing.

A third problem stemmed from changes in the families' situations, affecting the number, age and presence of their children, the location and characteristics of their accommodation, the presence of a spouse or cohabitee, etc. These changes frequently caused delays in the payment of benefits (from one to twenty-one months), and sometimes resulted in errors which meant that some families had to hand back considerable amounts of money that had incorrectly been paid to them.

It is therefore hardly surprising that all the 43 families whose situation was studied in depth had had to resort to social assistance at least once within a period of 18 months. Such assistance (in the form of *Aide Sociale à l'enfance* from the *Département* or *Aide Sociale Facultative* from the city hall) represented between 0.7 and 9 per cent of their income over the same period, with an average of 3.3 per cent. However, the proportion could reach 100 per cent for certain families at certain times. For many families, the main role of assistance was to provide emergency help so to remedy occasional malfunctions of the family benefits scheme.

Conclusion

The French policy package outlined above is obviously very different from its British counterpart. Compared with the latter, it has several advantages and one major shortcoming.

Foremost among the advantages is the fact that the various means-tested benefits are subject to different income ceilings — sometimes quite high ones — which means that the French system has not produced any obvious poverty trap. Correspondingly, nobody seems to be claiming that French social security or family benefits produce any disincentive to work. The major role played by family benefits — as opposed to assistance — means that relatively few people need to feel the stigma generally associated with claiming assistance, although this may in turn exacerbate the problem for those who need to claim. In addition, family benefits are financed entirely by contributions from employers and the self-employed, which reduces the risk of taxpayer resentment against families in general or low-income families in particular. Finally, payment of all benefits (except *Aide Sociale*) through the same agency (and office) encourages take-up by simplifying application and facilitating claims for more than one benefit.

The one obvious gap in the system is that certain households may be left without a regular income high enough to cover their basic needs. Nevertheless, some progress has been made. In 1976, the *Allocation de Parent Isolé* was created and *Supplément de Revenu Familial*, a new, wider ranging benefit has recently been introduced by the Act of 17 July 1980 mentioned above. As from 1 January 1981, the latter ensures that most families with three children have a minimum total income of 4200 FFr per month (approximately £102 per week). That guarantee, however, only applies to families whose average earned income over the preceding year reached the level of the national minimum wage (about £58 per week). Other low-income families with three dependent children only receive a lump sum of 210 FFr per month (about £5.10 per week).

This chapter has described arrangements designed to avoid or reduce family poverty in France. The *Supplément de Revenu Familial* is a further step forward in the same direction. Whether it would prove sufficient in the event of growing long-term unemployment remains to be seen. In any case, it reflects a remarkable continuity in French social policy which, over the last 50 years, has consistently put the emphasis on families and workers rather than on individuals or the poor generally. Whether the new Socialist government will seek to shift the emphasis we can only wait and see.

References

ATD (Aide à Toute Détresse — Quart Monde) 1980, *Familles pauvres de Reims: de l'argent pour vivre*, Institute de Recherche du Mouvement, ATD-Quart Monde.

Bradshaw, J. and Piachaud, D. 1980, *Child support in the European Community*, Occasional Papers on Social Administration 66, London, Bedford Square Press.

Debonneuil, M. 1978, *Les familles pauvres d'une Ville Moyenne*, Paris, INSEE.

Ellingson, L. M. 1979, 'Recent changes in French family allowance policy', *Social Security Bulletin*, vol. 42, no. 12, pp. 14—19.

Fabius, L. 1978, 'The economy and social security in a period of inflation and recession' in *Problems of Social Security under economic recession and inflation*, Studies and Research, 9, Geneva, International Social Security Association, pp. 38—50.

France 1978, 'La situation demographique de la France et ses implications économiques et sociales: bilan et perspectives', *Journal Officiel*, 10 August.

Gorce de la, P. 1965, *La France pauvre*, Paris, Bernard Grasset.

Klanfer, J. 1965, *L'exclusion sociale*, Paris, Bureau de recherches sociales.

Launay, J. 1970, *Le France sous-développée: 15 millions de pauvres*, Paris, Dunod-Actualité.

Lawson, R. 1980a, 'Social security, employment and the single-parent family' in A. Samuels (ed.), *Social security and family law*, London, Oceana Publications.

Lawson, R. 1980b, *The structure of social assistance in 1979: France*, Mimeo.

Lenoir, R. 1974, *Les Exclus: Un Francais sur Dix*, Paris, Editions du Seuil.

Lion, A. 1980, 'Une politique contre la pauvreté?', *Economie et Humanisme*, 254, pp. 35—40.

Parodi, M. 1969, *'France' in low income groups and methods of dealing with their problems*, Paris, OECD.

Questiaux, N. and Fournier, J. 1978, 'France' in S. B. Kamerman and A. J. Kahn (eds), *Family policy: government and families in fourteen countries*, New York, Columbia University Press, pp. 117–82.

Scardigli, V. 1970, *Social policies and the working poor in France*, Paris, CREDOC, Mimeo.

Sinfield, A. 1980, 'Poverty and inequality in France' in V. George and R. Lawson (eds), *Poverty and inequality in Common Market Countries*, London, Routledge and Kegan Paul.

8 The Netherlands: Family Benefits
Wim Huizing*

The concepts of poverty and the poverty line, and the notion of a 'fight against poverty' are unheard of in Dutch politics and have played no part in recent developments in social policy. Albeit, social minima have been evolved in the years since 1969 which guarantee minimum incomes — now linked to the minimum wage — for all sections of the population (see Chapter 4). However, while the existence of these minima, together with the general level of affluence, may explain why poverty is not part of political discourse, they should not be interpreted as a response to the problem of poverty.

The deteriorating economic situation may bring about a change. The first few months of 1981 saw the attention of policy-makers focused on the worsening circumstances of families solely dependent on a single minimum income. Such families had been hardest hit by the fall in consumer purchasing power which occurred in 1980 and 1981, and as a response they were to be granted a one-off lump sum payment in autumn 1981 varying in amount from f250 — for a childless family — to f450 for a family with two or more children. This development is completely new in The Netherlands and it may be an indication that poverty will begin to feature in the political debate in future years.

The family allowance scheme is not aimed at combating poverty. Equal allowances are paid regardless of income to bring about a horizontal redistribution of income rather than a vertical one. The remainder of this chapter will describe the development of family allowances, explain the present scheme and finally consider plans for its future development.

The Development of Family Allowances and Child Tax Relief
Family allowances were first introduced in 1941 giving employees the right to family allowance for their third and subsequent children and by 1946 entitlement had been extended to all children. 1951 saw coverage

*I would like to thank Ruud Timmer for his help and advice in the preparation of this chapter.

of the family allowance scheme extended to restricted categories of the self-employed with very low incomes who were to receive benefit on third and subsequent children, although the amount of allowance payable was only half that for wage earners.

Major legislation was introduced in 1963 which initiated four new schemes:

(a) The General Family Allowances Act (*AKW, Algemene Kinderbijslagwet*) gave all inhabitants entitlement to allowance for the third and subsequent child;

(b) The Family Allowances Act for Wage Earners (*KWL, Kinderbijslagwet voor loontrekkenden*) provided family allowances for the first two children of employees (other than civil servants) and of a few other categories of citizen;

(c) The Family Allowances Scheme for Civil Servants (*KTO, Kindertoelageregeling voor Overheidspersoneel*) similarly provided civil servants with family allowances for their first two children; and finally

(d) The Family Allowances Act for the Self-Employed (*KKZ, Kinderbijslagwet voor kleine zelfstandigen*) made allowances payable for the second child of self-employed persons with incomes (1979) between f21 150 and f21 800, and for the first two children of self-employed persons with lower incomes.

[The 1963 legislation seems to have been designed both to broaden the base of eligibility for family allowances and further to standardise provision. Nevertheless, the antecedents of the legislation were evident in the existence of a separate scheme for civil servants, which could be traced back to a time when the salaries of civil servants included an allowance for children, and in the provisions for the self-employed which made entitlement subject to income. Payments under all schemes were indexed to wages and, with the exception of KKZ, financed by a levy on incomes payable in the case of employees by their employers — editors' note.]

The next change occurred in 1974. Prior to that, family allowance counted as taxable income against which was set a child tax relief (i.e. relief on income). In 1973, family allowance was made tax-free and the child tax-allowance reduced by an amount equivalent to family allowance. The change was neutral in fiscal terms but meant that from 1973 child tax relief consisted of a tax-free allowance equivalent to family allowances (i.e. corresponding to family allowances) and a residual tax relief equal to the difference between the child tax-relief obtaining in 1972 and the family allowance. The system was indexed such that the net benefit of the combined family allowance and residual tax relief kept pace with prices. Because family allowances for the second and subsequent children were indexed to wages, which increased faster than prices, the residual tax relief was gradually eroded and, in the case of the fourth and subsequent children, eventually eliminated in 1977. At the same time, however, tax-relief for the first child increased since the value of family allowances in this case was frozen at 1972 levels.

Between 1978 and 1980 the system was changed yet again. The AKW provisions were extended to the first and second child, thereby superseding the other three schemes. Moreover, the residual income relief remaining in relation to the first three children was abolished and partially compensated for by increases in family allowances.

The AKW provisions were further amended in 1978 and 1979 as part of the government's programme of measures in response to the faltering economy announced on 30 June 1978 ('*Bestek 81*' — a blueprint for 1981). The government argued that collective expenditures had to be curtailed so as to reduce the rise in labour costs, increase incentives and thereby promote investment and new employment. The family allowance scheme bore a significant part of the f3500 million cuts in social security provisions on the grounds that they provided supplementation rather than income support and that the effect of reductions would be spread across all income groups.

The Current System of Family Benefits

Family allowances

From 1980 the family allowance system has had the following features:

(a) All inhabitants with children entitled to tax-free family allowance for first and subsequent children;

(b) No child tax allowances (although tax relief follows from the tax-free nature of family allowance);

(c) Family allowances payable quarterly to the parent responsible for maintaining the children (generally the father), although a Bill is in preparation to accord entitlement, in the first instance, to the parent responsible for looking after the children (generally the mother);

(d) Family allowance paid for children up to and including the age of 16, unconditionally; from 16 to 17 if in full-time education, disabled or running the house; from 18 to 26 if in full-time education or running the house. A means-tested student grant may also be paid if the student is between 18 and 26;

(e) For children up to the age of 18 living away from home a double family allowance is paid;

(f) A double family allowance is also paid for children between the ages of 18 and 26 who are living at home; if not living at home a triple benefit may be paid if the parents are not providing maintenance;

(g) Family allowance varies according to the position of the child in the family, the allowance increasing with the number of children (see Table 8.1);

Table 8.1   The value of family allowances in The Netherlands
1 January 1980

	Annual family allowance:		b as % of:	
	(a) per child (f)	(b) cumulative (f)	(c) net minimum wage[1]	(d) net modal wage[2]
First child 0—2 years born after 1.1.79	520	520	3	2
1st child born before 1.1.79	1036	1036	6	5
2nd child	1680	2716	16	12
3rd child	1692	4408	25	20
4th child	2044	6452	37	30
5th child	2044	8496	49	39
6th child	2256	10752	62	49
7th child	2256	13008	75	59
8th and subsequent children	2484	15492	90	71

1 The net minimum wage for employees aged 23 and over is f17 300 per annum.

2 The 'modal wage' (*modaal inkomen*) is an administrative concept introduced by the Central Planning Office. It is regarded, broadly speaking, as the commonest wage in The Netherlands earned by employees with two children below the age of 16. At f21 870 net per annum it is just below the level at which maximum compulsory health insurance premium is payable.

(h) The allowance for the first child is relatively low because allowances for the first child have been frozen since 1973 and are to remain so until 1 January 1982; the allowance for a first child born after 1 January 1979 is half the general rate of family allowance for the first child until the age of three. These measures are purely money-saving devices;

(i) Allowances for second and subsequent children will be adjusted in line with wage increases at six monthly intervals. From 1 January 1982 all allowances will be adjusted in line with the Domestic Retail Price Index.

The AKW is executed by 22 Boards of Labour (*Raden van Arbeid*) who also administer old-age pensions, widows' and orphans' pensions.

Payment is by money-order cashable at a Post Office (20 per cent), to Girobank (40 per cent) and direct to a bank (40 per cent) and the award lasts for only three months after which the beneficiary has to submit a quarterly renewal declaration. The Boards of Labour are independent of the Ministry of Social Affairs and are under the direction of the Social Insurance Bank (*Sociale Verzekeringsbank*), the board of which is composed of representatives of employers and employees and appointees of the Minister of Social Affairs. The Social Insurance Bank administers the family allowance fund but contributions are levied and collected by the Inland Revenue Department. Supervision of the Social Insurance Bank rests with the Social Security Council (*Sociale Verzekeringsraad*).

It is estimated that the cost of family allowances in 1980 was f7310 million out of which f3800 million (52 per cent) was funded by central government and the rest from social security contributions. Contributions are paid by employers on behalf of their employees and are equal to 2 per cent of the gross wage up to f46 400 per annum (1980) with the effect that, in total, the system is regressive.

The Dutch system of family allowances achieves a horizontal distribution of incomes for the benefit of families with children. This may best be illustrated with reference to the self-employed who are responsible for their own contributions. A self-employed individual with the national modal income (approximately f31 500) pays f630 per annum in social contributions. With one child the same person receives f1036 in family allowances so that practically all self-employed individuals with children benefit on balance from family allowances. An exception — resulting from economy measures introduced in January 1979 — is the individual with one child under the age of three born after 1 January 1979 who receives only f520.

The fact that family allowance contributions are paid by employers does not necessarily mean that employed persons have a structural advantage over the self-employed. In practice, it is impossible to determine whether the incidence of contributions falls on the employer or on the employee. However, it is quite conceivable that gross wages would be higher if social contributions were paid by employees leaving 'net real disposable wages', the central focus of wage negotiations in The Netherlands, unchanged.

Other provisions for children
All employed persons who earn f40 250 or less (1980) are compulsorily insured under the Health Insurance Act (*ZFW, Ziekenfondswet*). This insurance covers medical, pharmaceutical, dental and hospital care and is administered by Health Insurance Funds, which are themselves

financially dependent upon the General Health Insurance Fund. Contributions are paid at a rate of 4.05 per cent of wages up to an annual wage ceiling of f32 500 (1980). The children of the insured are insured free of charge as is a wife if she is not in paid employment. Persons with incomes above f40 250 who are thereby not covered by ZFW, generally take out private health insurance.

Education is free in The Netherlands up to the age of 17 when fees become payable based on an assessment of parental income. Children are also indirect beneficiaries of government grants to local authorities, housing associations and private landlords for housing construction and of an extensive system of rent control. Means-tested rent allowances (*Individuele Huursubsidie*) are also available to those with incomes not exceeding f32 000 (1979) but, while the allowance takes account of rent, it does not vary according to the number of children.

Finally, to consider the position of a low-income worker after 1 January 1980, let us assume that a family earning the minimum wage has two children, aged 14 and 16, both of whom attend junior vocational school. The family allowance for this family would be f2716 per annum (see Table 8.1). In addition, the children would receive free compulsory health insurance. The total amount paid out under the Health Insurance Act by way of medicines, medical assistance, prescriptions, etc. is f6820 million per annum. Since the total number of insured parties, including the members of insured families, is approximately 7 million, the *per capita* payment is f975 per annum.

The family would also be entitled to grants towards the educational costs for the 1979—80 school year amounting to f350 for the child aged 14 and f1750 for the child aged 16 (dependent upon the parent's income, the form of education, the age of the children and the composition of the family). Therefore, the maximum that the family would receive in benefits is:

Family allowances	f2716
Health insurance payments	f1950
Education grants	f2100
	f6766

Altogether these benefits would constitute 39 per cent of the family's net income with family allowances providing 16 per cent.

A New Family Allowance System
The changes that occurred in the family allowance system in The Netherlands between 1978 and 1980 did not generally affect the level of allowances or the differentials. However, both the Dutch Parliament

and the Social and Economic Council (*SER, Sociaal-Economische Raad*), an advisory body to government comprising representatives of trade unions and employers and members appointed by the Crown, have strongly urged that the structuring of family allowances should be taken further in these respects. Opinions are divided as to the manner of change required. Many liberals and employers favour abolition of family allowance for the first child on the grounds that the high standard of living enjoyed in The Netherlands has made it superfluous. Trade unions and many others on the political left are not convinced by this line of argument and further point out that family allowance for the first child has been frozen since 1973 and should be increased in line with the family allowance for subsequent children. The left-wing opposition in Parliament and the trade unions also want family allowance to be income-related so as to achieve some degree of vertical income redistribution but the government parties in Parliament, the government itself and employers are strongly opposed to this.

Ideas on differentiation according to the position of the child in the family configuration also vary considerably — from maintaining the *status quo* (i.e. the family allowance per child increasing with the number of children) to a diminishing payment for each child. The view taken often depends on whether emphasis is placed on the costs-per-child theory or the family welfare theory of family provision (see below). Finally, there is a large group who feel that family allowances should be differentiated by age because the costs of older children are greater than those for younger ones. On 31 March 1980, in accordance with the established system of consultation, the Dutch government submitted a request to the SER for recommendations on the restructuring of family allowances (The Netherlands 1980). The content of this request is of interest for the purposes of international comparison in that it reveals the government's views on the future development of family allowances. Moreover, it further develops the objectives, basic premises and theoretical basis of the family allowance scheme.

Objectives, premises and parameters

In its request for recommendations to the Social and Economic Council the government formulated the aim of family allowances as follows: 'To correct the distribution of incomes for the benefit of families with children and thus to foster the children's opportunities for development' (The Netherlands 1980). In addition, seven basic premises and three conditions were stipulated. The premises stated that:

(a) All inhabitants of The Netherlands who are responsible for children should be entitled to family allowances;

(b) Entitlement to family allowances should start with the first child;

(c) Entitlement to family allowances should continue until the children are aged 18;

(d) Family allowances should be tax-free;

(e) Age-related differences in costs should be reflected in the level of allowance;

(f) The level of family allowances should be such that the parent continues to bear some financial responsibility for child-rearing;

(g) The level of allowance should be related to differences in the capacity of parents to maintain their children resulting from variations in family size.

The three conditions imposed were that:

(a) The new system should not cost more than would have been the case if policy had remained unchanged (see Figure 8.1);

(b) A revival of tax relief for children must not become necessary which means that family allowances ought not to be income-related;

(c) The system must remain simple both in terms of legislation and implementation;

Condition (b) requires further explanation. One fundamental premise of Dutch fiscal policy is that differences in financial capacity resulting from differences in incomes should be reflected in tax rates and not in the tax-free threshold. Therefore, while people with incomes below the tax threshold are considered to be unable to pay tax because they lack the capacity, the level of the threshold is determined by factors such as civil status and not by the size of income. Differences in financial capacity associated with income are accommodated by progressive tax rates.

The difficulty posed by non-taxable family allowances is that any change in level represents a change in tax-free income (i.e. the tax threshold). Consequently, if family allowances were to be differentiated by income, the tax threshold would also be related to income which runs counter to the premise cited above. The view of the Dutch Parliament — which now has statutory force due to the passing of an amendment to the Act governing the restructuring of family allowances — is that if this should happen, tax relief for children would have to be reintroduced to correct the situation.

There is a further objection to income-related family allowances. The marginal burden of tax and social security contributions is a minimum of 45 per cent up to incomes of around f50 000 and gradually increases above this figure. A system of income-related family allowances would increase this marginal pressure. If, for example, family allowances were

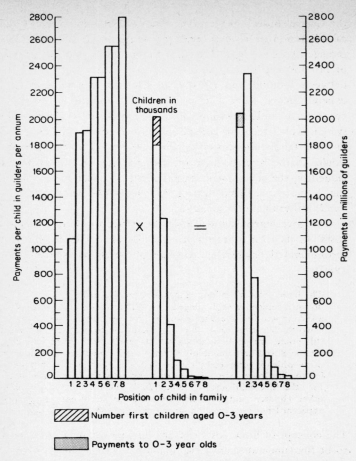

Figure 8.1   *Cost and structure of current family allowance scheme
projected for 1982*

Source:

to be reduced by f150 for each f1000 increase in income, the *effective*
marginal rate of tax would increase from 45 to 60 per cent.

The concept of basic costs

Family allowances are designed to contribute to the costs of children and
it is therefore important which concept of cost is applied. The current
system is based on research on family budgets in which actual expenditure on children is measured (SER 1964). However, studies have shown
that absolute expenditure on children rises with income. For example,

the Central Bureau of Statistics is shortly to publish a report on the costs of children in which it emerges that expenditure on two children below the age of six averages f3265 per annum for households with an income of f16 000 per annum and rises to f6407 for households with incomes between f30 000 and f37 000 (1974 figures net amount). Similarly expenditure on older children is found to increase in proportion to income. Such studies call into question the theoretical basis of the current system which rests on expenditure. Furthermore, a new system which involved family allowances rising in direct proportion to parental income would not be received with great enthusiasm in The Netherlands. Consequently, the government feels that the new system should be based on the 'basic costs of child rearing' (*noodzakelijke kosten van levensonderhoud*) rather than on expenditure.

The government acknowledge the difficulty of the concept of 'basic costs' in its formal request to the Social and Economic Council for recommendations on the structure of family allowances (Netherlands 1980):

> The basic costs of child-rearing is a normative concept that has everything to do with subjective value judgements. What one person considers a minimum, a second will find reasonable and a third excessive. Nevertheless, it would be a worthwhile exercise to have experts in the field of family budgeting study this point, and to have the standards which they devise critically evaluated by the Social and Economic Council. This could then provide an objective norm which is accepted by the Council, a body of broad composition. According to the Government's line of thinking, only the basic costs of child-rearing for the first child need be established. The basic costs of child-rearing for other children and also the differentiation according to age will then be apparent from the ratios that are found for expenditure on children.

The concept of basic costs warrants further examination since it is likely to be fundamental to any development in Dutch family provisions. Three postulates are predicted to hold for the basic costs of child-rearing:

(a) They rise with the age of the child;
(b) They decrease per child as the number of children in the family decreases;
(c) They are independent of the income of the parents.

In addition, the following postulates hold true of the relationship between the basic costs of child-rearing, family size and income:

(d) The capacity of the parents to contribute to the basic costs decreases as the number of children increases;
(e) The capacity of the parents to contribute to the basic costs of child-rearing increases as income increases.

Postulates (a) and (c) define what is termed the 'costs-per-child theory', postulate (d) the 'family welfare theory' and postulate (e) 'the income theory'. The government wishes to base the future system of family allowances on a combination of the costs-per-child theory and the family welfare theory. The incomes theory is excluded for the reasons already detailed.

Despite the fact that actual expenditure is known to be related to income while basic costs are deemed not to be so, the official view is that ratios found between actual expenditure on children of different ages, or in different positions within the family configuration, hold also for basic costs. Two studies can be cited as circumstantial evidence in support of this contention (DFC 1977; CBS 1979). Both demonstrate that actual expenditure is correlated with age of the child but also that the ratio of expenditure between different age groups is virtually independent of income.

Models for the restructuring of family allowances

In its request to the SER, the government proposed three models for re-structuring family allowances (Netherlands 1980). Each model incorporates:

(a) Differentiation by age of child.
(b) A new method of differentiation by position within the configuration of the family, and
(c) The abolition of the system whereby family allowances are reduced by 50 per cent for the first child when aged 0 to 2 years.

Differentiation by age is according to the ratios 70:100:130 for the age groups 0 to 5, 6 to 11, and 12 to 17 years respectively. These ratios are consistent with findings from empirical studies of family expenditure although information is not available for age groups as small as a single year (DFC 1977; CBS 1979). However, the 'Costs of Children' study which considered seven categories of expenditure suggests that spending increases gradually with age. The categories of food, housing, clothing and footwear, and hygiene and medical care account for most expenditure (reducing from 90 to 75 per cent with increasing income) and would be unlikely to change abruptly when a child reaches a certain age. Furthermore, detailed study of the other categories of expenditure: education; leisure and social life; social obligations and insurance; and miscellaneous indicates a gradual increase in expenditure with age.

The combination of differentiation by position in the family configuration and age creates technical difficulties because children are likely to change their position within the family. For example, in a two-child family, once the elder (i.e. first) child ceases studying and thereby becoms ineligible for family allowance, the younger (i.e. second) child becomes the first child. Thus differentiation by position in the family is influenced by the size of family and not by features of the individual child as is the case with differentiation by age. This difficulty is resolved by operating family allowances on the basis of family size as shown, using fictitious figures, in Table 8.2. Under the current system, a family with two children receives 2 × 110 = 220 units and under the new system for two children aged six to eleven the family receives 2 × 110 = 220 units. Also, as the table shows, it is simple to differentiate family allowances by age under the new system.

Table 8.2   Comparison of the current and proposed systems of
family allowances in The Netherlands

Illustrative units

Family allowances payable under:		Age of child (years)		
(a) Current system	(b) New system	0—5	6—11	12—17
1st Child 100	Families with 1 child	70	100	130
2nd Child 120	Families with 2 children	77	110	143

All three models also include the abolition of the current halving of family allowance for the first child aged under three which was introduced by Parliamentary amendment as an economy measure. This change is necessary on both technical and theoretical grounds. If the 0—2 age group were not subsumed under the 0—5 category, an extra age differential would continue to exist and would, in addition, affect the position within the family configuration. The resulting system would also lack consistency since the provision relates to young, first children and the first child is relatively expensive whereas younger children are relatively inexpensive.

The distinctive features of the three models proposed are as follows:

Model 1: age differentiation is incorporated into the current system;

Model 2: age differentiation is incorporated into a system into which differentiation by position within the family is abandoned;

Model 3: age differentiation is incorporated into an entirely new system of differentiation by position; this new system is based on total reimbursement of the basic costs of child-rearing with corrections to account for the parents' financial contributions and to ensure that the cost of the system remains unchanged.

Model 1

Model 1 would be too expensive to introduce assuming that differentiation by age was according to the ratio of 70:100:130. This is largely due to the recent fall in the number of births, which has resulted in an increase in the proportion of older children. Therefore, the introduction of Model 1 on a non-cost basis would require the overall level of family allowances to be reduced by 3.3 per cent or by 5.2 per cent if the 50 per cent reduction for the first child was abolished (see Table 8.3).

Table 8.3   *Family allowances in The Netherlands according to proposed Model 1, 1982*

Annual value of family allowances (f) payable under:					
(a) Current system			(b) Model 1		
For:		less 5.2%	per child for families with:	Age of child (years)		
	(f)	(f)		0—5 (f)	6—11 (f)	12—17 (f)
1st child	1071	1015	1 child	711	1015	1320
2nd child	1899	1800	2 children	986	1408	1830
3rd child	1912	1813	3 children	1080	1543	2006
4th child	2513	2193	4 children	1194	1705	2217
5th child	2513	2193	5 children	1262	1803	2344
6th child	2551	2418	6 children	1334	1905	2477
7th child	2551	2418	7 children	1385	1979	2573
8th child	2810	2664	8 children	1445	2064	2683

A further problem with Model 1 is that it could radically alter the incomes of sizeable numbers of families so that its introduction would have to be accompanied by transitional arrangements. The effect of implementing Model 1 would be to reduce the income of families with young children and to increase that of those with older ones. If introduced on 1 January 1982 it would mean a reduction in family income of as much as f4003 per annum in the least favourable case and an increase of f2231 per annum in the most favourable.

Model 2

Model 2 is not discussed further since it is the least well-argued and probably, therefore, the one with the least chance of being implemented.

Model 3

A number of arbitrary assumptions are necessary if the potential value of this model is to be adequately demonstrated:

(a) Basic subsistence costs for a first child aged six to eleven years are taken to be f2500. Although this assumption is crucial it is not based on empirical data and implementation of Model 3 would have to be preceded by thorough research.

(b) Basic subsistence costs vary in the ratio of 100:85:79:73:69:67:65:63 for the first through to the eighth child in a family. These ratios are derived from an early study of expenditure patterns (SEC 1964).

(c) Basic subsistence costs vary according to age in the ratio 70:100:130 for children aged 0–5, 6–11 and 12–17 respectively.

Table 8.4 illustrates the scheme which would result from acceptance of the above assumptions with full reimbursement for the basic costs of child-rearing. However, such a scheme would fail to meet the government's requirements on two grounds. First, parents would not be bearing any financial responsibility for their children and secondly, the scheme would be much more expensive than the present one.

Table 8.4   Family allowances in The Netherlands according to proposed Model 3, assuming full reimbursement of basic costs, 1982

Annual family allowances (f) per child for families with	Age of child (years)		
	0–5 (f)	6–11 (f)	12–17 (f)
1 child	1750	2500	3250
2 children	1619	2313	3007
3 children	1540	2200	2860
4 children	1474	2106	2738
5 children	1421	2030	2639
6 children	1300	1971	2562
7 children	1345	1921	2497
8 children	1315	1878	2441

The scheme outlined in Table 8.4 would cost f9265 million in 1982, taking account of the end of the 50 per cent allowance for first children and the increased proportion of older children, compared with f5815 million made available by government. Given that the task of establishing the degree of financial responsibility to be met by parents is inevitably an arbitrary one, a pragmatic solution is to match parental contributions to the f3450 million shortfall in available finance. Table 8.5 shows the effects of apportioning the shortfall equally between all (i.e. 2 021 000) families so that each would be deemed to contribute f1707 per annum to the basic cost of child-rearing. In this example, differences in the amount of family allowances payable to families with four or more children are so small that a single rate of family allowance would be justified for these groups.

*Table 8.5   Family allowances in The Netherlands according to
proposed Model 3, assuming family contribution to basic costs, 1982*

Annual family allowances (f) per child for families with	Age of child (years)		
	0—5 (f)	6—11 (f)	12—17 (f)
1 child	555	793	1031
2 children	1021	1459	1097
3 children	1142	1631	2120
4 children	1176	1680	2184
5 children	1182	1689	2196
6 children	1180	1686	2192
7 children	1175	1678	2121
8 children	1166	1665	2165

Postscript

On 7 April 1981, the SER published interim advice on the introduction
of family allowances differentiated according to the age of child (SER
1981). They agreed unanimously with the proposal to differentiate
family allowances as from 1 January 1982 in accordance with the ratio
70:100:130 outlined in page 222 above. (A recommendation on older
children was delayed pending the introduction of a new system of study
grants.) On the other hand, the SER rejected proposals for a six-year
transitional period which would have limited the provisions of the new
scheme to children entering the three age cohorts. Instead, the SER
recommended that the benefit levels be gradually adjusted for all children over the same transitional period (see Table 8.6).

*Table 8.6   Transitional arrangements for family allowances in
The Netherlands proposed by the SER*

	Family allowance payable as a % of that for the 6—11 age group				
	Age of child (years)				
Year of transition	0—5 (born before 1982)[1]	0—5 (born in 1982 or later)[1]	0—5 (first child-ren 0—2 years)	6—11	12—17
1982	95	70	50	100	107.5
1983	90	70	60	100	115
1984	85	70	70	100	120
1985	80	70	70	100	125
1986	75	70	70	100	127.5
1987	70	70	70	100	130

1 Excluding first children aged 0—2 years.

Conclusion

Family allowances are unique in The Netherlands in that an attempt has been made to provide an area of social security policy with a sound theoretical base. Any scientific approach is based on a marriage between assumptions and data. In practical politics the assumptions must inevitably derive from social and political premises or parameters.

In this chapter, a theoretical underpinning has been sought within the set of social premises presented. Two theories which are consistent with the political parameters laid down by government, family welfare theory and the cost-per-child theory, have been applied in developing proposals for the reform of family allowances. In Model 3, the most radical of the proposals considered, a viable scheme was made possible by the pragmatic response of setting the need for a nil-cost solution against the desire to ask parents to accept partial responsibility for the costs of children.

The approach implied by an alternative theory, the income theory, was rejected not because it was intrinsically unsatisfactory but because it is inappropriate in the context of Dutch social policy. Likewise, little emphasis has been given to the role of family provision in alleviating poverty. This is because the concepts of poverty and the poverty line have little visibility in the politics or social policy of The Netherlands. Indeed, even the concept of minimum incomes, which is important in other areas of Dutch social security, is largely irrelevant to the debate on family allowances.

The family allowance system envisaged by the Dutch government and described in this chapter has been systematically assembled. Premises, parameters and theory have been combined and married, on occasion, with necessary pragmatism. Lessons to be learned from the Dutch system are not confined to the UK but apply to several other countries as well. The premises and parameters of social policy will vary from one country to another and the family allowance system will differ accordingly. However, if the desirability of changing the family allowance system is recognised, then the Dutch system could perhaps provide pointers towards reform.

References

CBS 1979, *Persbericht van het Centraal Bureau voor de Statistiek*, no. 09016—79— DS, Voorburg, 28 December.

DFC 1977, *De kinderbijslag-en kinderaftrekregelingen nader bekeken*, Nederlands Gezinsraad, The Hague, 1977.

Netherlands 1980, *Adviesaanvrage aan de Sociaal-Economische Raad over de structuur van de kinderbijslag*, The Hague, 31 March.

SER 1964, *Advies over de hoogte van de kinderbijslagen*, The Hague, Sociaal-Economische Raad, no. 4.

SER 1981, *Interimadvies structuur kinderbijslag*, The Hague, Sociaal Economische Raad, no. 6.

9 West Germany: Poverty and the Family
Helmut Hartmann

Introduction

It is only during the past decade that poverty has been 'rediscovered' as a significant socio-political problem in the Federal Republic. The extraordinary economic growth of the 1950s and 1960s, together with the establishment of a comprehensive social security system, created the impression that poverty was almost a thing of the past. What remained of the problem appeared to be largely an unavoidable aftermath of the war, which it was generally assumed would soon be overcome. This optimism began to be questioned at the end of the 1960s and in the early 1970s, as evidence appeared of 'concealed poverty' among pensioners and of the problems of homeless families and foreign workers. However, these were still mostly interpreted as relating to special cases or to be problems of *Randgruppen*, the small number of people on the periphery of society. Such views were not seriously challenged until the publication in 1975 of a report on 'Poverty in the Welfare State' by Heiner Geissler, a prominent Christian Democratic politician (Geissler 1975; see also Chapter 12). According to the report, in 1974 the incomes of around 2 million households — about 9 per cent of all households — containing 5.8 million people, fell below the official poverty line, the living standard associated with last-resort social assistance. As the opening sentence of the report put it, 'Poverty, a theme long since thought dead, is an oppressive reality for millions of people.'

Although the reliability of Geissler's estimates has been strongly disputed (see Lawson 1980), concern about poverty has grown appreciably in the Federal Republic since the report was published. It must be stressed, however, that much of the debate and literature on the subject has dealt with methodological and conceptual issues, especially the difficulties of defining poverty and of interpreting statistical information on incomes. Discussion of the causes of poverty, the social structure of that part of the population considered to be poor, and the options for actively combating poverty has been much less adequate. Moreover, such discussions have largely been restricted to considerations of income poverty with very little attention being given to other aspects of disadvantage —

in housing, education, medical care, etc. – or to their association with lack of income.

While this chapter is also confined to discussion of income poverty, it addresses a subject that has been largely neglected at least until very recently. Family poverty first received official mention in 1979 in a report produced for the Federal Government by a commission of experts (Germany 1979b). However, as we shall see, other official data, particularly that relating to social assistance, reveal that increasing numbers of families with children are facing financial and social difficulties, especially with rising unemployment and the growing numbers of one-parent households.

Social Assistance Levels and Family Poverty

In the Federal Republic, as in the UK, most investigations of the extent of poverty have adopted as their main yardstick the scale of eligibility for means-tested social assistance. Under the Federal Social Assistance Law, local authorities are required to provide *Sozialhilfe* to cover the minimum needs of those with inadequate incomes and to enable them 'to lead a life that corresponds to the dignity of man' (BSHG 1961). Unlike the British supplementary benefits scheme, *Sozialhilfe* is available whether or not a claimant is in paid work. Indeed, paid work, including part-time work is actively encouraged and a special wage earners' supplement is paid both as an incentive and to cover work expenses.

Most claimants receive regular monthly allowances which vary according to the size of the household, the ages of household members and a number of other special circumstances. The principal components of the allowances are:

(a) *Base rates* for adult householders, which are derived from an official 'basket of goods' covering food, clothing, household equipment and personal needs. Amounts vary slightly in different parts of the Federal Republic, mostly as a result of differences in local living costs. In 1980, the Federal average rate was 309 DM a month.

(b) *Dependants' allowances* calculated as percentages of the base rates, the proportions being fixed by the Federal Law. Children under 8 years of age receive 45 per cent of the base rates, children between 8 and 11 years 65 per cent, children between 12 and 15 years 75 per cent, and children between 16 and 21 years 90 per cent. Other adults receive 80 per cent of the householder's rates.

(c) *Additional 'extra needs' allowances* for certain groups of persons (over 65s, blind and disabled persons, wage earners and lone parents). In the case of lone parents these amount to 30 per cent of the base rate where there are two or three dependent children and to 50 per cent if the parent is responsible for four or more children.

(d) *Housing costs* (including fuel costs) are normally met in full.

(e) *Further supplements* are granted for larger expenditures and non-recurring payments. Although difficult to estimate, it is generally assumed that these amount on average to approximately 15 per cent of the base rate.

Table 9.1   Sozialhilfe *limits (poverty line) for two households in 1980*

	Lone parent with 2 children (8 and 14 years) (DM/mth)	Married Couple with 3 children (6, 8 and 14 years) (DM/mth)
Flat rate for head of household	309	309
Flat rate for adult (80%)	–	247
Flat rate for 6-year-old child (45%)	–	139
Flat rate for 8-year-old child (65%)	201	201
Flat rate for 14-year-old child (75%)	232	232
Additional rate for extra needs (30%)	93	–
Rent (estimate)	250	250
Additional rate for large expenditures (15% of the sum, except rent)	125	169
Social aid limit	1210	1547

Table 9.1 gives an indication of the levels of assistance in 1980 for two model households. The assistance limit of 1210 DM per month for a couple with two children compares with an income (net of tax and social security contributions, plus child benefits) of just over 2000 DM for a family of the same composition but where the husband is on average earnings (Bradshaw and Piachaud 1980). Taking account of a fuller range of income sources, social assistance payments have have been estimated to average approximately one-third of the mean income of private households in the Federal Republic (Hartmann 1979). Relative to average earnings, West German benefit rates for householders are set well below the British levels (Table 2.15 above; also Lawson 1980), although the West German equivalence ratios for children are considerably more generous than those in Britain. Consequently, in relative terms, West German benefits appear to be lower for smaller families and higher for larger ones.

How many families depend on *Sozialhilfe* and what have been the trends in recent years? The most up-to-date information available from the Federal Statistical Office is for 1978, when more than 190 000 families with children received regular monthly social assistance payments. The numbers had risen substantially since the early 1970s: in 1972, 105 000 families received assistance and, in 1975, 156 000 families. Part of this increase is accounted for by improvements in the real value of social assistance benefits and by more liberal procedures and greater publicity given to the scheme (Ehrenburg and Fuchs 1980). Nevertheless, it is also a reflection of the increasing vulnerability of certain households with children.

Table 9.2   Family characteristics of households receiving Sozialhilfe, 1965—80

Type of household	Numbers receiving Sozialhilfe *as a % of all households on* Sozialhilfe			
	1965	1970	1975	1978
Married couple with 1 to 2 children	2	2	4	4
Married couple with 3 or more children	2	2	3	3
Lone parent with 1 to 2 children	8	8	12	14
Lone parent with 3 or more children	4	5	5	5

Source: Germany 1978.

Table 9.3   The 'risk of families being dependent on Sozialhilfe, 1970, 1978

Type of family	% of each family type receiving Sozialhilfe	
	1970	1978
Married couple with 1 to 2 children	0.1	0.5
Married couple with 3 and more children	0.4	1.1
Lone parent with 1 to 2 children	2.8	7.7
Lone parent with 3 and more children	12.9	19.3
All households	1.9	3.0

Source: Germany 1970, 1972, 1978, 1979a.

Tables 9.2 and 9.3 examine this change in more detail. They reveal a particularly high rate of increase among smaller families (i.e. those with less than three children). However, lone parents with dependent children were most at risk during this period and are more likely to depend on social assistance than any other group in the Federal Republic. Moreover, the extent of their dependence grew dramatically between 1970 and 1978.

In addition to recipients of *Sozialhilfe*, account has to be taken of those people who, although eligible for assistance, do not claim it. Unfortunately, by their very nature statistics relating to what has come to be called 'concealed poverty' are inadequate. As already noted, the Geissler study (1975) has been criticised for overestimating assistance levels as has another by Kögler (1976; see Hauser and Krupp 1979). A study by Erhard Knechtel (1960) has better stood the test of time although it focused solely on complete families with under-age children. It concluded that, in 1956/7, 2.8 per cent of such families had resources below *Sozialhilfe* limits, a figure which rose to 4.3 per cent for three-child families and to 15.6 per cent for families with five or more children.

However, a very different picture emerges from preliminary analyses for the European Commission National Poverty Study (Hauser and Krupp 1979) which is only partly explained by the estimated fall in concealed poverty. According to the National Poverty Study, 1.7 per cent of households in 1969 had incomes below *Sozialhilfe* levels compared with 3.4 per cent in 1963. Moreover, couples with children accounted for only 6.3 per cent of the concealed poverty and had a below-average risk of poverty (0.2 per cent overall compared to 1.5 per cent) regardless of the number of children. The risk of poverty was greater for lone parents but even so was much less than for households with a head aged over 65 who accounted for 71.6 per cent of the concealed poverty. Analysis based on 1973 data yielded similar results.

The National Poverty Study findings are themselves markedly at odds with those recently published by the *Institut für Sozialforschung und Gesellschaftspolitik* at Cologne (Hartmann 1981). These show that as many households live in concealed poverty as receive social assistance and that approximately two-fifths of the households have children, the majority including two parents.

Causes of Family Poverty

Poverty cannot be explained by any one cause. Rather, in a society like the Federal Republic, it results from the cumulative effect of various, often interrelated, factors. Certain of these factors as they affect families with children can be discerned from Tables 9.2 and 9.3. First, the risk of material need increases with the number of children and, secondly, the absence of one parent — be it through separation, divorce or death —

often severely affects the financial situation of the family. Whereas the number of large families has declined during the past decade or so, the number of broken families has grown considerably as a result of the high increase in divorce (approximately a two-fold increase between 1965 and 1976). However, the fact that a family has several children or is separated does not automatically lead to poverty. It follows that such factors can be regarded as secondary causes of poverty and that a further precondition is necessary. This, it must be presumed in the absence of precise information, is related to class in that the majority of potentially poor families are drawn from lower socio-economic groups with insufficient financial resources to provide against contingencies such as divorce, etc. In this context income poverty may seem to result from the interplay of a further two factors:

(a) The family's income from employment is insufficient or, for reasons of sickness, invalidity, unemployment, etc. non-existent, to defray the cost of living. A low income and a large number of family members both lead to financial difficulties.

(b) The social transfers from the State are inadequate to compensate for low income and family commitments.

A clue to the importance of these factors is provided by the official social assistance statistics, which list the sources of income (other than *Sozialhilfe*) of families drawing benefits. Table 9.4 shows that around a fifth of the families with children receiving *Sozialhilfe* have an income from employment and that this changed little between 1970 and 1977 despite the substantial growth in the numbers receiving *Sozialhilfe*.

Table 9.4   Sources of additional income for Sozialhilfe *recipients, 1970, 1977*

| Family type | Year | % of each family type receiving income from: | | | | |
		Employ-ment	Social insurance pension[1]	Unemployment benefit	Private alimony payments	Other income[2]
Married couple with children	1970	19	35	5	—	81
	1977	20	14	38	—	100
Lone parent with children	1970	13	9	1	21	87
	1977	15	5	5	28	98

1 Statutory accident, pension and sickness insurance.
2 Including child benefits.

Source: Germany 1970, 1977.

Significant numbers receive social insurance pensions, for disability, etc. and unemployment benefits. While the former were less significant in 1977 than in 1970, the latter were more so on account of the rise in unemployment. When insurance benefits are less than *Sozialhilfe* it is frequently because claimants fail to fulfil all the conditions of entitlement and consequently receive only partial payments (see Chapter 5).

To summarise, it is possible to make four broad observations about families in receipt of *Sozialhilfe* and, thereby, about a substantial part of the family poverty in the Federal Republic:

(a) the vast majority of claimants are dependent on *Sozialhilfe* because they have no income through employment. Nevertheless, substantial numbers draw *Sozialhilfe* because of:
(b) insufficient earnings or
(c) inadequate benefits; unemployment in particular contributes considerably to the impoverishment of married couples with children;
(d) many families, including large numbers of lone parent families, dependent on *Sozialhilfe* have no other income apart from child benefit which is, itself, insufficient to cover family needs.

While these conclusions are preliminary and subject to further research, they provide some reference points for evaluating the measures taken to combat poverty.

Measures to Combat Poverty

Sozialhilfe is, in principle, an important instrument for preventing material and non-material need in the Federal Republic. In practice, it cannot be regarded as a solution to the problem of poverty. As we have seen, it fails to reach some of the poorest families, while many of those who are claimants receive only meagre allowances. The task of social assistance is also limited: it does not consist of providing a minimum income on a permanent basis. According to paragraph 1 of the Federal Social Assistance Act (BSHG 1961), the aim is to help the recipient to become self-supporting as soon as possible. The assistance is thus designed primarily as a temporary financial aid for poor people. Above all, however, the increasing dependence of families on social assistance is a challenge to state social policy. It suggests serious deficiencies in the system of family and child support.

Family policy has expanded considerably since the early years of the Federal Republic, when it was characterised by parsimony and non-intervention largely in reaction to the blatantly pro-natalist policy of the National Socialists before the war (see editors' review to Part III). When family allowances were first introduced in 1954 they were low by

European standards, payable only for the third and subsequent child and financed by employers' contributions. Family allowances were regarded as supplementing employees' normal earnings to form a 'family-wage' although much greater emphasis was in fact placed on child tax allowances. A considerable change has occurred since the second half of the 1960s, particularly since the formation of the Social Democratic-Liberal coalition government in 1969, with a movement away from the post-war preoccupation with family cohesion and integrity toward the newer concept of child support as part of social investment in the new generation (Parker 1980). A typical characteristic of the new family policy has been the greater recognition and acceptance of 'irregular' forms of family life, though this is more evident in changes in family law than in social security. Examples of the new aim of 'protecting the institution of the family' include vesting illegitimate children with equal rights (1970), reform of naming for partners after marriage (1976), the reform of marriage law (elimination of 'moral guilt' as a criterion for alimony payment obligations) (1976), reform of family law relating to parental prerogative (1979) and a model programme providing day foster-mothers (*Tagesmütter*) for working mothers (1974–8). Alongside these developments more attention has been paid to families affected by cumulative social problems. The principal target groups of these measures and programmes have been large families, especially among homeless people, immigrants and other marginal groups.

For families generally the most important change in social policy was the reorganisation of child benefits under the Child Benefit Act 1974. In January 1975, the previous system of child benefits and tax allowances was replaced by a new universal child benefits scheme, under which benefits are payable for every child in the Federal Republic regardless of the family's socio-economic status. Most tax allowances for families were also abolished though certain important reliefs have remained, including a marriage tax relief which benefits richer families. Policy responsibilities were vested in the Federal Ministry of Youth, Family and Health although the Ministry of Labour and Social Affairs retained responsibility for administration.

The scale of the change is evident in the 'social budget': expenditures on child benefits rose from 2.8 billion DM in 1970 to 15 billion DM in 1978. Table 9.5 gives the new benefit rates since 1975, which show how the measure has been aimed particularly at larger families (see also Tables III.2 and III.3). There is no variation in benefit according to the age of the child, but considerable increases for families with three or more children. Benefits are normally payable until the age of 18 but, subject to means-test, may be extended to 27 or even 29 for students and trainees.

Table 9.5   *Rates of child benefits, 1975—81*

Number of children	1975—77 (DM/mth)	1978	1979 (to 1 July) (DM/mth)	1 July 1979 1980 (DM/mth)	1981 (DM/mth)	1982 (DM/mth)
1	50	50	50	50	50	50
2	120	130	130	150	170	150
3	240	280	330	350	410	370
4	360	430	530	550	650	610
Increase for a family with . . . . . children (1975 = 100)						
2	100	108	108	125	142	125
3	100	117	138	146	171	154

The child benefit payments since 1975 have undoubtedly helped to combat poverty among certain families. The social assistance statistics reveal a slight decline by 1978 in the number of married couples with children receiving assistance who had other sources of income, such as unemployment insurance payments supplemented by child benefits. However, the new scheme has clearly done less to alleviate the problems of lone parents with children or smaller families with low earnings. Indeed, for such families the effects of the reform have been far more modest than was originally intended. In the discussions leading up to the reform, the government appeared to have accepted the idea that parents should be relieved of at least half the costs of raising their children, but this has not been achieved. Similarly, except for families with three or more children, child benefit rates have not been adjusted in line with changes in earnings or in adult tax allowances since 1975 (Parker 1980).

For these reasons a further increase in child benefits would certainly be welcome. However, with the financial problems now facing the Federal government, no increases in universal social security benefits can be expected. Indeed, as part of a cost-saving exercise in January 1982, child benefit for the second and third child was reduced and the age limit cut to 16. It has recently been suggested within the Social Democratic party that in future all child allowances, or any further increases in child allowances, should be means-tested. Such an approach would be a more effective way of combating poverty, but there is no guarantee that an overly complex scheme and low take-up could be avoided.

Other recent developments in family policy have included a considerable expansion of educational grants and housing allowances. Under the 'Social-Liberal' coalition *Wohngeld*, the unified means-tested housing allowance has become a central instrument of both housing and social security policies for families with modest incomes. It is available to both tenants and owner-occupiers dependent on qualifying housing costs, household size and income. The cut-off point for a two-child two-parent family is about 14 per cent above average earnings and may, in certain circumstances, be higher (Parker 1980). It still suffers, however, from many of the problems associated with means-testing.

Another measure, aimed particularly at poor families, is an Act passed in 1979 regulating maintenance payments in advance for lone parents. This came into force in January 1980 and grants lone parents payments in advance when the absent spouse does not fulfil his or her maintenance obligations to other members of the family. This applies only to parents with children up to six years of age and only when a court decision is made in favour of the lone mother (or father).

Despite such developments, lone parents remain one of the most vulnerable groups in the Federal Republic. A recent official commission argued that the existing financial provisions for lone parents are 'disharmonious' and largely insufficient (Germany 1979b). Others have described lone parents as one of the forgotten groups in the West German welfare state (compare Lawson 1979). Their plight has worsened with the economic recession, since job opportunities for women with children (particularly those looking for part-time work) are now very limited. The Federal Labour Office tends also to take an ambiguous approach to the task of finding employment for single mothers, because of their obligations in the household and for the care of their children. Despite the efforts of some national organisations, single parents have also lacked a powerful political lobby. Any future anti-poverty programmes, and family policy in general, will need to pay much more attention to the hardship of such families.

References

Bradshaw, J. and Piachaud, D. 1980, *Child support in the European Community*, London, Bedford Square Press.
BSHG 1961, *Bundessozialhilfegesetz*, BSHG.
Geissler, 1975, *Die Neue Soziale Frage*, Bonn, Zahlen, Dokumente, Fakten.
Ehrenberg, H. and Fuchs, A; *Sozialstaat und Freiheit*, Frankfurt, Suhrkamp, 1980.
Germany 1970, *Fachserie Sozialhilfe*, Wiesbaden, Statistisches Bundesant.
Germany 1972, *Statistisches Jahrbuch*, Bonn.
Germany 1977, *Fachserie Sozialhilfe*, Wiesbaden, Statistisches Bundesant.
Germany 1978, *Fachserie Sozialhilfe*, Wiesbaden, Statistisches Bundesant.
Germany 1979a, *Statistisches Jahrbuch*, Bonn.
Germany 1979b, *Dritter Familienbericht, hrsg. v. der Sachverständigenkommission der Bundesregierung*, Bundestagsdrucksache, 8/3121, 20 August.

Hartmann, H. 1979, 'Standort und Perspektiven der Sozialhilfe im System der sozialen Sicherung', *WSI-Mitteilungen*, 12.

Hartmann, H. 1981, *Sozialhilfebedürftigkeit und 'Dunkelziffer der Armut'*, Forschungsbericht des Instituts für Sozialforschung und Gesellschaftspolitik (ISG), Cologne.

Hauser, R. and Krupp, H. J. 1979, *Interim report concerning the national report on poverty in the Federal Republic of Germany*, Frankfurt, Arbeitsgruppe Armutsforschung.

Knechtel, E. 1960, 'Die Zahl der einkommensschwachen kinderreichen familien in der Bundesrepublik', *Soziale Welt*, 11.

Kögler, A. 1976, *Die Entwicklung von Randgruppen in der Bundesrepublik*, Schriften der Kommision für Wirtschaflichen und Soziale Wandel, Band 87.

Lawson, R. 1979, 'Western Europe: a Comparative Study' in Samuels, A. (ed.), *Social Security and Family Law*, London. British Institute of International and Comparative Law.

Lawson, R. 1980, 'Poverty and inequality in West Germany' in R. Lawson and V. George (eds), *Poverty and inequality in Common Market Countries*, London, Routledge and Kegan Paul.

Parker, H. 1980, 'West Germany' in J. Bradshaw and D. Piachaud, *Child support in the European Community*, London, Bedford Square Press.

Part IV Poverty, Social Security and the Elderly

Editorial Overview

One of the most important factors contributing to the enormous growth of social welfare expenditures in Western Europe since the Second World War has been the increase in the costs of pensions and other social provisions for the elderly (see Chapter 2). Expenditure on the elderly is by far the largest item in most countries' social budgets, and in many countries has risen more than twice as fast as the national product over the past 30 years. Moreover, despite recent efforts everywhere to contain these costs, they seem likely to grow significantly during the 1980s and 1990s both as a result of demographic and social changes, and because of funding difficulties associated with unemployment and inflation. The evidence points to a growing discrepancy throughout Europe between increased welfare commitments to the elderly and a workforce that is shrinking in relative terms and which therefore faces a rising burden of costs (Rohrlich 1980).

The demographic and financial pressures have also served to highlight the shortcomings of post-war policies, particularly as regards the poor. One of the disturbing findings of the reports prepared for the European Commission's anti-poverty programme is the persistence of a surprisingly high incidence of poverty among elderly persons in most EC countries, even in countries like West Germany where expenditures and 'average' benefits are among the highest in the world (EC 1981d; see also Chapter 2). Much of this poverty appears to be rooted in traditional inequalities of social status, class and sex which social security systems have often tended to legitimize and reinforce. However, it also reflects the shortcomings of policies as new problems have emerged, especially those associated with the growing divisions between the newly retired and the very old, changes in family structures and the prestige and authority enjoyed by the aged.

We begin this section by exploring further some of the demographic and social changes affecting the elderly, and by way of introduction to

*Roger Lawson took lead responsibility for this overview.

the rest of the section we also examine briefly certain similar and different national responses to their needs. The three chapters that follow then present a more detailed analysis of policies in France, The Netherlands and West Germany. Both the French and West German chapters focus mainly on the problems of developing an adequate social security system and some of the reasons for the persistence of income poverty among the elderly. While discussing these issues, the Dutch chapter focuses on the relationship between disability and poverty in old age, and examines why The Netherlands has the world's highest percentage of old people in institutional care.

Demographic and Social Changes

In Western Europe a general aging of the population has been evident for more than a century, but this accelerated appreciably in most countries between the 1930s and mid-1970s (Clark and Spengler 1980). In the early 1930s, persons aged 65 and over comprised just under 8 per cent of the total population of Northern and Western European countries. By 1950, the proportion had risen to 10 per cent and by the end of the 1970s to 14 per cent. The detailed reasons for this increase need not concern us. However, they clearly include falling birth rates, which have affected the numbers of young people, as well as the advances in medicine and general improvements in living standards that have enabled many more people to survive into old age.

Table IV.1 reveals some interesting differences in the trends experienced by countries examined in this volume. By European standards generally, the rise in the proportion of old people has been particularly sharp in West Germany and the UK. However, whereas in Britain population aging was most pronounced between the 1930s and 1950s, in West Germany this occurrred between the mid-1950s and mid-1970s. In France, by contrast, the recent rate of increase in the proportion of old people has been well below the European average. This is partly because of higher post-war birth rates but also because France was one of the first countries to experience a significant decline in fertility and natality and already had a substantial proportion of elderly people by the early decades of this century. Developments in The Netherlands have also differed from the general European pattern, but for opposite reasons to those in France. During the first half of this century the Dutch experienced the lowest fall in fertility in Europe so that The Netherlands has a relatively small proportion of elderly people. However, this is now changing and within the next 20 years the proportion will be close to those in Britain.

Some of the implications of these differences will become evident in the national chapters, but certain general points are worth making here.

Table IV.1   Proportions of elderly persons in the total population in selected European countries, 1930–90

(a) % aged 65 and over

	1930	1950	1975	1990
France	9.2	11.7	13.3	13.1
West Germany	–	9.4	14.3	14.3
The Netherlands	6.2	7.8	10.8	12.3
UK	7.3	10.7	14.0	14.9

(b) % by age and sex

	Age 65–74		Age 75 and over	
	Males	Females	Males	Females
France				
1950	3.1	4.5	1.5	2.6
1975	3.6	4.7	1.6	3.4
1990	3.0	3.9	2.1	4.1
West Germany				
1950	3.0	3.7	1.2	1.5
1975	3.9	5.7	1.5	3.2
1990	2.8	5.0	1.9	4.6
The Netherlands				
1950	2.6	2.8	1.1	1.3
1975	3.0	3.8	1.9	2.4
1990	3.2	4.1	1.8	3.2
UK				
1950	3.1	4.1	1.4	2.1
1975	3.9	5.1	1.6	3.4
1990	3.7	4.8	2.1	4.3

Sources: UN 1980; EC 1981a.

First, demographic change, while important, only accounts for part of the recent growth in expenditure on the elderly (OECD 1976; Rohrlich 1980; Judge 1981). During the 1960s and early 1970s, population aging explained only 40 per cent of the increase in expenditure on pensions in OECD countries when expressed as a share of GDP. In Britain, the ratio was somewhat higher than this and in West Germany it exceeded 50 per cent while in The Netherlands and France it was slightly lower. Moreover, over the post-war period as a whole, demographic trends have probably been even less important.

Anxiety about the effects of an aging population has at times encouraged negative attitudes to the elderly, or at least acted as a constraint on policy developments. There is evidence of this today in many countries and it is exemplified in the more general 'burden of welfare' thesis. In the past, such concerns have had a considerable impact on policies in Britain and France. In Britain, they influenced the Beveridge Report and help to explain the low rates of benefit obtainable through the post-war state social security system (compare Titmuss 1963). In France, demographic fears arising from the trends earlier in this century have had a more profound effect. The French chapter suggests that they have left a 'particularly unfortunate inheritance', which has changed only slowly, in which the elderly have been viewed as contributing to a lack of dynamism and forward thinking in society. It may be argued, too, that the elaborate family policies developed as part of *'une politique demographique active'* have served to divert resources to the young and have lent support to the traditional view that the family rather than the community should be primarily responsible for supporting the old and disabled (Lawson and Reed 1975). In West Germany, there has been much discussion of the *Rentenberg*, a term literally meaning 'pension mountain' but carrying connotations of the increasing 'burden' of dependency. However, until recently, fears about this appear to have been allayed by economic growth and perhaps also by the fact that the provision of decent pensions has been considered as much a part of good industrial relations as of policy towards the elderly.

Table IV.1 also illustrates the considerable shift which has been occurring recently throughout Western Europe in the age structure of the elderly population and which will be even more pronounced during the next 20 years or so. Over the past decade, the proportions of 60 to 74-year-olds have remained more or less constant, and this is likely to continue, during the 1980s and 1990s, though again with some variations between countries. However, a 25 per cent rise has already occurred in the past decade in the proportion aged 75 and over and a further marked increase is projected for the remaining years of this century. This will result in increased numbers of old people living alone and/or in poor health because of their advanced age. Moreover, the majority will be women and this in turn means increasing numbers of widows. On average, women already represent two-thirds of the over-75s in Western Europe, and about a quarter of women over 75 years old are widows. Furthermore,

> more than a quarter of all the over-75s, men and women together, live alone, on account of either widowhood or of the general evolution of family structures and the fall in the birth rate. In France, it is estimated that almost 27% of the over-80s did not, or no longer, have children. (Laroque 1979)

Recent studies have emphasised, too, the regional disparities in the proportions of the aged, especially the very old. There is not only a high proportion of older people in the larger cities, mainly the inner areas, but also in many of the more underdeveloped rural parts of Europe (Amann 1981; Laroque 1979).

The emergence of this 'new class of the very old' (Amann 1981) is of immense significance to the future of social policy. Not only are there obvious financial implications for social security, health and welfare but the shortcomings of existing policies are revealed in stark terms, particularly those arrangements under which men have traditionally gained higher pensions and benefits than women and also greater access to resources generally. That this has contributed to the creation of a severely disadvantaged minority among the very old, especially elderly widows, is now amply documented throughout Europe and will be discussed in the national chapters. It is also evident that, despite recent efforts to improve their prospects, the very old have been hardest hit by inflation, while their access to many newly emerging resources, such as improved occupational pensions and saving schemes, is restricted (Walker 1980). Naturally, too, their problems and needs suggest that 'in future social policy for the elderly will increasingly have to reckon with the physical, mental and social changes of old age, with the "risks of old life"' (Amann 1981).

However, the challenge of meeting these needs is greatly complicated by another, on the face of it paradoxical, development. At a time when the very old are growing in numbers, changes in retirement practices have produced a dramatic decline in the proportions of the 'young old' who are employed and a rapid increase in the proportions claiming pensions. In the UK the economic activity rates of men aged 65 and over fell from 31 per cent in 1951 to 15 per cent in 1978, and in the same period the proportion of the elderly in receipt of pensions rose from 62 to 91 per cent (Judge 1981). Similar trends are found in most other European countries (Townsend 1979). Indeed, Eurostat estimates reveal that activity rates among the younger elderly, especially in the age group 60–4, are much lower in most EC countries than in Britain (see Table IV.2).

A number of different factors have contributed to this development and their relative importance is far too complex a subject to examine here. Not surprisingly, however, most surveys point to the worsening economic conditions since the mid-1970s (compare Tracy 1979; Walker 1980; Judge 1981). Before the recession, improvements in pensions and the introduction of more flexible retirement conditions, particularly for workers in poor health, seem to have been important. But since then the political need to alleviate severe unemployment and the fact that older workers have been over-represented in those branches of industry most affected by recession have been decisive, and this in turn has meant a

Table IV.2   Proportions of persons aged 60–9 in the labour force and receiving pensions, 1977

	% of activity rates[1]			% pensioners[2]		
	Total	Male	Female	Total	Male	Female
Age 60–4						
France	36.4	48.0	26.3	47.3	57.3	38.7
West Germany	29.8	53.2	13.8	52.3	52.3	52.3
The Netherlands	32.7	61.6	7.4	–	–	–
UK	57.1	80.1	26.7	42.6	26.2	57.1
Age 65–9						
France	13.4	18.2	9.6	79.8	90.1	71.4
West Germany	8.3	13.8	4.7	80.4	93.0	72.1
The Netherlands	7.4	13.7	2.3	–	–	–
UK	18.2	27.2	10.9	86.9	84.5	88.9

1 Labour force as a percentage of the total population of the same age and sex.
2 Persons receiving one or more pensions as a percentage of the total population of the same age and sex.

Source: EC 1981b.

distinct shift from voluntary to 'compulsory' retirement. As Anton Amann has argued, the recent trends towards even earlier retirement seem to be based on assumptions that these are emergency solutions to what is, at worst, a medium-term phenomenon.

> But what – one must ask – will happen if it turns out that unemployment must be recognised as a long-term phenomenon in economic and social policy? . . . Whose resources will be sacrificed in whose favour, if the resources are too scarce to ensure the accustomed level? (Amann 1981).

Policy Trends and their Implications
According to the OECD study of income maintenance, the principal factors behind the rise in expenditures on the elderly have been improvements in the scope and levels of social protection (OECD 1976). This conclusion is reached, too, in a recent analysis of post-war trends in state pensions in Britain (Judge 1981). A number of comparative policy studies have also emphasised the progress made during the past 30 years or so in setting new standards of social security and welfare for the elderly, particularly as a result of the new pension strategies developed in this period. This new approach to pensions represents, in Heclo's words, 'probably the most technically complex social policy ever undertaken by national governments. In its long-term implications it may also be one of the most important' (Heclo 1974). How then can one summarise briefly the objectives and implications of these developments, and the principal differences between countries?

In most countries, state old-age pensions were originally developed as a kind of supplement towards subsistence. They were designed essentially to aid the family in supporting its aged members and to provide a form of relief which was clearly distinct from the poor laws. Although this conception changed gradually in the first half of this century, pensions remained small and provided for the basics of life (e.g. the Beveridge minimum). Above this minimum there might or might not be private provisions, but this was for the most part a voluntary matter, not a concern of the State. With the new pension strategies, by contrast, the starting point of the calculation has been the idea that pensioners should not suffer a significant reduction in their former levels of living. In the words of a West German economist, 'The mission of social security is no longer to offer protection against destitution and the like, but to safeguard an acquired social status' (Liefmann-Keil 1959). The concern with status implies, too, a commitment to the dynamic principle, the regular adjustment of pensions in line with changing living standards or some notion of the general prosperity of a country.

Another important aspect of the new pension strategies is a blurring of the boundaries between state provisions and the private sector, especially private occupational pensions. In many countries, the target of pension policies is now a 'replacement ratio' for the average wage earner of between two-thirds and three-quarters of previous earnings. However, it is also assumed that private pensions ought to contribute to the attainment of this desired level. This in turn has led to much more government involvement in encouraging the spread of occupational pensions and other forms of savings and in setting minimum standards in these areas. In several European countries, too, collective agreements involving entire industries have brought about a substantial extension of compulsory private pension coverage, as well as other advantages such as the transferability of pension rights. In France, almost all employees in the private sector belong to a 'complementary' occupational scheme, the main provisions of which are settled centrally by representataives of employers and workers and are then given legislative backing (OPB 1981). In the Netherlands, where 80 per cent of the workforce are already covered by 'second-tier' private schemes, the establishment of a universal and integrated system of occupational pensions has now been agreed in principle. Pension policy in the UK was slow to follow the new European strategy. Instead, the emphasis continued to be one of supporting minimum pensions and, as in the case of unemployment benefit, the introduction of a graduated (i.e. earnings-related) scheme had more to do with economical means of raising pensions than with attempts to maintain living standards. Moreover, although occupational pensions were encouraged, private pensions were viewed as optional supplements rather than as an integral component of pensions for all. Consequently, coverage remains limited and is generally restricted to higher income groups. The Pension Act of 1975, however, represents a step towards 'harmonisation' with the situation in other countries.

Broadly speaking, the main thrust of modern pension strategies has been to apply to many ordinary workers and their families principles similar to those which have long governed the pensions of civil servants and many salaried and professional groups (Marshall 1975). In this sense, they have sought to promote greater equality of treatment among employees, as well as to reduce the risk of poverty for many ex-workers. The Netherlands, in common with Denmark and Sweden, has also placed considerable emphasis in its policies on counteracting other inequalities, by setting decent minumum standards of income and welfare for the elderly. The Dutch chapter shows, too, how special welfare services for disabled and infirm elderly people have sought to treat dependence in old age 'more within a normal context and less as "failure" or "misfortune"'.

By contrast, the arrangements in West Germany and France, and in most other European countries, have done much less to reduce inequalities resulting from low pay and low status, sex discrimination and other labour market disadvantages. Indeed, despite all the achievements of recent years, the financial circumstances of many pensioners remain bleak. This is illustrated by Table IV.3 which shows that only in The Netherlands do state pensions currently guarantee benefits above the international poverty standard. Thus a Frenchman retiring on average earnings is unlikely to receive an income above this standard even if he is entitled to a typical occupational pension. Moreover, minimum pensions are very low indeed. Even in West Germany the average pensioner with both a state and occupational pension will not be much above the poverty standard, unless his wife has a pension in her own right. Widows and couples on minimum pensions are relatively no better off than their counterparts in France which, as the West German chapter shows, reflects long-standing attitudes to the relationship between work and welfare, which have led to traditionally high standards of protection for the 'good' worker but to less generous treatment of the poor. Similar attitudes are found in France, where the situation of the elderly has also been complicated by demographic issues and the difficulties of developing pension schemes for small farmers, agricultural workers and the self-employed.

The protection afforded against poverty by the basic UK pension is comparable to that provided by minimum rates in France and West

Table IV.3   State and occupational pensions in selected European countries, 1975, 1980

(a) State old-age pensions in 1980 as a % of average earnings[1,2]

	Ex-workers with average earnings		Minimum state pension	
	Single	Couple	Single man	Widow
France[3]	45.0	61.1	31.8	31.8
West Germany[4]	48.4	48.4	36.2	21.7
The Netherlands[5]	40.6	58.6	40.6	40.6
UK[6]	23.1	37.0	23.1	23.1

(b) State old-age pensions in 1980 as a % of international poverty standard[1,6]

	Ex-workers with average earnings		Minimum state pension	
	Single	Couple	Single man	Widow
France[3]	83.1	71.7	58.7	58.7
West Germany[4]	130.0	82.5	97.5	58.5
The Netherlands[5]	125.3	115.0	125.3	125.3
UK[6]	63.8	64.9	63.8	63.8

(c) Coverage and benefits of occupational pensions, 1975

	% of working population covered	Typical pension as % of earnings
France	80	8
West Germany	60	12—22
The Netherlands	80	7—11
UK	45	23

1 Figures refer to the pensions of persons retiring in July 1980.

2 Annual earnings are for April 1980.

3 Unlike the other countries, the French minimum pensions and supplements for wives are means-tested. Average pension levels assume a career of at least 37.5 years.

4 The West German estimates assume a career of 45 years, both for average wage earners and minimum pensions.

5 Both the British and Dutch figures are benefits provided by the universal flat-rate pensions.

6 International poverty standard as defined by Beckerman 1979; see also Annexes 2A, 2B.

Sources: EC 1981b; Haanes-Olsen 1978.

Germany. However, fewer Britons have occupational pensions and the state earnings-related scheme is less generous. The 1975 Pensions Act provisions promise to improve the prospects of future pensioners, particularly those who retire on full pensions after 1998.

Finally, Table IV.4 shows that the elderly constitute a substantial proportion of all households in poverty. Widespread reliance on minimum

Table IV.4   *Households in poverty with head aged over 65,
selected countries, mid-1970s*[1]

	% of poor households with head aged 65 or over	
	40% average equivalent disposable income level	*60% average equivalent disposable income level*
The Netherlands	20.5	29.3
France	10.4	34.9
West Germany	44.4	35.6
UK	13.8	49.6

1 See Chapter 2 for definitions

Source: EC 1981d.

pensions and assistance benefits in France and the UK mean that the
elderly are relatively better protected than certain other age groups with
respect to the severest definition of poverty (see also Table 2.21). But,
at the 60 per cent disposable income level, the elderly are the largest
group in every country, and in the UK, where pensions for average
earners are lowest, they comprise almost half of the poor.

The following chapters illustrate how post-war social security developments with their close links between employment, earnings and welfare,
have favoured the worker rather than the citizen. In practice, they have
benefited many in a wide middle stratum of society, while leaving largely
unresolved the problem of the *'mal protegés'* — the underclass of the
poorly protected and those disadvantaged in their working lives.

References

Amann, A. 1981, *The status and prospects of the aging in Western Europe*, Vienna,
European Centre for Social Welfare Research and Training.

Beckerman, W. 1979, *Poverty and the impact of income maintenance programmes*,
Geneva, ILO.

Clark, E. K. and Spengler, J. 1980, *The economics of individual and population
aging*, Cambridge, CUP.

EC 1981a, *Demographic strategies*, Luxembourg, Eurostat.

EC 1981b, *Pensioners in the European Community, 1977*, Luxembourg, Eurostat.

EC 1981c, *Comparative tables of the social security systems of the European Communities*, 11th edn, Luxembourg.

EC 1981d, *Final report from the Commission to the Council on the first programme
of pilot schemes and studies to combat poverty*, Brussels.

Haanes-Olsen, L. 1978, 'Earnings-replacement rate of old-age benefits, 1965—75,
selected countries', *Social Security Bulletin*, January.

Helco, H. 1974, *Modern social politics in Britain and Sweden*, New Haven, Yale
University Press.

Judge, K. 1981, 'State pensions and the growth of social welfare expenditure', *Journal of Social Policy*, vol. 10, no. 4.

Laroque, P. 1979, 'Social protection and the over 75s: what are the problems' in *Social protection and the over 75s*, Geneva, International Social Security Association.

Lawson, R. and Reed, B. 1975, *Social Security in the European Community*, London, Chatham House, PEP.

Liefman-Keil, E. 1959, 'Index-based adjustments for social security benefits', *International Labour Review*, May.

Marshall, T. 1975, *Social policy*, 3rd edn, London, Hutchinson University Press.

OECD 1976, *Public expenditure on income maintenance programmes*, Paris.

OPB 1981, *Improved protection for the occupational pension rights and expectations of early leavers*, London, HMSO, Cmnd 8271.

Rohrlich, G. 1980, 'Maintaining social security pension schemes adequate and solvent — a transnational synopsis of problems and policies', *International Social Security Review*, vol. XXXIII, no. 2.

Titmuss, R. 1963, 'Pension systems and population change' in *Essays on the welfare state*, London, Allen Lane.

Townsend, P. 1979, *Poverty in the United Kingdom*, London, Allen Lane.

Tracy, M. 1979, *Retirement age practices in ten industrial countries 1960—76*, Geneva, International Social Security Association.

Walker, A. 1980, 'The social creation of poverty and dependency in old age', *Journal of Social Policy*, vol. 9, no. 1.

UN 1980, *Demographic yearbook*, New York.

10 France: The Elderly
Doreen Collins

The Socio-economic Background

On 1 January 1980, the total French population was estimated at 53.6 million persons and, like most Western European countries, France has a large population of elderly persons both in absolute and in relative terms (Table 10.1). The expectation of life has increased significantly at birth as well as in middle and later years so that, today, at the age of 65 a man

Table 10.1 *The elderly population in France, 1980*[1]

Age group	Men	Women	Total
60−4	750 700	859 800	1 610 500
65−9	1 056 200	1 328 900	2 385 100
70−4	856 200	1 202 100	2 058 300
75−9	597 900	980 700	1 578 600
80−4	294 800	634 800	929 600
85+	141 100	442 000	583 100
Total over 60	3 696 900	5 448 300	9 145 200
Over 65s as a % of total	11.2	16.8	14.0
Total	26 253 000	27 330 000	53 583 000

Source: EC 1982

may expect to live a further 13 years and a woman over 17 (Table 10.2). There has been a particularly noticeable increase in the number of French men and women aged 75 and over of whom the great majority are women (Tables 10.1 and 10.3).

Marital status is often taken as a crude indication of social isolation and thus of the capacity of an individual to live an independent life of reasonable quality. Significant numbers of the over 65s do not have a current marriage partner and, in percentage terms, the partnerless state increases with age (Table 10.4).

So far, basic demographic factors appear to follow a broadly similar

Table 10.2   Life expectancy in France

Sex	Date	0 years	Expectation of life at age 50 years	65 years	75 years
Male	1933–8	55.9	20.4	11.1	6.3
	1952–6	65.0	22.4	12.1	6.8
	1975	69.0	24.0	13.2	7.8
Female	1933–8	61.6	24.0	13.1	7.5
	1952–6	71.2	26.7	14.8	8.3
	1975	76.9	29.9	17.2	10.1

Source: France 1978a: 47.

Table 10.3   Growth of the elderly population in France, 1901–80

Year	Men total	65–74 men (000s)	75+ men (000s)	Women total (000s)	65–74 women (000s)	75+ women (000s)	Men and Women as % total population 65–74	75+
1901	18 938	1072	419	19 548	1222	542	6.0	2.5
1950	20 005	1296	582	21 642	1866	983	7.6	3.8
1966	23 833	2588	716	25 121	2252	1483	7.7	4.5
1977	25 949	1894	915	27 026	2510	1896	8.5	5.3
1980	26 253	1912	1034	27 330	2531	2058	8.3	5.8

Table 10.4   Marital status of French elderly in 1975

Marital status	Age group 65–99 yrs (Nos)	(%)	75–99 yrs (Nos)	(%)
Single	685 145	9.2	279 955	9.5
Married	3 722 875	50.0	988 955	33.4
Widowed	2 862 885	38.4	1 639 355	55.4
Divorced	178 100	2.4	52 075	1.7
Total	7 449 005	100.0	2 960 340	100.0

Source: Parant 1978: 385.

pattern to those in the UK but greater divergences can be seen in relation to two further points which it is convenient to make at the outset. The first relates to the occupational structure. Although France is now an industrial nation, the occupational structure is characterised by features which are not matched in the UK. A much higher proportion of the working population is self-employed, and is concentrated particularly in agriculture, small businesses, professional occupations and family firms (Table 10.5). The range of employment patterns, as well as the variations within the self-employed group itself, are of particular importance in relation to pensions which are based on previous earnings. Earned incomes

Table 10.5   French occupational groups, 1975

Occupational group	Number	%	Women as % group
Exploitants	1 650 865	7.6	34.3
Salariés agricoles	375 480	1.7	11.6
Patrons — industrie et commerce	1 708 925	7.8	33.4
Profs. lib. et cadres supérieures	1 459 285	6.7	23.2
Cadres moyens	2 764 950	12.7	45.2
Employés	3 840 700	17.6	63.9
Ouvriers	8 207 165	37.7	22.4
Service	1 243 420	5.7	77.9
Autres	524 000	2.4	19.1
Total		99.9	

Source: France 1977.

in agriculture and *petit bourgeois* occupations are notoriously low in relative terms and the problem is made worse by the fact that both these categories are important outlets for women's employment. As an average, men still earn about one-third more than women in comparable jobs. There are also important regional variations in earnings. Thus, in 1973, the average wage in the Ile de France was 128.5 per cent of the national wage level but only 85.4 per cent in Languedoc.

Secondly, a special mention must be made of the geographical distribution of the elderly. A particular feature is that of the rural population. The density of the population in France is much less than in the UK, and outside the well-known city conurbations, a large number of people live in rural and semi-rural conditions. The rapid exodus from agriculture that has occurred in the previous generation has left cantons in the heart of the countryside where up to 30 per cent of the population may be over 65 years old and in La Creuse, the *département* with most elderly, nearly 25 per cent of the population is over 65 including 10 per cent over 75. In general, the pockets of highest concentration of rural ageing are found in central and southern France. Not only are individual incomes and living standards relatively low but the least prosperous areas are left with the greatest burden in terms of the development of supportive services. This problem is compounded by geographical isolation which can make it difficult for the elderly physically to reach services and by the general lack of infrastructure in the form of adequate roads, public transport and telephones.

Parts of Paris illustrate the opposite problem of the elderly in urban city centres, left high and dry as patterns of development move the younger generation and employment outlets away and redevelopment isolates the elderly in outmoded accommodation with little community support. Although there is some movement at the point of retirement away from Paris towards the suburbs and the southern sun this seems a minority choice, primarily amongst the middle classes, most people preferring to remain where they have spent their working lives '*Mais les personnes agées restent encore plus volontiers à Paris*' (Bureau n.d.: 13). Information collected in 1977 from people between the ages of 50 and 70, both working and retired, concerning intentions about moving at retirement and moves actually made, reported that 60 per cent of those still working intended to stay where they were and that 70 per cent of the retired had actually done so. Whilst the results were related to income groups they were also strikingly related to regions. Above all, it is people in Paris and the Paris basin who look forward to moving although in the event fewer make the move they had previously considered (Monnier 1980). The idea that all French people are hankering to return to that part of France from which they and their family sprang as soon as they have wrung a pension or *rente* from a hard-faced employer seems a myth at the present day.

The implications of these factors are obvious. The cost of pensions and support services is heavy. Elderly women are especially vulnerable either because they are concentrated in low-paid occupations during working life or because widows' pensions have traditonally been low, yet they are the larger section of the elderly population. The elderly are particularly affected by redevelopment schemes that isolate them, which lead to a pattern of urban life where they have no part, and by the population movements which have changed the nature of rural life. If we add to these pressures the further one that encourages a lowering of the retirement age, then it seems clear that social and economic forces, coupled with social and economic policies, together work to push the elderly away from the mainstream of society.

French policy towards the elderly has had a clear theoretical base throughout the whole of the post-war period. Its objective has been to maintain social integration and to develop services which express this goal (France, 1962). Practical achievement has often fallen short of this ideal. For many years, priority in social policy was deliberately given to the younger age groups, and particularly to child-rearing. This has been important for resource allocation and for the development of attitudes which have inhibited the acceptance of the elderly as a group with a rightful social place and a contribution to make to social well-being. It was not until the 1970s that a reasonably firm grasp of the problems was shown by central government — by which time, of course, deterioration of the economic climate made fulfilment particularly difficult. By then, however, we can define the goals of social policy towards the elderly as consisting of improved living standards, notably pensions, the build-up of support services in order to maintain the elderly in the local community, and a recognition of the importance of maintaining individual autonomy and decision making instead of developing services for a group wrongfully and inadequately described as dependent on the younger groups. Whilst these goals have been imperfectly achieved, there has been a considerable redirection of social spending towards the elderly in recent years until by 1980 they were estimated to absorb 43.1 per cent of the French social budget (EC 1979).

Pension Policy

Due to historical and political factors the structure of French pension schemes is extremely diverse. This makes it difficult to generalise about the condition of pensioners. However, it would be wrong to suppose that there is no overall government policy towards pension levels. Such policy is designed to ensure a framework within which schemes operate, to achieve a minimum pension level and to accept the financial responsibility necessary to ensure the fulfilment of political goals without destroying the structural variations and the independence of decision possessed by different schemes. Balancing these objectives leads to a situation of great complexity. The idea of 'national solidarity', which has been so important in French social policy, is helpful here. Policy is not aimed to achieve equality in the sense of uniform pensions for all, but to provide a guarantee that overall policy regarding pension levels is achieved and to provide the necessary support for groups so that they may continue to reach the goal in their own way.

Before the Second World War, pension provision was still patchy and spasmodic but the principle of a pension paid in return for work done and linked to retirement from it had been established for certain groups. This applied in particular to those who could claim to have served the State and to whom therefore the State had an obligation so that the *fonctionnaires* (roughly translated as 'civil servants') and the armed forces early established rights. Their example was followed by the nineteenth-century *élite* groups of industrial workers such as railwaymen and coal miners with the result that a number of occupational groups have their own pension arrangements. Today, these pension arrangements relate to industries in public ownership and are usually referred to as the special schemes. (See list in Table 10.7 but note that some authors include only schemes for groups (c) to (e) under *régimes statutaires*, e.g. France 1978b.)

Special schemes take the place of the *régime général* (see below) for workers in appropriate industries. Such groups continue to receive pensions on relatively favourable terms as is indicated by the comparison with private industry in Table 10.8 (Columns 6, 7 and 8). It can be seen that 51 per cent of pensioners in private industry fall into the two lowest pension categories compared with 25 per cent from the nationalised industries and 10 per cent of *fonctionnaires*.

Private industry began to follow suit although only in a limited way. It maintained an uneasy relationship with developments in the public sector and government did not succeed in establishing the beginnings of effective arrangements in the private sector until 1930. From this time, it is possible to speak of a structure which ensured pension coverage for the bulk of the wage-earning population on a contributory basis. However, a further significant step was taken as a result of agreement, in 1936, between the employer associations and the main trades unions, which expressed a joint wish to create pension schemes for those in private industry. This was to prove of great subsequent importance for the establishment of the *régimes complémentaires* (complementary or occupational schemes, see below).

The post-war reforms which affected pensions did not sweep these arrangements away. The special schemes remained in existence but the social assurance scheme for private industry was significantly extended in the *régime général*. However, this was established in such a way that it would not undermine the developing *régimes complémentaires*. Instead, both *régime général* and appropriate complementary schemes together provide the pension coverage for workers in private industry, and the maintenance of this dual system is an integral part of public policy. Government has constantly to balance the needs of the *régime général* with those of the complementary schemes and has to control and extend the coverage of the latter so that they play their allotted part. Although most workers in private industry had acquired membership of a scheme by the early 1960s this was not made fully comprehensive until 1972. There have therefore been considerable numbers of pensioners relying mainly or entirely on the *régime général* in the past but this situation is becoming less important.

Outside the structure for private industry are the special schemes, already mentioned, and particular arrangements for major groups of the self-employed. It is the totality of schemes mentioned in this and the preceding paragraph which constitute the French pension structure with the result that conditions for the receipt of benefit, as well as pension levels, vary considerably between occupational groups. (Underlying these arrangements there continues to be a residual local assistance service but it is of declining importance as a source of cash benefits for the elderly and it is not discussed here.)

The post-war period opened with many of the elderly in a difficult position. The principle of the *régime général* at that time was to provide a pension of 40 per cent of previous earnings at the age of 65, based on 30 years' contributions, a condition which many could not meet. (This has now been increased to 50 per cent of previous earnings based on 37½ years' contributions.) A ceiling on assessed income kept the maximum pension low, but, since the finances of the *régimes complémentaires* were built on assumptions concerning the ceiling, changes in it were both difficult and limited. Neither the impact of inflation nor rising expectations could be readily accommodated within the rules. Outside the general system, the position of pensioners of the special schemes and from the public service was relatively favourable but the circumstances of small farmers and of the *petit bourgeois* generally was particularly poor.

It therefore became necessary to bolster the position of those at the lowest level and this was done through a variety of means-tested allowances, carried on both government and base pension-scheme funds (i.e. all pension schemes excluding the complementary). It is through these allowances, including the minimum pension, that a basic minimum standard (*minimum vieillesse*) has been achieved and in recent years policy has been devoted to lifting this minimum in preference to financing other possible policy choices, notably a general reduction in the retirement age.

Minimum Vieillesse

The *minimum vieillesse* consists of two elements: a base element which itself may be composed of both an insurance and assistance component, and an allowance from the National Solidarity Fund (*Fonds nationale de Solidarité, FNS*). The base may consist solely of the contributory pension under the *régime général*, a special scheme or one of the schemes for the self-employed. However, if resources of the pensioner are below a given level or no pension has been earned, an assistance type payment is made. Consequently, those with only token membership of their scheme will be eligible for a relatively larger assistance element in addition to any contributory pension they receive. The assistance element will be paid in one of several forms which are assimilated to the *Allocation aux Vieux Travailleurs Salariés, AVTS*. The base benefit is thus itself a fairly complex structure. Moreover, if resulting resources for the individuals do not reach a given limit, the second element — an assistance supplement from the NFS — comes into play. At present, this is carried on governmental funds for schemes other than the *régime général*. The two elements together form the minimum standard (*minimum vieillesse*), which is underwritten by central policy and the objective has been to allow this to reach half the current rate fixed for SMIC (*salaire minimum interprofessionel de croissance*). Table 10.6 shows that this policy objective was first achieved in 1978.

Table 10.6   The value of the Minimum Vieillesse, *1950 – 1979*

Year	Minimum vieillesse France p.a.	Income ceiling for single person's eligibility FFr p.a.	Minimum vieillesse as % SMIC (SMIC before 1970)
1950	450	—	—
1955	658	1440	26.0
1960	1036	1940	31.1
1965	1700	2010	42.4
1970	2900	3200	42.6
1975	6800	4400	48.4
1977	9000	8950	48.4
1978	11000	11900	52.6
1979	12900	13800	54.8

Source: private communication

The number of pensioners receiving FNS does not seem to vary greatly from year to year. In 1976, there were 1.8 million beneficiaries (i.e. 17 per cent of pensioners, see Table 10.7, column 3) compared with 1.7 million in 1975 and 1.9 million in 1972 (France 1978a). Beneficiaries of FNS are eligible to receive certain other benefits such as a housing allowance, reduced rates for electricity and gas, and exemption from local taxes.

Pension Schemes

Table 10.7 illustrates the very great variation in the size of pension schemes, their relative burden of pensioners, their general financial health and the level of pension payable. Those, notably the special schemes, with a very high ratio of beneficiaries to contributors, do not necessarily pay low benefits that must be supplemented by FNS. The situation is

Table 10.7   *French retirement pension schemes, 1976*

Scheme	1 Number contributors	2 Number beneficiaries	3 Beneficiaries receiving supplement (FNS)	4 2 as % 1	5 3 as % 2
General *régime*	13 045 000	4 254 000	801 000	32.6	18.8
Régime Agricole	719 000	846 500	111 000	117.6	13.1
Merchant Marine	79 000	94 000	5 000	118.9	5.3
Clercs de notaire	38 000	14 000	–	36.8	–
Mines	125 000	372 000	3 000	297.6	0.8
Fonctionnaires	1 842 000	1 073 000	–	58.2	–
Agences des collectivités locales	738 000	217 000	3 000	29.4	1.4
SNCF (rlys)	272 000	410 000	7 000	150.7	1.7
Special schemes					
EDF-GDF (Electricity and Gas)	136 000	100 000	1 000	73.5	1.0
Ouvriers de l'Etat	89 000	105 000	2 000	117.9	1.9
RATP (Paris transport)	36 000	37 000	–	102.7	–
Others	28 000	70 000	1 000	250.0	1.4
Self-employed					
Exploitants Agricoles	2 217 000	1 836 000	798 000	82.8	43.5
ORGANIC (*industrie et commerce*)	712 000	681 000	76 000	95.6	11.2
CANCAVA (artisans)	561 000	385 000	65 000	68.6	16.9
Liberal profs.	218 000	67 000	2 000	30.7	3.0
Total	3 708 000	2 969 000	941 000	80.0	31.7

Source: France 1978a: 166.

very different for the self-employed among whom the burden of pensioners and of supplementation is heavy for all groups except the liberal professions. Supplementation is also necessary for large numbers of beneficiaries under the *régime général*, although legislation passed in 1972 that provided for compulsory membership of occupational schemes (*régimes complémentaires*) should gradually reduce the proportion claiming FNS.

The *régimes complémentaires* apply to those who work in private industry. Managerial grades began to be covered in 1947, other employees in 1962 and since 1972 membership of the relevant pension scheme has been legally compulsory. By 1976, there were 17.3 million contributors and 4.7 million beneficiaries (excluding dependants) in these schemes (France 1978b). The schemes are funded by contributions from employers and employees (at a given percentage of annual earnings up to a minimum amount) which are used to purchase pension units according to rules that allow for yearly revaluation by the schemes in conjunction with government. There are many different pension schemes in existence but transferability is not an issue. The French accumulate pensions from more than one source, the value of each complementary pension being maintained through the yearly revaluation of the holding of pension points. Although the basic principle is the same for all, there are important differences between the arrangements for managerial and other employees. The percentage contribution paid by employers and employees, and the income limit, are higher for managerial grades and the pension unit is valued differently. The aim of government policy today is to ensure that a pension of at least 20 per cent of previous earnings can be drawn from an occupational scheme after 37 years' contributions. (Many schemes pay a good deal more but it will be some time before the schemes are fully mature.) Since the *régime général* is now geared to the payment of a pension of 50 per cent of previous earnings after the same period of time, government policy anticipates a total pension of 70 per cent of previous earnings for this section of the working population. During 1971/2 the method of calculating pensions in the *régime général* was also reformed so that pension levels are now linked to the wages earned in the 10 best years and improved arrangements were established for the payment of widows' pensions.

Other groups of workers do not belong to occupational schemes. They may be members of the special schemes which already give very favourable terms. Alternatively they may belong to one of the schemes for the self-employed groups and perhaps have little pension entitlement because of low earnings. The self-employed fought hard to retain their separate identity but have gradually had to accept the constraints that arise from playing a part in the official social security structure. They still retain considerable individuality and a certain freedom of action but impoverishment is the outstanding characteristic of some of the schemes today and this has resulted in a most complex rescue operation (see below). All schemes available to the self-employed must now pay the minimum pension and also have arrangements whereby additional contributions can be paid to purchase higher pensions. However, the schemes vary from those professions which pay good pensions, such as for the liberal professionals, to those of the small farmers and businessmen which have a high proportion of pensioners at the minimal level and whose pensions can be honoured only because of the transfers now being operated through the social security system. Table 10.8 indicates how recipients of pensions for the artisans and business schemes are concentrated at the bottom end

Table 10.8 Pensions according to occupation group, economic sector and sex

Monthly pension (FFr)	Ouvriers (et pers. de service)	Employés moyens	Cadres moyens	Cadres sup. prof. liberales	Commerçants artisans	Salariés du secteur privé	Salariés du secteur nationalisé	Fonctionnaires	Male	Female	Total
	(1)	(2)	(3)	(4)	(5)	(6)	(7)	(8)	(9)	(10)	(11)
Number in sample group	(454)	(107)	(125)	(99)	(139)	(468)	(116)	(174)	(550)	(403)	(953)
Number in sample group											
1250 and less	24	19	5		34	25	9	2	11	31	20
1250–1750	28	28	5	2	16	26	16	8	18	22	20
1750–2250	24	27	9	2	20	16	38	14	21	16	19
2250–2750	13	10	14	4	9	10	15	14	12	10	11
2750–3250	6	7	28	9	10	9	11	17	11	10	10
3250–3750	2	6	18	8	2	3	3	18	7	5	6
3750–4250	2	1	13	8	4	3	2	10	6	3	4
4250–4750	1	1	2	13	1	1	1	5	2	1	2
4750–5250			4	10	2	2	1	4	3		2
5250–7250		1	4	27	2	3	3	7	5	2	4
7250 or more			1	17		2	1	1	4		2
Total	100	100	100	100	100	100	100	100	100	100	100
Non-response (%)	8	7	7	6	8	9	5	3	8	7	8
Average pension FFr	1840	1905	3080	5175	2005	2195	2340	3250	2790	1975	2425

Source: Monnier 1980.

of the pension scale whilst the liberal professions cluster, with the *cadres supérieures*, at the top. Table 10.7, it will be recalled, shows the importance of supplementation for the self-employed categories, reflecting the steady economic decline in these occupations.

During the 1970s, it was realised that, if the principle of paying a basic minimum at an improved level was to be achieved for all the elderly, the problem of the financial capacity of certain schemes would have to be faced and the schemes brought into a more unified financial structure. (This plan excluded the *régimes complémentaires* which are the concern of employers and their workforces.) Already some financial transfers had been insisted upon from the *régime général* to some of the self-employed but the worsening situation in some schemes made it necessary to establish more elaborate transfer arrangements. Therefore, a new policy was introduced in 1974 and from that date it is possible to speak of a generalised financial system underlying the various schemes but only up to a limited pension level. The system consists of mutual financial compensation between schemes which depends upon both financial and demographic factors and, in practice, now results in transfers largely from the *régime général* into certain of the schemes for the self-employed. However, this in no way implies the application of identical rules for contributions or for pension determination. At the same time, government accepted responsibility for reimbursing the *régime général* for the outgoings for which it finds itself responsible in this connection. This policy was announced as a temporary measure only and it remains an open question whether it represents a significant change in the financing of retirement pensions through making the state a more significant contributor than hitherto. The State may, of course, retreat once the demographic problem has righted itself, for traditionally the State's financial role has been strictly limited and the French still hold to the primacy of the contributory principle. The role of government has been to determine the principles of policy, such as the pension level, to insist upon a basic minimum, and to ensure that the various agencies can fulfil their role whilst itself financing only those functions which it has agreed to underwrite.

The policy of subsidy of the inadequate schemes by those whose schemes have a more favourable financial and demographic profile aroused considerable resentment but it demonstrated an important approach in French social policy which attempts to balance overall community responsibility for a need with the retention of considerable autonomy for the various social elements. No scheme can be left to flounder unable to fulfil its basic obligation, and this requires the application of the principle of national solidarity. It does not mean, however, a move towards equality of pensions or in the means of achieving them.

The Retirement Age

Considerable argument has revolved around the question of the age of retirement. The issue is complicated by the fact that in many of the special schemes it is possible to retire from the age of 55 on relatively generous terms whilst the *régime général* and occupational (complementary) schemes are based on the assumption of retirement at 65 on full pension, although there is the possibility of retirement at 60 with a reduced rate of pension. About 20 per cent of the labour force is eligible for a half-pay pension equivalent to 50 per cent of former earnings at the age of 60, if not earlier, and there has been strong pressure, particularly as unemployment has mounted, to extend this principle to the *régime général* to which the bulk of the workforce belongs. So far, this has been resisted by the government primarily for financial reasons although the move is also opposed on the grounds that it is not being necessarily in the interests of the individual worker and encourages social isolation which policy is trying to overcome. The evidence for what happens in practice and for what people really want to do is both patchy and variable but suggests that the creation of conditions under which effective individual choice can be made would be a desirable policy goal. (See discussion in Monnier 1979 and Fournier and Questiaux 1978: 597–611).

Whilst the decision was taken to concentrate on improving the level of the lowest pensions rather than bringing the age of retirement down for all, the terms upon which a full pension might be drawn from the *régime général* at the age of 60 were considerably improved during the years 1971–6. The groups which benefited under these arrangements include women, persons defined as incapable of work largely because of indifferent health and lack of suitable work, persons with bad war-time experiences and manual workers in arduous jobs. Working mothers, for instance, in manual occupations who have raised three children need a contribution record of only 30 years. Arrangements have existed for some time under the unemployment benefit scheme for private industry whereby workers between 60 and 65 who stop work are guaranteed 70 per cent of their previous pay and remain members of the social security system (see Chapter 3). They cannot, however, take paid work and continue to draw the benefit whereas retirement pensions are not subject to an earnings rule.

Pension Levels

The Monnier survey undertaken in the latter part of 1977 demonstrated a considerable variation in pension levels resulting from their relationship to previous earnings. These results (Table 10.8) supplement Tables

10.6 and 10.7 which show 1.8 million beneficiaries at the level of the *minimum viellesse* (assessed for 1977 at 9000 FFr per year). If we assume a rate for SMIC of 18 668 FFr per year during 1977, columns 9 and 10 below suggest that between 29 and 50 per cent of men and 53 and 69 per cent of women were below the minimum wage level. (SMIC moved from 7.89 FFr per hour in January 1977 to 10.06 francs per hour in December. A 40-hour week is assumed above.)

Respondents were also asked their views concerning the adequacy of their pension and although the majority felt it was sufficient, significant numbers were less satisfied (Table 10.9). Not surprisingly, those who thought their pension insufficient or very insufficient averaged much lower pension incomes. If this result is related to the bunching of pension incomes evident in Table 10.8, it is possible to conclude that dissatisfaction is greater among women than men, in the private sector more so than in the public and particularly widespread among former unskilled workers and among the *petite bourgeoisie*.

Table 10.9   *Assessment of pension sufficiency by retired people*

Assessment categories	Assessment of efficiency (%)	Average monthly pension (FFr)
Sufficient	54	2950
Insufficient	36	1850
Very insufficient	5	1400
No reply	5	–
Total	100	2425[1]

1 Excludes no replies

Source: Monnier 1980.

Broader Policy Towards the Elderly

The sixth and seventh economic and social plans (1971–80) devoted considerable attention to the needs of the elderly and the seventh plan in particular had to recognise that the accepted goal of social integration was not being achieved, or even effectively pursued. It was realised that most of the elderly were too poor to be considered full members of a consumer society; community developments in urban planning and transport ignored them and specific services for the elderly often led to their physical exclusion from society at large. The swing away from the large residential unit and the geriatric ward to the old people's home had already begun to move towards more open homes and forms of semi-independent living rather than the traditional residential unit. The seventh plan strengthened this direction in policy and at the same time stressed the importance of domiciliary and community support so that the elderly might live actively in their own local circles. A feature was the attention paid to the need to involve the elderly themselves in the arrangements made.

This policy was translated into the specific targets of holding the number of people in nursing homes and old people's homes at the 1968 level through bringing more people in the community into contact with services designed to prevent their admission. It was envisaged that services should be seen in an across-the-board fashion to include the improvement of incomes, housing, health care, light infrastructure and neighbourhood services.

Although unremarkable in objective, the implications of this policy were quite significant. In France especially, the tradition of a strong centralising bureaucracy cuts across the lines of modern policy which are designed to bring different institutions together at local level to make coherent neighbourhood plans, to allow these local groupings to have a real control over policy, to encourage the involvement of the elderly and local inhabitants and, generally, to adapt services to the consumer rather than the other way round.

The policy was strengthened with the creation of local administrative sectors in which social security funds, local authorities, hospitals and governments were expected to work together in a co-ordinated way. Each sector was made responsible for a housing programme and for services designed to improve the possibility of participation in social and cultural life, facilities which could range from light maintenance work to the provision of leisure activities. In addition, each sector was required to have at least three programmes from a defined list which included information and preventive services, the improvement of domiciliary aids including telephones or specially trained home helps, more catering services (not only meals but help with shopping and nutritional advice), domiciliary health care and various forms of support services to achieve better liaison of services and more effective use of voluntary workers. Central government provided a system of incentive grants to stimulate these activities, particular help being directed to operating expenditure rather than capital costs in order to reverse the emphasis on institutional care in the public provision of services.

A second facet of policy was the attempt at a more meticulous definition of the role of residential care with recognition that the seriously infirm and the very old constitute a significantly sized group of which considerable numbers will require this form of help. It was recognised that the task, as the community services developed, would be more specialised than hitherto and that the same principle of autonomy and individual decision taking should be applied within such units as for the fitter and more active elderly living outside.

A first evaluation of progress has suggested only modest success in achieving policy goals both on the criterion of a shift in the emphasis in services and on that of improving lifestyles both for those in their own homes and those in residential care (OECD 1979). The priority action programmes in the seventh plan were designed to overcome structural weaknesses in the local administrative sectors and achieve services which can change and adapt but this appears to remain a significant stumbling block.

Thus the themes of *la politique de la vieillesse* have still some way to go but the twin ideas of social integration and of the right of the elderly to determine their own lives run counter to strong economic, social and historical forces. It was realised long ago that industrial society tends to exclude the elderly from the work process and that this required a policy towards pensions, but less attention has been paid to the more difficult issue of the place of the elderly in society as growing numbers of people can expect to live for many years beyond retirement. France has, perhaps, a particularly unfortunate inheritance in that her demographic fears have encouraged her to adopt a negative attitude to the elderly who have often been viewed as a burden on the active, inhibiting dynamic and forward thinking. Public policy has tried to take a different view and, after years of delay, has begun to develop. How successful it will be in achieving its goals is by no means solely a question for the services themselves but, far more, for the public at large in the attitude it adopts towards the elderly.

References

Bureau n.d., *La Population Agée de Paris en 1968*, Paris, Bureau d'Aide Sociale de la Ville de Paris.

EC 1979, *The European social budget 1980–1975–1970*, Brussels, Commission of the European Communities.

EC 1982, *Demographic statistics*, 1970–1980, Luxembourg, Eurostat.

Fournier, J. and Questiaux, N. 1978, *Traité du social; Situations, Luttes, Politiques, Institutions*, Dalloz.

France 1962, *Rapport de la commission d'etude des problèmes de la vieillesse*, (Usually referred to as the Laroque Report), Paris.

France 1977, *Economie et statistique*, July–August.

France 1978a, *Annuaire statistique*, Paris.

France 1978b, *Données sociales, edition 1978*, Institut National de la Statistique et des Economiques.

Monnier, A. 1979, 'Les limites de la vie active et la retraite', *Population*, Paris, July–October, pp. 801–22.

Monnier, A. 1980, 'Les limites de la vie active et la retraite', *Population*, Paris, January, pp. 109–35.

OECD 1979, *Socio-economic problems of the elderly*, Paris.

Parant, E. 1978, '*Les personnes âgées en 1975 et la vieillissement démographique en France (1931—75)*', *Population*, Paris, March, p. 385.

11 The Netherlands: Poverty and Disability in Old Age

*Peter Coleman**

It is not an easy matter to represent accurately another country's welfare policy and provision. Brief factual statements may be misleading unless the total frame of reference, including most importantly the historical context, is adequately explained. Provisions must be seen in relation to each other and in relation to their historical forebears.

The Dutch provisions for their elderly population provide good illustrations of these points. As a welfare state, The Netherlands is known to be generous to its inhabitants and the elderly are no exception to this. Yet an Anglo-Saxon visitor might be startled to find that The Netherlands has the highest percentage of institutionalised elderly people of any country in the world (13 per cent of those aged over 65). How, might he ask, can that be a good thing?

Our visitor's perception would probably stem partly from the negative connotation which attaches to the term 'institution' in Britain and the USA. While the British have yet to develop an adequate philosophy of long-term care for elderly people, the critical examinations of standards of care, following Peter Townsend's *The Last Refuge* (1962), have stimulated a search for alternatives to institutions rather than a wish to improve the quality of care given within them. If anything, the American experience has been even more negative (Vladeck 1980).

However, the foreign visitor to Dutch old people's homes needs to be prepared to reconsider the value of residential care. It is not only that Dutch homes are of a higher quality and descend from a wholly different historical tradition; they also reflect different values held with regard to the 'security' of their elderly population. A Dutch visitor to Britain would likely as not be startled by our apparent 'neglect', which we might call 'tolerance', of disabled elderly people living in risky situations in the community. This reflects the greater stress which the British seem to place on the importance of maintaining an 'independent' life.

*I would like to acknowledge all that I have learned from my ex-colleagues at the Gerontological Centre in Nijmegen, and especially Joep Munnichs and Paul Remmerswaal, and also my gratitude to the latter for his helpful comments on an earlier draft of this chapter.

Indeed, when talking about comparative social policy it is difficult to escape talking about values, the relative importance given to different aims in different societies. The Netherlands, though a close neighbour of Britain, is a different society and we cannot expect Dutch policy-makers to have seen things in quite the same ways as their British counterparts. In regard to measures to combat poverty and disability in old age they have both seen and acted very differently.

The Significance of Disability in Old Age

There are a number of factors which threaten living standards in old age. Loss of income following retirement is obviously a major factor, but quality of life is diminished by many other losses as well: bereavement, isolation, loss of contact with family and other people, and loss of participation in the wider community. The most crucial factor is probably the increase in occurrence of diseases affecting both physical and mental capacities. Although some people remain fit and active right into advanced old age, and perhaps many more would if we paid proper attention to factors in middle age related to the onset of disease in old age, others suffer badly from poor health and the quality of their lives is greatly affected. Health status, therefore, is a major source of inequality in later life and demands some reaction from society, some 'compensation' for the loss incurred.

The incidence of disability increases with advanced age. Studies in the UK, The Netherlands and other Western countries show that up to 30 per cent of those over 65 years of age exhibit a degree of disability requiring some form of assistance (Akhtar *et al.* 1973; Gemeente Rotterdam 1970; Hofman *et al.* 1979; Hunt 1978; Isaacs and Neville 1976). This rises from between 15 and 20 per cent in the 65 to 74 age group, to between 35 and 40 per cent in the 75 to 84 age group, and to over 60 per cent in the above 85s.

The Dutch reaction has been to provide institutional care for frail and infirm elderly people with the aim of ensuring a supportive environment for every older person who for reason of infirmity no longer wishes to live independently. Current estimates suggest that 3 per cent of the Dutch elderly population live in 'nursing homes' and 9–10 per cent in so-called 'caring homes'. In Britain, by contrast, provision of institutional care remains very limited and the proportion of elderly living in long-term accommodation, private nursing homes, and residential homes provided by local authorities and by private and voluntary organisations is well below 5 per cent. Though it is true that domiciliary services and warden-monitored sheltered housing schemes play a more significant role in the UK, the British system is still dependent on the care given to very large numbers of extremely disabled elderly people by families rather than by professional carers.

Indeed in recent years the British emphasis has increasingly been placed on caring for elderly people in the community, translated in terms of improved domiciliary services and greater — though still insufficient — support for families caring for their elderly relatives. The rationale for this is very clear. When there are so many elderly people and their families in need, it is better to spread resources thinly so as to support large numbers of elderly people in their own houses rather than to focus all care on the smaller number living in institutions. The option of spending a great deal more money on the welfare of the elderly no longer seems open.

The Dutch, however, have already managed to make a much more generous provision for their elderly population and have removed the necessity for intensive support by families and the domiciliary services with the result that old age appears less problematic in The Netherlands. This is not to say that every elderly person in need receives the most appropriate help at the right time, nor that residential care is always perceived by disabled elderly people as the most appropriate solution to their problems. Moreover, some would argue that Dutch intramural provision is too large. Nevertheless, in comparison with Britain a much more determined effort has been made to meet perceived needs, not only in regard to institutional care but also with respect to the whole range of welfare provisions for the elderly.

The Development of Pensions and Social Assistance

The major legislation and government action that has been carried out on behalf of elderly people in The Netherlands since the Second World War is set out in Figure 11.1. As in the UK, the main impetus in The Netherlands came during the war and immediately afterwards although it is difficult to trace exactly when and how people became aware of the developing problems associated with an increasingly large number of elderly people in the population (see Table 11.1).

However, the Dutch were not initially at the forefront in developing provisions for the elderly. Although a measure was adopted in 1947 whereby assistance was given to very poor elderly people (this was essentially a means-tested subsistence payment), it was not until 1957 that the AOW (*Algemene Ouderdomswet*), the 'General Old Age Pension Act', came into force. The idea that care of elderly people was primarily the responsibility of the family and of their children in particular was very firmly embedded, and the dominant Catholic and Protestant political parties feared that loss of concern would follow loss of responsibility.

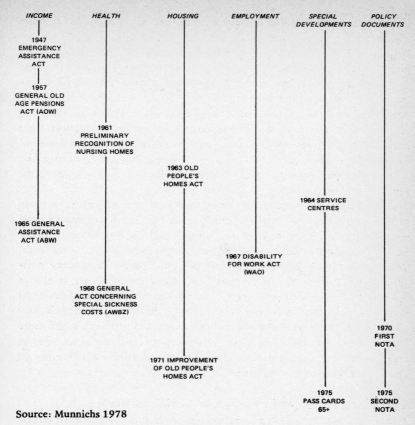

Source: Munnichs 1978

Figure 11.1   *Development of services for the elderly in the Netherlands in the post-war years*

Table 11.1   *Actual and estimated proportions of elderly people, The Netherlands and Great Britain, 1899–2001*

Country	Year	% of total population aged over:		
		65 years	*75 years*	*85 years*
The Netherlands	1899	6.0	1.8	—
	1930	6.2	1.9	—
	1950	7.7	2.4	0.3
	1975	10.7	4.0	0.7
	2000	13.2	5.6	1.2
Great Britain	1901	4.8	—	—
	1931	7.4	2.1	0.2
	1951	10.9	3.6	0.4
	1976	14.2	5.1	0.9
	2001	13.6	6.0	1.3

The Liberals also opposed a general pension provision on the grounds that it would diminish individual responsibility to make provisions for old age. Only gradually did these views give way to arguments from the socialist side (Drees 1979). A further reason for the delay was the resistance of individual firms and enterprises which already administered and financed their own pension schemes (Menzies 1974). Indeed, the history of all welfare provision for the elderly in The Netherlands is characterised by the wish of individual organisations to maintain their autonomy. This in itself reflects the important role they have played and still play in developing provisions.

The pension provision when it was made was very generous in conception and the forerunner of other generous legislation (Riemen 1979). As in the UK a flat-rate payment was introduced but in The Netherlands this was payable to all people who had reached the age of 65, regardless of status or whether or not they had worked. It was, therefore, and remains a genuinely national insurance (*'volksverzekering'*). The pension is financed mainly by a levy on wages which all working people are obliged to pay.

In the first instance, the level of benefit chosen was that equivalent to the highest rate payable under the 1947 provision. In the 1960s and 1970s, the level of pension was gradually raised to the level of the minimum wage (a real increase of some 70 per cent in the period 1968—78), and now follows changes in the minimum wage, which is itself linked to the cost of living index. Essential to the system is a spiral whereby rising pensions mean higher contributions leading to higher wages and thus another rise in pension levels (Menzies 1974). Present payments (at 1.7.80) are f1553 a month for a married couple and f1082 for a single elderly person, nearly twice the state pension in the UK at current exchange rates.

Initially, it was conceived that the state pension would be supplemented by occupational schemes, and a goal was envisaged whereby any worker with 40 years' service could claim a pension equal to 70 per cent of his wages prior to retirement (Riemen 1979). The gradual raising of the basic AOW payment made this more feasible and a large number of Dutch elderly people enjoy such a pension. Nevertheless the policy has not been completely successful. In the first place not everybody is involved in such additional occupational schemes (for example, many unmarried women) and indeed the census of 1971 showed that 36 per cent of people aged over 65 had only a basic state pension, sometimes supplemented by other forms of state assistance (Fiselier and Kraft 1978). Further, because of the great variety of different occupational pension schemes in operation, change of employment often means loss of pension rights that have previously been built up. Serious thought is now being given to a general employees' pension which would guarantee a 'complete' pension on retirement.

Other hopes for the future include the lowering of the pension age from 65, particularly for single women. The EEC directive of 1978 on equal treatment of men and women in regard to social security obliges some change in the payment of pensions before the end of 1984. However, it is very unlikely for financial reasons that the scheme will be changed to allow both man and wife to receive the same AOW payment as a single elderly person (Riemen 1979).

Some evidence of the improvement in pension provisons is provided by the fact that the numbers of elderly people living in their own homes and receiving social assistance decreased markedly in the 1970s, from 90 000 (i.e. 7 per cent of the elderly population) in 1969 to 39 000 in 1977 (just over 2 per cent) (see Table 11.2). This, however, has to be set against the fact that the numbers within residential homes receiving social assistance have increased (see below).

Table 11.2   Number of elderly receipients under the ABW,
The Netherlands, 1965—77

Year	Number (000s) of elderly ABW recipients by residence in:		ABW paid on behalf of 'caring home' residents (million guilders)
	Own home	Caring home	
1965	48	43	57
1966	57	47	84
1967	61	44	117
1968	76	50	149
1969	90	55	186
1970	89	62	263
1971	86	83	333
1972	83	93	433
1973	81	100	562
1974	75	106	753
1975	78	101	1081
1976	55	106	1278
1977	39	109	1469

Source: Ministerie van Cultuur, Recreatie en Maatschappelijke Werk.

The ABW (*Algemene Bijstandswet*: General Assistance Act) was drawn up in 1963 and ensures every adult an allowance in cases of extraordinary expenses if the necessity for maintaining a tolerable level of living can be duly demonstrated. This law finally broke the dependence of elderly people on their children and stimulated the growth of special provisions for the elderly, particularly residential care.

The conception of the ABW like the AOW was generous and has been succeeded by other generous legislation relating to chronic sickness and to disability. The AWBZ (*Algemene Wet Bijzondere Ziektekosten*: General Act Concerning Special Sickness Costs) of 1968 established a method of financing old people to stay in the recently established nursing homes, and the WAO (*Wet Arbeidsongeschiktheid*: General Disability for Work Act) of 1967 allowed people to retire early on the grounds of ill health and to receive up to the equivalent of 80 per cent of their last working salary. Together these pieces of legislation provide substantial compensation for the losses in living standards suffered by disabled elderly people. However, the developments have not been free of problems, and these will be considered in the following sections.

Verzorgingstehuizen (Caring Homes)

The large number of places provided in old people's homes, now commonly called 'caring homes', is probably the most controversial issue in Dutch policy towards the elderly. Thanks to the activity of the postwar era, 140 000 Dutch elderly people (9 per cent of the population aged over 85) now live in such homes. This is four to five times as many as live in any form of residential care in the UK and is a much higher percentage than is found in any other country.

There are a number of explanations for this growth. First it is important to recognise that there is a long tradition of residential care in The Netherlands related to the importance of voluntary associations in the provision of social welfare (de Wolf 1977). These organisations have maintained their independent character and influence despite all the modern developments in systems of welfare.

Even before the Second World War there were substantial numbers of religious and communal associations providing elderly people with board and lodging. Though greatly lacking by modern standards these homes were quite unlike the Britsh 'workhouse'. As one American observer has commented:

> Aged homes in The Netherlands have a long tradition of descent from medieval 'guest homes', the Dutch version of the poor-house. Perhaps because these institutions were privately supported and church related, rather than tax supported and governmental as in England and America, they seem to have escaped some of the nastier, punitive features of the Elizabethan 'poor house'. An example, the sexes were separated and uniform dress was required, but the men's uniform included both a top hat and watch chain. (Wershow 1979).

The very concept of residential care that the post-war Dutch policymakers stimulated was thus quite different to the one of British and American traditions. The majority of Dutch homes today are still independent institutions run by religious or other voluntary foundations, though subject to inspection from the provincial authorities. Of the 1600 homes in existence, the vast majority (1500) belong to the four main organisations of old peoples' homes (Catholic, Protestant, humanist and general) which themselves form the LSB (*Landelijke Samenwerking Bejaardentehuisorganisaties*), the 'National Co-operative Association of Organisations of Old People's Homes'. Control by individual organisations is generally thought preferable to control by local authorities (van Gestel 1980).

National policy in regard to caring homes is the responsibility of what used to be the Ministry of Social Welfare and which since 1965 has been re-formed as the Ministry of Cultural Affairs, Recreation and Social Work. Legislation carried out in 1963 (*Wet op de Bejaardenoorden*: Old People's Homes Act) established the standards that the provincial authorities were obliged to monitor. Living in dormitories became impossible and features such as lifts were insisted on, as was the fulfilment of certain safety requirements. Most homes are modern and purpose-built (see Figure 11.2) and in them residents usually have their own rooms which

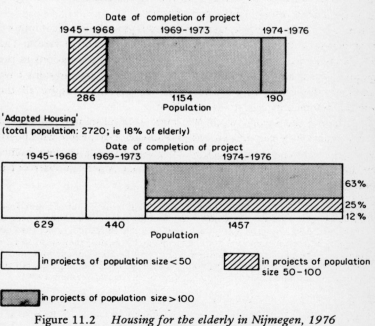

Figure 11.2   *Housing for the elderly in Nijmegen, 1976*

Notes: Population of Nijmegen 142 000 Elderly (65+) number 12 000 (8—9 per cent of total population).

Source: Coleman 1977

they furnish themeselves. There are also communal areas which are often attractively laid out but, because of the freedom people have to live in their own rooms, they do not have the same atmosphere as the 'day rooms' found in residential institutions for the elderly in other countries.

In understanding the growth in residential care in the 1960s and 1970s it is also important to appreciate the particular social problems which the Dutch faced after the war. They experienced a dramatic increase in the birth rate — much greater than in neighbouring countries — and a concurrent shortage of housing especially for young couples. One solution to the problem was the development of special housing for the elderly, leaving more family homes free for young families and at the same time providing elderly people with greater security. Stated simply, this may sound a rather cynical policy but from looking at records and talking to the policy-makers involved, it is clear to the present writer that there was a genuine conviction that the development of residential homes was also the right strategy for older people.

However in so doing the Dutch policy-makers also severed the ties of dependency between elderly people and their children. The significance of this was probably not realised at the time (Munnichs 1977). Far more than in England (Laslett 1976), Dutch elderly people traditionally lived with their children or had their children live with them. Indeed the term 'independent living' has a special significance in Dutch, meaning living on one's own, and as applied to elderly people in particular, living independently of children. Therefore, encouraging elderly people to move to an old people's home rather than live with children was to encourage them to live independently, quite the opposite to the meaning given to this term in English where it is so often used to refer to living outside of an institution.

The idea of three generations living under one roof also lost its attractiveness for other reasons. Most houses built in the post-war era were only suited to nuclear families. Increased mobility also played a part, as did the improved pension provisons. The figures for single elderly living alone illustrate the trend. In 1960, 101 000 elderly people (10 per cent of the elderly population) lived entirely alone, but by 1970 this number had risen to 215 000 (16 per cent) and to 360 000 (25 per cent) in 1976 (Munnichs 1978). Whereas it had been possible in the past for elderly people to continue living with their children if they became disabled, it was quite a different matter to go and live with them precisely because of the onset of infirmity.

Payment for Residential Care

The one piece of legislation which confirmed the status of 'caring homes' as the proper residence for disabled elderly people was the *ABW*

(*Algemene Bijstandswet*), the General Assistance Act of 1963 which came into effect in 1965. Whether it was foreseen or not, the most frequent application of the bill has become the payment by the State of all expenses associated with living in a 'caring home' wherever an elderly person is unable to pay. By so doing it guaranteed the financing of 'caring homes' on a large scale and resulted in a large increase in homes during the late 1960s and early 1970s (see Figure 11.2 for the example of one particular city).

Both the number of people living in homes who receive help from the ABW and the amount of money paid out on their behalf have soared, from 43 000 people and 57 million guilders in 1965, to 83 000 people and 333 million guilders in 1971, and to 109 000 people and 1469 million guilders in 1977 (see Table 11.2). Moreover, the cost has risen exponentially, quite out of proportion to the number of beneficiaries. By 1979, the average cost of residential care had risen to f1730 a month for a single person and f2976 for a married couple (Federatie LSB 1980) which very few elderly people can continue paying for long. The ABW takes over payment when income (including pension) and capital are diminished to f4050 for a single elderly person and f8100 for a married couple (figures at 1 July 1980). Residents are then allowed to keep the remaining capital and, if all other income is used in payment of the costs of residential care, are entitled in addition to a monthly payment ('*maandgeld*') to cover personal expenses, holidays and light meals (f661 maximum for a married couple and f380 for a single elderly person at 1 July 1980).

The percentage of elderly people living in homes drawing help from the General Assistance Act rose to 80 per cent in 1980 (Federatie LSB 1980). This contrasts markedly with the position of elderly people living in their own homes whose demand on the ABW, as mentioned earlier, has fallen. In part, this is due to the movement of infirm elderly people into homes, but also reflects improved pension provisions and the introduction of rent subsidies for those on low incomes. While the ABW guarantees the security of residents of 'caring homes', there is some resentment that so many elderly people are thus made dependent on the state (van de Lisdonk 1980). Certainly one can genuinely question the psychological costs of depriving so many people of financial independence and of the associated feelings of self-respect and freedom, freedom for instance to leave the home and live in the community again. Moreover, residents of homes, the major recipients of aid under the ABW, have not benefited from recent changes whereby elderly people living outside institutions can receive assistance while retaining significant amounts of capital.

The national policy on residential care first began to be called into question in the early 1970s. Opinions were expressed that elderly people were made unnecessarily dependent; that they could better maintain their own lifestyles in their old environments; and that residents of homes tended to be belittled or treated like children. The homes were themselves criticised on the grounds that their rules were too restricting and that they were too separated from the rest of society.

It was evident also that many elderly people who were still in good health were nevertheless applying for places in homes. Indeed, this was often encouraged by policies on admissions which tended to discriminate against elderly people who were in visibly poor health or deteriorating. The elderly were also encouraged in their early application by their children and doctors since the home had become the normal destination for elderly people. All these considerations, together with the soaring costs of residential care have led recent Dutch governments to seek a change of policy.

(*Verpleeghuizen*) Nursing Homes

In addition to 'caring homes' the Dutch have also developed 'nursing homes' for disabled elderly people. These are the responsibility of the Ministry of Public Health and Environmental Hygiene. Like 'caring homes' these need to be distinguished carefully from their British counterparts. The small British nursing home is a very insignificant part of the total health service for the elderly in the UK, most elderly patients being found in hospitals. This is certainly not the case in The Netherlands.

The Dutch did not develop a National Health Service after the war but instead developed a system whereby those below an income threshold pay compulsory state health insurance while those above it are obliged to make arrangements with private insurance companies. Similarly, the Dutch did not follow the British in developing a speciality of geriatric medicine to deal with the problems of the frail elderly within the hospital services (van Zonneveld 1975). Instead, a need was seen for institutions which could cater for patients who required a long period of medical and nursing care. The hospital became more and more a place for short-stay treatment and assessment while patients needing rehabilitation or long-term care were placed in 'nursing homes' which rapidly increased in number.

Dutch 'nursing homes' were first organised into an association in 1953, became increasingly recognised by the health insurance systems and finally in 1968 were firmly established by the AWBZ (*Algemene Wet Bijzondere Ziektekosten*: General Act Concerning Special Sickness Costs) which established as a general principle the state funding of residence in 'caring homes'. In 1976, 41 000 beds in 297 nursing homes were paid for under this legislation, 19 000 in institutions for the physically infirm, 9000 in institutions for the mentally infirm, and 12 000 in mixed institutions (Ministerie van V en M 1980). In practice 'nursing homes' cater mainly for very old and infirm elderly people, some of whom are admitted for convalescence and rehabilitation, some for long-term care and some for terminal care. Many people in the UK with equivalent levels of disability would be found in long-stay hospital beds — geriatric or psychogeriatric — but equally many would be found in residential homes or living in the community supported by relatives. Some authorities have queried whether The Netherlands, with 3 per cent of its elderly population in 'nursing homes', has too many nursing home places (Munnichs 1978). Such an expensive resource has to be used to capacity but some existing residents might be adequately catered for elsewhere. Moreover, many elderly people (and their relatives) prefer 'nursing homes' to 'caring homes' since stay in the former is completely paid for under the AWBZ, whereas ABW payments for residence in 'caring homes' are available when people have little or no means.

Recent Developments

Dutch policy towards the elderly has come in for much scrutiny in recent years as a result of which important developments have occurred. Demographic projections indicate a rapid increase in the number of old people, particularly very old people. Because of a high birth-rate in the post-war years the proportion of elderly in the population has not yet increased to the same extent as in the UK and some other Western countries. However, the rate of increase is now accelerating and by the end of the century the proportion of elderly people in the Dutch population will be very similar to that in the UK.

The increase in the over-75s causes policy-makers most concern since this group exerts the heaviest demand on services (for example, more than 80 per cent of people in 'caring homes' are aged over 75). Between 1975 and 2000 the proportion of the total population aged over 75 is expected to increase by 40 per cent and the proportion over 85 by 60 per cent (see Table 11.2).

Not surprisingly, successive Dutch governments have become increasingly concerned at the prospect of meeting the demand implied by these figures and have sought to bring down the numbers of elderly people requesting places in 'caring homes' by offering alternative sources of security. The first major development, which reflected a greater emphasis on community services, was the introduction of 'service centres' in 1964. These are situated in individual neighbourhoods and are meant to serve as information centres and co-ordination points for services such as home help or home nursing, social security enquiries, luncheon clubs, laundry service, chiropody and so on. However, the service centres have failed to attract a sizeable clientele which suggests that, at least in The Netherlands, life linked to a service centre does not always seem preferable to life in an old people's home.

A second development has been the increased provision of special housing accommodation for the elderly by housing associations and local authorities (see Figure 11.2), but again this has not reduced the popularity of 'caring homes'. Although 15 per cent of those aged over 65 now live in 'sheltered' housing, there is a steady turnover of people wishing to move on to 'caring homes', with more than a third eventually making the move (which is, incidentally, a much higher rate than in the UK; Coleman 1975; 1976). Clearly, 'sheltered' housing in The Netherlands does not provide the necessary security required by Dutch elderly people and if its importance is to increase, new developments are necessary, including, perhaps, an enhanced caring role for staff such as wardens employed on the premises.

It is important to appreciate how firmly established 'caring homes' have become as the major source of security for elderly people in The Netherlands. When people think of provisions for the elderly at home is uppermost in their minds. While the family has declined as a source of support, the old people's home has strengthened. Against this background, initiatives taken to develop community services and special housing have not been sufficiently convincing. Many elderly people wish to enter a home not because they feel already disabled but out of a concern for the future and an unwillingness to live alone. This need for security strikes an outside observer as being very deep-grounded in The Netherlands. Perhaps it is associated with the need to build dykes to protect against flooding; the provision of residential homes is a very powerful dyke!

The changing economic situation has, however, accelerated some decisions. The government has declared its intention to bring down the norm for the proportion of elderly people living in 'caring homes' to 7 per cent, and no permission is now given for new building in areas which already exceed the norm. Renovation is only approved if it results in a reduction in the total number of places available. Moreover, after a period developing the necessary machinery, the government finally issued a statutory measure in 1977 obliging all local authorities to set up indexing boards, which have responsibility for examining all applications for places in 'caring homes'. Only where there is a demonstrated need for admission can people be placed on the official waiting list from which homes are obliged to draw their admissions.

Most homes, however, are badly equipped to handle an increasing level of disability among their residents. For a number of years the government has fixed a maximum personnel ratio of one staff member to every three residents. This is still the official rule. Homes are entitled to apply for permission to have more personnel, but this requires a painstaking and time-consuming procedure to convince the administrative authorities. The major part of this procedure involves completing a form for each resident, indicating his or her need of help in relation to 33 daily activities (Remmerswaal 1979).

At present, there is much concern about the lack of positive elements in the current policy of the Ministry of Culture, Recreation and Social Welfare in regard to provisions for the elderly. Although the policy note of 1975, which first defined the 7 per cent norm, indicated that there would be an increase in extramural provisions, nothing of the sort has yet happened (Leenaerts 1980). It is clear too that the norm must be sensitive to the increasing numbers of very old among the elderly population. The Ministry seems to be awaiting the evaluative reports of the first few years' operation of the indexing boards.

The Future

Although the Dutch are not confronted by the same problems as the British, for example, that of maintaining very disabled elderly people in the community, they too face severe difficulties which are likely to increase in the future. The high expectation of the family's role in caring for the elderly, which is still a very important feature of services in the UK, has disappeared during the last 20 to 30 years. Even if one wanted to reverse such trends, it would be difficult to do so. People in The Netherlands pay generously, through taxes and pension contributions, to support the elderly population. That is right and proper since those who are now old are the source of the country's present prosperity. However, it may not be sufficient contribution to the care of the elderly.

The proportion of the very old and disabled in the population is increasing even more dramatically than in the UK and 'caring homes' will have to change into somewhat different institutions so as to cope with the demand. A central problem, too, is finding sufficient numbers of well-motivated staff to work in them. More needs to be done to encourage elderly people to continue to live independently in the community.

The UK has for long taken a different path, and the increasing economic preoccupations of the last years have reinforced the emphasis on community care. A great deal of imaginative thinking is now being given to better support services for disabled elderly people and their families in the community in the form of day care, relief-admissions into hospitals and residential homes and community orientated geriatric and psycho-geriatric services. The services fall a long way short of meeting need but at least it is being recognised that the family and all other interested people are integral to services for disabled elderly people, and that they may need support in their own right. If we are to succeed in maintaining the quality of life of people who become infirm in old age we need to be very aware of this mesh of formal and informal support networks.

We cannot just assume that families in future will be prepared to continue to shoulder the burdens of supporting their elderly relatives without a lot more support. The Dutch have already recognised this, but they have taken the much more costly path of trying to care for their disabled elderly people outside of the context of the family and the close community. That course of action has its problems too.

Nevertheless, it is clear that the Dutch have been generous to their elderly population. There is a widely shared feeling that old people should be enabled to continue to share in the general benefits of society. The pension provisions which are much higher than in the UK help towards this end. As far as disabled and infirm elderly people are concerned, less stress has been put on maintenance of independence, but much more on the preservation of a decent standard of living (e.g. in comfortable surroundings, in privacy, and with one's own possessions around one). As a result, dependence in old age is seen more within a normal context and less as 'failure' or 'misfortune'.

It has also been recognised that retired people deserve extra opportunities. Mention has been made earlier of the lack of success of service centres, but this seems in part due to the limited conception of providing only 'services for the elderly'. More and more it is being realised that old people want to be part of the general society, and to take the opportunity provided by retirement of broadening interests. A significant development in more recent years has been the introduction of pass cards which allow people to use transport, cinema, theatre, museums and so on at lower prices after retirement. For reasons of this kind the placement of 'social welfare' within the same government ministry as 'culture' and 'recreation' seems a happy one.

Fundamental to any reform in the situation of the elderly is a more positive image of and attitude to old age. So many provisions stigmatise the elderly as a separate disadvantaged group and the process of growing old as the acquisition of negative traits. Even some of the most well intended legislation in The Netherlands has reinforced this negative image. For instance, it is due to the workings of the WAO (the Disability for Work Act) that approximately equal numbers of people now retire early on grounds of ill health as retire at the 'normal' age of 65. Generous though this legislation is, it also encourages an association between growing old and being disabled. It is true that disability is more frequent in old age but ageing is also a time with great potential for positive developments. It would seem far better to persist with the experiments under way in certain industries which offer early retirement to all who want it, thereby providing them with the opportunity and means to live their old age as they would like. Thus old age would commence on a positive note and not a negative one.

References

Akhtar, A. J. *et al*, 1973, 'Disability and dependence in the elderly at home', *Age and Ageing*, 2, p.102—11.

Coleman, P. G. 1975, 'Bejaardenwoningen: een mogelijkheid tot langer zelfstandig wonen?' *Nederlands Tijdschrift voor Gerontologie*, 6, pp. 172—80.

Coleman, P. G. 1976, *Bejaardenwoningen in Amersfoort: een eerste evaluatie*, Nijmegen, Stichting GITP (Oude Kleefsbaan 10, Berg en Dal).

Coleman, P. G. 1977, 'Balanced provision of sheltered housing and residential homes for the elderly. Contrasts between Britain and The Netherlands', *Concord. The Journal of the British Association for Service to the Elderly*, 7, pp. 53—9.

Drees, W. 1979, 'Noodregeling ouderdomsvoorziening 1947; AOW 1957', *De Bejaarden*, 19—20, pp. 366—7.

Federatie Landelijke Samenwerking Bejaardentehuisorganisaties 1980, *Statistiek bejaardentehuizen 1978*, Federatie LSB, Postbut 84393, 2508 AJ The Hague.

Fiselier, A. A. M. and Kraft, H. L. P. R. 1978, 'Achterblijven als moderne armoede', in C. J. M. Corver, A. M. van der Heiden, C. de Hoog, L. Th van en Leeuwen, (eds), *Gezin en samenleving* Assen, Van Gorcum, pp. 129—47.

Gemeente Rotterdam 1970, *De Rotterdamse bejaarden, een onderzoek naar hun levensomstandigheden en behoeften*, Deel 2 Lichamelijke huishoudelijke en psychische validiteit, Gemeente Rotterdam.

Gestel, J. D. van 1980, 'Verzorgingstehuizen wel of niet onder gemeentelijk beheer', *Senior*, 22, pp. 468—9.

Hofman, A., Tanja, T.A. and Valkenburg, H.A. 1979, 'Een epidemiologisch onderzoek onder bejaarden (EPOZ) 1: Algemene karakteristieken van bajaarden in de open bevolking', Nederlands *Tijdschrift voor Gerontologie*, 10, pp. 187—94.

Hunt, A. 1978, *The elderly at home*, London, HMSO.

Isaacs, B. and Neville, Y. 1976, 'The needs of old people. The "interval" as a method of measurement', *British Journal of Preventive and Social Medicine*, 30, pp. 79—85.

Laslett, P. 1976, 'Societal development and ageing' in R. H. Binstock and E. Shanas, (eds), *Handbook of ageing and the social sciences*, New York, Van Nostrand Reinhold, pp. 87—116.

Leenaerts, W. A. F. 1980, 'Provinciale planning voor de bejaardenoorden', *Senior*, 4, pp. 71—3.

Lisdonk, C. van de, 1980, 'Bijdrage bejaardenoord onbehoorlijk geregeld', *Leeftijd*, 2, pp. 41—2.

Menzies, A. M. 1974, 'The Netherlands' in T. Wilson, (ed.), *Pensions, inflation and growth*, London, Heinemann, 110—54.

Ministerie van Volksgezondheid en Milieuhygiëne 1980, *Statistiek verpleeghuizen 1976*, Staatsuitgeverij, afdeling Verkoop, Christoffel Plantijnstraat 1, The Hague.

Munnichs, J. M. A. 1977, 'Linkages of old people with their families and bureaucracy in a welfare state, The Netherlands', in E. Shanas and M. B. Sussman, (eds), *Family, bureaucracy and the elderly*, Durham, N. C., Duke University Press, pp. 92—116.

Munnichs, J. M. A. 1978, 'Sociale gerontologie in Nederland. Een schets van haar ontwikkeling' in *Gerontologisch Centrum Nijmegen Tien Jaar Gerontologisch Centrum Nijmegen 1967—1977*, Nigmegen, Katholieke Universiteit, pp. 7—40.

Remmerswaal, P. W. M. 1979, *Caring in homes for the aged: interdependency of residents and personnel*, Paper presented at the Kassel Symposium Nijmegen, Stichting GITP (Oude Kleefsebaan 10, Berg en Dal).

Riemen, A. P. A., 1979, 'De AOW, een motor in ons sociaal zekerheidsbestel', De Bejaarden, 19—20, pp. 412—3.

Townsend, P. 1962, *The Last Refuge*, London, Routledge and Kegan Paul.

Vladeck, B. C., 1980, *Unloving care. The Nursing Home Tragedy*, New York, Basic Books.

Wershow, H. J., 1979, 'The outer limits of the welfare state: discrimination, racism and their effect of human services', *International Journal of Ageing and Human Development*, 10, pp. 63—75.

Wolf, H. C. de 1977, *58 miljoen Nederlanders en hun bejaarden*, Amsterdam, Amsterdam Boek BV.

Zonneveld, R. J. van, 1975, 'The Netherlands', in J. C. Brocklehurst (ed.), *Geriatric Care in Advanced Societies*, Lancaster, MTP.

12 West Germany: Social Security, Social Status and the Elderly
Roger Lawson

The Germans have long enjoyed a reputation for high standards of social security, especially for the elderly. However, the ideas and objectives underlying their policies have often differed markedly from those in other countries with ambitious and sophisticated welfare provisions. From the days of Bismarck to the Federal Republic, the Germans appear to have been concerned less with establishing comprehensive national minimum standards for all citizens or redistributing income in favour of the poor than with protecting the different rewards, privileges and social status acquired through economic activity and public service. Hence, rather than aiming to diminish economic inequalities, their policies have often sought to perpetuate them or to 'solidify rather than alter the economic basis of the social structure' (Rimlinger 1971). In West Germany, these priorities were particularly evident during the 1950s and 1960s, when the main governing party was the conservative Christian Democratic Union (CDU). They were also most clearly expressed in a far-reaching and much publicised reform of the statutory pension system in 1957.

Between 1969 and 1982, when the coalition of Social Democrats (SPD) and the small Free Democrats (FDP) was in office, West German social policies assumed a rather more egalitarian character and a number of important reforms sought to improve the prospects of previously neglected and underprivileged groups. On the whole, though, the Social Democrats tended to adopt a more pragmatic than doctrinaire approach to social policy and were reluctant to depart too swiftly or radically from the German welfare traditions. In their social as well as economic policies they also attempted to find a common ground for agreement between business, trade unions and the government; and undoubtedly met with more success in this than many other Western governments. Nevertheless, like other governments, they faced a growing 'crisis of the welfare state' from the mid-1970s, with the declining rates of economic growth and rapidly rising social expenditures. The financial crisis in turn exposed other contradictions in their policies and particularly the wide disparities that still exist in the distribution of social benefits, despite the more egalitarian trends of the 1970s. A number of recent studies have focused attention, too, on the relative poverty of an unorganised and poorly represented 'underclass' of West Germans, mainly the poorest pensioners and others outside the labour force, who have not only benefited much less than others from the elaborate and costly social provisions but have suffered more from the process of bureaucratisation in social welfare.

In this chapter, I want to examine more closely the ideas underlying the development of the main state pension and social assistance provisions for the elderly and to discuss some of their consequences. From a comparative point of view, it is clearly of interest to know what lessons can be learned from the West German emphasis on preserving social status and on policies which have been closely tied to questions of economic production. The chapter begins with an account of developments before the 1957 pension reform. It then discusses this reform and its consequences, and looks finally at the trends and problems of the 1970s.

Developments Before 1957

Until the 1957 legislation, much of Germany's statutory pension system had managed to survive without a major reorganisation since before the First World War. It contained two 'general' social insurance schemes, one covering all manual workers and first established in 1889 as part of Bismarck's reforms and the other a scheme for salaried employees with earnings below a prescribed amount which was set up in 1912. Both schemes provided old-age pensions at the age of 65, disability and survivors' pensions, and a number of other, mainly discretionary, welfare benefits. There were also other social insurance pension provisions for miners and self-employed craftsmen, the only self-employed persons with compulsory insurance, and special state-financed schemes existed for certain war victims and refugees. In addition, civil servants and state officials, who had always enjoyed special rights and privileges in West Germany, had their own separate and generous non-contributory pension scheme. As well as these pension arrangements there was also a public assistance service, which had replaced the Poor Law in 1924. This was run by the individual states (*Länder*) and local authorities, quite separately from the rest of the social security system, and provided basic subsistence benefits and certain welfare services on a means-tested basis, in principle for anyone in need. Unlike Britain's reformed national assistance scheme, however, public assistance was often only granted to old people whose children or grandchildren were unable to support them. In other respects, too, the code of relief ensured that it was essentially a last-resort defence against poverty, still associated in many people's minds with inferiority and shame.

The two main social insurance pension schemes had been established at a time when West German social policy was predominantly concerned with securing the allegiance of the new working classes to the state and preserving the existing social order against the disruptive forces of socialism. Moreover, those who had advocated social insurance had always presented it as a means of reconciling principles of mutual aid and social solidarity with respect for individual incentive, personal discipline and the status which people had earned by their own efforts. The provisions were said to combine an 'educational function' — moral elevation through the reward of work — with the material improvements of workers' and pensioners' conditions. These principles, which were given much more prominence in West Germany than in many other countries, were reflected in a number of features of the pension schemes, such as the way pensions were assessed. An old-age pension was made up of a basic minimum amount, payable to all who had contributed at least 15 years, and a *personal* supplement related to an individual's earnings and contributions record. Although the benefits paid out in the early years of this century tended on the whole to be small, a worker with the prospect of a full insurance 'career' and good earnings could theoretically reckon on a pension which would not only remove any threat of poverty but would contribute significantly to maintaining his living standards. After 40 years, for instance, an insured person was to achieve a pension of 70 per cent of the average of the earnings for which contributions had been paid (Jantz 1961).

While there were no major pension reforms in the inter-war years, there were important developments with serious implications for the pension schemes. Two trends in particular were later to have a profound effect on policies in the Federal Republic. On the one hand, the real value of most pension rights being built up in this period was steadily eroded, first of all by inadequate re-evaluations after the drastic inflation of the 1920s, then by the spells of unemployment experienced by many workers, and later by the wage and social policies of the Nazis. The average pensions paid out in 1937 were a mere 20 per cent of the national average wages at the time. On the other hand, the State assumed much more direct control than previously over the pension schemes. In the Weimar Republic this resulted from attempts to safeguard the poorest pensioners, by raising minimum pensions and increasing state subsidies to pay for this, while under the Nazis social insurance was naturally adapted to the wider objectives of the totalitarian state. The Nazis had plans, too, for a fundamental reform of pensions to make them even more compatible with their ideology which they claimed would be given priority in their new post-war society (Rimlinger 1971). This was to replace social insurance altogether with a new centralised and more comprehensive system, financed by the State, and paying uniform benefits to all who had 'done their duty to the community'.

The war itself and the events of the early post-war years brought chaos to the pension system and consequently acute hardship for many old people. Much of the original social insurance character of pensions was effectively destroyed with the loss of a large part of the pension fund reserves and as emergency regulations were introduced to deal with the many lost or incomplete pension records, including those of the refugees who flooded into West Germany after the war. Most of the regulations sought to relax or remove entirely insurance conditions and guarantee at least minimum pensions. Even so, the pensions paid out during and after the war (and many claims remained unprocessed) were often desperately small. Most old people had to supplement their benefits by working, by seeking help from their families and friends or from charities, or by resorting to the much-despised public assistance. To make matters much worse, many people of course lost their property or savings during the war. If they were among the more fortunate then, any remaining savings were wiped out in the post-war inflation or by the Currency Reform of 1948, when the mark was revalued at only one-fifteenth of its nominal value (Wallich 1955).

Despite this, the problems of the elderly were given low priority in the early post-war years, though this was due partly to a more general uncertainty about the future of all social security provisions. Immediately after the war, for example, the Allies briefly attempted to introduce a Beveridge-style reform, and Beveridge himself expounded his ideas in a lecture tour of a number of German cities in 1946. The plans were soon withdrawn, however, as it became evident that they were widely regarded as alien to the German traditions of social welfare and quite inappropriate for a country which had just experienced the abuse of centralised state power. The fact that there were similarities with the Nazis' plans hardly helped matters (Hockerts 1977; Hockerts 1981). Moreover, for many Germans, particularly in the newly formed CDU and smaller Liberal-Conservative parties, the solution of the crucial social problems facing the country lay, first and foremost, in the creation of a more liberal economic order and in economic revival, even when this meant delaying much needed social reforms and adding initially to the hardships of the economically weak. This was the main theme of Konrad Adenauer's first official statement as Federal Chancellor after the CDU emerged as the dominant party.

However, this had already become official policy following the Currency Reform a year earlier. In the most critical reconstruction phase, between 1948 and 1950, virtually all efforts were directed towards dismantling wartime and post-war controls and generally 'raising production incentives by keeping down the burden of carrying the unproductive part of the population' (Wallich 1955). Industrial investment was stimulated with elaborate tax concessions for which many pensioners paid heavily, because of the high rates of taxation on basic necessities. After 1950, the adverse social implications of these policies were to some extent compensated by improvements in the general level of pensions and other social benefits. Nevertheless, as Henry Wallich showed in his study of the 'German miracle' written in 1955, the policies pursued throughout the reconstruction period remained harsh on pensioners, who he described as 'a socially and financially submerged group that forms the lowest layer of German society. Here are the real stepchildren of the German recovery' (Wallich 1955). Their plight was highlighted, too, in the first post-war official inquiry into the social security system in 1953 (*Statistiches Bundesamt 1953—5*). This was set up in response to growing demands for a comprehensive reform of the whole system, but the results helped instead to focus debate on the urgent need to improve the lot of the elderly and disabled. They left little doubt that this would have much wider implications for the general standard of living, since so many pensioners were dependent on their children and families for support. In 1953, the average old-age pensions paid out by the main social insurance schemes, which made no provision for any additional payment for pensioners' spouses, amounted to less than one-third of national average earnings. Many old people received much less than this, especially widows who were only entitled to 60 per cent of their husbands' pensions. In spite of this, the inquiry revealed that only 3 per cent of pensioners in the manual workers' scheme and 1 per cent in the white-collar scheme were obtaining additional benefits from public assistance.

In retrospect, these early post-war developments may, of course, be seen in a different light, since West Germany's remarkable economic recovery clearly laid the foundations for major improvements in social security. Moreover, it may be argued that, partly because of the priority given to economic growth and the consequent delay in social reform, measures like the 1957 pension reform were in many ways much better attuned to post-war economic and social conditions than, for example, the Beveridge reforms in Britain. Moreover, despite the ideological commitment in West Germany to private property rights and free enterprise, a feature of the debates before the pension reform was the widespread acceptance that state pensions, rather than private occupational provisions or personal savings, should play the leading role in providing for the vast majority of the elderly. Comparative studies of the 'civic culture' conducted at the time show, too, how West Germans' expectations of government differed in this respect from those of the British or Americans: the West Germans placed considerably more emphasis on the government's role as a guarantor of economic stability and social security (Verba 1965). This may be attributed partly to a general sense of the individual's helplessness resulting from the experiences of inflation and war. Undoubtedly, though, it also reflected a return to traditional attitudes towards the State, after a period of uncertainty immediately following the war. As Nevil Johnson (1973: 19) has observed, this influence is difficult to define satisfactorily, but there clearly has been in the Federal Republic

> a predisposition to accept the desirability of public regulation on a consistent and equal basis of a wide range of activities which in other countries are left entirely unregulated . . . a continuing sense of the state's necessity for individual well-being.

In the 1950s, these attitudes were particularly important in determining the governing CDU's commitment to the pension reform and they were also strongly represented in the German civil service.

The 1957 Pension Reform and its Consequences

The Christian Democrats' approach to the pension reform may be seen as an interesting attempt to reconcile a liberal position on economic and social affairs with the more traditional attitudes to social protection, as well as with Christian (mainly Catholic) social teaching. In practical terms, it also involved seeking compromises between the party's neo-Liberals led by the Economics Minister, Ludwig Erhard, who insisted that any advances in social welfare should be 'market conforming' and designed to promote the responsibility of the individual for his welfare, and the more ardent advocates of positive social programmes in the Christian Social camp of the party. The strong leadership of Chancellor Adenauer also played a significant role in the reform (Hockerts 1977). Adenauer appears to have been anxious to associate his chancellorship with the tradition of social protection dating back to Bismarck: it was, he argued, one of the few state traditions Germans should 'hold on to . . . and be proud of'. His views on social policy were profoundly conservative, but it was a conservatism which stressed the need for decent standards of social welfare so as to promote social harmony and stability and good industrial relations. Hence his objectives in pension reform, like Bismarck's aims in the 1880s, were as much concerned with the expectations of workers as with improving the lot of the elderly and disabled. He was extremely sensitive, too, about the division of Germany and argued for social reform that would ensure that 'the Federal Republic remains attractive to the people of the (Soviet) Zone'. Another crucial consideration was the fact that 1957 was an election year and the opposition SPD were clearly aiming to make social reform a central election issue.

Studies of the pension reform have also emphasised the importance, in shaping the attitudes of Adenauer and his government, of a report published in 1955 by Professor Wilfrid Schreiber of the politically influential Federation of Catholic Employers (Schreiber 1955). Schreiber advocated immediate and substantial increases in pensions designed to guarantee that they would not merely prevent poverty but help maintain the 'acquired social status' of individuals and their families. Moreover, to maintain the collective status of pensioners as a whole, he called for a guaranteed 'dynamic' adjustment of pensions in payment in line with the general standard of living and increasing national prosperity. This 'new' concept of pension insurance' required in turn radical changes in the methods of financing pensions, with the principle of funding replaced by a pay-as-you-go approach in which the pensions of the current aged population were paid for directly by the current working population. Schreiber referred to this as a new 'solidarity contract' between the generations. He argued that these innovations were essential, given the changes in workers' conditions and family life in the twentieth century and the catastrophic consequence of the inflations, wars and the enforced movement of large sections of the population. Just as catastrophic, however, had been the intrusion into social insurance of authoritarian and dirigist elements, which had blurred the distinction between insurance principles and state-controlled assistance and had stifled personal initiative and incentive. A new pension programme, therefore, needed to apply 'individual' insurance principles more firmly than previously and to conform more with the tenets of the free market economy. Old-age pensions should be financed solely by the contributions of the insured and their employers; benefits should be firmly based on the principle of 'achievement at work' (*Leistungsprinzip*); and the task of securing a minimum income or redistributing income in favour of the poor should be a function of residual social assistance, not of the main social insurance provisions. In Schreiber's (1955: 15) view:

> The active person of today . . . should expect from the State, Parliament, Government and Administration nothing more than contractual help, an organisational service; but no direct material assistance . . . .. To make excessive demands on the State always implies artificially inflating the State, and in turn becoming its slave.

Another interesting feature of the Schreiber plan and other similar arguments put forward at the time, especially when compared with liberal conservative arguments in countries like Britain, is that they were framed not in terms of freedom of choice as regards form of provision, but rather in terms of freedom of choice in the disposal of personal income. It was felt that the ability to choose to what use a pension should be put would be provided only if the income level was more than sufficient to meet basic subsistence requirements. (Menzies 1974: 57).

This in turn meant giving priority to social security cash benefits over other forms of social welfare. Indeed, measures like rent controls and subsidies that might have benefited the elderly were explicitly rejected since they were not 'market-conforming', while both liberal and Catholic social doctrines were agreed that special welfare services should be provided primarily by voluntary organisations of a religious or non-denominational nature. Voluntary efforts could be subsidised by local authorities, as they had been in the past, but direct public provision of welfare services should as a rule follow the principle of 'subsidarity': i.e. be made on a selective, means-tested basis for those lacking adequate family support or charitable aid.

These, basically, were the guiding principles underlying the 1957 reform and other developments at the time in social assistance. Many of the details of the reform are too complex to summarise briefly and we will focus here mainly on the changes in the methods of calculating pensions in the manual workers' and salaried employees' schemes. The new legislation considerably improved the living standards of most pensioners drawing benefits from these schemes. The average pensions paid out by the two schemes were increased immediately by 65 per cent, since anyone with at least 15 years' contributions became eligible for the new pensions at the full rate. They were, in effect, credited with additional contributions and, to guarantee pensions of a reasonable size, credits were given for periods of unemployment, sickness, wartime service, etc. (Menzies 1974). The increases also meant that the average old-age pensions in the two schemes were raised from 34.5 per cent of the average wage in 1956 to almost 50 per cent in 1958.

A much publicised aspect of the reform was the new *dynamic* principle of adjusting pensions in payment in line with average earnings. Under pressure from the neo-liberals and business interests, however, the original bill providing for the automatic annual adjustment of pensions was amended, and a specially constituted Social Advisory Board was required to study the case for increases each year and to submit recommendations to the government, which in turn had to seek Parliament's approval. In practice, until the financial crisis of the second half of the 1970s pensions were always raised annually in line with the general movement of earnings; but, as a concession to fears about the macroeconomic effects of the new principle, the earnings base used was the average gross earnings of all insured persons in the three years prior to any adjustment. Thus, when earnings rose rapidly, as they did for most of the 1960s and early 1970s, annual pension increases lagged behind annual increases in gross wages and salaries. On the other hand, the rate of growth of pensions in payment in this period was more than two and a half times that of the cost of living index. In most years between 1965 and 1977, pensions also grew faster than the net earnings of wage and salary earners, who were subject to increasing taxes and contributions partly to pay for the growing costs of pensions.

The most distinctive feature of the 1957 legislation was, however, the strengthening of the 'individual' nature of pensions. As one of the civil servants closely involved in the reform put it:

> The essential innovation of the German pension reform is that both pension and wage are seen in a new relation to work. The man whose working life is behind him deserves a pension corresponding to the work he had performed, just as he had always received an appropriate reward for his efforts during his working life in the form of wages. . . . Wage and pension are both paid in acknowledgement of work. (Jantz 1961: 138)

As this implies, the reform strongly differentiated among workers and pensioners by linking pensions much more closely than previously to lifetime earnings and work records and, unlike state pensions in many other countries, no provision was made for a minimum pension nor for any weighting of benefits in favour of the low paid. Moreover, in line with the traditional rules in West German social insurance, there was no supplement in the scheme for wives and a widow continued to receive 60 per cent of her husband's pension. To be more precise, the very complex formula adopted in 1957 sought to determine an individual's economic status by calculating his earnings in each year of insurance as a percentage of the average earnings of all insured wage and salary earners. These percentages were then averaged and, to preserve a person's 'status', the resulting amount was related to the average earnings of all insured persons during the three years preceding the year of retirement. This lag was again included to assuage fears about the pension's economic effects. The calculations produced a pensioner's *personal* wage base, and for each year of insurance an individual was entitled to an old-age pension equal to 1.5 per cent of this base. Thus, after 30 years the pension amounted to 40 per cent, after 40 years to 60 per cent, and after 50 years to 75 per cent of the personal wage base. These replacement rates only applied, however, to earnings up to a ceiling equal to twice the average earnings, beyond which the rates fell progressively.

In practice, because of the time lag in the formula, the *standard* old-age pension paid to an individual after 40 years on average wages amounted to 51 per cent of the current average earnings in 1958. This proportion subsequently fell during the 1960s and early 1970s with the more rapid rises in earnings but was to some extent offset by improvements in pensioners' contribution records. By the 1970s, almost 55 per cent of men drawing pensions had more than 40 years' contributions and over 40 per cent had contributed for more than 45 years. At the same time, however, more than one-third of male pensioners and the vast majority of women had contributed for less than 35 years. In the case of the men, these included a surprisingly high proportion of workers forced to retire early on a low pension because of illness and disability. A survey in the Ruhr district in the mid-1960s put the proportion at 42 per cent for all manual workers, and at 54 per cent for the lower paid unskilled and semi-skilled workers (Roth 1974). Although the situation has undoubtedly improved since then, disability among workers and industrial accident rates in West Germany still appear high by comparison with other countries.

At the time of the pension reform it was always envisaged that the new state pensions would be 'first-tier' provisions and would be supplemented, mainly by private occupational pensions but also with private savings, to achieve the overall aim of maintaining customary living standards and status. In fact, official statements in 1957 suggest that the state pensions were designed to provide two-thirds of most pensioners' incomes. This implied an ultimate replacement goal of 75 per cent of income, the amount received by most civil servants and, from the early 1960s, most other public sector employees. Outside the public sector, higher paid employees were expected to rely more heavily on private initiative, because of the earnings ceiling in the pension formula and also because the compulsory insurance of salaried employees was still restricted to those with salaries below a prescribed amount. This limit was raised, however, in 1957 to incorporate 95 per cent of white-collar employees and it was finally abolished in 1967. Although the growth of occupational pensions was encouraged by tax concessions, comparatively little attention was paid to their development during the 1960s. The trade unions, in particular, appear to have shown little interest in campaigning for their improvement, but to have concentrated their efforts in social security on the state sector (Menzies 1974). Hardly any detailed information was available about occupational pension coverage or benefits until an official survey was undertaken in 1970. The results indicated that they were by no means fulfilling their objectives, at least for manual workers. Not only were the majority of workers not covered by the schemes, but two-thirds of those with coverage were likely to lose their claim to a pension if they left their firm before retirement.

Another aspect of the 1957 legislation, which should be mentioned since it filled an increasingly serious gap in social security, was the creation of a new pension scheme for independent farmers. This formed part of a much broader government-subsidised programme designed to bring about changes in the structure and efficiency of German farming, and the new pensions were based on quite different principles from the rest of the pension reform. With the farmers' scheme and the provisons for craftsmen, over 60 per cent of the self-employed were covered by national social security arrangements. The remainder included doctors, lawyers, journalists, etc., who had insurance coverage under *Länder*-wide or professional schemes, and others who had adequate private provision. However, there were still gaps in protection, particularly of small shop-keepers and businessmen with one or two employees who had tradition-ally resisted compulsory insurance but whose savings had suffered during and after the war. The persistence of poverty among the elderly after 1957 is also partly explained by the fact that in the 1920s and 1930s the self-employed (including 'family helpers') made up one-third of the West German labour force, whereas the proportion had fallen to one-seventh by the 1970s. Hence, during the past two decades a significant minority of old people have either not received social insurance pensions or have only limited rights because of poor contribution records.

As this suggests, West German policies after 1957 differed markedly from the policies pursued in countries, like Denmark and The Nether-lands, where high social expenditures on the elderly (broadly similar to the German expenditures) were associated with the development of generous universal citizenship pensions. The differential benefit structure in West Germany's state pensions also contrasts with the flat-rate benefits received by most old people in Britain, although differences in the treat-ment of pensioners in West Germany are far less significant than in Britain because of the much greater importance in Britain of the highly frag-mented private occupational sector with its numerous forms of discrim-ination and inequality. Moreover, because of the emphasis on maintaining living standards and status, West German policies after 1957 involved a commitment to a much more substantial transfer of income from the active population to the elderly than has ever occurred in Britain. This in turn has helped prevent the sinking of pensioners to the bottom of the socio-economic scale to the extent that has been evident in Britain. While comparisons of relative poverty naturally have to be treated with caution, most of the available evidence points to differences between the two countries similar to those revealed in an EEC survey in the mid-1970s (Willmott *et al.* 1978). In the survey, 15 per cent of West Germans over retirement age, as compared with 47 per cent in Britain, were living in households with incomes below two-thirds of the median incomes of all families interviewed.

The West German situation appears in a less favourable light, however, when one looks at the conditions after 1957 of the minority of old people expected to depend on means-tested social assistance to secure a minimum standard of living. Although the old public assistance scheme was replaced in 1961 by a more modern *Sozialhilfe* (social aid) services, the process of liberalising the conditions for receiving relief and improving benefits and welfare services, which was evident in most countries at this time, proceeded relatively slowly in West Germany. In fact, during the 1960s the value of 'subsistence aid' allowances (*Hilfe zum Lebensunterhalt*), the equivalent of the British supplementary benefits, declined steadily both in relation to the value of pensions and the general standard of living. When comparisons are made with national average wages, the average West German allowances for old people amounted to just over three-quarters of the British benefits at the end of the 1960s (George and Lawson 1980). To add to their difficulties, the poor in West Germany appear to have been under considerable pressure in the 1960s to keep silent about their poverty and forgo any claim for assistance, partly it seems because of the emphasis placed on achievement and merit in the main social security schemes. Moreover, very little was done to publicise rights and persuade people to exercise them and there was no counterpart in the Federal Republic of the British network of poverty lobbies. Indeed, until the 1970s there was hardly any public discussion of poverty or social assistance, particularly at a national level. One of the few poverty studies in the 1960s showed, too, that many of the poorest old people did not apply for assistance to avoid conflicts with their children and grandchildren, who could still be asked to refund any grants made to them (Blume 1970).

Throughout the period since the 1957 reform only 2—3 per cent of all people in the Federal Republic aged 65 and over (compared with around 25 per cent in Britain) have regularly received the basic social assistance allowances. However, according to recently published estimates based on the national Income and Consumption Surveys (similar to the British FES), in 1963 about 14 per cent of all old people had incomes at or below the social assistance levels, and in 1973 the proportion was probably 7—9 per cent (Klanberg 1979; George and Lawson 1980). The majority were women and mainly elderly women, but they also included, as one would expect from the structure of pensions, formerly unskilled and semi-skilled workers, some of the previously self-employed and others who had suffered during and after the war but had received little or no compensation from the special provisions made for war victims and refugees.

The Social Democrats and the Trends and Problems of the 1970s

The elections of October 1969 forced the CDU into opposition for the first time since the founding of the Federal Republic and led to the coalition of the SPD and the small Liberal FDP which governed the country until 1982. While this change in government had important repercussions in social policy, the policies of the new coalition also compromised in many ways with traditional aims and priorities, much more so than seemed likely when the SPD was in opposition in the early post-war years. In 1952, for example, as part of a wide-ranging social plan which specified that 'social security must be the foundation of socialist economic policy', the SPD had called for a fundamental reorganisation of pensions. Every aged and disabled person was to be entitled, as a basic citizenship right, to a minimum pension paid for out of general taxation; to maintain living standards, this was to be supplemented by earnings-related benefits provided by a new unitary national insurance scheme (Rimlinger 1971). By the end of the 1950s, however, the party had dropped this social plan, along with its more socialist economic programmes, in favour of pragmatic reformist policies pursued under the slogan 'Competition as far as possible — Planning as far as is needed'.

This change was clearly reflected in the SPD's approach to pensions after the 1957 reform. Partly under pressure from the trade unions, who had generally welcomed the reform, it accepted more than previously the notion of linking pensions closely with wages and work records and abandoned the idea of a universal minimum pension. Instead, it was argued that it was 'the duty of the SPD . . . to put into effect more than hitherto the social principle alongside the insurance principle' (Rimlinger 1971). These ideas were developed further in the SPD's *'Die Volksversicherung'* (people's insurance plan) of 1965 (SPD 1965). This contained proposals for amending the 1957 legislation to provide a minimum pension for workers with 'a full working life', more protection for manual workers against the lowering of wages in later working life, and for changes in the age at which pensions could be drawn to give workers greater latitude in making the retirement decision. It also sought to widen social insurance to cover all the self-employed and give housewives some protection and, to secure a more just pooling of risks, to extend compulsory insurance to all salaried employees. This last proposal was enacted when the SPD first entered government in the controversial 'Grand Coalition' with the CDU between 1966 and 1969. As the SPD's 1969 election manifesto stressed, however, in this period its main role as regards pensions was to defend the dynamic principle against growing opposition within the CDU after the recession of 1966—7. Significantly, too, the manifesto emphasised the need to maintain close links between the aims of social policy and the essentially free market economic policies.

A number of the proposals in *'Die Volksversicherung'* found their way onto the statute books in 1972, with some modifications in what was described as the 'Second Pension Reform'. The changes in 1972 included the extension of state pension coverage on a voluntary basis to all the self-employed and to housewives and an alteration of the formula for assessing and adjusting pensions which effectively raised benefits by lessening the time-lag between wage changes and benefit increases. However, the principal innovations were the introduction of a new minimum pension for workers with at least 25 years' insurance and the policy on 'flexible retirement'. The minimum pension was achieved by weighting the benefit formula in a way explicitly rejected in 1957, though the changes were by no means a radical departure from the principles underlying the 1957 reform. Under the new formula an insured person who qualifies for a minimum benefit is assumed to have a personal income status, or wage base, equal to 75 per cent of that of an average wage earner. In practice, this means that the pension levels of low wage earners with full working life of 40 years or more are now much closer than previously to the average pensions. But the minimum pensions for anyone with 25 to 35 years' insurance are still relatively low and below the minimum income levels of social assistance. This is true also of many widows' pensions which remained after 1972 at 60 per cent of a husband's entitlement, including any entitlement to minimum pension.

The new policy on flexible retirement has had more significant repercussions, though again mainly for those with good working records. The 1972 Act made it possible for all insured persons with at least 35 years' contributions to retire at the age of 63, instead of 65. It also enabled disabled persons to draw an old-age pension under favourable conditions at the age of 62, and improved provisions made to the 1957 legislation permitting older workers unemployed for more than a year to receive a pension at the age of 60. In 1972, it seems to have been envisaged that a large number of workers would take advantage of these provisions, but that most would prefer the incentive of a higher pension at the age of 65 or later. However, the vast majority of West German workers now appear to be retiring at 63, partly because of their good pensions but also because they have often had little choice since the beginnings of the recession in 1974. More recently there has been much discussion of a new phenomenon — the '59-ers'. These are workers made redundant at the age of 59, under collective agreements and often with good lump-sum leaving payments, who draw unemployment insurance benefits for a year and then become eligible for an early old-age pension as well as being able to do certain part-time work. Although estimates of the numbers involved vary, West Germany's largest firms, especially in the car and chemical industries, seem increasingly to be adopting this policy. Indeed, some firms now appear to be under considerable pressure from the trade unions to extend such provisions to workers below the age of 59.

As in Britain, the unions have played a much more active role recently in the development of occupational pensions and there have been some significant new state initiatives here. A 'Law to Improve Occupational Old Age Pensions' (*Gesetz zur Verbesserung der Betrieblichen Altersversorgung*), passed in 1974, created a new statutory framework for the schemes which sought to promote their growth while at the same time co-ordinating them more closely with state pensions and setting minimum standards as regards benefit levels and the preservation of pension rights. An important ruling by the Federal Labour Court in 1977 has also increased pressure on employers to improve benefits, particularly to adjust them regularly in line with cost of living changes. According to a report to the *Bundestag* on the effects of the 1974 Act, by the end of 1976, 65 per cent of employees in the private sector were covered by occupational schemes and more than two-thirds of them were eligible for benefits equal to more than 15 per cent of their earnings at retirement (Bericht 1978). The proportions were significantly lower, however, among lower paid workers and less well unionised workers in medium-sized and smaller firms.

During the past decade, more progress has also been made in improving social assistance and other means-tested welfare and housing benefits. A number of important changes in social assistance law were contained in a revision of the Federal Social Aid Act (*Bundessozialhilfegesetz*) in 1974 (BfJFG 1977). This relaxed and simplified certain of the conditions for receiving assistance, including family maintenance obligations which are now restricted to the children of old people. It also sought to promote more social work and welfare services for the elderly and disabled, particularly home-care services, and generally to place more emphasis on the *right* to assistance and welfare. In the early 1970s, there were large increases, too, in the basic 'subsistence aid' allowances which compensated for the erosion of their value in the 1960s. Since then the *Länder*, who still set the scale rates of assistance, have raised them at the beginning of each year and have adapted them more closely than previously to the general standard of living. Another recent development has been the enlargement of the national housing allowances scheme, which had been introduced in 1965 mainly to offset rent increases following the ending of most private sector controls (Lawson and Stephens 1974). Under the

'Social-Liberal' coalition the scheme's benefits have been raised significantly and its means-test simplified. The government has tended to view the allowances as a form of supplementary income for poorer pensioners and low wage earners, which helps reduce the need to claim social assistance, as well as a means of compensating for high housing costs.

With these developments, however, there has also been more public discussion and awareness of the limitations and contradictions of these policies. More generally, the extent and significance of poverty and the need for social assistance have become much more controversial issues during the past decade, particularly since the publication in 1975 of a report on poverty in the welfare state by Heiner Geissler, a leading Christian Democratic politician (Geissler 1976). The Report drew attention both to the relatively meagre standards of social assistance, in spite of the improvements in benefits, and, more significantly, to the persistence of substantial 'hidden poverty' due to non-claiming of assistance. It estimated that in 1974 the incomes of 9 per cent of all West German households or of 5.8 million people fell below the poverty line associated with the social assistance level of living. This included 14.5 per cent of all pensioner households, containing 2.3 million persons: almost four times the numbers regularly receiving 'subsistence aid'. These calculations were in turn used as evidence of the emergence of a 'new social question' affecting those sections of society excluded from the levelling tendencies of the modern Social State because of their lack of organisation and protection by trade unions and other powerful interest groups and associations. Indeed, according to Geissler, the fate of this 'underclass' in West German society is now being determined by the new balance of power between the well-organised majority of workers and the interests of capital since

> in the tug of war between unions and employers in an inflationary society it is no longer possible for either side to wrest permanent advantages at the expense of the other. It is the non-organised people at whose expense such advantages are gained. (1976: 15).

There is clearly much truth in arguments like these, and they can of course be extended further to embrace other 'new' social problems resulting from the construction of the modern welfare state. As a number of Geissler's critics have pointed out, however, it is nevertheless important to recognise the extent to which the problems of the poorest sections of West German society are rooted in more traditional patterns of social inequality and sexual discrimination, which social provisions like pensions, with their emphasis on the achievement principle, have tended to support and reinforce. Moreover, the other main national poverty study undertaken in recent years, which contains a more detailed analysis than

Geissler's based on more reliable data, has produced significantly lower estimates of poverty. This is the study mentioned earlier based on the income and consumption surveys, which reveals a marked decline in the incidence of 'hidden poverty' (*Dunkel Ziffer*) between 1963 and 1973. It suggests that, in 1973, 2.4 per cent of all West German households had incomes below the social assistance minimum, compared with Geissler's 9 per cent (Klanberg 1979; George and Lawson 1980). Nevertheless, this study still indicates that more than 60 per cent of elderly people eligible for social assistance were not claiming it, and other more recent local studies which have examined this problem in greater detail have come up with similar findings (Bujard and Lange 1978). They show too that as well as lacking information regarding their eligibility, many elderly people still fear the pressures that officials may bring to bear on their immediate relatives and are generally unwilling to see the benefits as more than a last resort.

It is difficult to assess the likely influence on policy of evidence like this with the recession and the expenditure crisis in social policy. However, a further reform of pensions is promised following an important ruling by the Federal Constitutional Court in 1975 declaring the treatment of widows in the state pension schemes incompatible with the Basic Law (*Grundgesetz*) or Constitution. The Court's ruling requires the provisions to be altered, by 1984 at the latest, to produce equality in treatment between the sexes after the death of one partner. This decision, which was itself partly influenced by the growing evidence of the plight of many elderly widows, has in turn led to demands for a more far-reaching reform of the social security rights of women and also for the introduction of a 'social minimum' pension. On the other hand, a committee set up by the government to consider the implications of the Court's decision has recommended a more limited change in pension rights, involving improving the provisions made for working women to include special 'baby year' allowances for each child they have and a splitting of pension rights after the death of one partner (Standfest 1979).

Even such a modest reform would add to the difficulties now facing the West Germans in maintaining the levels of benefits and services for the elderly. In recent years, the elaborate and costly commitments made during the period of rapid economic growth have had increasingly serious repercussions, especially since the recession has been accompanied by a steady increase in the number of persons drawing pensions as well as a shrinking in the number of contributors to social insurance. Moreover, between the beginnings of the recession in 1974 and 1977 the dynamic adjustment of pensions, in line with gross earnings and with its built-in lag, produced average annual increases in benefits of more than 11 per cent, whereas net wages and salaries rose annually by an average of 6.7 per cent and the cost of living for pensioner households by 5.5 per cent. By the end of the 1970s, expenditure on statutory pensions, including disability as well as old-age benefits, amounted to over 15 per cent of West Germany's GDP, more than twice the proportion in the mid-1950s. To finance these benefits, the combined insurance contributions of employers and employees, which were set at 11 per cent of earnings in 1955, had risen to 18 per cent at the end of the 1970s. But, in addition to this, 45 per cent of expenditures were financed out of general taxation, a much higher figure than was ever envisaged by those responsible for the 1957 pension reform. To add to the seriousness of the problems now facing the government, demographic forecasts point to a further significant increase in the numbers of pensioners in the 1980s and 1990s, when there are also likely to be demands to allocate more resources in social policy to the unemployed and to younger families.

The Social-Liberal coalition's main response to these problems was to raise the contribution rate by a further 0.5 per cent with effect from the beginning of 1981, and, more controversially, to suspend the dynamic adjustment of pensions. No increases were made in pensions between July 1977 and January 1979 and in the next three years pensions were raised annually at rates of 4.5, 5 and 5 per cent. This policy has, however, proved unpopular and in the Federal elections both the SPD and CDU appeared to be committed to reintroducing the dynamic principle in 1982. Options now being considered by the new CDU—FDP government to achieve further savings include cutting back on the costly pensions for public servants, the introduction of pensioners' contributions to the national health insurance scheme and the raising of the pension age for women from 60 to 63. Unless there is a dramatic economic revival, however, it seems inevitable that pressures will grow during the next decade for a more fundamental reappraisal of policies towards the elderly and, indeed, of the commitments of the 'Social State' as a whole.

References

Bericht, 1978, *Bericht der Bundesregierung über die Erfahrungen bei der Durchführung des Gesetzes zur Verbesserung der betrieblichen Altersversorgung*, Bonn.

Blume, O. 1970, 'The poverty of old people in urban and rural areas' in P. Townsend (ed.), *The concept of poverty*, London, Heinemann Educational Books.

Bujard, O. and Lange, U. 1978, *Theorie und Praxis der Sozialhilfe*, Stuttgart, Kohlhammer.

Bundesministerium fur Jugend, Familie und Gesundheit (BfJFG), 1977, *Leistungen der Bundesregierung fur ältere Bürger in der BRD*, Bonn.

Geissler, H. 1976, *Die Neue Soziale Frage*, Freiburg, Herder.

George, V. and Lawson, R. (eds) 1980, *Poverty and inequality in Common Market countries*, London, Routledge and Kegan Paul.

Hockerts, H. G. 1977, 'SozialPolitische Reformbestrebungen in den frühen Bundesrepublik', *Vierteljahrshefte für Zeitgeschichte*, January, pp. 341–72.

Hockerts, H. G. 1981, 'German post-war social policies against the background of the Beveridge plan. Some observations preparatory to a comparative analysis' in W. Mommsen (ed.), *The emergence of the welfare state in Britain and Germany 1850–1950*, London, Croom Helm, pp. 315–39.

Jantz, K. 1961, 'Pension reform in the Federal Republic of Germany', *International Labour Review*, no. 83.

Johnson, N. 1973, *Government in the Federal Republic of Germany*, Oxford, Pergamon Press.

Klanberg, F. 1979, 'Einkommensarmut 1969 und 1973', *Sozialer Fortschritt*, Heft 6.

Lawson, R. and Stephens, C. 1974, Housing allowances in West Germany and France, *Journal of Social Policy*, vol. 3.

Menzies, A. 1974, 'The Federal Republic of Germany' in T. Wilson (ed.), *Pensions, inflation and growth*, London, Heinemann Educational Books, pp. 45–109.

Rimlinger, G. V. 1971, *Welfare policy and industrialisation in Europe, America and Russia*, New York, Wiley.

Roth, J. 1974, *Armut in der Bundesrepublik*, Frankfurt, Fischer.

Schreiber, W. 1955, *Existenzsicherheit in der industriellen Gesellschaft*, Cologne, Bachem.

SPD 1965, *Die Volksversicherung*, Bonn.

Standfest, E. 1979, 'Zur Diskussion um die soziale Sicherung der Frau und die Reform der Hinterbliebenenversorgung', *WSI Mitteilungen*, December, pp. 682–8.

Statistisches Bundesamt 1953–5, *Die sozialen Verhältnisse der Renten- und Unterstützingsempfänger*, Wiesbaden.

Verba, S. 1965, 'Germany — the remaking of political culture' in L. Pye and S. Verba (eds), *Political Culture and Political Development*, Princeton.

Wallich, H. 1955, *Mainsprings of the German revival*, New Haven, Yale University Press.

Willmott, P. Willmott, P. and McDowell, L. 1978, *Poverty and social policy in Europe. A pilot study in the United Kingdom, Germany and France*, London, Institute of Community Studies.

Part V   Lessons from Europe

13   Lessons for the UK
Roger Lawson and Robert Walker

It is commonly believed that the fight against poverty has been fought more successfully in Europe than in the UK and critics of British social policy frequently support their case by reference to Europe. In fact, the evidence assembled in this volume indicates that, despite a rapid growth in welfare expenditure, poverty remains widespread throughout Europe.

The European Commission's national poverty studies reveal that in all countries the income of more than one household in eight falls beneath the '60 per cent personal disposable income' poverty line. (It will be recalled that in Britain the '60 per cent personal disposable income' line closely approximates to supplementary benefit levels; (see Table 2.25.) Moreover, since the data for those studies was collected in the 1970s, it is certain that the economic recession has brought about a marked increase in the prevalence of poverty. Statistics based on average rates conceal the greater risk of poverty faced by certain groups especially those outside the labour market including the retired, the sick and the unemployed. Moreover, employment does not necessarily guarantee protection against poverty since wages in agriculture and in other declining industries are often low while short-term contracts and part-time working also frequently undermine financial security. Women in particular continue to be disadvantaged in the labour market and this disadvantage is frequently replicated by social security. Families which do not conform to traditional expectations, the divorced, lone parents and families with many children, for example, face greater risks of poverty because support systems are narrowly constrained or inflexible in the face of changing social norms and patterns of behaviour.

As already explained (Chapter 2), the '60 per cent personal disposable income' line is not a wholly satisfactory measure of relative poverty. There is a need to examine whether such an income actually allows family or social needs to be met and, in Chapter 1, Peter Townsend advocates the search for an independent criterion of income level chosen to represent the start of more severe forms of deprivation or multi-deprivation. Nevertheless, in the light of facts such as these, it is not surprising that the final poverty report from the European Commission should call for 'resolute action' grounded not on 'any crude calculation of costs or benefits' but:

> on equality, compassion and solidarity and the evident need to give new hope to the 30 million people in the Community who are currently denied social justice. (1981c)

It is debatable whether supra-national organisations or, indeed, national governments have the political will to meet this challenge. In Chapter 1, Peter Townsend grounds a structural explanation of poverty in the workings of the world economy and points to the responsibilities of multinational corporations and international cartels as well as those of national governments. In particular, he draws attention to the limited commitment shown by the European Community to social policy and further warns of the possibility that national welfare systems may deteriorate in their ability to provide protection against the effects of changes in the global economy.

Table 2.25 above shows that, in 1975, one in six households in Britain had incomes below the '60 per cent personal disposable income' line. This was fewer than in either West Germany or France. Moreover, with respect to the more stringent '40 per cent personal disposable income' line the proportion of 'poor' households in Britain was even lower than in The Netherlands. It must be stressed, though, that both measures concern relative poverty and in absolute terms represent a lower material standard of living in Britain than in the other countries. This reflects Britain's lower national income.

The comparative success of the UK (at least up to the mid-1970s) in maintaining a low incidence of extreme relative poverty may seem surprising given that so small a proportion of national income is devoted to welfare expenditure (e.g. see Table 2.10). It will be recalled that in this respect the UK resembled the two countries poorer than herself, that is Italy and Ireland, rather than those marginally more prosperous, namely The Netherlands and Belgium. One reason may be that the reduction of poverty has been more prominent in the political rhetoric of Britain than in that of Europe and has come to assume a central importance among the objectives of social policy. In most other European countries, as contributors to this volume have emphasised, the relief of poverty has rarely been more than a subsidiary element in a social policy that is more concerned to regulate the relationship between capital and labour, foster solidarity, and to maintain the acquired living standards of those no longer in employment. Significantly, the European Commission's poverty studies were undertaken in response to the export of ideas from the UK via Eire (see Chapter 1; also James 1980).

In accord with the British emphasis on poverty relief, a national system of last resort has been established that offers relatively higher benefits than social assistance in Europe. This serves to minimise the numbers with very low incomes as distinct from those with low incomes. At the same time, first line-income support benefits are not as generous nor as comprehensive in Britain as on the Continent. As a result, many more people are dependent on means-tested assistance or have incomes only marginally above assistance levels. For this reason estimates of poverty for the UK are particularly sensitive to the positioning of the poverty line. A 5 per cent increase above supplementary benefit rates has been shown to increase the number of individuals in poverty by 41 per cent and a 20 per cent increase by 167 per cent (Beckerman 1979).

The reliance on assistance and on means-testing also raises problems of a more profound nature. The numbers failing to claim the benefits to which they are entitled are likely to be increased. A poverty trap is created because claimants are faced with high marginal rates of taxation as benefits are withdrawn. The dependency status of the poor is increased by the need to submit themselves to investigation into their eligibility in order to qualify for benefit while widespread use of discretion raises issues concerned with social control and regulation of the poor. Moreover, there is, in Britain, a unique importance attached to work and employment status in determining the type of income maintenance available to the poor. This relates, in part at least, to a concern that benefits should be received only by the 'deserving poor' which in turn explains the emphasis given to minimising the disincentives to work caused by social security provision.

Also, associated with the emphasis on poverty relief in Britain is the limited role played by trade unions and employers in the development of social policy. Here the 'social wage' was taken seriously only briefly during the mid-1970s whereas it is often integral to wage negotiations and economic planning on the Continent. European trade unions (and employers' organisations) are often actively engaged in the provison of welfare benefits whereas in Britain, to take but one example, the newly constituted Social Security Advisory Committee has a single trade union representative. The failure to involve labour in social security decisions on the same scale as in Europe may have served further to marginalise the poor in Britain.

The intention in the remainder of this chapter is further to consider British policies to combat poverty in the light of European experience.

The aim is not to look to Europe for simple solutions to problems of the UK. As we recognised in the Preface to this volume, any welfare system is the organic product of a socio-political process which is in turn grounded in cultural perceptions and economic realities. As such, policies cannot generally be successfully transplanted from one country to another. Moreover, as we have seen, no European country has success-fully dealt with the problems of poverty. However, this is not to say that welfare assistance evolved in complete isolation from developments abroad, nor that it is impossible to learn from international comparisons. Indeed, without such comparison, it is difficult to assess what has been achieved or to establish realistic goals for the future.

The structure of this chapter reflects that of the book as a whole. It is divided into four parts. The first two concern unemployment and low pay respectively; the third considers child support and family policy; and the fourth focuses on the elderly.

Unemployment

The growth in unemployment throughout Europe during the 1970s and especially since 1980 has brought about a marked change in the structure of poverty and contributed to its wider impact. The UK was the first to be affected and still suffers higher levels of unemployment than most of her competitors. Moreover, there is substantial evidence that even during the 1970s, unemployment significantly increased the number of young families in poverty. Between November 1972 and November 1980, the number of unemployed men with families in Great Britain increased by approximately 126 000 (or 68 per cent) and the number of children affected from 194 000 to 611 000. As a result of the 34 per cent increase in unemployment during 1981, the number of unemployed men with children may have risen to 450 000 by early 1982. Over half of these families would probably have been eligible for supplementary benefit and virtually all will have fallen below Beckerman's international stan-dard poverty line (see Table 2.1). (Beckerman's standard is similar to the '60 per cent personal disposable income line', see Chapter 2). Also, the disproportionate rise in unemployed youngsters, while possibly having a less significant impact on the number in poverty, will inevitably have reduced the income of families with teenagers and deprived some parents of their only period of relative prosperity (CPRS 1980).

Between 1974 and 1977 the proportion of married couples with child-ren having incomes below 120 per cent of supplementary benefit in-creased from around 4 per cent to over 10 per cent, a larger increase than for any other group and due in large part to the rise in unemployment. Similarly, whereas in 1974 couples with children constituted only 18.6

per cent of people in poverty, by 1977 this proportion had risen by 28.8 per cent. The drop in unemployment during 1979 reduced the number of poor families but recent rises will have reversed this trend once more (DHSS 1982).

The impact of unemployment on poverty is not restricted to the present. The risk of poverty in future years is greatly increased by the extent to which the unemployed have fallen into debt or needed to replace consumer durables, have used up their savings, or suffered a deterioration in health or a loss of self-esteem. The process is exacerbated by the British social security system which, for example, makes full entitlement to certain national insurance benefits dependent on employment of a year's duration. Similarly, because the 1975 pension scheme does not credit periods of unemployment, retirement pensions stand to be affected. Whether present unemployment will have an effect on future generations is more questionable but this is already a concern of the French government (see Chapter 3).

The growth in unemployment throughout Europe has been associated with a slow-down in economic growth and increased sensitivity to inflationary pressures following substantial increases in oil prices, combined with adverse demographic trends and structural shifts in employment (see Part II). In Britain, these factors have been compounded by a long history of low growth and, recently, by vigorously restrictive fiscal and monetary policy. Negative growth was recorded for six consecutive quarters in 1980/1 and the positive growth in early 1982 was at an annual rate of less than 0.5 per cent (CSO 1982). If growth were to continue at less than 1 per cent for the next decade, the inevitable improvements in productivity could cause a further loss of 1.5 million manufacturing jobs at a time when the labour force would have been expected to grow considerably. Unemployment would continue to rise though it is likely that the real value of aggregate wages would increase — at the same rate as national income. This would result in a divergence in the living standards of those in work and those without employment (Coutts *et al.* 1982).

Without a return to sustained growth, therefore, it is hard to see how conflict and social unrest can be avoided. Growth, the present government believes, will follow naturally from tight monetary policy although many would disagree (e.g. Meade 1982; CEPG 1982; NIESR 1982). What is clear is that under any of the economic strategies currently under discussion, unemployment is likely to drop only slowly so that ways of distributing the costs of unemployment more fairly must be found. This will mean increased financial protection for the unemployed and a substantial sharing of existing employment.

Unemployment benefits

In most respects, the financial protection afforded the unemployed is already much greater in Europe than in Britain. Earnings-related benefits have traditionally been important in Europe whereas flat-rate benefits have been favoured in Britain since the early years of the century. Beveridge reinforced the principle when he argued for a scheme with flat-rate contributions that offered flat-rate benefits 'to be sufficient without further resources, to provide the minimum income needed for subsistence in all normal cases' (Beveridge 1942: paragraph 307). This attempt to establish social minima through the insurance system (which incidentally explains the unique system of child additions, see below) contrasts with the continental view that benefits should aim to minimise the personal upheaval resulting from job loss. Whereas in Europe it was accepted that welfare services should expand with increasing national prosperity, both political parties in Britain were wedded to centralised acts of charity (Shonfield 1968). When an earnings-related scheme was finally introduced in the UK in 1965, it was justified as an attempt to take account of people's financial commitments and as a method of encouraging workers to accept necessary redundancies rather than as an extension of the insurance contract between state and workers (Kaim-Caudle 1973). In practice, very few of the unemployed — 25 per cent of unemployed men in November 1980 — received earnings-related supplement (ERS) and many of them received very small amounts. As part of the public expenditure cuts, ERS was abolished in January 1982 although contributions continue to be earnings-related. This further undermined any notion of a contractual relationship. It also reduced the maximum benefit payable to a two-child couple to 63 per cent of the international poverty standard (compare Table II.3).

As a consequence of the difference in emphases, replacement ratios have been generally much higher on the Continent than in the UK since benefits are designed to maintain living standards rather than to support a minimum income. Even before the abolition of ERS, replacement ratios were much less than in Denmark or The Netherlands (see Table II.2) although for the small minority receiving the supplement (and providing they had sufficient children) they were comparable with those in West Germany and France. However, ERS was payable only for six months — a much shorter period than in the other countries — and the numbers unemployed for longer than six months in Britain have increased dramatically. The abolition of ERS and the 5 per cent reduction in the real value of benefits implemented in the Social Security (no. 2) Act 1980 have reduced replacement ratios still further. Nonetheless, the British system still affords many of the lowest paid larger social insurance and assistance payments in unemployment than either their West German or French counterparts.

Table II.2 shows that replacement ratios are maintained for considerably longer in Europe than in the UK. Similarly insurance benefits are payable for longer in Denmark, The Netherlands and West Germany (but see Chapter 5) so that fewer of the unemployed are dependent on social assistance. The qualifying conditions necessary for receipt of unemployment benefit are also much more stringent in the UK, particularly for lower paid workers (DHSS 1980).

In turn higher replacement ratios and longer periods of entitlement on the Continent reflect a much more relaxed attitude (at least until very recently) to the disincentive effects of high benefit levels. It is hard to explain why disincentives are taken so seriously in Britain unless the concern is construed as part of the 'policing' necessary to deter the 'undeserving poor' from claiming a benefit available on the basis of 'need'. ('Blaming the victim' does, however, seem to be a peculiarly British pastime, see Table 2.19.) Certainly, the evidence shows that very few of the unemployed receive benefits in excess of former earnings while many people are prepared to accept jobs which pay lower wages than they were previously earning (SBC 1980; Moylan and Davies 1981; Bradshaw 1982). In theory, child additions payable on unemployment benefit add to disincentives and this factor is not present in other countries, at least until entitlement to insurance benefit is exhausted and assistance benefits become payable. However, a falling proportion of the unemployed have children and by February 1982 only one in eight of those receiving unemployment benefit (excluding supplementary benefit recipients) were entitled to child additions (Trinder 1982). This change is due to the high proportion of school leavers who cannot find work. In the British context, additions paid during unemployment for children are vitally important in that they help to maintain the incomes of the low-paid people on the margins of poverty who become unemployed. To an extent, therefore, child additions serve to compensate for low basic rates of benefit (Tables II.2 and II.3).

Although evidence is scanty, greater stigma would appear to attach to unemployment and to the unemployed in the UK than in the other countries. Take-up of benefits is also lower. This may once again reflect the need-based nature of British insurance benefits, but equally important is the fact that many more of the unemployed in Britain depend on social assistance which generally attracts greater stigma than insurance-based benefits (EC 1981c). The latter factor arises not only because unemployment benefit is payable for a relatively short period but also because the basic flat-rate benefit is frequently insufficient on its own for subsistence without access to means-tested supplementation. The trouble is that large proportions of those eligible for means-tested benefits do not in fact receive them. By 1979, government estimates of the shortfall were 1 200 000 (including 130 000 unemployed). Independent estimates are generally higher. For 1979, it was officially estimated that an additional £355 million could have been claimed by those eligible to such benefits (DHSS 1982).

Higher levels of unemployment on the Continent have recently increased reliance on social assistance but not to the same extent as in Britain. Moreover, cuts in the real value of insurance benefits in Britain have exacerbated the problem (SSAC 1982). Between 1980 and 1982, the numbers of people dependent on supplementary benefit increased from 4.5 million to 6.5 million. There is evidence of deterioration in the immediacy and quality of the 'safety net' of assistance. While the number of claimants has swollen, staffing levels have actually fallen with strikes in offices and the payment elsewhere of emergency benefits. There have been more delays and mistakes in payment. The government's widely publicised 'crackdown on scroungers' with the doubling of the number of unemployment review officers in 1980 and other measures have very probably deterred people in great need from claiming benefit and have certainly increased acrimony between claimants and staff.

A Different Approach

At attempt to emulate the best of European provision requires a substantial rise in the level of benefit in order to enhance income replacement ratios and to reduce dependency on social assistance. This may only be more feasible potentially through the establishment of a fully earnings-related scheme. Such a scheme could offer equity in the maintenance of living standards and rationalises the relationship between benefit levels and earnings. In addition, a genuine contractual relationship might — in small measure — help to erode the stigma still attaching to benefit receipt.

But an earnings-related system can result in very low benefits being paid to the low-paid. This occurs in France and West Germany although in Denmark and The Netherlands it is prevented both by setting minimum benefit levels and by high minimum wages. Indeed, it is at least arguable that low pay is a problem to be tackled through the wage bargaining system and should not be used to justify distortions in social security. Moreover, earnings-related benefits do at least ensure that the unemployed share the increased earnings of those in employment providing, that is, their value is maintained in payment.

The cost of reintroducing ERS would be small while the additional costs of a thorough-going earnings-related scheme would not be substantial in relation to the total outlay on unemployment benefits and could ultimately be made self-financing. Part of the cost might be met by abolition of the ceiling on national insurance contributions for which there seems to be little justification.

West Germany excepted, the unemployment funds in the other countries are administered by semi-autonomous bodies comprising representatives of both sides of industry with the role and financial contribution of government varying considerably. The origins of this approach, which differs so markedly from the UK system, in part reflect the important role played by trade unions in the development of unemployment cover. To suggest that the UK adopt this continental model would necessitate a considerable reorganisation and segmentation of the existing national insurance scheme and a substantially enhanced role for the trade union movement. Also, many trade unionists might fear the potential loss of independence in representing the rights of labour, while the interests of less powerful groups and non trade unionists would have to be protected in the same way as in Europe. However, such a scheme might attract a government determined to reduce its responsibilities but, more importantly, it would lead to the direct involvement of employers and employees – already the prime financers – in determining the specifics of policy and being responsible for its successes and failures. Both sides would also have a vested interest in reducing outlays from the fund which, European experience suggests, would result not in lower benefits but in co-ordinated pressure and action to maintain high levels of employment and in favour of effective rehabilitation, training etc.

An alternative proposal, which though less radical is nevertheless consistent with European practice is that tripartite discussion on wages policy involving employers, employees and government, should include consideration of benefit levels and conditions (see below).

All the above proposals seek to link the financial circumstances of the unemployed to the outcome of industrial negotiations. The European model is that by 'demarginalising' the position of the unemployed their financial circumstances will be improved and thereafter protected. However, the financial protection afforded the unemployed in the UK in many cases falls so far behind that in Europe – even accounting for the UK's limited resources – that more immediate improvement is called for. Moreover, to the extent that unemployment is an inevitable consequence of policies designed to increase future national wealth, common justice demands that the nation should be prepared to minimise the hardship suffered by those affected. This would involve at the very least a restoration of the 5 per cent cut in unemployment benefits and payment of the higher rate of supplementary benefit to the long-term unemployed.

Job creation and work sharing

The lessons to be drawn from European experience are much less clear with regard to job creation and work sharing. All the countries studied have responded to unemployment in a largely *ad hoc* fashion and, until very recently, it has been assumed that unemployment is a short-term problem. Not surprisingly, therefore, many of the measures implemented have been overtaken by the increasing scale of unemployment. Moreover, macro-economic differences combined with inadequate information, make it impossible to gauge the efficacy of the national responses.

Whereas West Germany and Denmark have concentrated on measures to redistribute labour and to regulate its supply and demand, Britain has, like The Netherlands, concentrated on measures to increase labour demand although with less reliance on public sector job creation. The thrust of British policy has been through selective subsidies to employers which in theory not only increase jobs but redistribute employment in favour of the most disadvantaged, thus helping to reduce poverty. The impact on inflation and on the balance of payments should also be less than for general subsidies (see Part II above). In December 1980, 700 060 people were within the scope of the special employment measures (Tables 13.1 and II.1).

Table 13.1   Special employment measures in December 1980, Great Britain

	December 1980 (nos)	March 1982 (nos)
Temporary short time working compensation scheme	509 500	175 000
Job release scheme	63 300	63 000
Youth opportunities programme	155 000	215 000
Community industry	6 300	7 100
Special temporary employment programme/ community enterprise	11 400	27 500
Training for skills programme (end of October)	22 200	—
Young workers scheme (starting January 1982) and Enterprise Allowance Scheme	—	41 750
	767 000	564 350

Source: MSC 1981, 1982.

As the Manpower Services Commission readily admits, the net effect of its measures may be less than Table 13.1 would suggest (MSC 1981). Some participants would have been recruited anyway, some would have been recruited at the cost of displacing others, while some employers have simply replaced regular employees with temporary workers financed under the special schemes. In such cases the measures have as much to do with work sharing as with job creation.

Denmark and, to a lesser extent, the other three countries have placed greater emphasis on implicit measures to redistribute employment. An example in Britain is the scheme for job splitting announced by the British government in July 1982, though the nature of jobs amenable to part-time working probably limits the redistributional impact of the scheme. Also, the scheme has met considerable trade union resistance (Forester 1982). Nevertheless, other avenues are worthy of exploration. The working week on the continent is generally shorter than in the UK (EC 1981a) and the French government, under Mitterrand, is committed to further reductions with a view to increasing employment prospects. Similarly, Denmark has increased holiday entitlement for the same reasons and is considering limiting overtime. Finally, measures to facilitate flexible retirement are more comprehensive and generous in The Netherlands, West Germany and Denmark (see Chapters 4, 5 and 6 respectively) than in the UK where activity rates among the over-60s, are still exceptionally high (EC 1981b).

European evidence testifies to the difficulty of implementing measures to redistribute employment (see Chapters 3, 5 and 6 and EC 1981c). Unilateral action which increases labour costs may lead to a decline in international competitiveness. Likewise, any increase in labour costs relative to capital may be at the expense of employment opportunities. However, it may be possible to minimise increases in labour costs by permitting employees to choose those arrangements which give them greatest personal benefit and for which they are prepared to forgo income. Moreover, government would save unemployment benefit and employers might not always pass on additional costs into prices (Coutes *et al*. 1982). Another problem is that the ratio of new to old employment generated by job-sharing measures may be significantly less than unity unless measures are adequately policed. Furthermore, any scheme which involves income sharing in addition to job sharing, e.g. across-the-board limitations in overtime, would present serious problems for the low paid, while early retirement schemes may serve to reinforce the dependency status of the elderly (see below).

Job-creation and work-sharing schemes are no substitute for economic growth. Nevertheless, while unemployment remains high, such schemes will need to be vigorously pursued on a larger scale than hitherto, not as a means of reducing the unemployment statistics but in order to share the burden of unemployment and to prevent the emergence of an underclass who are permanently denied employment. The final report of the European Commission's Programme to Combat Poverty also emphasised the importance of work-sharing policies and urged international co-operation on a Community-wide basis facilitated by transfers of resources to the weaker economies within the Community (EC 1981c). Certainly, at the time of writing, Britain's employment programmes had not yet begun to amount to the creation of permanent jobs on a substantial scale.

Low Pay

The growth of unemployment has tended to distract attention from low pay as a cause of poverty. Nevertheless, the two are intimately connected and low pay is a significant problem affecting many families in the UK (Pond 1981). There is considerable evidence that low earners run substantially increased risks of unemployment and tend also to have worse national insurance records and lower savings with which to preserve their standard of living. Paradoxically, however, unemployment may be a financial blessing for the few whose incomes in work are less than benefit levels.

Since 65 per cent of low wage earners working full-time are female (Pond 1981), the importance of low pay as a cause of poverty has sometimes been questioned (e.g. Miller 1981). Such questioning assumes, first, that female wages are merely supplementary to male earnings and, secondly, that it is the male wage which should be sufficient to support a family (Bennett 1981; Land 1981). Leaving aside the fundamental issue of equity, and holding judgement as to how far family support should be financed through the wage system, the 1971 Census found that one in six households, excluding pensioner households, were dependent on women for their main sorce of income (Bennett 1981). Moreover, it has been estimated that the number of households in poverty would treble were it not for the contribution made by wives' earnings (Hamill 1978). Clearly, low pay cannot lightly be dismissed as a cause of poverty.

Whether the circumstances of the low paid worsened during the 1970s is a matter of some dispute. In real terms, the gross earnings of the lowest decile which increased in the early 1970s for both sexes declined sharply between 1977 and 1982. Differentials between the skilled and the unskilled narrowed in the years 1973—6 in response to egalitarian pay policies involving flat-rate increases. However, the differentials have since widened (see Table II.5 and Marsden 1980) and it is clear that the earnings of low paid men and women are continuing to fall in the 1980s (Atkinson 1982).

Net pay is, of course, a more realistic index of living standards than gross earnings. Between 1970 and 1977 tax thresholds fell markedly from 58.4 per cent of average gross earnings to 47.9 per cent for a two-child couple, thus bringing more low wage earners into tax. In theory, the increased taxes were more than offset, in the case of families with children, by the introduction of child benefits and family income supplement (Piachaud 1980). In practice, however, family income supplement exacerbated the poverty trap while, in addition, many families failed to claim the new benefit. Fiscal changes since 1979, taking account of indirect as well as direct taxation, appear to have caused a drop in the net incomes of low wage families both in real terms and in relation to families on average incomes (Meacher 1982; Field 1981).

It is impossible to be certain whether the problem of low pay is worse in the UK than elsewhere in Europe. Much depends on indirect employer benefits as well as exact interpretation of the social wage. Comparison, restricted to skill and industry differentials, indicates that the number of working poor and the extent of their deprivation may be greater in France than in the UK but much less in Denmark and The Netherlands. The situation in West Germany approximates very closely to that in the UK (see Figure 2.1; Tables II.4 and II.5).

A minimum wage

France, Denmark and The Netherlands have adopted a minimum wage to which certain social security benefits are related. In Denmark, the minimum wage is no longer statutory although, as in The Netherlands, it forms an integral part of collective wage agreements. In both countries, minimum wages rose faster than average rates during the 1970s (see Chapters 4 and 6). In France, where the minimum wage has a special political significance, minimum wage rates have also increased steadily although they remain below those in Denmark and The Netherlands even after the increases implemented by the Mitterrand government (see Chapter 3 and Part II).

In the UK, on the other hand, policies have failed to improve, or even to protect, the position of the low paid (Metcalfe 1980b; Berthoud *et al.* 1981). Minimum pay levels are set by wage councils for about 2.75 million employers in nearly 400 000 establishments. In 1980, male manual workers in sectors covered by wages councils were over three times as likely as other groups to earn less than the wage equivalent of supplementary benefit for a two-child couple. Moreover, their position worsened relative to other manual workers during the decade (Metcalfe 1980b). The ineffectiveness of wage councils is due in part to the effect of wage restraint (wages councils tended to abide by government guidelines), to the failure to set targets for minimum wages and to the lack of real enforcement.

At the very least, any serious attempt to tackle the low-wage problem requires a complete overhaul of the wage council system with a view to making it more coherent, more effective and more forceful. One object-ive should be to link wage council minima to average wages with a com-mitment, over a specified period of time, to raise minima to at least two-thirds of average male workers and perhaps ultimately to Dutch levels.

A parallel extension of the coverage of wages councils would lay the basis for the introduction of a national minimum wage which must be a major priority. A minimum wage will not in itself eradicate the poverty arising from low wages because poverty depends crucially on the number of children and dependants in a family and on the number of wage earners. However, it does provide the foundation for a co-ordinated policy of income support across the employment divide that would facilitate a reduction of means-testing, lessen the poverty trap and permit a more even progression of income on entering the labour market. Such a policy would also require a systematic strategy of family support (see below).

One objection to a minimum wage is that it would price marginal groups out of employment although this problem may be reduced by tapering the minimum wage as described in the national chapters (see Chapters 3, 4 and 6). Another argument is that its introduction would be expensive and lead to proportional rises in all wages, rather than to a contraction of differentials. This is certainly a danger although continen-tal experience seems to be that it is not a major problem (see Chapters 3, 4 and 6). One possible solution is to incorporate decisions about mini-mum wages into wider tripartite negotiations about wages between representatives of employers and trade unions, with government as a junior partner. The scope of these negotiations would include con-sideration of the social wage since it would be the intention to co-ordinate wage and benefit levels though not to make them mutually interdependent (see Chapter 4 for a discussion of the 'carousel effect'). In effect, this is to suggest a movement towards the 'social contract' model adopted by Denmark and The Netherlands. (The West German system, which is very different in formal structure, in practice operates in a not dissimilar fashion since trade unions are few in number, their actions tend to be orchestrated and virtually all benefits are linked to wages.)

The idea of a social contract might not find favour among those in the UK who believe in wage bargaining at the level of the local plant irrespective of any wider repercussions. Nevertheless, it is axiomatic that, even in an atmosphere of free collective bargaining, wage agreements are influenced by the going rate. Moreover, there are clearly better criteria for establishing a norm than the position of certain key groups in the pay round and it is certainly questionable whether the low paid, hard working and skilful groups made greatest headway during the 1970s (Saunders, 1980). The choice of appropriate norms would clearly be governed by macro-economic considerations, not least the objective of facilitating the highest employment for a given level of inflation (see Metcalfe 1980a), but attention would also be focused explicitly on desirability of existing differentials.

To the extent that benefit levels are linked to wages or prices, the level of the social wage is already largely determined by pay bargaining. However, there are major advantages in making this link explicit, the most important being that it could lead to the reintegration of dependent groups into the economic fabric, thus fostering solidarity rather than separation. The equation between the level of benefits and welfare expenditure would be discussed in the context of the relative position of deprived groups and the social wage would be presented as a logical extension of the industrial wage, with receipt recognised as a social right rather than as a privilege. Social and economic policy would be conceived as a whole.

Child Support and Family Policy

In Britain, the financial impact of low wages and unemployment is most severe when the household afflicted includes children. The wages system fails to provide adequate income for many families even allowing for supplementation by the State (e.g. see Table 2.20 above). Likewise the social security system, most notably supplementary benefit, offers child allowances which recent research has shown to be insufficient to meet the basic requirements of children (Piachaud 1981).

In this instance, the lessons to be drawn from Europe are not comforting. This volume has shown that levels of child support are low in a number of countries, even in relation to poverty standards, and that large and lone-parent families face a significantly enhanced risk of poverty (e.g. see Part III and Table 2.26 above). Nor surprisingly, the Final Report of the European Commission's national poverty studies concluded that in most countries family support policies were not being used to the best effect and should be strengthened. Its recommendations include:

> Indexation to the cost of living (where this is not already undertaken), the use of differential allowances by age or by size of family (rather than a flat-rate for each child), a re-examination of the pros and cons of family allowances related to income rather than allowances made on a universal basis, and a review of the way total 'investment' in families is allocated to ensure that the outlay is weighted in favour of the poorest families. (EC 1981c)

In addition, action is urged to raise tax thresholds for low wage earners and to avoid policies which produce a proliferation of means-testing.

Post-war trends in Britain

While Part III shows that in the mid-1970s much of Britain's child support compared relatively favourably with that of West Germany and The Netherlands, if not with that of France, recent developments in Britain take on a special poignancy when set against the Commission's recommendations. Families with children have generally fared badly over the post-war period compared with other sections of the population. Whereas pensions and many other benefits have improved relative to wages (with some decline in the late 1970s and early 1980s), this has not been the case with most children's allowances. Indeed, the latter have often failed to keep pace with rising prices (see Table 13.2; also SSAC 1982). Despite the improvements made with the introduction of the new child benefit scheme between 1977 and 1979, the real value of child benefit is now significantly lower than the combination of family allowances and child tax allowances in the 1950s. Moreover, it is worth recalling that when family allowances were first introduced they were set at only 62 per cent of the level recommended by Beveridge (Kaim-Caudle 1973). Child benefits, like family allowances before them, are not differentiated by household size nor age of child (again contrary to Beveridge's recommendation) and while differentiation is characteristic of the supplementary benefit provisions, it was reduced in 1980. The burden of taxation on families with children has also increased disproportionately, particularly for those on average and below average earnings (see Table 13.3). Indeed, the tax threshold for many of the poorest families is now set below the supplementary benefit and family income supplement levels (SSAC 1982). Finally, the reduced subsidy for school meals, combined with the withdrawal of obligations on local authorities to provide free meals at school for low-income families not dependent on supplementary benefit or FIS has reduced the living standards of many families with young children relative to other households.

An even more disturbing trend has been the failure to adapt the social security 'safety net' provided by supplementary benefits to changing family responsibilities and the growing costs of child-rearing. It is true that the restructuring of supplementary benefits in 1980 was accompanied by much needed improvements in the benefit scales for children, most notably for the under 5s and 11- to 12-year-olds. However, these rates fell relative to prices in 1981 and still appear to be seriously inadequate to meet even frugally defined minimum needs. Piachaud (1981) has estimated that the children's scale rates in 1981 ranged from 64 to 90 per

Table 13.2 The real value of child support and relative to retirement pensions, 1946–81[1]

	1946 (%)	1955 (%)	1960 (%)	1965 (%)	1970 (%)	1975 (%)	1980 (%)	1981 (%)
Real value of child support[2] as a % of November 1981 value.								
Married couple with:								
1 child under 11	86.9	107.6	88.4	89.9	70.9	65.7	101.3	100.0
3 children under 11	107.0	131.2	111.8	110.5	87.2	82.3	101.3	100.0
1 child aged 11–16	86.9	107.6	109.5	109.5	86.5	75.0	101.3	100.0
3 children aged 11–16	107.0	131.2	129.3	129.3	102.9	92.0	101.3	100.0
Child support[2] as a % of a married couple's retiremnet pension								
2 children under 11	57.1[3]	58.5[4]	44.3[4]	32.3[4]	25.9[4]	20.9[4]	21.9	22.2
2 children aged 13–15	57.1[3]	58.5[4]	53.5[4]	38.3[4]	30.9[4]	23.4[4]	21.9	22.2

1 November of each year unless otherwise stated.
2 The combined value to standard rate taxpayers of child tax allowances, after clawback, and family allowances or child benefit.
3 July 1948.
4 April.

Source: SSAC 1982

Table 13.3   *Increases in income tax and national insurance from 1960/1*

Percentages

| Income | Increase in the % of income paid in income tax and national insurance [1] | | | | |
	Single person	Childless couple	Couple + 1 child [2]	Couple + 2 children [2]	Couple + 4 children [3]
1960/1 to 1980/1					
½ average earnings	80	100	115	111	112
¾ average earnings	78	118	222	356	366
Average earnings	63	93	166	277	639
2 × average earnings	29	35	51	70	148
1960/1 to 1982/3					
½ average earnings	99	136	152	146	146
¾ average earnings	92	141	257	407	407
Average earnings	74	110	190	308	697
2 × average earnings	39	46	63	83	166

1 Income includes family allowance or child benefit as appropriate. Employees are not contracted out of the earnings-related state pension scheme.
2 Children aged under 11.
3 Two children aged under 11; two children aged 11–16.

Source: Hansard 22 January 1980, columns 177–188; 21 December 1981, columns 300–2; 2 April 1982, columns 211–4.

cent of the basic costs of younger children, while the amounts available for teenagers 'must mean that many of them living in families on supplementary benefit suffer severe deprivation'. This is all the more serious since, as already noted, the number of children living in families dependent on supplementary benefits has increased rapidly with the growth of unemployment.

Another feature of Britain's child support policies during the past two decades has been the increasing reliance on means-tested allowances for the 'working poor'. To some extent this has served to offset the erosion of the other benefits and, judged individually, allowances such as the family income supplement and rent and rate rebates have been of considerable value to families who have successfully claimed them. Taken together, however, the spread of these provisions has produced serious and intractable problems, particularly by exacerbating the poverty trap and reinforcing tendencies to segregate the poor from the rest of society. The latest available information on 'take-up' for these benefits shows that this is still a major problem: according to DHSS estimates, family income supplement is received by little more than half of the families who are eligible (SSAC 1982).

Despite the introduction of new benefits, the system of family support in the UK has generally been slow to adapt to changing social and demographic circumstances, notably the increase in lone-parent households and working wives. Table 2.26 above shows just how great the risk of poverty is for lone parents, both in relation to other groups and compared with lone parents abroad. About half of them claim supplementary benefit — the number of lone-parent claimants has increased threefold since 1966 — and a further 6 per cent receive family income supplement (half of all families dependent on family income supplement, SSAC 1982). Both schemes contain special provisions for lone parents but even so lone-parent recipients of supplementary benefit would find it difficult to supplement their living standards to any great degree by working, while lone-parent families on family income supplement face a considerable poverty trap, particularly if they receive passport benefits. With regard to working wives, support through the tax system is anachronistic in that all wives are treated as dependants and the married man's allowance is payable irrespective of whether the wife is working, while the provisions of the supplementary benefit system may encourage wives with unemployed husbands to cease employment.

Towards a British family policy

It would seem, therefore, that British policy of family support has developed in directions which are opposite to those recommended by the EC's Final Report. This would be less important if British policy was far advanced or even if it had evolved in relation to coherent objectives. For the UK, the main lesson to be drawn from the chapters on family poverty contained in this volume concern the benefits and means of developing a more conscious and clearly defined 'family policy' (compare, e.g. Bottomley 1981; Rodgers 1975). The restructuring of family benefits under discussion in The Netherlands, and described in some detail in Chapter 8, is especially interesting. It has involved a systematic official review, of a kind which has never taken place in Britain, of the concept of the basic costs of children and of the capacity of parents to contribute towards these costs. This in turn has underlined the need to adapt policies more to lifecycle changes in family needs and resources and highlighted the crucial importance of horizontal as well as vertical redistribution of income in favour of families.

Likewise, the main thrust of the well-developed French family policy has concerned horizontal rather than vertical redistribution. One aspect of this, though admittedly associated also with pro-natalist considerations, is the much greater support given to large families than to small ones as compared with the UK (or indeed West Germany or The Netherlands). This has effected a substantial reduction in the additional risks of poverty traditionally experienced by large families (compare Tables III.2 and 2.26 above). Other important features of French policy are the administrative uniformity, with all benefits for children being the responsibility of one agency, and the involvement of employers, trade unions and voluntary organisations in the local funds (*Caisses*, see Chapter 7 above). Finally, despite the horizontal emphasis of *la politique familiale* the net outcome of policies appears to be vertically more progressive than in the UK (see Table III.2).

In West Germany, too, more thought has recently been given to what constitutes a 'rational' family policy. During the past decade there has also been greater recognition of the needs of disadvantaged families and of the importance of making special provisions for single parents and their children, as exemplified by the advanced maintenance payments which came into force in 1980. However, it is West Germany's social assistance benefits which have most to teach us. Even allowing for the relatively low level of German assistance payments, allowances for children are much more generous than under supplementary benefit. For instance, a child aged 10 is eligible for an allowance equal to 65 per cent of the single householder's rate in West Germany and 34 per cent in Britain; a child aged 14, 75 per cent in West Germany and 51 per cent in Britain. This may, of course, partly reflect differences between the countries in the relative cost of raising children. But it is significant that the West German authorities conduct regular and thorough investigations into these 'equivalence ratios', and this forms part of a much fuller enquiry into the needs of people forced to depend on social assistance.

European experience certainly suggests that, as a first step towards developing a coherent policy on child support, it is essential to establish the costs associated with children. Equally necessary is debate, followed by explicit decisons, as to how costs of children should be apportioned between individuals and the State, parents and non-parents, wealthy and less wealthy, and employer and employee. In a number of countries the State, non-parents, employers and, to a lesser extent, the wealthy have contributed more than in the UK. A fundamental review of child support would also need to consider why, in contrast to many European countries, British family income support differs markedly according to whether or not an adult member is in work. Whereas in the UK, supplementary benefit claimants must not be in full-time employment, social assistance on the Continent is available for non-workers and workers alike. Similarly, most housing allowances and special provisions made for lone parents in other countries are awarded irrespective of employment status. As a consequence, much of the complexity inherent in the British system is avoided, the significance of the unemployment and poverty traps is much reduced and individuals are freer to choose how best to support their children.

The employment/non-employment distinction in the UK could be greatly reduced by introducing a minimum wage, increasing child benefit and certain non means-tested benefits received by adults, but also by raising the level of supplementary benefit for single and married persons and by making it available to people in employment when necessary. Much of the 'cost' of this change would have to be borne by employers through increased minimum wages (see above) which would reduce the numbers of low paid who would otherwise become eligible for benefit. All child support would be provided through a much enhanced child benefit which for the non-taxpayer would cover a child's minimum needs with the result that child additions under national insurance benefits and supplementary benefit would disappear. The child benefit would be taxable as would virtually all forms of income including national insurance benefits. There would need to be a truly universal housing benefit. The tax threshhold would equate with supplementary benefit levels for a couple or a single person (as the Royal Commission on Taxation recommended as long ago as 1954) and the income tax system as a whole would have to be more progressive, especially in the middle income bands. Such a scenario — which has much in common with some social dividend schemes (see Collard 1980) — could not, of course, be achieved immediately nor does it yet exist in any European country. Nevertheless, other European countries are striving towards a more unified or integrated system of family support and none is burdened by an emphasis on employment status which continuing high levels of unemployment make ever more anachronistic.

Social Security and the Elderly

From a British perspective, international comparisons of pension provision reveal a failure, after the impressive developments immediately following the war 'to consolidate and build further on foundations that had been established ... in advance of other countries' (Shonfield 1965). This was most evident between the 1950s and early 1970s, when economic growth and rapidly rising living standards were accompanied in a number of countries by important pension reforms. State pension schemes, in particular, were remodelled to make a more substantial contribution towards maintaining the living standards and status of pensioners. Public policies became increasingly committed to providing the average wage earner with a pension, after a normal working life, equal to approximately two-thirds of his pre-retirement earnings and which was regularly adjusted in line with average wages or some index of the living standards of the active population. Countries such as The Netherlands and Denmark also placed considerable emphasis on the achievement of decent universal minimum standards for the elderly.

In Britain, a number of schemes were proposed during this period for similarly transforming the structure of pensions, but none was successful until the 1975 Pensions Act. British policies were distinguished instead by reliance on occupational pensions to supplement low national insurance benefits and on means-tested social assistance for those without adequate pensions. In practice, because of inflation and the slow and uneven growth of occupational pension rights, many elderly people came to rely heavily on the State for their income. By the second half of the 1970s, little more than one-third of state pensioners also had occupational pensions (OPB 1981). Moreover, the proportion of the workforce building up private pension rights, which had advanced rapidly after the war, also declined during the 1970s so that in 1975 almost 7.5 million workers had no private pension rights. Overwhelmingly, those without occupational pensions are lower paid manual workers in private industry and commerce, with many women among them (Field 1981). Further disparities of treatment exist according to age, sex, length of employment, occupation, size of firm, job changes, etc. which greatly disadvantage certain groups. Such disparities have been of less importance on the Continent, mainly because higher state benefits reduce the significance of the occupational pension component of pensioners' incomes.

Another feature of British provision is the large number of old people dependent on basic means-tested assistance which is many times greater than in The Netherlands or West Germany (see Table 2.16). In Great Britain, 2 million old people, almost a quarter of all pensioners, are currently in receipt of a weekly supplementary pension and the latest available official figures suggest that in 1979 there were another 900 000 pensioners who, although eligible for supplementary benefit, did not claim it. Indeed the take-up of supplementary pensions dropped from 72 per cent in 1977 to 65 per cent in 1979 (DHSS 1982; New Society 1982). In The Netherlands, where social assistance payments based on the statutory minimum wage are set at higher levels than in Britain, only about 3 per cent of old people living at home receive these allowances. While this is partly due to the larger numbers in institutional care, the contrast with Britain undoubtedly mostly reflects the differences in pensions. In West Germany, there is more evidence of hardship amongst pensioners, especially elderly widows, and if comparisons are made with average wages social assistance rates for old people fall below the British levels. Even allowing for this, however, West German policies have clearly prevented the sinking of pensioners to the bottom of the socio-economic scale to the extent apparent in Britain.

The new pension scheme

How far then will this be changed by the 1975 Pensions Act? With the new scheme, with its entitlements to new earnings-related benefits as well as the existing flat-rate pensions, Britain has at last begun to develop a substantial pension system which includes important features intended to break the link between poverty and old age. As well as being weighted in favour of low-income groups, the new state pension is based on a person's best 20 years of earnings, which should benefit women and those whose earnings have passed their peak by the time they retire (Field 1981). When it reaches maturity the scheme certainly promises a new deal for many old people. In a detailed analysis of the scheme, taking all sources of income into account, Ermisch suggests that 50 years from now 'most of the elderly will be replacing over three-quarters of their net final earnings at retirement. . . . Half could have replacement ratios in the region of 0.9 or more' (Ermisch 1982).

Compared with pensions in a number of other countries, however, the scheme has certain major weaknesses. First, there is a long transition period, so that many of those currently at work, let alone existing pensioners, have no prospect of ever gaining much higher benefits than at present. In fact, during the next 20 years, when the new pension rights are being accrued, the state earnings-related scheme will have little impact on most pensioners' incomes and no decline can be expected in the numbers dependent on supplementary benefits (Altmann and Atkinson 1982). Moreover, in this period improvements in occupational pensions and other sources of incomes are unlikely to benefit much those with low earnings or insecure employment during their working lives. The scheme will also widen discrepancies between the newly retired and older pensioners — an injustice which will have become strikingly evident by the end of the century. Needless to say, the financial needs of many pensioners actually increase with age since they are less frequently able to supplement their income by working and may face additional costs associated with failing health. The main improvements in pensioners' incomes are likely to take place after the turn of the century. Even then it will be some time before those depending entirely on state pensions fully benefit from the 'best 20 years' rule since pensions are based only on earnings after 1978 (Ermisch 1982). Likewise, there will still be a large number of elderly pensioners, particularly widows, who have no benefits or very inadequate pensions under the 1975 Act.

Under the present arrangements, therefore, many old people would continue to rely on supplementary benefits at least until the second and third decades of the twenty-first century. Already, however, pressures exist for a more effective guaranteed minimum income and are likely to grow much stronger as the inequities of the transition period become obvious. Altmann and Atkinson (1982; compare Field 1981) have shown how increases in the basic pension or the development of tax credits for the elderly could substantially reduce dependence on supplementary benefits. The initial costs would be high, but by no means excessive, and in both cases they would fall steadily as the pension scheme approaches maturity. Other options include the introduction of a disability allowance, which would help older pensioners in particular, combined with special allowances for the over 75s.

Older pensioners are most likely to suffer, too, from the second weakness of the new scheme, which is clearly apparent from comparisons with other countries. A feature of European pension developments since the 1950s has been the acceptance of the *Dynamische Rente* (dynamic pension) principle, the regular adjustment of pensions in payment in line with average national earnings. This is widely seen as the fairest means of attuning pensions and other benefits to changing national prosperity, though there is now growing controversy in a number of countries (e.g. West Germany and The Netherlands) about whether indexing should follow gross or net earnings. However defined, the principle is now conspicuously absent from the British arrangements, which merely contain guarantees against price inflation. In practice, it is difficult to believe that the basic social security pensions will not keep pace, more or less, with earnings. But further and perhaps far-reaching reforms, particularly in the financing and structure of occupational pensions, would be required if this principle were adopted for the earnings-related components. Without this, however, even on maturity the 1975 scheme will be associated with steadily declining living standards during retirement. Alternatively, as has happened in the past, the basis of the scheme might be gradually undermined by *ad hoc* attempts to compensate for these defects.

A third weakness of the new strategy concerns occupational pensions. While the role of state pensions has been enlarged, great reliance continues to be placed on membership of occupational pension schemes. Unfortunately, several difficulties inherent in these provisions have yet to be tackled effectively, most noticeably (apart from the indexing issue) the problem of preserving the rights of those who leave employment before retirement. Under the present arrangements, 'early leavers' receive frozen benefits based on wages and salaries at the time of leaving, with no guarantee of any further adjustment. Indeed, in 1980, 73 per cent of all occupational pension schemes gave no increases at all on deferred pensions and, in the private sector, only 18 per cent of schemes improved benefits for early leavers (Times 1982). Moreover, the problem affects the growing numbers of unemployed and redundant workers as well as those who are merely changing jobs.

The Occupational Pensions Board (OPB) has recently called for urgent action to protect the value of preserved benefits arguing that

> The obective set out in the 1971 White Paper that job mobility should not undermine occupational schemes as a major form of provision for retirement has not been achieved, and the concentration of benefits on stayers limits the effectiveness of the contribution which occupational schemes make to the welfare of the population in retirement. (OPB 1981).

It recommended, therefore, that preserved benefits should be increased 'as far as possible in line with the movement of national average earnings'. However, because of the possible cost to employers, a majority of the OPB proposed a ceiling of 5 per cent per annum on such increases which, incidentally, would have entailed a fall of over 50 per cent in the real value of a pension between 1974 and 1982. This is a bare minimum proposal without which there can be no real prospect of reaching the accepted standards of provision in a number of other countries. But, as the OPB makes clear, European practice points to more radical alternatives.

One such strategy might be to increase the state pension to a level comparable with that in other countries. This would reduce the significance of occupational pension provision since most schemes would probably adjust their benefits downwards to take account of the enhanced state pension. This would be much simpler to administer, cheaper and facilitate mobility between jobs. Another option would be to extend occupational provision to a point where it was effectively universal and to co-ordinate the provisons of individual schemes such that schemes would have to conform to state rules. This is already the position in France and is an objective of Dutch pension policy. Such arrangements facilitate subsidisation of declining industries with older age structures by growth industries with younger ones. They also lend themselves to the protection of individual rights and reflect a view of occupational pensions as deferred pay which is only slowly gaining acceptance in the UK. The French system shows, too, that occupational schemes need not be fully funded but may be run on a 'pay as you go' basis provided they are to some extent financially interdependent. Attempts at reform along these lines would doubtless meet much resistance in Britain and would not be free of costs, either financial or institutional. This is illustrated by the fact that negotiations towards a comprehensive system have been under way in The Netherlands for over a decade and different interests still remain to be reconciled.

Early retirement

Another pressure increasing pension costs, and adding greatly to the policy difficulties posed by an aging population, is the movement towards early retirement. This is already further advanced on the Continent than in the UK. It is part of a long-term secular trend so that in the UK between 1931 and 1971 the proportion of men aged 65 and over who were retired increased from under 50 to 78 per cent, and by 1980 the figure was 91 per cent (Lewis 1975; Fogarty 1982). More recently, however, governments, employers and unions have been encouraged by high levels of unemployment to introduce early retirement schemes which raise profound issues concerning the status of the elderly and the possible conflict of interests between old and young. Those who retire before normal retirement age, and who are encouraged to do so by special schemes, comprise primarily the unskilled, sick, disabled, unemployed and those in irregular employment (see Chapters 7, 8, 9, 10 and 12). This has tended to underline associations between old age, redundancy and obsolescence (Walker 1980). So, too, have job-release schemes designed, as in the British case, 'to create vacancies for unemployed people by encouraging older workers to leave their jobs' (DE 1980). Furthermore, the incomes of the early retired tend to be low since even 'generous' early retirements plans are usually dependent on former wages and work records which, for those retiring prematurely are often poor. Certainly this was the case in Britain during the 1970s when many more were dependent on means-tested benefits (Altmann 1982).

These pressures for early retirement are unsatisfactory in other respects. Recent studies have shown that many older workers would prefer to continue working as long as possible, not least because it is the best means of maintaining their incomes. As Fogarty (1982) has argued,

> from the point of view of individual employers, the employment of older workers is economic, and . . . neglect of the maintenance and further development of their capacities from middle age onwards has cumulative and costly consequences for employers as well as for the workers themselves, and also consequences for pensioners' capacity to cope and remain active in retirement.

There are also sound macro-economic reasons for seeking to counter this trend. 'Shifting unemployment from 16 year-olds to 60 year-olds may cut Britain's dole queues, but it will not save money. It will do the reverse.' (*Economist* 1981).

Finally, unless wholesale early retirement is resisted, the outlook for the future development of pensions is bleak. This is now gradually being recognised in a number of European countries, where pressures are growing to include the 'right to work' of the elderly in future employment plans. It is also increasingly acknowledged that further important changes in pension schemes will be required both to give more scope to gradual or 'flexible' retirement plans and at the same time to transfer resources to the increasing numbers in the 'fourth generation'. Options being considered include the introduction of two-tiered pensions. The first tier would consist of basic pensions, awarded perhaps from the age of 65, with opportunities being provided for part-time work: fully earnings-related pensions, the second tier, would then become payable at a later age, perhaps 69–70. This would not preclude selective, and more generous, early retirement schemes for reasons of ill-health or disability. In a British context, this may also be the only effective way of remedying the defects of the present pension strategy (e.g. see *Economist* 1981).

Postscript

International comparisons of social welfare are inevitably comparisons in imperfection and, in seeking lessons for the UK, the imperfections of British policy have been highlighted. Undoubtedly, other European countries would have something to learn from British experience, but that should be the subject of another book.

This volume has shown that, at least up to the late 1970s, Britain had managed to restrict the numbers in *extreme* relative poverty. However, a price has been paid by the large number of people in Britain (6.5 million in 1982) who are forced to rely on the supplementary benefit scheme or family income supplement for what is surely a barely adequate minimum standard of living. It is then evident that the unemployed, lone parents, some large families and a substantial number of pensioners have been less well served by the Welfare State in Britain than many of their counterparts in other European countries. Moreover, the importance attached to these means-tested benefits in British social policy has exacerbated the 'poverty-trap', fuelled fears about disincentive effects and scroungers, and helped to marginalise the needy. The resultant unsympathetic and, sometimes, hostile political environment has limited improvements in the circumstances of the poor in a way that is rare elsewhere in Europe. Turning to the future, and perhaps to a world where unemployment opportunities are less abundant, the British system, if unaltered, is destined to create two nations: one privileged by work, the other impoverished and disparaged by its absence.

The continuing increase in unemployment, particularly in the numbers unemployed for more than a year, together with the rise in the numbers who are low paid or who are prematurely retired, is already undermining the achievements of the post-war period and portends a return to mass poverty in a country renowned only a generation ago for its leadership in social welfare. Restrictions on the rights of citizenship and the definition of need are likewise creating situations of deprivation which were barely discernable only a few years ago.

We have, therefore, offered a number of suggestions for improving British provisions based on European experience. The suggestions are not, in the main, nil-cost solutions but then Britain fails to match the welfare expenditure of even the poorer European countries. The most important are:

(a) Priority should be given to the introduction of a national minimum wage, which would provide the foundation for a coordinated policy on income support across the employment divide. This in turn would facilitate the reduction of means-testing.

(b) This should be complemented by a much more generous, systematic and coherent strategy on family income support, with benefits better attuned to the basic costs of children and changes in the family lifecycle.

(c) While unemployment remains high, job-creation and work-sharing programmes, of a kind now being explored in many countries, must be more vigorously pursued, leading to the creation of permanent jobs in all sectors of the economy. However, such measures should recognise the 'right to work' of the elderly as well as the young and of women as well as men.

(d) The Nation should also seek to minimise the hardship of the un-employed, by emulating the higher unemployment benefits and less stringent qualifying conditions found in most other countries.

(e) Steps must be taken to remedy the deficiencies in Britain's pension strategy. In particular, measures are required to compensate for the inequities arising during the long transition before the new state pension reaches maturity. Improvement of occupational schemes is also necessary, most notably the protection of the rights of 'early leavers'.

References

Altmann, R. 1982, 'Incomes of the early-retired', *Journal of Social Policy* vol. II.

Altmann, R. and Atkinson, E. 1982, 'State pensions, taxation and retirement income 1981–203–' in M. Fogarty (ed.), *Retirement policy: the next 50 years*, London, Heinemann.

Beckerman, W. 1979, *Poverty and the impact of income maintenance programmes*, Geneva, ILO.

Bennett, F. 1981, 'Family wage?' *Low Pay Review*, 4.

Berthoud, R., Brown, J. C. and Cooper S. 1981, *Poverty and the development of anti-poverty policy in the United Kingdom*, London, Heinemann.

Beveridge, W. 1942, *Social insurance and allied services*, London, HMSO, Cmnd 6404.

Bottomley, P. 1981, 'Tax and benefit over the family cycle', *Poverty*, 50.

Bradshaw, J. 1982, 'The unemployment trap', *New Society*, 7 January.

Bryne, D., Pond, C. and Sullivan, J. 1983, 'Low Wages in Britain', *Low Pay Review*, 12.

CEPG 1982, 'Policy assessment', *Cambridge Economic Review*, 8, 1.

Collard, D. 1980, 'Social dividend and negative income tax' in C. Sandford, C. Pond and R. Walker (eds), *Taxation and social policy*, London, Heinemann.

Coutes, K., Cripps, F., and Ward, T. 1982, 'Britain in the 1980s', *Cambridge Economic Policy Review*, vol. 8, no. 1.

CPRS 1980, *People and their families*, Central Policy Review Staff, London, HMSO.

CSO 1982, *Economic trends*, 345, July, London, HMSO.

DE 1980, *Job release scheme*, London, Department of Employment.

DHSS 1980, *Social benefit tables for member states of the European Communities, position at 1 January 1980*, London, Department of Health and Social Security.

DHSS 1982, *Low income families — 1979*, Department of Health and Social Security, March.

EC 1981a, *Wages and incomes*, Rapid Information, Luxembourg, Eurostat, February.

EC 1981b, *Pensioners in the European Community, 1977*, Luxembourg, Eurostat.

EC 1981c, *Final report from the Commission to the Council on the first programme of pilot schemes and studies to combat poverty*, Brussels, European Commission.

Economist 1981, 'Grandmothers' chickens', *Economist*, 29 August.

Ermisch, J. 1982, 'Resources of the elderly — Impact of present commitments and established trends' in M. Fogarty (ed.), *Retirement policy: the next 50 years*, London, Heinemann.

Field, F. 1981, *Inequality in Britain*, London, Fontana.

Fogarty, M. 1982, 'The work option' in M. Fogarty (ed.) *Retirement policy: the next 50 years*, London, Heinemann.

Forester, T. 1982, 'Job creation: Unable to cope', *New Society*, 2 September.

Hamill, L. 1978, *Wives as sole and joint breadwinners*, London, DHSS, Economic Adviser's Office.

James, E. 1980, 'A role for Europe', paper to a conference on responses to poverty in European countries, Civil Service College, Sunningdale.

Kaim-Caudle, P. 1973, *Comparative social policy and social security*, London, Martin Robertson.

Land, H. 1981, 'The mantle of manhood', *New Statesman*, 18–25 December.

Lewis, P. 1975, 'Off the scrapheap', *New Society*, 6 February.

Marsden, D. 1980, *Study of changes in the wage structure of manual workers in six Community countries since 1966*, Eurostat, Sussex European Research Centre.

Meacher, M. 1982, 'Why the poor are getting poorer faster, *The Guardian*, 8 February.

Meade, J. E. 1982, *Stagflation: wage-fixing*, London, George Allen & Unwin.

Metcalfe, D. 1980a, 'Comments on Chapters 2 and 3' in F. Blackaby (ed.), *The future of pay bargaining*, London, Heinemann.

Metcalfe, D. 1980b, 'Must the low-paid always be with us?', *New Society*, 16 October.

Miller, R. 1981, 'Low pay, no pay, minimum wages and wages councils', *The Journal of Economic Affairs*, vol. 1, no. 3.

Mommsen, W. (ed.) 1981, *The emergence of the welfare state in Britain and Germany*, London, Croom Helm.

Moylan, D. and Davies, B. 1981, 'The flexibility of the unemployed', *Employment Gazette*, vol. 89, no. 1.

MSC 1981, *Manpower Review 1981*, London, Manpower Services Commission.

MSC 1982, *Annual Report*, London, Manpower Services Commission.

New Society 1982, 'Poverty — the growth industry', *New Society*, 22 April.

NIESR 1982, 'Summary and appraisal', *National Institute Economic Review*, 100, February.

OECD 1979, *Socio-Economic policy for the elderly*, Paris.

OPB 1981, *Improved protection for the occupational pension rights and expectations of early leavers*, HMSO, Occupational Pensions Board, Cmnd 8271.

Piachaud, D. 1980, 'Taxation and social security' in C. Sandford, C. Pond and R. Walker (eds), *Taxation and social policy*, London, Heinemann.

Piachaud, D. 1981, *Children and poverty*, London, Child Poverty Action Group.

Pond, C. 1981, 'Low-pay — 1980s style', *Low Pay Review*, 4.

Rodgers, B. 1975, 'Family policy in France', *Journal of Social Policy*, vol. 4 no. 2.

Saunders, C. T. 1980, 'Changes in relative pay in the 1970s' in F. Blackaby (ed.), *The future of pay bargaining*, London, Heinemann.

SBC 1980, *Annual report 1979*, London, Supplementary Benefits Commission.

Shonfield, A. 1965, *Modern capitalism*, Oxford, OUP.

Sinfield, A. 1981, *What unemployment means*, London, Martin Robertson.

SSAC 1982, *First report of the Social Security Advisory Committee 1981*, London, HMSO.

Times 1982, 'The pension trap', *Times*, 25 June.

Trinder, C. 1982, 'Why not work?', *New Society*, 26 August.

Walker, A. 1980, 'The social creation of poverty and dependency in old age', *Journal of Social Policy*, vol. 9, no. 1.

Walker, R. 1980, 'The policy debate: where do we go from here?' in C. Sandford, C. Pond and R. Walker (eds), *Taxation and social policy*, London, Heinemann.

Williams, F. 1982, 'The twin dangers that could wreck the Welfare state', *The Times*, 3 August.

Index